D0206167

An Unseen Light

An Unseen Light

Black Struggles for Freedom in Memphis, Tennessee

Edited by
Aram Goudsouzian
and
Charles W. McKinney Jr.

UNIVERSITY PRESS OF KENTUCKY

Scholarly publisher for the Commonwealth,
serving Bellarmine University, Berea College, Centre College of Kentucky, Eastern
Kentucky University, The Filson Historical Society, Georgetown College, Kentucky
Historical Society, Kentucky State University, Morehead State University, Murray
State University, Northern Kentucky University, Transylvania University, University
of Kentucky, University of Louisville, and Western Kentucky University.
All rights reserved.

Editorial and Sales Offices: The University Press of Kentucky
663 South Limestone Street, Lexington, Kentucky 40508-4008
www.kentuckypress.com

Library of Congress Cataloging-in-Publication Data

Names: Goudsouzian, Aram, editor. | McKinney, Charles Wesley, 1967- editor.
Title: An unseen light : black struggles for freedom in Memphis, Tennessee /
   edited by Aram Goudsouzian and Charles W. McKinney Jr.
Other titles: Civil rights and the struggle for Black equality in the
   twentieth century.
Description: Lexington, Kentucky : The University Press of Kentucky, [2018] |
   Series: Civil rights and the struggle for Black equality in the twentieth
   century | Includes bibliographical references and index.
Identifiers: LCCN 2017058296| ISBN 9780813175515 (hardcover : alk. paper) |
   ISBN 9780813175539 (pdf) | ISBN 9780813175522 (epub)
Subjects: LCSH: African Americans—Civil rights—Tennessee—Memphis—History.
   | African Americans—Political activity—Tennessee—Memphis—History. |
   African Americans—Tennessee—Memphis—History. | Memphis (Tenn.)—Race
   relations—History. | Civil rights movements—Tennessee—Memphis—History.
   | Memphis (Tenn.)—Politics and government.
Classification: LCC F444.M59 N489 2018 | DDC 323.1196/073076819—dc23
LC record available at https://lccn.loc.gov/2017058296

Member of the Association
of University Presses

Contents

Introduction

Aram Goudsouzian and Charles W. McKinney Jr.

Richard Wright was walking down Beale Street in a tattered overcoat, lugging a cardboard suitcase. It was a cold, gusty Sunday morning in November. He was seventeen years old, a migrant from Mississippi. Leery of sordid tales about Memphis, he had strapped all his cash to his body, even if all that sin was just a scent in the air, a remnant of Saturday night carousing.[1]

Beale Street was famous for its con men and crap games, its saloons and scamps, its pickpockets and prostitutes. It was also the place where W. C. Handy wrote "Memphis Blues" and "St. Louis Blues," launching a new American musical tradition. It was the place where Robert Church Sr. laid the foundation for his economic empire, becoming the nation's first black millionaire, and where Robert Church Jr. built a political machine, leveraging black votes for influence with the city's "boss," E. H. Crump. It was the place where Ida B. Wells published her crusading newspaper *Memphis Free Speech,* and where a mob deposited the severed head of a black lynching victim named Ell Persons. Beale Street condensed the entire African American experience into a few blocks of bars, bordellos, shops, and offices.[2]

Wright had lived in Memphis once before, arriving with his family in 1911, when he was just three. In his memoir *Black Boy,* he described this initial stint as a baptism in depravity. He wrote of murdering a kitten, of fighting for his grocery money against a band of tough boys, of entertaining saloon crowds by getting drunk. His father, a victim of Beale Street's temptations, abandoned the family. His mother, unable to feed her kids, sent them to an orphanage. When he was eight or nine, she gathered them again and headed for Elaine, Arkansas, another stop along the lower Mississippi River, part of a long wandering loop in search of a better life.[3]

When Wright returned in 1925, Memphis was a center of southern industry, with about 160,000 residents, one-third of whom were black. The city's downtown boasted the new twelve-story Peabody Hotel and impressive edifices such as Lowenstein's Department Store, the Cotton Exchange Building, and the Union Planter Bank Building. If Memphis had a reputation as the murder capital of America, it was also a land of opportunity, drawing migrants from the rural plantations of the Mississippi Delta. Wright soon found respectable lodgings and a decent job at an optical company.[4]

For Wright, though, Memphis was a cruel riddle. Jim Crow asked terrible questions that had no good answers. Surviving the South meant hiding behind a mask. White people could never know your frustrations, your fears, your aspirations, or your intelligence. At the optical company, the white men told Wright that another young man wanted to kill him, and they told the other worker the same thing—they just wanted to see two black boys fight. That racism, and the corresponding poverty, poisoned his fellow blacks. The elevator operator at the company, an otherwise smart and proud man named Shorty, would shuck, jive, and let white people kick him in the rump for a quarter, rationalizing that "my ass is tough and quarters is scarce."[5]

Reading was Wright's salvation, his gateway to a wider world. One day he read an editorial in the *Commercial Appeal* that chastised H. L. Mencken. He grew curious. Who was this prickly social critic, and how had he inflamed these white southerners? Satisfying his curiosity meant wearing another mask. To be allowed to check out books from the Memphis Public Library, Wright forged a note from a white man: *Dear Madam: Will you please let this nigger boy have some books by H. L. Mencken?*

He had to leave the South. If he accepted his inferior station, he would hate himself. If he succumbed to booze and sex, he would be just like his father. If he turned into an angry revolutionary, the racists would kill him. He read Mencken and then Theodore Dreiser and Sherwood Anderson and Sinclair Lewis, and although they described essentially alien worlds, "these writers seemed to feel that America could be shaped nearer to the hearts of those who lived in it." And so in 1927 Richard Wright boarded a train for Chicago. Those novels and essays had served as an inspiration, like "a tinge of warmth from an unseen light."[6]

But Wright could not see the lights that shone in Memphis. His zeal to migrate north blinded him to the various ways African Americans had shaped the politics and culture of this city at the crossroads, sitting atop a Mississippi River bluff, with the fertile and oppressive Delta fanning to its south. Black Memphians found salvation and independence in churches. They did the courageous and calculated work of political organizing. They made music that became a seminal American art form with global impact. And they forged a brilliant, complicated, dynamic movement for freedom. Wright could see only the shadow that racial oppression cast over this variegated history; he could not see the ways in which black people survived, accommodated, subverted, battled, and wrestled with the persistence of racial subordination. Throughout these struggles, black Memphians forged stories as individuals and as a people.

This book tells some of the stories of those "unseen lights."

"Something is happening in Memphis," intoned Martin Luther King. "Something is happening in our world." Outside, the skies were filled with ominous rumbles of thunder, crackling lightning, and violent sheets of rain, but inside Mason Temple, he recalled great periods in human history, from the biblical Exodus through Franklin D. Roosevelt's inaugural speech. Despite the crises of the present time, he cherished the moment. Throughout the world, people were yearning to be free. "I'm just happy that God has allowed me to live in this period to see what is unfolding," he said. "And I'm happy that He's allowed me to be in Memphis."

The date was April 3, 1968, and this was King's final speech. He had come to support the city's striking sanitation workers. Their struggle reflected the larger plight of black people in Memphis and beyond. King used the occasion to remind the packed church about sacrificing for the common good, about using their economic leverage, and about maintaining the discipline of nonviolence. He spoke, too, of the threats on his life—"but it doesn't really matter to me, because I've been to the mountaintop." Even if he did not complete the journey himself, his people would get to the Promised Land.[7]

King was shot and killed the next day. The assassination rocked the nation and hung like a gloomy cloud over Memphis. With some justification, that singular tragedy dominates the memory of the city's civil rights struggle—in one way or another, most history books on race in Memphis revolve around 1968. That moment in time was further memorialized with the construction of the National Civil Rights Museum, a monument erected at the Lorraine Motel, the site of the killing. Yet this iconic moment rested on an expansive history of black struggles for freedom—struggles that were born in the dawn of freedom and would continue long after King's death. *An Unseen Light* provides context for understanding this rich history of African Americans in Memphis, beyond King's murder. It is not a comprehensive history, but it includes intriguing stories, profiles of compelling people, and portraits of a city that suggest both remarkable progress and unfinished work. And as we look back, we hope the essays in this book provide some lessons to carry us forward.

While it has been long recognized as a major epicenter of black life, history, and culture, Memphis remains one of the more underresearched (or "unseen") major cities in the United States. This unfortunate reality belies a rich history worthy of critical intellectual scrutiny. Starting in the second half of the nineteenth century, Memphis became the most populated—and most vibrant—metropolitan area for black people in the entire Mid-South region. The congregation of recently freed African Americans led to the development of a civic, political, cultural, religious, and economic universe whose impact reverberated far beyond the boundaries of the city's black communities. In the crucible of segregation, African Americans in Memphis took on the task of reshaping the city—and the nation—to better conform to the principles of equality. They were creating a "light" of their own in the Bluff City.[8]

For decades, the population of Memphis surpassed that of other New South cities such as Atlanta, Richmond, and Birmingham; only New Orleans counted a larger population among Mid-South and Deep South cities. Blacks in Memphis rightly regarded northern cities such as Chicago, Detroit, and Washington, DC, as their city's cultural, economic, and political peers. When it came time to locate the headquarters of the largest black evangelical denomination in the country—the Church of God in Christ (COGIC)—Charles Mason built its base of operations in Memphis. Scores of black-owned businesses, such as banks and insurance companies, anchored the economic vitality of the city. Beale Street, the iconic center of black culture, nurtured generations of musicians and attracted a spectacular array of talent that included Robert Johnson, Ma Rainey, B. B. King, Howlin' Wolf, Carla Thomas, and Isaac Hayes. The city's African American activists cultivated one of the nation's largest and most active chapters of the NAACP.[9]

Blacks in Memphis also nurtured a large constellation of civic and community organizations. Rooted in religious, fraternal, civic, and political networks, this wide assortment of black women and men formed groups, worked together, contended for space and recognition, and ultimately drove momentum in the effort to attain racial equality. While grappling with the constraints of gender, class, and race, labor activists carved out a space for union activity that helped shape the economic, social, and racial contours of the city. This vibrant movement for justice spanned the twentieth century.[10]

In the past few decades, historians have crafted a body of work that has extended and improved our collective understanding of the African American pursuit of equality in the nation's urban centers. Scholars in fields such as politics, culture, labor, modernity, activism, and internationalism have illuminated the lives of black folks. Much of this work has been geographically specific, tending to focus on major cities with large black populations. These cities have much to tell us about the inner workings of black communities, how those communities made sense of the world around them, and how they constructed collective movements for freedom and equality. Recent works on New York, Chicago, Oakland, Atlanta, Washington, DC, and a few other cities perform crucial work in this regard.[11]

It is our hope that *An Unseen Light* will help situate Memphis alongside these other cities in the critical conversation about the nation's African American experience. It builds on the work of a generation of historians of Memphis, many of whom are contributors to this volume. They have enriched, deepened, and complicated our understanding of the city by employing many of the lenses that inform how historians approach the larger black freedom struggle: an emphasis on a "long civil rights movement," an appreciation for the centrality of women and gender, a focus on local movements and grassroots activism, an examination of the interplay between politics and culture, and a determination to avoid a triumphalist narrative that wraps America's history of racial inequality in a tidy box. This book brings together their perspectives.[12]

In the essay that begins this collection, Brian D. Page investigates black life in the aftermath of the Memphis Massacre of 1866, chronicling how new migrants helped reconstitute cultural life and political strength. His examination reveals that an alliance with white elites during the 1876 election reflected not only a practical accommodation to political reality but also a staking of black independence.

Deep into the twentieth century, black life in Memphis was marked by violent repression. Yet African Americans refused to be passive victims. In 1917 a white mob lynched a black woodcutter named Ell Persons. Darius Young chronicles not only this brutal injustice but also black political resistance: "Black Memphians silently refused to enlist in the military, mobilized the vote, and used the national platforms of civil rights organizations to voice their opposition to the lynching and white intimidation." Almost two decades later, a fire destroyed the headquarters of the Church of God in Christ. Elton H. Weaver III describes how, despite public scorn, the church remained a resilient presence in the black community of Memphis, challenging the white political establishment while freeing its congregants' souls.

In the decades prior to World War II, the political machine of "Boss" E. H. Crump provided opportunities for black advancement, even as it enforced black subservience. From different angles, David Welky and Beverly Greene Bond illuminate those contradictions. Welky describes the aftermath of the 1937 Ohio-Mississippi River flood, when the government provided relief for both black and white flood refugees, yet structured it through patterns of racial segregation. Key black political figures protested a roundup of forced labor to stanch the flooding. Bond tells the story of L. O. Taylor, a unique figure in the city's history. He was a preacher, writer, photographer, and filmmaker who avoided any direct challenge of the Crump machine yet delivered sermons and produced art that emphasized black humanity, creating a subtle insistence on racial equality.

Historians have viewed the war years as a racial crucible—amidst the battle to destroy fascism abroad, black Americans shifted their consciousness, firming strategies to combat racism at home. Yet Jim Crow eroded slowly, in jagged chunks. Jason Jordan tells the story of the 1940 "Reign of Terror," a three-month police occupation of black neighborhoods that brutally obstructed their surging political independence from Boss Crump's machine. Yet as Jordan notes, this effort was the "wild thrashing of a dying regime." Laurie B. Green shifts the focus to the protest initiatives of working-class women and men, holistically considering their struggles against workplace discrimination, racist stereotypes, police brutality, and sexual abuse. Green's essay deftly foregrounds the surging momentum of the early movement years by looking backward, into the activism of black workers during wartime.

During the years of the civil rights movement, Memphis had a reputation as a relative oasis of peace—neither a crucible of activism, like Nashville or Atlanta, nor a hotbed of violence, like Birmingham or the Mississippi Delta. Elizabeth Gritter and Steven A. Knowlton both explain and complicate this depiction. Training her lens on formal politics, Gritter examines the history of the Shelby County Democratic Club from 1959 to 1964, when the city's black political establishment turned out black voters, forged ties with John F. Kennedy's administration, and built a power bloc in local politics. Knowlton's essay concerns the fight to desegregate Memphis libraries, which encompassed not only legal challenges but also a 1960 sit-in campaign that inspired direct action protests throughout the city. Although there were no fire hoses or police dogs at Cossitt Library, the tale highlights key themes of the civil rights struggle: a tradition of black activism, various forms of segregationist resistance, eventual desegregation, and continued patterns of racial inequality.

No element of Memphis life promoted the myth of racial harmony more than its groundbreaking music industry. From Sun Records and the birth of rock and roll to Stax Records and the heyday of southern soul, a popular story has been that Memphis music transcended boundaries of race. Yet as Charles L. Hughes shows in his portrait of Rufus Thomas, the local music scene reflected and perpetuated the second-class status of African Americans. Thomas touched every important development in the history of Memphis music, and his personal accounts contradict the racial myths surrounding him.

The 1968 sanitation strike and assassination of Martin Luther King focused national attention on the Memphis movement. In his essay on the 1966 Meredith March against Fear, Aram Goudsouzian surveys a prologue of sorts, when Memphis experienced the aftermath of a dramatic shooting, an influx of national leaders, critical debates about civil rights and Black Power, and local activism that revealed a wide range of white attitudes and black experiences. Anthony C. Siracusa carries the narrative toward the tumultuous moment of 1968 but places it within the longer historical context of a War on Poverty program that included an unlikely alliance between nonviolence icon James Lawson and the Invaders, a Black Power organization. Siracusa argues that the FBI's counterintelligence program (COINTELPRO) not only fomented disruption during the sanitation strike but also contained a wider agenda to discredit black antipoverty organizing.

While the national spotlight shifted away from Memphis after 1968, the city's black population mobilized in new and powerful ways. James Conway and Shirletta Kinchen explore local strands of this movement. Conway tells the story of the "Black Monday" school boycotts of 1969, when the NAACP incorporated aspects of Black Power while allying with a host of community groups, winning concrete gains while also inspiring a backlash. "The Black Monday protest," writes Conway, "demonstrated how black Memphians had more control over their community than at any other time in the city's history." Kinchen traces Black Power at Memphis State University. In 1970 Maybelline Forbes was the university's first black homecoming queen. This achievement stemmed from the activism of the Black Student Association, and it infused a black aesthetic onto the campus.

Finally, Zandria F. Robinson and Michael Honey link the past to the present. Robinson's ethnographic study of the Soulsville community reminds us that for all the global popularity of the southern soul sound, it was rooted in historic patterns of racism and resiliency in this South Memphis neighborhood. As residents claim that musical history, they also claim a stake in Soulsville's revitalization. Honey's labor history of the city stretches deep into the past, and it arrives in the twenty-first century to find glimpses of optimism against a backdrop of a gutted labor movement and a diminished capacity to confront ever-expanding economic inequality.

"The issue is injustice," continued Martin Luther King in that final speech at Mason Temple. He was talking about the striking sanitation workers, but he was also talking about the fight for a greater freedom. Yes, he called for more nonviolent marches, but he also implored black Memphians to boycott the goods of companies that discriminated against black workers. He called for people to buy their policies from black-owned insurance companies, to deposit their money in the black-owned Tri-State Bank. And he called for a reorientation of national priorities. "God has commanded us to be concerned about the slums down here and His children who can't eat three square meals a day," he said. "It's all right to talk about the new Jerusalem, but one day God's preacher must talk about the new New York, the new Atlanta, the new Philadelphia, the new Los Angeles, the new Memphis, Tennessee."[13]

Taken together, the essays in this volume reveal the determination of African Americans to craft a new Memphis. That struggle spanned centuries, and it is ongoing. It reminds us that while Memphis is still scarred by King's assassination, it is more deeply haunted by its failure to heed King's call for true equality.

Notes

1. Richard Wright, *Black Boy* (1945; reprint, New York: Harper and Row, 1966), 228.

2. Preston Lauterbach, *Beale Street Dynasty: Sex, Song, and the Struggle for Memphis* (New York: W. W. Norton, 2015).

3. Wright, *Black Boy*, 16–43.

4. Michel Fabre, *The Unfinished Quest of Richard Wright*, trans. Isabel Barzun (New York: William Morrow, 1973) 60–65; Hazel Rowley, *Richard Wright: The Life and Times* (New York: Henry Holt, 2001), 42–43.

5. See Robert Felgar, *Understanding Richard Wright's* Black Boy (Westport, CT: Greenwood Press, 1998); Katherine Fishburn, *Richard Wright's Hero: The Faces of a Rebel-Victim* (Metuchen, NJ: Scarecrow Press, 1977), 6–13; Timothy Dow Adams, "I Do Believe I Know Him though I Know He Lies: Lying as Genre and Metaphor in Richard Wright's *Black Boy*," in *Richard Wright: A Collection of Critical Essays*, ed. Arnold Rampersad (New York: Longman, 1994), 83–97.

6. Wright, *Black Boy*, 228–85.

7. Martin Luther King Jr., *I Have a Dream: Writings and Speeches that Changed the World* (San Francisco: Harper San Francisco, 1992), 194–203.

8. Kenneth Goings and Gerald Smith, "Duty of the Hour: African American Communities in Memphis, 1862–1923," in *Trial and Triumph: Essays in Ten-*

nessee's African American History, ed. Carol Van West (Knoxville: University of Tennessee Press, 2002), 227–43; Armstead Robinson, "Plans Dat Comed from God: Institution Building and the Emergence of Black Leadership in Reconstruction Memphis, 1865–1880," in *Toward a New South? Studies in Post–Civil War Southern Communities,* ed. Orville Burton and Robert C. McMath (Westport, CT: Praeger Press, 1982); David M. Tucker, *Black Pastors and Leaders: Memphis, 1819–1972* (Memphis, TN: Memphis State University Press, 1975).

9. Elizabeth Gritter, *River of Hope: Black Politics and the Memphis Freedom Movement, 1865–1954* (Lexington: University Press of Kentucky, 2014); Kenneth W. Goings and Gerald L. Smith, "'Unhidden' Transcripts: Memphis and African American Agency, 1862–1920," *Journal of Urban History* 21, no. 3 (1995): 372–94. On the history of the Church of God in Christ, see Calvin White Jr., *The Rise to Respectability: Race, Religion, and the Church of God in Christ* (Fayetteville: University of Arkansas Press, 2015). On the vitality of Beale Street, see George W. Lee, *Beale Street: Where the Blues Began* (New York: R. O. Ballou Press, 1934); Lauterbach, *Beale Street Dynasty;* Roger Biles, *Memphis in the Great Depression* (Knoxville: University of Tennessee Press, 1986); Charles Hughes, *Country Soul: Making Music and Making Race in the American South* (Chapel Hill: University of North Carolina Press, 2015).

10. Gritter, *River of Hope;* David Tucker, *Lieutenant Lee of Beale Street* (Nashville, TN: Vanderbilt University Press, 1971); David Tucker, *Memphis since Crump: Bossism, Blacks and Civil Reformers, 1948–1968* (Knoxville: University of Tennessee Press, 1980); Gloria Brown Melton, "Blacks in Memphis, Tennessee, 1920–1955: A Historical Study" (PhD diss., Washington State University, 1982); Ralph J. Bunche, *The Political Status of the Negro in the Age of FDR,* ed. Dewey Grantham (Chicago: University of Chicago Press, 1973); Annette E. Church and Roberta Church, *The Robert Churches of Memphis* (Ann Arbor, MI: Edwards Brothers Press, 1974); Lester Lamon, *Blacks in Tennessee, 1791–1970* (Knoxville: University of Tennessee Press, 1981).

11. On the black freedom struggle in New York City, see Clarence Taylor, *Civil Rights in New York City: From World War II to the Giuliani Era* (New York: Fordham University Press, 2011); Martha Biondi, *To Stand and Fight: The Struggle for Civil Rights in Post-War New York City* (Cambridge, MA: Harvard University Press, 2006); Shannon King, *Whose Harlem Is This, Anyway? Community Politics and Grassroots Activism during the New Negro Era* (New York: New York University Press, 2017). For Chicago, see Marcia Chatelain, *Southside Girls: Growing up in the Great Migration* (Durham, NC: Duke University Press, 2015); Davarian Baldwin, *Chicago's New Negroes: Modernity, the Great Migration, and Black Urban Life* (Chapel Hill: University of North Carolina Press, 2007); Jakobi Williams, *From the Bullet to the Ballot: The Illinois Chapter of the Black Panther Party and Racial Coalition Politics in Chicago* (Chapel Hill: University of North Carolina Press, 2015). For Oakland, see Robert O. Self,

American Babylon: Race and the Struggle for Postwar Oakland (Princeton, NJ: Princeton University Press, 2005); Robyn Spencer, *The Revolution Has Come: Black Power, Gender, and the Black Panther Party in Oakland* (Durham, NC: Duke University Press, 2016). For Atlanta, see Maurice Hobson, *The Legend of the Black Mecca: Politics and Class in the Making of Modern Atlanta* (Chapel Hill: University of North Carolina Press, 2017); Tomiko Brown-Nagin, *Courage to Dissent: Atlanta and the Long History of the Civil Rights Movement* (New York: Oxford University Press, 2012). Other notable studies of American cities include Natalie Hopkinson, *Go-Go Live: The Musical Life and Death of a Chocolate City* (Durham, NC: Duke University Press, 2012), and Patrick D. Jones, *The Selma of the North: Civil Rights Insurgency in Milwaukee* (Cambridge, MA: Harvard University Press, 2010).

12. See Laurie B. Green, *Battling the Plantation Mentality: Memphis and the Black Freedom Struggle* (Chapel Hill: University of North Carolina Press, 2007); Gritter, *River of Hope;* Michael K. Honey, *Going down Jericho Road: The Memphis Strike, Martin Luther King's Last Campaign* (New York: W. W. Norton, 2007); Michael K. Honey, *Black Workers Remember: An Oral History of Segregation, Unionism, and the Freedom Struggle* (Berkeley: University of California Press, 1999); Michael K. Honey, *Southern Labor and Black Civil Rights: Organizing Memphis Workers* (Urbana: University of Illinois Press, 1993); Hughes, *Country Soul;* Zandria Robinson, *This Ain't Chicago: Race, Class, and Regional Identity in the Post-Soul South* (Chapel Hill: University of North Carolina Press, 2014); Shirletta Kinchen, *Black Power in the Bluff City: African American Youth and Student Activism in the Memphis, 1965–1975* (Knoxville: University of Tennessee Press, 2015); Darius Young, "'The Gentleman from Memphis': Robert R. Church Jr. and African American Leadership during the Early Civil Rights Movement" (PhD diss., University of Memphis, 2011); Elton H. Weaver, "'Mark the Perfect Man, and Behold the Upright': Bishop C. H. Mason and the Emergence of the Church of God in Christ in Memphis, Tennessee" (PhD diss., University of Memphis, 2007); James David Conway, "Moderated Militants in the Age of Black Power: The Memphis NAACP, 1968–1975" (PhD diss., University of Memphis, 2015).

13. King, *I Have a Dream,* 196–200.

"In the Hands of the Lord"

Migrants and Community Politics in the Late Nineteenth Century

Brian D. Page

On December 9, 1874, a coalition of African American benevolent associations announced their decision to align themselves with former slave owners in Memphis. Commenting on the contentious battles over city elections during Reconstruction, their proclamation suggested a new direction in local politics: "After long years of citizenship, without evil intent on our part, we find ourselves . . . estranged from our best interests, and in a most bitter antagonistic relation to the true people of the south—the owners of the soil—through whom alone we could only hope for prosperity in this section of the country."[1]

The events surrounding this alliance were indicative of changes taking place in southern communities at the end of Reconstruction. The Republican Party's failure to sustain a viable political alternative in the South led black southerners to look for new ways to maintain their influence in the political arena.[2] In the months following the declaration, elite white southerners' support for the black community's efforts to appoint black teachers and their support for an African American female teacher in a dispute with a white school principal seemingly solidified the alliance between former slaves and "the owners of the soil."[3] As a result, in the 1876 city election, elite Memphians' candidates for office were elected.[4] It had been ten years since the end of federal occupation of the city, but members of the white antebellum elite finally regained control of the city government with support from the black community.

At first glance, the alliance between former slaves and elite Memphians fit well with the Reconstruction narrative. While violence, fraud, and intimidation proved to be an expedient recourse for southern Democrats to reclaim political control, practical concerns often led elite white men to consider conciliatory gestures toward black southerners, so long as these alliances did not challenge white supremacy.[5] The alliance also reiterated the conclusions of scholarship on the trajectory of African American politics. In the years following enfranchisement, African Americans became disenchanted with the Republican Party's moderation and failure to fight for permanent reforms.[6] But by allying themselves with white southerners, African Americans helped create what Laurie Green identifies as a "plantation mentality." This political culture upheld a racist ideology that promoted white domination and black subservience.[7]

Yet a closer examination of the events surrounding this alliance suggests that although African Americans in Memphis appeared to be accommodating to elite white domination, their actions were consistent with the formerly enslaved migrant populations' struggle for independence. For example, the association of black mutual aid societies credited with facilitating the alliance between former slaves and elite white Memphians had little to do with the debate over the appointment of black teachers. Rather, this coalition of mutual aid organizations comprised benevolent associations from the northern and eastern periphery of the city—rural areas where individuals were dependent on agriculture for employment—while the conflict over black teachers represented a community debate transpiring in the urban working-class neighborhood of South Memphis.

African American political struggles, therefore, cannot be easily classified as either accommodation or resistance en masse. An examination of postemancipation political events in South Memphis reflects the diverse interests of African Americans as they looked for ways to assert their autonomy.[8] For migrants, the city symbolized the possibilities of a life free from white supervision and social control on southern plantations. As a result, long-term black residents and Republican activists utilized the political process to promote racial equality, whereas incoming migrants were often more willing to challenge white supremacy on a daily basis. The migrant population was not monolithic, however. In South Memphis, a community-oriented migrant population approached politics as one way to express its independence. By demonstrating its desire for freedom, it was equally critical of the political culture of white supremacy.

Wartime Migration

How enslaved men and women approached the Civil War provides insight into the continuity of family, kinship, and community throughout the war. Memphis's central location in the Mid-South, surrounded by cotton-producing counties with enslaved majorities, made the city a destination for wartime migrants. On June 6, 1862, the city fell to federal troops; migrants received additional protections in October 1862 when the federal government took over local law enforcement and ordered slaves to be treated as free persons. In addition, the city contained three contraband camps, and it was a center for the recruitment of black soldiers, with three regiments of black soldiers stationed at Fort Pickering in South Memphis.[9] As a result, between 1860 and 1865, the black population of Memphis increased from 3,882 to over 16,000.[10]

The advancement of the Union army often informed slaves' approach to the war.[11] Julius Jones, a former slave from Arkansas, observed that on his plantation, "all of the men on the place run off and joined the northern army" once the war began.[12] Similarly, in southwestern Tennessee, John Houston Bills complained that the region's slave population was "desiring an excuse to run away and join the Northern Army," which "many of them are doing." In one instance, he observed, more than 900 slaves were carried away on a train to Memphis.[13] In northern Mississippi, one white southerner reported that more than a thousand slaves accompanied the Union army when it left the area.[14] Those that did not join the Union army were often taken to the contraband camps in Memphis. Sally Dixon's family was taken to Memphis, where, she noted, "they had a place for us to stay." And although many black men chose to join the army voluntarily, evidence suggests that some may have been conscripted. Dixon recalled that, once in Memphis, "they made my father a soldier, and he stayed in the army in Memphis til the war was over."[15]

Incoming migrants approached emancipation in ways that were congruent with the communal networks that had informed their daily lives as slaves.[16] "They just passed the word 'round," Anna Hall remembered. Similar to the oral traditions sustained outside the supervision of white southerners, knowledge about the war was shared clandestinely. Emma Barr, a former slave from Arkansas, remembered that slaves on the plantation gathered to talk about freedom. Not unlike religious gatherings during slavery, "they turned an iron pot upside down in the room" to prevent others from overhearing their discussion.[17] Similarly, according to Laura Abromson, during the war slaves "stole out in some of their houses and turned the washpot down at the door" and prayed for freedom.[18]

Slaves' decisions to migrate might be made individually or communally. Evie Herrin observed that as soon as her family learned about freedom, they left, and Maria White remembered that, "quick as ma heard it, she left de place."[19] For others, the decision to leave the plantation was a collective endeavor. For example, in Bolivar, Tennessee, slaves from four plantations simultaneously abandoned their owners late one evening.[20] Some, as Violent Shaw observed, "got on the road just walking."[21] Susan Jones of Panola County, Mississippi, remarked that one Sunday morning, everyone on her plantation walked together to Hernando, Mississippi, where they stayed all night before they "walked to Memphis the next day."[22] According to Louis Hughes, as a result of these wartime migrations, "the city was filled with slaves from all over the south, who cheered and gave us welcome."[23]

Countless migrants chose not to join the Union army or to live in contraband camps under the supervision of federal authorities. They inhabited crowded tenements and makeshift huts on the southern periphery of the city near Fort Pickering. The close quarters provided friends, relatives, and newcomers the opportunity to reconstitute communities.[24] Since most freed people arrived in Memphis with few material possessions, they made do with whatever building material they could find. Not unlike the customary rights claimed by slaves on southern plantations to furnish their cabins and feed their families, military officials observed that freed people "carry off axes, shovels, spades, and picks where they can be found, to use in building, and maintaining these households." Others pooled their resources to survive. It was here, outside the supervision of federal authorities, where slave neighborhoods were "enlarged and re-created" with the arrival of migrants, forming an intricate network of kin and new neighbors.[25]

While incoming migrants relied on past practices to navigate their new terrain, they also looked to shed their slave status. Male migrants found work as barbers, carpenters, shoemakers, and draymen, while women labored as cooks or did washing and ironing. In response to migrants' efforts to assert their independence, authorities required every former slave living and working in the city to carry a pass attesting to his or her employment. Many refused, and in the summer of 1863 black migrants were ordered to register their employment with the provost marshal. Those without proper documentation would be arrested and removed to contraband camps.[26] In the summer and fall of 1865 federal authorities made a concerted effort to relocate the "surplus" population of former slaves to rural areas. Despite these efforts, General David Tilson observed, most former slaves refused and preferred to "rely on such a precarious living as they can make in the city."[27]

Incoming migrants' desire for independence undoubtedly escalated social tensions in the city, contributing to the Memphis Massacre of 1866.[28] On May 1, 1866, a physical altercation between the city's predominantly Irish police force and a group of recently discharged African American soldiers escalated into three days of rioting that targeted the newly formed migrant community in South Memphis.[29] Members of the Joint Congressional Committee sent to investigate the massacre concluded that forty-six African Americans had been killed and five African American women had been raped, in addition to the destruction of ninety-one homes, four churches, and twelve schools.[30] The violence was concentrated in the Sixth and Seventh Wards along South Street, where the majority of new migrants resided. The massacre, Altina Waller concluded, was not a citywide conflict but a "neighborhood event."[31]

Individual and collective responses to the violence underscore divisions within the black community. Immediately following the massacre, the city's "most influential colored citizens" petitioned the Freedmen's Bureau to designate them as labor agents for the city. They planned to "induce the surplus portion of the colored population" to enter into contracts with planters in the region to mitigate racial tensions.[32] These actions reflected the antebellum black population's discomfort with the burgeoning migrant population, which threatened their precarious social position in the city. Migrants did indeed choose to flee the city. The Reverend Ewing O. Tade, a member of the American Missionary Association and the pastor of Lincoln Chapel, observed that a "majority of the working class were afraid to be seen, and hid themselves," while others "left the place by cars and boats." Some members of his congregation "have gone away and have not come back."[33] Likewise, Henry Porter, the owner of a black community store, noted that many of those who lost their homes during the massacre were "gone."[34]

Events surrounding the massacre and its investigation revealed the limits of federal, state, and local authorities' commitment to protecting the migrant community. Three weeks after the massacre, one military official observed that, "although many of the perpetrators are known, no arrests have been made, nor is there now any indication on the part of civil authorities that any are mediated by them."[35] Even though the congressional report identified almost seventy known perpetrators, none was ever brought to justice. Meanwhile, in the months following the massacre, the state of Tennessee ratified the Thirteenth Amendment, passed legislation allowing blacks to testify in court, and created a new Metropolitan Police Force, resulting in the professionalization of the force. The Freedmen's Courts were disbanded by the end of May.[36] In July 1866 Tennessee ratified the Fourteenth Amendment and was readmitted to the Union.[37] As a result, in the fall of 1866 the military restored full authority to the citizens of Memphis, just six months after one of the bloodiest episodes in post–Civil War history.[38]

In spite of the unwillingness of authorities and residents to protect migrants, many chose to remain and rebuild. Although no one was held accountable, the Freedmen's Bureau did take steps to rebuild the schools that had been burned down. African Americans, however, provided the labor. The *Memphis Daily Post* observed in early May that a large crowd of African American carpenters "numbering from one hundred and fifty to two hundred" showed up for these jobs. As a result, on May 28, 1866, the *Post* reported that a new schoolhouse was reopened in South Memphis. These schools and churches symbolized hope and a rejection of the past. Lincoln Chapel, for example, was one of several churches burned down by the mob. Members expressed both disbelief and a resolve to remain in Memphis. "Quite a number of the parents came out, and a large number of children," Reverend Tade observed, to view the destroyed church. They "seemed to be very troubled on account of it" and "expressed strong feelings of attachment." As they gathered, Reverend Tade encouraged them not to be "discouraged," assuring them that "there were enough ashes there to build another Lincoln Chapel." One week after the massacre, close to 100 members met to worship at an alternative location.[39]

Evidence suggests that black migrants' responses to the massacre strengthened the bonds of fellowship and the desire to build a community.[40] Associational networks expanded after the massacre. In the summer of 1866, for example, Joseph Colwell and other leading black Memphians organized the Colored Mechanics Benevolent Association. In addition to Colwell, whose building was burned during the massacre, its members included Wesley Ware, who, along with his wife, had been targeted by the mob.[41] Migrants also reaffirmed their commitment to these newly formed communities. Men and women from the local Methodist and Baptist congregations established mutual aid associations to build new churches. These included the Avery Chapel Building Fund and the Daughters of Zion Building Fund No. 1 for the First Baptist Colored Church.[42]

Avery African Methodist Episcopal (AME) Chapel was one of the most prominent congregations in Memphis. Horatio Rankin, a northern African American missionary, helped establish the church during the Civil War. Avery Chapel would become a center for black Republican activism. Its members included middle-class black Memphians, former Union soldiers, and working-class migrants. Teachers, barbers, carpenters, and draymen attended, in addition to members of the antebellum free black community. Members Catherine West and Anna Jackson were both former slaves from the southern interior who washed and ironed clothes, and the pastor, Page Tyler, was a former slave from Arkansas.[43]

Members of Avery Chapel demanded that either the federal government or the city of Memphis compensate the congregation for its losses. The Freedmen's Bureau refused to provide funds for "the erection of churches" and argued that "the city of Memphis should pay the losses sustained by your congregation." In a July 30, 1866, letter to Rufus McCain, a prominent member of the congregation, the agency clarified its position, noting that while it believed the city "ought to pay," the congregation should not expect any compensation.[44] Instead, Horatio Rankin traveled north to raise funds, and the congregation appealed directly to the local black community.[45] In the fall of 1866 the congregation bought a lot and organized a fair to raise money to go toward "paying off the debt of the church and for the lot and building now complete." The congregation raised more than $1,000. Afterward, leaders of the congregation attributed their success to the fact "that members of the said church turned out and built and established the foundations of said church, by and with their own labor."[46]

In contrast, although members of the First Baptist Church did not formally protest the attacks on their community, their actions after the massacre were political, as they expressed their autonomy. Austin Cotton, a twenty-nine-year-old migrant and church member, expressed the sentiments of many African Americans during his testimony to the Joint Congressional Committee. Cotton, who had been beaten over the head with a pistol by a policeman while walking home from work, took the opportunity to relate specific incidents during the massacre to larger questions about equality. Though he had never been abused prior to this attack, Cotton observed, "The colored people do not have any rights; if one of them lifts his fingers he will be fined five dollars, when he would not have been if he had been a slave." In the end, he noted, all he could do was leave it "in the hands of the Lord."[47] Cotton's seeming resignation reflected not only a belief that the Lord would judge those responsible but also the independence of the congregation and its distrust of white authorities.

Despite efforts to limit the autonomy of the migrant population, the First Baptist congregation grew. Morris Henderson, a slave from Virginia who migrated to Memphis in 1847, held religious services in the basement of a white church until the congregation decided to abandon it and move to a "brush arbor."[48] Throughout the Civil War era, periodic revivals and mass baptisms brought newcomers into the community. Julius Jones, a former black soldier from Louisiana who had been discharged in Memphis, noted that soon after the war, he attended his first meeting at a Baptist church in a "brush arbor." He recalled, "when the call came for moaners, I went to the bench and when I said 'amen,' I couldn't rise from the seat."[49] During the fall of 1866 the Beale Street Baptist Church organized a revival where former slaves shared similar conversion experiences, resulting in the baptism of more than 100 new members.[50] Soon thereafter, Henderson's congregation raised $5,000 and, in October 1866, purchased a lot on Beale Street for a new church in South Memphis.

The proliferation of African American churches and benevolent associations strengthened the social and economic foundations of the migrant community. By 1875, there were eighteen African American churches in Memphis.[51] These neighborhood churches were spread throughout the city to accommodate the residential patterns of black Memphians. It was at church where newcomers were introduced to the community and established the foundation of black organizational life. Church members often designated their pastor as their primary beneficiary, leaving him their assets upon their death. For example, Lizzie Fisher, a washerwoman from Fayette County, Tennessee; Lucinda Holmes, a seamstress from Mississippi; and Richard Reedus from Limestone County, Alabama, all listed Reverend Henderson as the beneficiary of their deposits in the Freedmen's Savings Bank. African Americans established a broad spectrum of almost 100 different church groups, benevolent societies, trade associations, Masonic orders, and social organizations. In an examination of more than 200 deposits made by such organizations to the Freedmen's Savings Bank between 1866 and 1874, 51 percent of these groups were identified as working-class mutual aid associations. Political leadership came from the more skilled and entrepreneurial classes rather than the religious and benevolent societies led by the new migrant population.[52] Though not part of the core group of black Republican activists, the community-oriented migrant population helped shape the trajectory of political debates throughout the late nineteenth century.

African American Electorate

Black benevolent societies provided a link among community, culture, and politics in the postslavery era. Associations such as the Sons of Ham and the United Benevolent Societies regularly sponsored commemorations of emancipation, the anniversary of the federal occupation of Memphis, and the Fourth of July, as well as neighborhood picnics designed to build community and mobilize voters.[53] Voluntary organizations helped bring rural migrants into the electoral process by making these gatherings distinctively African American events. The music, dancing, and parades that characterized these events were undoubtedly familiar to the migrants in attendance. Participants "drawn up in line and decorated with regalia of their several orders," accompanied by fife, drum, and fiddle music, marched down the city streets and, as local newspapers reported, sometimes danced in a "ring."[54] Whether this "dancing ring" mirrored the counterclockwise African dance is not clear, but the songs and rituals engaged in during these community events provided space to carve out a political ethos that appealed to the migrant community.[55]

African Americans responded enthusiastically to their enfranchisement by the state of Tennessee in February 1867. In May 1867, for example, 4,562 African Americans from Shelby County registered to vote in Memphis.[56] As a result of this enthusiasm, the chairman of the Republican Committee in Shelby County reported that 7,140 African American men had registered to vote by the end of the summer.[57] Based on calculations from the 1870 census, this suggests that every potential black male voter registered in Shelby County. Yet voter turnout never approached the 100 percent registration rate tallied for Memphis and Shelby County. In fact, in some instances, electoral results indicated that as few as 33 percent of potential voters participated in local contests.[58]

Who were these new voters?[59] Several of the first registered voters were residents of the antebellum free black community. Frank Talley and Joseph Clouston, free blacks, were among the first 102 African Americans registered in Memphis. Both men took leadership roles in public life and voted regularly. Other longtime residents among the first voters were most likely former slaves. They included Edward Gibson, a sawmill laborer born in Missouri; he had lived in Memphis for almost twenty years before the war and belonged to Collins Methodist Episcopal Church, the oldest African American congregation in Memphis. In an examination of almost 1,200 voters in Memphis, of the 327 whose pre–Civil War residence could be determined, 13 percent lived in Memphis before the war.[60] More likely to be literate, these individuals' organizational ties to the antebellum population solidified their connection to the community, placing them in contact with established social networks that kept them politically informed.[61]

The majority of African American voters were, however, wartime migrants. Although social status was the clearest indicator of divisions within the black community, these newcomers also approached politics differently based on their personal histories and social ties in the community. Based on the available biographical information, it appears that most newly registered voters shared a common past as laborers on the cotton plantations in the Mississippi River Valley. For instance, Joseph Thomas, a fifty-four-year-old blacksmith born in South Carolina, lived in Vicksburg before migrating to Memphis. Henry Hunt, a former Union soldier, was born in Missouri and was later sold to a Mississippi plantation owner at one of the slave markets in Memphis. In all, 49 percent of newly registered voters had been born in either Tennessee or Mississippi. And where antebellum residence could be determined, 73 percent had migrated to Memphis from elsewhere in Tennessee or from Mississippi, the majority from counties in close proximity to the city. A majority of these incoming migrants struggled for economic survival as manual laborers. Not surprisingly, unskilled day laborers were less likely to be identified as part of the electorate than were members of the entrepreneurial and professional class in Memphis.[62]

For a core group of black Republican activists, participation in politics represented a continuation of their collective efforts during the war. Black soldiers played an early organizational role in politics. In addition to defending the city at Fort Pickering, they engaged in armed confrontations with Confederate soldiers. This included the battle in defense of Fort Pillow, where a regiment led by Memphian General Nathan B. Forrest massacred black troops after they surrendered. Their experiences in the Union army undoubtedly played a role in their political mobilization. William Williams, for example, was wounded during the siege on Fort Pillow, while Kane McClellan, another former soldier, suffered a gunshot wound in Tupelo, Mississippi, while fighting Confederate forces. In total, former soldiers represented 10 percent of the urban electorate.[63]

While former soldiers were responsible for early efforts to register new voters, the new independent churches and cooperative networks had more of a long-term impact on black politics in Memphis. Religious and community associations provided social places to educate voters about the democratic process, establish political strategies, and hold leaders accountable. At least 20 percent of black voters had some ties to community organizations. An analysis of specific organizations suggests a direct correlation between civic life and political involvement. Sixteen of the twenty-three known leaders of the Sons of Ham were among the elector-

Beale Street Baptist Church. (Courtesy Memphis and Shelby County Room, Memphis Public Library)

ate. Made up primarily of carpenters, draymen, and plasterers, its members took an active role in public life, organizing social events and political rallies. In addition, nine of thirteen representatives from the Young Men's Associations participated in electoral politics. They included Joseph

Clouston and Rufus McCain, who were members of the professional and entrepreneurial class and prominent political activists.[64]

Though many newly registered migrant voters were not part of the core group of political activists, their affiliation with the independent congregations and mutual aid societies informed their community-oriented approach to politics. Associated with Beale Street Baptist Church and Salem Baptist Church in the South Memphis and Fort Pickering neighborhoods, these associations originated from the influx of former slaves into the southern periphery of the city. It was not uncommon for these organizations to participate in political rallies, but they were rarely the architects of political events, as they tended to keep their distance from both black and white Republican leaders. The majority of representatives from the Sons of Zion did, however, cast ballots at the polls. They included Thomas Green and Solomon Green, day laborers who migrated to Memphis during the Civil War era. In addition, twenty of thirty-six identified members of the social benevolent societies and eleven of twenty-three Union Forever Society representatives were among the electorate.[65] Though little information is known about these organizations' membership, it was not uncommon for 200 to 300 individuals to belong to an organization. Therefore, when new voters came to the polls, they did so not just as former slaves or Republicans but as members of expansive social networks with their own traditions and community interests.

Community Politics

Migrants exhibited a political ethos of independence that confounded the Republican leadership in Memphis. After the enfranchisement of African Americans on February 26, 1867, a voting constituency of approximately 2,000 black Memphians embraced their entrance into the political arena. African American voters gained their most monumental electoral success in the Shelby County elections in the spring of 1868, contributing to a landslide victory for the Republican Party.[66] Yet despite these successes, Republican leaders expressed frustration at the degree of independence black Memphians exhibited. In anticipation of state elections in the fall of 1868, one prominent white Republican lamented his failure to mobilize African American voters because he lacked the resources and the "time to run after them and see to them." "I could control them," he wrote, "if I had the time."[67]

Clear divisions were apparent between established black political activists and the community-oriented migrant population. After the state of Tennessee passed a law allowing African Americans to hold public office, black Republican activists began to demand federal posts and elected offices.[68] White Republican leaders often opposed these efforts. Hannibal Carter, for example, a former soldier and Republican activist, was promised the position of assessor for the US Internal Revenue Department in West Tennessee. But the position was given to a white Republican instead, while Carter became the deputy assessor.[69] In response to party officials' unwillingness to recognize black leaders as equals, a group of prosperous black Memphians led a movement to elect Edward Shaw, the city's most prominent black political leader, to the US Congress. On September 27, 1870, a black Republican delegation held a political gathering at Colwell's Hall, which had long served as a meeting place for affluent black residents of Memphis. There, Shaw criticized white Republicans' unwillingness to recognize African Americans as equals and asked those present to teach white Republicans a "lesson."[70] Despite an active campaign, Shaw garnered only 167 votes.[71]

Why was Shaw unsuccessful? In 1869 conservative Democrats returned to power in the state of Tennessee, ending the Republican Party's control of state and national elections there. However, Shaw's vote total fell well below the 1,802 ballots cast for the designated Republican congressional candidate.[72] The outcome suggested black political activists' inability to put forth an argument that appealed to the community-oriented migrant population. Supported by prominent members of the antebellum community and business owners such as Joseph Clouston and Robert Church, Shaw was a relative newcomer with limited ties to the migrant community in South Memphis. Clouston, an antebellum free black and one of the city's wealthiest residents, lived next door to Shaw and was a member of Avery Chapel. Church had made a name for himself not only as a business leader but also as a political activist who challenged white discrimination by refusing to stand on the platform outside a streetcar in 1867.[73] More so than personal relations, the campaign's focus on elected office and criticism of Republican paternalism proved ineffective in mobilizing the migrant population. Between 1870 and 1879, political events demonstrated that migrants were more likely to respond to local issues centered on neighborhood interests. While, on the surface, the alliances created appeared to represent an accommodation to racial subservience, for the community-oriented migrant population, these alliances were consistent with their long-standing desire for autonomy and distrust of political authorities.

A coalition with Irish Americans in the municipal elections demonstrated African American voters' potential to transform the political landscape. In Memphis, the conservative electorate was divided among working-class and middle-class white southerners, elite ex-Confederates, and a constituency of Irish and German Americans. The Civil War and Reconstruction disrupted the antebellum political order, allowing middle-class immigrants to establish a political presence in local governance. With the return of ex-Confederates to the political process, a constituency of disgruntled Irish Democrats looked to maintain their political influence. In preparation for city elections in 1872, white conservatives lamented that these disgruntled Irish Americans threatened to upset the social order by putting "Ireland to bed with Africa."[74] To solidify a wide range of community support, the coalition constructed a biracial ticket composed of an Irish American for mayor and Irish, German, and African American candidates for City Council in 1872 and 1874.

More so than elected officials, the coalition campaigned on a promise to integrate the city's police force. Given the long-standing coercive relationship between African Americans and white southerners, this proposal undoubtedly appealed to black migrants' desire for self-determination. Conservative Democrats and the city's "best citizens" put forth a People's ticket in opposition to the alliance. Candidates attended meetings at Zion Hall in South Memphis. To minimize the effectiveness of the coalition, conservatives drew on recent history by revisiting the Memphis Massacre.[75] The *Memphis Daily Appeal* encouraged Irish Americans to remember that they were "not negroes" and that the "negro is your natural and inevitable enemy and competition in every department of labor."[76] Despite this effort to "incite a riot" that, as observed by one longtime white Republican leader, "united the whites violently against the blacks," African Americans expressed a different narrative of the massacre rooted in the historical efforts of immigrants and native whites to resort to violence to marginalize African Americans.[77] Edward Shaw, who was running for wharf master, noted that although there were "Irishmen in the mob," it contained "citizens of all classes."[78]

Underlying the political discourse of race and class, therefore, were long-standing community conflicts over the social and cultural autonomy of the residents of South Memphis. While African Americans accounted for 49 percent of the population in the Seventh Ward, for example, almost 20 percent of the Irish immigrant population also lived in the ward. Evidence suggests that the success of the coalition was dependent on political support from the community-oriented migrant population. On the eve of the 1872 municipal election, the *Daily Appeal* observed, "most of the negroes have registered within the last three days," and election returns indicated a high African American turnout, resulting in the defeat of a ticket of ex-Confederates.[79] Responding to a letter written to the Reverend Morris Henderson of Beale Street Baptist Church that was critical of black support of the coalition, one unidentified African American affirmed the independence of the black community, noting that its members were "free" and proposed to "have some influence in deciding who shall lead." Furthermore, he continued, "no man can so delude the colored people as to compel them to support a candidate whose recommendation is not endorsed by the colored people."[80]

The results achieved by the coalition raised questions about the accountability of elected officials to African American voters. Supporters of the coalition elected a new mayor, an African American wharf master, and six African American councilmen.[81] The newly elected councilmen moved quickly to ensure that the new administration lived up to its promise to know "no nationality or color" in public hiring.[82] Thomas Moon motioned that the mayor and the police board "appoint representatives on the police from all nationalities without regard to creed or color," while James Thomas proposed a resolution to place "10% Italians, 20% Irish, 20% Germans, and 50% Americans, white and black, without discrimination as to color," on the police force. This proposal was followed by a resolution by Joseph Clouston to appoint twenty African Americans to the police force.[83] Yet the mayor remained reluctant to offer his full public support, and no political officers were appointed. Migrants undoubtedly interpreted the outcome as a reason to distrust political leaders' commitment to their community.

At the same time, a dispute between Sarah Thompson, an African American teacher, and J. H. Barnum, a northern missionary and principal of Clay Street School in South Memphis, created neighborhood outrage and led to an unlikely alliance between former slaves and ex-Confederates. Barnum charged that Thompson was a constant source of disruption, failed to follow proper procedures for addressing grievances, and was an inadequate teacher. In response, Thompson criticized the management of black public schools and echoed the demands of migrants in South Memphis for the hiring of more African American teachers.[84] The dispute between Thompson and Barnum was the part of a long-standing debate over African American control and influence in the public schools of South Memphis.

Two years before the Thompson-Barnum controversy, community leaders had expressed their dissatisfaction with white northern teachers. In the summer of 1873 civic leaders at a neighborhood meeting held in Zion Hall on Beale Street resolved "that, in view of the fact white teachers in our colored schools have failed . . . [we] respectfully ask that the services of those teachers be dispensed." More importantly, they sought community control over local schools: "That, in view of the fact that we are prescribed by law to separate schools for our children upon the presumption of 'inferiority' we respectfully ask that we may have the benefit in full, and that every teacher, from principal down, be elected from the prescribed class."[85]

Long-term residents and members of the black political class, however, tempered this protest. At a separate meeting held in the hall of the Sons of Ham, participants rescinded the original resolution against white teachers and proposed a measure that favored the selection of "competent teachers without regard to 'race, color, or previous condition.'" Evidence suggests that the final resolution was a product of negotiation and collaboration with migrants in South Memphis. Participants proposed that "when there is a white and a colored applicant for our colored schools that colored teachers may have the preference when his or her competency and qualification in every respect are the same."[86]

Migrants' protests against the employment of white teachers in their schools were revitalized by efforts to remove Thompson from her teaching position. A report drafted by the "friends of Thompson" accused Barnum of "cruel and inhumane treatment to pupils; of clandestinely seeking the disparagement of colored teachers." More to the point, this association of pastors, teachers, and community leaders demanded Barnum's removal from "any position in the colored public schools" and petitioned the Board of Education to appoint African American teachers whenever a vacancy occurred.[87] The demands of the migrant community were criticized, however, by an association of established black Memphians who referred to themselves as the "old citizens of Memphis." They criticized local efforts over the past two years "to try and take control of schools" and advocated for Thompson's removal, claiming that her actions were disrespectful to Barnum's longtime commitment to the uplift of the black community. Instead, they argued, only when it was possible to train and prepare a sufficient number of black teachers should control be placed under the supervision of the black community.[88] The dispute between Thompson and Barnum exposed long-standing divisions between the community-oriented migrant population of South Memphis and a segment of the black political establishment.

The South Memphis migrant community had the unlikeliest of allies: elite white Memphians. In addition to a white and a black lawyer, Sarah Thompson was represented by Minor Meriwether in front of the Board of Education. A former slave owner and Confederate officer, Meriwether was also a leading supporter of the People's Protective Union, an association of elite white Memphians looking to regain control of local government. On January 7, 1875, a report from the People's Protective Union gave credence to the charges made by Thompson's supporters, criticizing the tactics used by Barnum to alienate and discredit Thompson. Students from other rooms had been placed in Thompson's class "to swell the number to ninety or more, constituting five different classes or grades," intending to "injure the teacher."[89] By supporting Thompson, elite Memphians were able to criticize northern influence in local affairs. These efforts were also part of elite white Memphians' long-standing criticism of a local government controlled by a political class, resulting in the mismanagement of city affairs and an unfair tax burden on the city's "best citizens" as a result of legislation implemented during Reconstruction.

Migrants' efforts to assert the independence of their community, therefore, influenced local political debates. Although Thompson was ultimately removed from her teaching position, in July 1875 a black principal was appointed at Clay Street School, along with African American teachers.[90] Throughout the summer of 1875 elite white conservatives continued to reach out to the African American population, participating in black voluntary organizations' Fourth of July celebrations and encouraging African Americans to vote for the "best man" for office.[91] More than an accommodation of white southern paternalism, the alliance between African Americans and "the owners of the soil" reflected the diverse interests of the black community, the failure of political leaders to produce tangible results, and the independence of the migrant community of South Memphis. In preparation for the 1876 municipal election, the People's Protective Union nominated a mayoral candidate to ensure that the Democratic Party assumed "full responsibility for the management and control of the affairs of the city," since current policies had been created by a government "under the rule of the bayonet."[92] In the end, an estimated 1,500 African American voters helped elect the conservative candidate as mayor of Memphis.[93]

Yet, even with control of the city seemingly restored to white elite Memphians, the migrant populations' independence remained in conflict with the elite view that only the "best men" deserved to rule. In the 1878 election, another coalition of African Americans and Irish Americans under the leadership of a Workingman's Party challenged conservative authority by electing candidates to office.[94] Municipal reform proved to be the most effective recourse for elite residents to redeem Memphis. A devastating yellow fever epidemic in the summer of 1878 encouraged popular support for a proposal by elite Memphians to revoke the city's charter. In 1879 a new Board of Commissioners was created, replacing ward politics with state-appointed and citywide elected officials.[95] As a result, although African Americans continued to vote throughout the late nineteenth century, the new city government weakened the influence of black voters.

African Americans in South Memphis remained independent. Rather than accommodating to white domination, South Memphis became the social and economic center of the black community. There, outside the control of white Memphians, the black population created a vibrant network of black-owned businesses, churches, and social institutions. In 1892 the lynching of three successful black owners of the People's Grocery Store in South Memphis underscored the ongoing challenges African Americans faced in claiming their independence in a culture predicated on white supremacy.[96] Yet the city remained a destination for black migrants looking to escape the countryside and shed their enslaved status. In the late nineteenth century the African American population increased to almost half the city's total population, and Memphis became the third largest city in the South. Centered around the music and dance establishments on Beale Street, South Memphis provided incoming migrants with the social space to challenge white supremacy. And while religious organizations and voluntary associations continued to hold politicians at arm's length, they established the foundations of an independent community that refused to accept a culture of dependency on white southerners. In 1873 members of the Sons of Zion pooled their resources to purchase land in South Memphis that would become the city's first African American cemetery.[97] Centered on the cooperative interests of incoming migrants, they cared for their community in both life and death, long after Reconstruction ended in the American South.

Notes

1. *Memphis Daily Appeal,* December 9, 1874.

2. Eric Foner, *Reconstruction: America's Unfinished Revolution, 1863–1877* (New York: Harper and Row, 1988); William C. Harris, *The Day of the Carpetbagger: Republican Reconstruction in Mississippi* (Baton Rouge: Louisiana State University Press, 1979); Michael Perman, *The Road to Redemption: Southern Politics, 1869–1879* (Chapel Hill: University of North Carolina Press, 1984); Sarah Wiggins, *The Scalawag in Alabama Politics* (Tuscaloosa: University of Alabama Press, 1977).

3. Beverly G. Bond, "Troublesome Times: African American Women in Memphis, Tennessee, 1820–1905" (unpublished manuscript, 1996), 193–208. Also see Kathleen C. Berkeley, "Like a Plague of Locust: Immigration and Social Change in Memphis, Tennessee, 1850–1880 (PhD diss., University of California at Los Angeles, 1980); David M. Tucker, *Black Pastors and Leaders: Memphis, 1819–1972* (Memphis, TN: Memphis State University Press, 1975).

4. *Memphis Daily Appeal,* January 14, 1876.

5. Laura Edwards, *Gendered Strife and Confusion: The Political Culture of Reconstruction* (Urbana: University of Illinois Press, 1997); Glenda Gilmore, *Gender and Jim Crow: Women and the Politics of White Supremacy in North Carolina, 1896–1920* (Chapel Hill: University of North Carolina Press, 1996).

6. Edwards, *Gendered Strife and Confusion;* Thomas C. Holt, *Black over White: Negro Political Leadership in South Carolina during Reconstruction* (Urbana: University of Illinois Press, 1977); Otto Olsen, *A Carpetbagger's Crusade: The Life of Albion Winegar Tourgee* (Baltimore: Johns Hopkins University Press, 1965).

7. Laurie B. Green, *Battling the Plantation Mentality: Memphis and the Black Freedom Struggle* (Chapel Hill: University of North Carolina Press, 2007).

8. Kenneth W. Goings and Gerald L. Smith, "'Unhidden Transcripts': Memphis and African American Agency, 1862–1920," in *The New African American Urban History*, ed. Kenneth W. Goings and Raymond Mohl (Thousand Oaks, CA: Sage, 1996); Green, *Battling the Plantation Mentality.*

9. Kevin R. Hardwick, "'Your Old Father Abe Lincoln Is Dead and Damned': Black Soldiers and the Memphis Race Riot of 1866," *Journal of Social History* 27 (Fall 1993): 109–28.

10. A census ordered by the City Council concluded that there were 10,995 African Americans in Memphis out of a total population of 27,703. See Job Bledsoe, Census of Memphis, 1865, Memphis and Shelby County Public Library. However, a census taken by the Freedmen's Bureau concluded that the total black population in Memphis and on President's Island numbered 16,509. See Freedmen's Bureau Census, Records of the Memphis Sub-District, reel 1, Memphis and Shelby County Public Library. An examination of 1,957 Civil War–era residents for whom biographical data were available from deposit ledgers of the Freedmen's Savings and Trust Company revealed that African Americans migrated to Memphis from more than 450 different counties throughout the American South. The majority were from Tennessee and Mississippi, including 40 percent who migrated to Memphis from the counties of southwestern Tennessee and northern Mississippi. See Registers of Signatures of Depositions in Branches of the Freedmen's Savings and Trust Company, 1865–1874, Memphis, Tennessee, Record Group 101, National Archives.

11. In an examination of wartime migration patterns from the Mississippi River Valley to the Upper Midwest, Leslie Schwalm identifies three distinct paths: slave flight, relocation organized by white soldiers, and relocation of fugitive slaves to northern employers. See Leslie Schwalm, "'Overrun with Free Negroes': Emancipation and Wartime Migration in the Upper Midwest," *Civil War History* 50, no. 2 (2004): 145–74. Similarly, in Memphis, the advancement of the Union army, geographic proximity, and social structures in the slave community influenced the pattern of wartime migration to Memphis. In Tennessee, for example, 20,000 African American men joined the Union army. See John Cimprich, *Slavery's End in Tennessee, 1861–1865* (Tuscaloosa: University of Alabama, 1985).

12. George P. Rawick, *An American Slave: A Composite Autobiography*, 41 vols. (Westport, CT: Greenwood Press, 1972–1977), vol. 8, pt. 3.

13. John Houston Bills's Diaries, Tennessee State Library and Archives.

14. *Memphis Daily Appeal*, July 24, 1863.

15. Rawick, *American Slave*, vol. 7, pt. 2, 625–30.

16. The social relationships and daily survival strategies of enslaved people placed African Americans, in the words of Stephanie Camps, on a path "closer to freedom," and they are therefore central to an understanding of wartime migration. Stephanie M. H. Camps, *Closer to Freedom: Enslaved Women and Everyday Resistance in the Plantation South* (Chapel Hill: University of North Carolina Press, 2004).

17. Rawick, *American Slave*, vol. 8, pt. 1, 119–21. For many slaves, "turning down the pot" was a cultural tradition designed to ensure secrecy. The origin of this tradition is unclear, but as Michael Gomez argues, these secret rituals were evidence of resistance and the shared cultural identify of African Americans. See Michael Gomez, *Exchanging Our Country Marks: The Transformation of African Identities in the Colonial and Antebellum South* (Chapel Hill: University of North Carolina Press, 1998), 200.

18. Rawick, *American Slave*, vol. 8, pt. 1, 8–10.

19. Ibid., supp. series, vol. 10, 2276–81; supp. series, vol. 8, 988–91.

20. Bills's Diaries.

21. Rawick, *American Slave*, vol. 10, 143–44.

22. Ibid., supp. series, vol. 8, 1256–60.

23. Louis Hughes, *Thirty Years a Slave: From Bondage to Freedom* (1897; reprint, Montgomery, AL: New South Books, 2002), 126–37.

24. Report of the Memphis Sub-District for the Month of August, September 10, 1866, Bureau of Refugees, Freedmen and Abandoned Land, reel 17, Memphis and Shelby County Public Library.

25. Anthony E. Kaye, *Joining Places: Slave Neighborhoods in the Old South* (Chapel Hill: University of North Carolina Press, 2007), 211.

26. *Memphis Daily Bulletin*, July 13, August 13, August 18, October 30, 1863.

27. General David Tillson, September 10, 1865, Records of the Memphis Sub-District, reel 1, Memphis and Shelby County Public Library.

28. For example, in 1862 Memphis passed an ordinance to increase the size of the police force from 32 to 100. As a result, the percentage of African Americans arrested during the war increased from less than 10 percent to 24 percent of total arrests. Although proportional to the overall population, the arrests of African Americans and confrontations between black migrants and local residents perpetuated fears that former slaves were prone to lawlessness. See *Memphis Daily Appeal*, August 8, 1862; Memphis Recorder's Court, Shelby County Archives.

29. Altina L. Waller, "Community, Class, and Race in the Memphis Riot of 1866," *Journal of Social History* 18 (Winter 1984): 233–46.

30. Immediately following the Memphis Massacre, a Joint Congressio-

nal Committee investigated the incident and interviewed witnesses, providing a detailed account of the episode in the records of the Thirty-Ninth Congress. Although the incident is commonly known as the "Memphis riot," the majority report of the Republican delegation referred to it as a "massacre," which I believe is a more appropriate characterization of the violence that took place in Memphis. See "Report 101 of the House of Representatives of the First Session of the Thirty-Ninth Congress," in *Memphis Riots and Massacres: Mass Violence in America* (Miami: Mnemosyne Publication, 1969).

31. Waller, "Community, Class, and Race in the Memphis Riot," 235.

32. Petition, June 4, 1866, Bureau of Refugees, Freedmen and Abandoned Lands, reel 16.

33. "Report 101," 95.

34. Ibid., 168.

35. "Report of an Investigation of the Late Riot in Memphis," Bureau of Refugees, Freedmen and Abandoned Lands, reel 34.

36. Clinton B. Fisk to Benjamin Runkle, May 19, 1866, Selected Records of the Tennessee Field Office for the State of Tennessee, Bureau of Refugees, Freedmen and Abandoned Lands, reel 1; Clinton Fisk to O. O. Howard, May 26, 1866, ibid., reel 34; Benjamin Runkle, Report for the Memphis Sub-District for the Month of May, May 31, 1866, ibid., reel 17; Waller, "Community, Class, and Race in the Memphis Riot."

37. Foner, *Reconstruction,* 261, 267.

38. Clinton Fisk to Madison Warren, October 7, 1866, Bureau of Refugees, Freedmen and Abandoned Lands, reel 1.

39. "Report 101," 95.

40. Armistead L. Robinson, "'Plans Dat Comed from God': Institution Building and the Emergence of Black Leadership in Reconstruction Memphis, 1865–1880," in *Toward a New South? Studies in Post Civil War Southern Communities,* ed. Orvil Vernon Burton and Robert C. McMath Jr. (Westport, CT: Greenwood Press, 1982), 82. See also Kathleen C. Berkeley, "Colored Ladies Also Contributed: Black Women's Activities from Benevolence to Social Welfare, 1866–1896," in *Church and Community among Black Southerners,* vol. 9, *African American Life in the Post-Emancipation South, 1861–1900,* ed. Donald G. Nieman (New York: Garland, 1994).

41. *Memphis Daily Post,* August 30, 1866; "Report 101," 343, 344, 346.

42. Registers of Signatures of Depositions in Branches of the Freedmen's Savings and Trust Company.

43. Ibid.

44. *Memphis Daily Post,* June 13, 1866; J. Jacobs to F. Palmer, July 26, 1866, Selected Records of the Tennessee Field Office for the State of Tennessee, reel 3; Clinton Fisk to Rufus McCain, July 30, 1866, ibid., reel 1; Clinton Fisk to Rufus McCain, July 30, 1866, ibid., reel 3.

45. *Memphis Daily Post*, May 15, 1866.

46. *Memphis Daily Post*, July 31, August 14, October 17, October 31, November 20, November 24, 1866; Avery Chapel Trustees to F. Palmer, November 1867, Records of the Memphis Sub-District, reel 11.

47. "Report 101," 102.

48. Robinson, "'Plans Dat Comed from God.'"

49. Rawick, *American Slave*.

50. *Memphis Daily Post*, September 10, September 17, October 1, October 15, 1866.

51. Boyle and Chapman and Company, *Directory of the City of Memphis for 1876*.

52. Registers of Signatures of Depositions in Branches of the Freedmen's Savings and Trust Company; Robinson, "'Plans Dat Comed from God.'"

53. Brian D. Page, "'Stand by the Flag': Nationalism and African American Celebrations of the Fourth of July in Memphis, 1866–1887," *Tennessee Historical Quarterly* (Winter 1999): 285–301.

54. *Memphis Daily Post*, July 5, 1867.

55. Sterling Stuckey, *Slave Culture: Nationalist Theory and the Foundations of Black America* (New York: Oxford University Press, 1987).

56. *Memphis Daily Post*, May 1–31, 1867. Similar to former slaves in other southern communities, both men and women participated and viewed the vote as a "collective; not an individual possession." See Elsa Barkley Brown, "Negotiating and Transforming the Public Sphere," in *The Black Public Sphere: A Public Culture Book*, ed. Black Public Sphere Collective (Chicago: University of Chicago Press, 1995), 128.

57. *Memphis Daily Post*, August 2, 1867. African American enthusiasm for enfranchisement was evident in other southern communities in the summer of 1867. See Julie Saville, *The Work of Reconstruction: From Slave to Wage Laborer in South Carolina, 1860–1870* (New York: Cambridge University Press, 1994).

58. *Memphis Daily Post*, January 2, 1868; *Memphis Daily Appeal*, January 8, 1869.

59. The names of the city's first black registered voters can be found in *Memphis Daily Post*, May 3, 1867. Although election returns are incomplete, poll records for local, state, and national elections held in the city of Memphis provide additional information on actual voters. See Poll Books, City of Memphis, Colored Wards 1–10, 1868–1872, Shelby County Archives. To compile a profile of the African American electorate in Memphis, these names were cross-referenced with the 1870 federal census, city directories, and deposit slips of the Freedmen's Savings and Trust Company. See Population Schedules of the Ninth Federal Census, City of Memphis, Wards 1–10, Shelby County Archives; Registers of the Signatures of Depositions in Branches of the Freedmen's Savings and Trust Company; and the following city directories: *Boyle and Chapman's Mem-*

phis Directory, 1873, 1874, 1876; *Edward's Annual City Directory,* 1870, 1871, 1872; *Sholes City Directory,* 1877.

60. Ibid.

61. Steven Hahn, *A Nation under Our Feet: Black Political Struggles in the Rural South from Slavery to the Great Migration* (New York: Oxford University Press, 2003), 121.

62 See note 59.

63. Ibid.

64. Ibid.

65. Ibid.

66. *Memphis Daily Post,* March 9, 1868.

67. Barbour Lewis to John Eaton, March 15, 1868, John Eaton Collection, Tennessee State Library and Archives.

68. Walter J. Fraser Jr., "Black Reconstructionists in Tennessee," *Tennessee Historical Quarterly* 34 (Winter 1975): 362–382.

69. *Memphis Daily Appeal,* July 12, 1872.

70. *Memphis Daily Avalanche,* September 27, 1870.

71. *Memphis Daily Avalanche,* November 9, 1870.

72. Ibid.

73. *Memphis Daily Avalanche,* October 6, 1870; Population Schedules of the Ninth Federal Census, 1870, City of Memphis, Wards 1–10; *Memphis Daily Post,* December 17, 1867, May 12, 1868.

74. *Memphis Daily Appeal,* December 16, December 17, December 22, December 31, 1871; January 1, January 3, January 4, 1872.

75. *Memphis Daily Appeal,* December 17, 1873.

76. *Memphis Daily Appeal,* January 2, 1872.

77. Lucien Eaton to John Eaton, June 7, 1874, John Eaton Papers, Tennessee State Library and Archives.

78. *Memphis Daily Avalanche,* December 10, 1873.

79. *Memphis Daily Appeal,* January 7, January 8, 1872; December 16, 1871.

80. *Memphis Daily Appeal,* December 11, 1873.

81. *Memphis Daily Appeal,* January 2, 1874.

82. Dennis C. Rousey, "Yellow Fever and Black Policemen in Memphis: A Post-Reconstruction Anomaly," *Journal of Southern History* 51 (August 1985): 357–74.

83. *Memphis Daily Appeal,* April 15, 1874.

84. Bond, "Troublesome Times," 193–208.

85. *Memphis Daily Appeal,* July 5, 1873.

86. *Memphis Daily Appeal,* August 8, 1873.

87. *Memphis Daily Appeal,* January 7, 1875.

88. *Memphis Daily Appeal,* January 26, 1875.

89. *Memphis Daily Appeal,* January 7, 1875.

90. Bond, "Troublesome Times," 193–208.

91. *Memphis Daily Appeal,* July 6, 1875.

92. *Memphis Daily Appeal,* November 28, 1875.

93. *Memphis Daily Appeal,* January 14, 1876

94. *Memphis Daily Appeal,* December 11, December 12, December 13, December 18, December 28, 1877; April 28, June 14, June 18, June 20, June 23, June 28, August 2, 1878.

95. Lynette Boney Wrenn, *Crisis and Commission Government in Memphis: Elite Rule in a Gilded Age City* (Knoxville: University of Tennessee Press, 1998).

96. Goings and Smith, "'Unhidden Transcripts.'"

97. United Sons of Zion, Deed Book 0094, p. 415, Shelby County Registrar of Deeds.

"The Saving of Black America's Body and White America's Soul"

The Lynching of Ell Persons and the Rise of Black Activism in Memphis

Darius Young

On Monday, April 30, 1917, at around six o'clock in the morning, Minnie Woods kissed her sixteen-year-old daughter, Antoinette Rappel, good-bye as she left for school. Woods stood on the front porch and watched Antoinette place her lunch and her books in the basket of her bicycle and ride away. Rappel was a beautiful blonde-haired, blue-eyed white girl who attended Treadwell High School on Highland Street, located approximately six miles from her house. Typically, she would ride the two and a half miles to the home of her uncle, William Wilfong, and wait there for the school wagonette. In the late afternoon, when Antoinette had not returned, her mother was not alarmed, as she often spent the night with the Wilfongs to avoid the lengthy trek to and from school. The following day, when she still had not seen or heard from her daughter, Woods began to worry. That evening, she went to her brother's house, and Wilfong told her that he had not seen Antoinette since Saturday. Woods suddenly became lightheaded and almost fainted. She began to sob uncontrollably and pleaded with her brother to find Antoinette.[1]

The next morning Wilfong, along with his neighbors Kelly Puryear, Dr. H. A. Johnson, and W. W. Grant, began to search for the girl. They retraced the route she took and stopped near the Wolf River Bridge. They asked a black worker in the area if he had seen a white girl riding her bike over the bridge. He replied that he had seen the girl, but there was no trace of her on either side of the mile-long structure. The men then began to search the dense brush beneath the bridge. They saw no sign of Antoinette, so the men got back in their car and turned down a blind road "leading down from the levee, when they noticed that the bushes on the right had been trampled down." Then they saw her bicycle leaning against a tree with the seat twisted to the side. Approximately three feet from the tree, they found a dark splotch of clotted blood and several "distinct imprints of an ax blade where it had missed its mark and buried itself deeply into the turf." Scattered on the ground were bloodstained flowers that Rappel had picked from her front yard to give to her teacher. The men then followed a trail through the underbrush and traveled about fifty feet, where they encountered a horrible, unthinkable, and ghastly sight. "Lying on its back, with arms and limbs outstretched, and with clothing torn and disheveled, the headless trunk of Miss Rapp[e]l's body was found. Near her right foot was the severed head, its golden tresses, clotted and gnarled with blood. The wide-staring blue eyes bore a frozen expression of horror."[2]

"Only God knows how a mother feels when her only child is taken from her in this way," said the teary, grief-stricken mother. "I am praying that they will catch him, whoever he is. . . . But I want them to get the right one though, for I don't want to see an innocent person suffer for something they did not do. I hope they get him—God knows I do," said Woods. She then reflected on her daughter's life by simply stating, "She was the best girl you ever saw."[3] Woods had been raising Antoinette as a single parent since the girl's father had died when she was only three years old. Woods struggled to cope with the reality of her daughter's death. She did not call for vigilante violence; instead, she trusted the legal system.

On May 3 the *Memphis Commercial Appeal* and *Memphis Press-Scimitar* whipped the city into a racial frenzy by not only reporting the gruesome details of the girl's slaying but also suggesting that black men had attacked her. The *Press-Scimitar* speculated, "every indication tends to fasten the crime to a negro wood cutter, or more likely two of them."[4] The *Commercial Appeal* hinted, "a large number of Negroes worked as wood cutters in the area."[5] The newspapers succeeded in planting the idea of a black assailant and capturing the imagination of whites in the area.[6]

Memphis Blues

"Memphis presented a strange paradox," wrote Gerald Capers. It was "a city modern in physical aspect but rural in background, rural in prejudice, and rural in habit."[7] By the start of the World War I era, the city boasted at least three colleges, a medical school, six hospitals, and three business colleges. Automobiles, paved streets, buildings, and city parks reflected an urban landscape. Aesthetically, Memphis seemed to be in the midst of an urban renaissance. It also provided a seeming refuge for rural African Americans escaping from the hostile racial atmosphere of the Mississippi Delta. Memphis was the only city in the region that had a substantial black professional class, and thanks to the activism of its African American leaders, black Memphians still had a political voice. Beale Street, once a posh, exclusively white residential area, now served as the "Main Street of Negro America."[8] On Beale Street one could find everything from the offices of leading black professionals to black-owned banks, auditoriums, music clubs, saloons, gambling dens, and restaurants. Musicians such as W. C. Handy, the "Father of the Blues," helped introduce a new musical genre to mainstream America. By the 1910s, Memphis offered an attractive alternative to the mundane country life of the Delta. With a sprawling downtown, a prominent skyline, new industries, a politically conscious black community, and a "progressive" mayor, Memphis in many ways epitomized the promise of a modern southern city.[9]

For many African Americans, Memphis represented a new beginning. Each decade, thousands of black people relocated to the Bluff City. Although Memphis provided an escape from their rural communities, African Americans soon realized that they could not escape the harsh realities of the Jim Crow South. In fact, the racial culture of Memphis reflected the traditions and ideologies of its rural neighbors. White Memphians, many of whom had also migrated from the Delta and other rural communities in Tennessee, remained resistant to change and brought their own system of values and beliefs. Religion, in particular, had an enormous effect on the southern way of life. The influential writer H. L. Mencken deemed Memphis the "Buckle of the Bible Belt," in reference to the unique form of evangelical Protestantism that permeated the area. Their religion led some white Memphians to reject certain characteristics associated with urban life, viewing them as a threat to their southern traditions. Living and working with African Americans caused tense race relations in the city. In particular, the notion of interracial sex caused white southerners to become even more consumed with the concepts of honor and the "right to vengeance." They considered it their sacred duty to protect their women and children from the moral and racial corruption of urban America.[10]

Black success also violated the racist laws that governed the region. White vigilantes often targeted black businessmen, doctors, lawyers, and other professionals for the crime of merely exceeding their white counterparts in wealth, education, and prominence. Some of the most notorious examples of white supremacists' attempts to keep black people "in their place" can be gleaned in the racial history of Memphis. For example, in early May 1866 a riot erupted in the city that left forty-six African Americans dead and numerous others injured. A little over a quarter century later, another riot erupted in a Memphis suburb commonly referred to as "The Curve." The three black owners of People's Grocery Company—Thomas Moss, Calvin McDowell, and Henry Stewart—were brutally murdered by a mob in 1892 after defending their property from white looters and rioters. The mob killed the three men for allegedly "taking up arms," but in reality, they were attacked because "they were succeeding too well. They were guilty of no crime but that."[11] The lynching prompted Moss's close friend, Ida B. Wells, to study lynchings for the rest of her career. She concluded that their murder had been "an excuse to get rid of Negroes who were acquiring wealth and property and thus keep the race terrorized and 'keep the nigger down.'" According to Wells, white vigilantes hid behind the threat of interracial sex and accusations of rape to hide their true intentions of preventing any perceived notions of "Negro supremacy."[12]

As more people, both white and black, migrated to Memphis at the turn of the century, the traditional values of white southerners were challenged, creating more racial tension in the city. As Amy Wood writes, white southerners "conceptualized the threat of black enfranchisement and autonomy as, above all, a dire moral threat to white purity, literally a physical assault on white homes and white women."[13] Therefore, even in a seemingly progressive city like Memphis, whites genuinely believed that it was their righteous duty to protect the sanctity of white supremacy by maintaining the racial hierarchy in the South from their inherently immoral neighbors.

By 1916, Memphis was a half century removed from the infamous race riot of 1866, and it had been more than twenty years since the city's last recorded lynching. That year, Robert Reed Church Jr. mobilized the black vote in Memphis and established himself as the preeminent black political leader in Tennessee. In the fall, he founded the Lincoln League of Tennessee in an effort to organize the black vote and to teach African Americans the "higher art of politics."[14] Church registered more than 10,000 black voters, and in local elections that year, they outpolled the lily-white Shelby County Republicans. Although the Democrats swept the elections, Church vowed to fight year after year "until the political chains are broken and colored men are treated as citizens." He continued, "If the League did nothing more than teach colored men the dignity of the ballot and white men that all colored men cannot be purchased and a great number misled that is enough for the first time."[15] Newspapers across the country commented on the Lincoln League's success that year, and Church's faction was recognized as the "Regular Republicans" in Tennessee. His political victories presented a clear challenge to white politicians in the city and, most important, violated the fundamental beliefs of white supremacists. The tension between the two races carried over into the next year and reached its peak that spring.

The newspapers' coverage of the murder of Antoinette Rappel transformed her from an innocent victim of a horrific attack into a symbol for white southerners to unite behind, with the intention of reestablishing color lines in the city. Just a few months prior, black Memphians had seemingly developed the blueprint for African American political participation in the South. They stood on the verge of fostering more interracial cooperation to protect their ability to vote freely in state and national elections. This development provides the context for extralegal violence in Memphis and the South. The African Americans' success in the 1916 elections enraged the white community. Newspapers created the false idea of a "negro takeover" that fed into white paranoia. Historian Claude Clegg notes, "even when a lynching was ostensibly a response to an alleged crime, the nature of this kind of murder could reveal larger communal anxieties about control over black labor, African American electoral power, shifting demographic trends, or black male access to white women." False images of black men lusting over innocent white women and attacking them became "instrumental in fracturing interracial political alliances and justifying for many the worst iterations of mob violence, including castrations, disembowelments, and burnings."[16] This proved to be true in Memphis during the summer of 1917.

Ell Persons

Shelby County sheriff Mike Tate led the investigation of the murder. The initial evidence suggested that a white male had committed the crime. Detectives Charles Brunner and John Boyle found Rappel's bicycle standing against a tree with the contents of her basket undisturbed. The rape and murder had taken place in a heavily wooded area; however, the foliage showed no signs of struggle. Also, her assailant had left a white jacket and handkerchief at the scene, attire not typically associated with the poor black woodcutters in the area. Based on their investigation, Brunner and Boyle concluded that Rappel probably knew her attacker. Dr. Lee A. Stone commented, "It is practically a certainty . . . that this terrible crime has been committed by a white man."[17]

As the days passed, Tate was under increasing pressure to find Rappel's killer. The community insisted that a black man had committed the crime. Instead of relying on the evidence, Tate succumbed to this pressure and interviewed black woodchoppers from the area. After randomly questioning these men, Tate interviewed one of the woodchoppers who claimed he had witnessed the murder. Dewitt Ford, an African American deaf-mute, worked as a woodcutter near the scene of the murder and allegedly reenacted the attack through an elaborate performance that involved a series of physical gestures and grimaces. Ford, also known as "Dummy" by his employer, had allegedly stood behind a tree and watched the entire attack. It appears that Ford may have implicated other woodchoppers during his interrogation, and Tate subsequently questioned several other suspects but was not satisfied with their testimonies. Finally, Tate questioned a thirty-something black woodcutter by the name of Ell Persons. He spoke with Persons twice and let him go each time. Tate believed a white man had committed the crime, but he tried to buy some time by interrogating the black "suspects" created by the media. The white community displayed its frustration with the investigation after a couple of weeks and at one point actually chased Tate out of town. After staying away for a few days, a desperate Tate returned to Memphis and decided to follow the advice of a New York criminologist who had told him to take a photograph of the victim's eye. According to the bizarre theory of French scientist Alphonse Bertillion, a person's retina retained the image of his or her killer. Officer Paul Waggener photographed Rappel's left eye because her right eye had decomposed. After he developed the film, Waggener asserted that he could see the forehead and hair of Ell Persons in Rappel's retina. This flimsy claim proved to be enough evidence for Tate. It sealed Persons's fate.[18]

On May 8, 1917, a grand jury indicted Ell Persons. The police immediately transported him to Nashville for his own protection as he awaited trial. Almost two weeks later, on May 21, two police officers were accompanying Persons back to Memphis for a court date when they were intercepted by a mob. The mob seized Persons without a struggle and began planning his murder. Someone leaked the details of the lynching to the *Commercial Appeal* and *Press-Scimitar*. The following day the newspapers advertised the location and time of the event with eye-catching headlines. The *Commercial Appeal* declared, "Mob Captures Slayer of the Rappel Girl: Ell Persons to Be Lynched Near Scene of Murder, May Resort to Burning." The previous night, an estimated 2,000 to 4,000 disappointed spectators had arrived at the Wolf River Bridge after hearing of his abduction. By the following morning, that number had increased to an estimated 10,000 men, women, and children. The atmosphere resembled a festival more than a public execution. Some people acted as police officers and directed traffic. Vendors set up concession stands and sold drinks, peanuts, cotton candy, and ice cream to the anxious onlookers.[19]

The proceedings began at around 9:00 a.m. One of the leaders of the mob walked Persons out in front of the waiting crowd, bound by a huge rope tied around his waist. He informed Persons that "he had only a few minutes to live, and that he had better tell the truth." After hours of torture the previous night, Persons stood on the rickety, makeshift podium and confessed to the crime. At the start of this highly organized ritual, a local white pastor attempted to pray with Persons before the mob proceeded with the lynching. As the pastor approached the condemned man, a heckler shouted that Persons had not allowed Rappel to pray and told the pastor to return to the crowd. The victim's mother, Minnie Woods, yelled, "Don't shoot him, please. . . . I want him to suffer 10,000 times more than did my little girl. Burn him, Burn him!" The police investigation and media stories had convinced Woods that Persons had killed her daughter, and the lynching was justified in her eyes. The mob respected her wishes. Some men flung the rope over a thirty-foot tree limb, raised Persons off the ground, dangled him over a pit filled with tree branches soaked in gasoline, and lowered him into the pyre.[20]

With his body ablaze and the air filled with the fragrance of burning flesh, the crowd sang "John Brown's Body" and "My Old Kentucky Home." When the fire died down, and with his body still smoldering from the ritualistic sacrifice, the crowd rushed to gather souvenirs from his charred corpse. Savagely, they cut off his ears, nose, lips, and fingers. Finally, someone decapitated Persons, as Rappel's killer had done to her. His severed head was then paraded around town, displayed outside the window of a car, and thrown onto Beale Street, not far from the offices of the city's black professionals and leaders.[21]

The significance of the Ell Persons lynching goes far beyond the retelling of this tragic episode in American history. It speaks to the cultural elements of this inhumane southern phenomenon. The Persons lynching was thoughtfully organized and carried out, and it demonstrates how commonplace lynchings had become in the region. It dispels the false idea that white southerners lynched blacks out of sheer raw emotion. White southerners were not consumed with vengeance to the point that they could not control their actions. It counters ideas that only poor, rural whites engaged in this type of behavior. This mob consisted of ordinary people and represented the entire social strata of white society. As W. E. B. DuBois observed, "its nucleus of ordinary men . . . continually [gave] the mob its initial and awful impetus."[22] Lynching no longer resided exclusively in the rural countryside; it had surfaced in one of the most thriving cities in the "New South." In addition, this type of spectacle lynching showcased white solidarity in its most dangerous form.

Although thousands of people witnessed the murder, no one identified the participants, no one testified, and no one was arrested. The carnival of violence that took place that day served as a clear illustration of the synonymous relationship between lynching and southern culture. In Memphis, no lynchings had been recorded since 1892. But twenty-five years later, thousands of people had gathered from the surrounding areas to participate without hesitation. People were not afraid, shocked, or appalled by the actions of the mob. Although most of the spectators at this event had probably never witnessed a lynching, they were familiar with the practice through word of mouth, family histories, newspapers, photographs, postcards, and stories.[23]

In fact, the city's urban, modern characteristics made it even more important for whites to define the color line in Memphis. Transportation, jobs, housing, and a growing black middle class continued to push the city's racial boundaries and threatened the separate black and white worlds created by Jim Crow. Members of the city's black elite had sufficient money and influence to infiltrate white spaces of consumption and leisure, though they were relegated to colored seating. For these reasons, by the turn of the twentieth century, many lynchings occurred outside of the rural countryside. Explains historian Grace Elizabeth Hale, "In the decades following 1890s . . . lynchers drove cars, spectators used cameras, out-of-town visitors arrived on specially chartered excursion trains, and the towns and counties in which these horrifying events happened had newspapers, telegraph offices, and even radio stations that announced times and locations of these upcoming violent spectacles."[24] By the 1910s, black and white southerners had unprecedented access to the details and images of lynchings, even though they occurred less frequently. Lynching was transformed from an isolated form of extralegal violence to a large spectacle of violence that reinforced the white power structure in the South.[25]

"Lynchings were rare in Memphis, but other forms of racial violence were not," according to historian Michael Honey.[26] Police brutality, bombings, and other forms of racial violence had already plagued the city and terrorized black Memphians long before the Persons murder. Although this was the first lynching in the city in more than two decades, Memphis's close proximity to Mississippi and Arkansas made blacks constantly aware of the possibility of being lynched. This often consumed their imaginations and paralyzed the black community with fear. Richard Wright, who lived in Memphis as a young man, wrote, "I had never in my life been abused by whites, but I had already become conditioned to their existence. . . . The white brutality that I had not seen was a more effective control of my behavior than that which I knew. The actual experience would have let me see the realistic outlines of what was really happening, but as long as it remained something terrible and yet remote, something whose horror and blood might descend upon me at any moment, I was compelled to give my entire imagination over to it."[27] Psychological repression was just as useful in maintaining white supremacy during the height of Jim Crow as the economic and political controls associated with the era. White southerners genuinely believed that fear of lynching was a more effective means of controlling black assertiveness than any formal legal system. Vigilante justice had the privilege of ignoring the constitutional rights of black men, and it could terrorize the black community in ways that other forms of systemic racism could not. As historian Jacquelyn Dowd Hall observes, black men could consciously avoid being arrested and landing in the court system, but "a lynch mob could strike anywhere, at any time." She continues, "Once the brush fire of rumor began, a manhunt was organized, and the local paper put out special editions announcing a lynching in progress, there could be few effective protestations of innocence."[28] The victim could be the guilty person or an innocent bystander.

Historians Kenneth Goings and Gerald Smith point out that no community group came to Persons's immediate defense. He did not belong to any defined group. He was not a member of the black professional class or the larger working class in Memphis. Instead, Persons "was an itinerant woodchopper, a migrant to the area who lived a relatively isolated existence in a woods outside of Memphis."[29] The city had a history of black activism, but for the most part, these activists geared their efforts toward problems within their own economic or social class. The Persons lynching revealed a fundamental flaw in the racial uplift strategy of the city's black leaders. As Goings and Smith state, the "Talented Tenth" in the city sought racial redress through legal and political action. Many of the city's leaders were not willing to jeopardize their lives because it

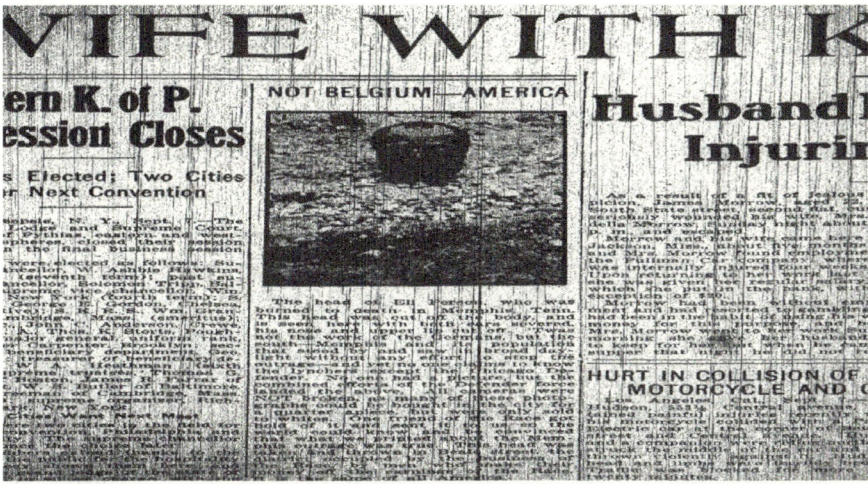

Newspaper depicting the severed head of Ell Persons.

would do nothing to "foster harmonious race relations." However, this is not to say that the black community merely acquiesced and did not resist in other subtle ways. As W. Fitzhugh Brundage notes, "we must rethink our preconceived expectations about the ways their protest may have been expressed."[30] The deference black Memphians displayed in the immediate wake of the lynching proved to be a guise for both the formal and informal political demonstrations that followed. Blacks never "knew their place," as Hall observes. "Lynching persisted as much to reaffirm solidarity and demonstrate power to whites themselves as to punish and intimidate blacks."[31]

In fact, it is the black community's reaction to the Ell Persons lynching that makes this story important. Black Memphians refused to enlist in the military, mobilized the vote, and used the national platforms of civil rights organizations to voice their opposition to lynching and white intimidation. Their reactions seemingly proved Wright's claim that the threat of lynching held more power over the black community when it existed only in their thoughts and imaginations. Now that it had become a reality, and black people had witnessed the worst of white vigilantism firsthand, they became more willing to mobilize and speak out against racial violence and white supremacy.

The Black Community's Response

By throwing Persons's head onto Beale Street, the mob made it clear that black success, wealth, and influence were violations of racial etiquette akin to physically assaulting a white woman. Just fifty years prior to the Persons lynching, the city's first black millionaire, Robert Church Sr., had been senselessly shot in the head after leaving a saloon he owned on Beale Street during the infamous 1866 Memphis riot. Although Church Sr. survived the attack, the painful migraine headaches he suffered for the rest of his life were constant reminders of that fateful night. The elder Church often refrained from public debates about race and politics and chose to put his energies into building his fortune through real estate ventures in Memphis.[32]

His son Robert Church Jr. inherited a life of luxury and privilege as the offspring of the city's most prominent black citizen. Initially, it appeared that he would follow in his father's footsteps as a real estate mogul and entrepreneur. He attended the prestigious Morgan Park Military Academy in Illinois, which was widely known as a preparatory school for the University of Chicago. From there, he attended Oberlin College in Ohio for two years and finally completed his studies at the Packard School of Business in New York. After returning home in 1907, Church worked as a cashier for his father's bank, the Solvent Savings Bank and Trust Company. By 1909, he was serving as its president while also managing his father's real estate holdings. As local educator and author Green Polonius Hamilton predicted, "In the natural course of time he will succeed his worthy sire as the wealthiest colored man in America." Church emerged on the Memphis scene as "a veritable chip off the old block" and began to carve his own legacy in the Bluff City.[33]

Despite his early success in the business world, Church remained passionate about politics. His father had dabbled in local politics but had never fully committed himself to the political arena. Church also corresponded regularly with his half sister, Mary Church Terrell, who had already established herself as one of the premier black women leaders of her generation and certainly served as a role model for him. Despite his family's ties to political movements, Church was initially reluctant to dedicate himself to politics, but that changed after his father died in August

1912. The following month, Ida B. Wells wrote him a letter of condolence and advised him "to fulfill your trust to the honor of your race and your generation."[34] Other leaders and family friends offered similar advice. Shortly thereafter, Church resigned from his position at the bank and became more involved in local, state, and national politics.

By 1917, he was a political force to be reckoned with in the city, gaining national attention after the 1916 elections. He responded to the Persons murder by becoming a more vocal critic of race relations in Memphis. In its aftermath, Church and his allies attempted to align themselves with larger organizations and institutions that had the resources to expose these southern traditions on the international stage. The white community perceived him as an enemy. Church became more expressive in his disapproval of these heinous crimes and directly challenged the tenets of white supremacy.[35]

Within days of the lynching, Church met with his longtime friend James Weldon Johnson. The National Association for the Advancement of Colored People (NAACP) had sent Johnson to Memphis to investigate the murder. On the day Johnson arrived, Church drove him to the lynching site. Johnson recalled, "A pile of ashes and pieces of charred wood still marked the spot." After envisioning this scene, Johnson stated, "I tried to balance the sufferings of the miserable victim against the moral degradation of Memphis, and the truth flashed over me that in large measure the race question involves the saving of black America's body and white America's soul."[36] Church served as Johnson's host and guide for the next ten days until he completed his report. Johnson interviewed Sheriff Tate, black and white residents, and newspaper reporters during his stay. His findings were later published in the *Crisis*, which reached thousands of readers across the country.[37]

Memphis's black community expressed interest in starting its own NAACP branch. Black Memphians were still excited about their accomplishments the previous year with the Lincoln League. League member Bert Roddy had been working since 1914 to establish an NAACP branch in Memphis after attending a meeting hosted by board chairman Joel Spingarn and W. E. B. DuBois. Johnson met with Roddy and Church to discuss the steps required to establish a branch in Memphis. On June 11, 1917, prior to Johnson's departure, Church provided the names and membership dues of fifty-three potential members, including himself, his wife Sallie, his mother Anna, and his sister Annette (they were the only women who signed the charter). Although members needed to submit only $1 to be considered active, over one-third of the applicants donated the maximum $5. The NAACP's national headquarters was impressed by their commitment, and it granted a charter to Memphis on June 26. Roddy served as the branch's first president, and Church served as chairman of the Executive Committee.[38] The Memphis branch played an integral role in expanding the NAACP's presence in the South.

However, not everyone was willing to join the NAACP or to live in a place where more than 10,000 people could participate in a lynching without any arrests being made. As the United States fought to "make the world safe for Democracy," black people did not feel protected in their own country. Black Memphians recognized the hypocrisy of President Woodrow Wilson's crusade and sought refuge. The week of Persons's lynching, 1,500 to 2,000 African Americans flooded the bus station in Memphis, hoping to purchase tickets to Chicago. On June 5 a recruiter came to Memphis with the goal of enlisting 8,000 black men in the US military. He had scheduled his trip to Memphis prior to the lynching and expressed disappointment at the turnout when only 3,000 men between the ages of twenty-one and thirty showed up. The *Commercial Appeal* noted that the few men who did enlist did so only to escape the city's racist atmosphere. Adriane Lentz-Smith writes of one disillusioned draftee, Sydney Wilson from Memphis, who, in the aftermath of the lynching, wrote to the Tennessee draft board and promised "to do what little fighting we is going to do in this country and not France." He continued, "once we gets through with you all, you wont be so anshous to draft the nigroes in any more." In a separate letter he warned the draft board that the war would not be over "until we straighten up" things back home.[39]

Church could not ignore the reactions of black Memphians, and he spoke out against the lynching. On June 29, 1917, 3,000 self-determining black men and women flocked to Beale Street and packed themselves into the cramped Church Auditorium for the first meeting of the Lincoln League since Persons's death. In the weeks since the burning, no local organization had publicly condemned the actions of the mob, no leader had come forward to offer advice or guidance, and no one had delivered a speech to provide hope and courage to those who desperately needed direction. A newspaper captured the moment: "The pent-up feeling of the patriots and patriarchs, together with a thousand women, found expression in a burst of cheers when Robert R. Church Jr. . . . took the gavel. What the people expected is exactly what they got."[40] Church told the crowd, "I would be untrue to you and myself as your elected leader if I should remain silent against shame and crime of lawlessness of any character, and I could not if I would hold my peace against either the lynching or burning of a human being." He encouraged the members, "We must not lose hope, but keep our eyes open and press forward." He concluded his speech by endorsing the work of the NAACP.[41]

Church's connections with the national NAACP and influential white politicians helped place Persons's murder into the national antilynching discourse. That summer, the Persons lynching served as one of the motivating factors for the New York Silent March, one of the first mass demonstrations in the nation's history. On July 28, 1917, an estimated 10,000 African American men, women, and children marched silently down Fifth Avenue to the sound of only muffled drums. A crowd of approximately 20,000 spectators consisting of both blacks and whites lined the streets as they too abided by the code of silence. There were no bands playing, no cheering or applause to break the monotony. Although no one spoke a word, the demonstrators conveyed their messages to the nation through numerous signs, some of which read: "Mother, Do Lynchers Go to Heaven?" "Mr. President, Why Not Make America Safe for Democracy?" "Race Prejudice Is the Offspring of Ignorance, and the Mother Is Lynching." Members of the Negro Boy Scouts distributed copies of a leaflet entitled "Why Do We March?" which stated:

> We March because by the Grace of God and the force of truth, the dangerous, hampering walls of prejudice and inhuman injustices must fall.
>
> We march because we want [to] make impossible a repetition of Waco, Memphis and East St. Louis by arousing the conscience of the country, and to bring the murderers of our brothers, sisters and innocent children to justice.

We march because we deem it a crime to be silent in the face of such barbaric acts.

We march because we are thoroughly opposed to Jim-Crow Cars, Segregation, Discrimination, Disfranchisement, Lynching, and the host of evils that are forced on us. It is time that the Spirit of Christ should be manifested in the making and execution of laws.

We march because we want our children to live in a better land and enjoy fairer conditions than have fallen to our lot.[42]

The activism displayed in Memphis encouraged other investigations in neighboring communities. In 1918 the NAACP's newly hired assistant field secretary, Walter White, traveled to Tennessee to investigate the lynching of Jim McIlheron in Estill Springs. Although it is unlikely that White stayed with the Churches during this investigation, he did so during other trips to the region. After a visit to the Churches in December 1918, White wrote to Anna to thank the family for their hospitality. "I have never enjoyed so thoroughly a visit in all my experience as I did the all too few days spent there and I shall always remember them with the keenest pleasure." Growing tired of his road travels, he jokingly concluded, "I suppose I'll get my resting in Heaven, if I ever get there, although I am afraid the Crackers won't let me."[43]

For his efforts to establish other NAACP branches in the region and to pass antilynching legislation, Johnson nominated Church to serve as a member of the NAACP's Board of Directors. Johnson, a native southerner, felt the South should have some representation on the board. In January 1919 the NAACP announced in its bulletin that Church had become the first exclusively southern member of the organization's Board of Directors. He had helped establish sixty-eight branches in fourteen southern states. He became the representative of 9,841 members in a region that had had virtually no branches just two years prior. Church had personally grown the Memphis branch to more than 1,000 members.[44] His success in the region established a trustworthy and capable liaison with the national office. Church would use his contacts in the region to provide news and information during preliminary investigations of lynchings, and he would use his influence to grow the NAACP in Tennessee and surrounding states.[45]

Church was now given the task of helping to establish more charters throughout the South. Newly appointed executive secretary John R. Shillady and NAACP president Moorefield Storey had devised plans for a membership drive that would attract 50,000 new members. They called on Church to assist. He invited Johnson and Shillady to speak at a meeting hosted by the Memphis branch and said he could get at least 2,000 or 3,000 people to attend. The meeting was billed as "A BIG Monster Mass Meeting" to be held at Church's Park and Auditorium. Its aim was to educate Tennesseans about the objectives of the NAACP.[46] Following the meeting, Church provided the names and addresses of several leading men in Chattanooga and Nashville who were eager to establish branches, despite the constant threat of violence that paralyzed the region. Church impressed the national office with his ability to mobilize large crowds on short notice, and much like the Republican Party, the NAACP's leaders in New York recognized that he could be a financial asset for the organization. The NAACP needed a respected black southerner who understood the culture of the South and could convince his peers to establish charters in their cities and towns. Following the meeting in Memphis, Church emerged as a key component in growing the organization and aiding its national anti-lynching campaign.[47]

In the years that followed, the Church family home often served as a headquarters for lynching investigations in Tennessee, Mississippi, and Arkansas. Church would dispatch informants and reporters to gather information about lynchings, riots, and other discriminatory practices and share those findings with the national office, preparing White or Johnson to undertake their own personal investigations. The NAACP's Executive Committee was always suspicious of infiltration and would instruct Church to monitor the behavior of individuals affiliated with the organization, such as branch leaders, attorneys, and investigators. They worried about correspondence between Church and the national office being intercepted and having their work sabotaged. Therefore, a select few members communicated in a secret code when discussing the details of certain lynchings. The NAACP's press official, Herbert Seligmann, created a system for gathering news from the South and urged Church to use the following codes:

CODE	EQUIVALENT
Purchased Memphis (or other city)	Man lynched at Memphis (or other city)
George purchased Memphis (or other city)	Woman lynched at Memphis (or other city)
1500 (or other number)	By mob of 1500 (or other number)
Cash	Charge of rape
Mortgage	Charge of attack on woman or other offense against woman
Clear	Charged with other offense
Sale Memphis (or other city) 100 (or other number of dollars)	Race riot Memphis (or other city) in which 100 (or other number) Negroes injured
Credit Memphis (or other city)	Your representative in Memphis (or other city)
Wire funds	Recommend immediate investigation
Forward shipment Memphis (or other city)	Advise by wire of developments at Memphis (or other city) and send clippings
Fred	Ku Klux Klan
Price raised Memphis (or other city)	Trouble threatened Memphis (or other city)
George Hill	H. J. Seligmann
Alfred Means	J. R. Shillady
Harold Phelps	J. W. Johnson
Joseph Wild	Walter White[48]

Church kept the national organization abreast of lynchings, riots, police brutality, white attitudes in the community, and the names of other southern black leaders who wanted to establish NAACP branches. Outside the offices in New York, Church emerged as one of the organization's most valuable members.

In the wake of Persons's lynching, black Memphians spoke out against this ritualistic practice that had become synonymous with southern culture since the end of Reconstruction. The NAACP, still in its infancy, used this lynching to expose the South's dirty secret and place the hypocrisy of the US government on the international stage during World

War I. It contributed significantly to the discussion of antilynching legislation, while shaming the barbaric actions of white southerners. Memphis became one of the most important cogs in the NAACP's strategy to extend its reach in the South, and it provided the foundation for the NAACP to become the preeminent civil rights organization of the twentieth century. It forced Church to transform from a champion of voting rights to a social activist. As his influence increased during the Republican presidential administrations of the 1920s, lynching remained one of the most prominent issues on his platform, and he advised each president to address the problem during his tenure. Persons's death, like that of so many other unintended martyrs during the black freedom struggle, helped awaken a passion within the black community to pursue equality and justice by directly confronting white supremacy during the height of Jim Crow. Persons did not lose his life in vain; his death forced the black community to mobilize in its own defense, and it forced the nation to come to terms with its conscience.

Notes

1. *Memphis Commercial Appeal,* May 3, 1917; *Memphis Press-Scimitar,* May 3, 1917; James Weldon Johnson, "The Burning of Ell Persons at Memphis: A Report Made for the National Association for the Advancement of Colored People," box 3, folder 28, Robert R. Church Family Papers, Mississippi Valley Collection, McWherter Library, University of Memphis; James R. Sweeney, "The Trials of Shelby County Tennessee: 'Judge Lynch' Presiding," *Tennessee Historical Quarterly* 63 (2004): 102–27; National Association for the Advancement of Colored People (NAACP), "The Lynching at Memphis," *Crisis,* August 1917, 185–88.

2. *Memphis Press-Scimitar,* May 3, 1917.

3. Ibid.

4. Ibid.

5. *Memphis Commercial Appeal,* May 3, 1917.

6. Amy L. Wood, *Lynching and Spectacle: Witnessing Racial Violence in America, 1890–1940* (Chapel Hill: University of North Carolina Press, 2009), 7.

7. Gerald Capers, *The Biography of a River Town: Memphis, Its Heroic Age* (Chapel Hill: University of North Carolina Press, 1939), 207; Kenneth Goings and Gerald Smith, "Duty of the Hour: African American Communities in Memphis, 1862–1923," in *Trial and Triumph: Essays in Tennessee's African American History,* ed. Carroll Van West (Knoxville: University of Tennessee Press, 2002),

231; James C. Cobb, *The Most Southern Place on Earth: The Mississippi Delta and the Roots of Regional Identity* (Oxford: Oxford University Press, 1992), 139.

8. Roger Biles, *Memphis in the Great Depression* (Knoxville: University of Tennessee Press, 1986), 88.

9. Ibid.; Paula Giddings, *Ida: A Sword among Lions* (New York: Harper-Collins, 2008), 615; Capers, *Biography of a River Town,* 207; Goings and Smith, "Duty of the Hour," 231; Biles, *Memphis in the Great Depression,* 88.

10. Wanda Rushing, *Memphis and the Paradox of Place: Globalization in the American South* (Chapel Hill: University of North Carolina Press, 2009), 44; Biles, *Memphis in the Great Depression,* 6; Wood, *Lynching and Spectacle,* 49; Giddings, *Ida,* 615.

11. Leon Litwack, *Trouble in Mind: Black Southerners in the Age of Jim Crow* (New York: Vintage Press, 1999), 156. See also Stephen V. Ash, *A Massacre in Memphis: The Race Riot that Shook the Nation One Year after the Civil War* (New York: Hill and Wang, 2013).

12. Giddings, *Ida,* 180–87.

13. Wood, *Lynching and Spectacle,* 49.

14. Lincoln League Meeting, November 1916, box 3, folder 25, Church Family Papers; Clarence L. Kelly, "Robert R. Church, a Negro Tennessean, in Republican State and National Politics from 1912–1932" (master's thesis, Tennessee Agricultural and Industrial State University, 1954), 28. The Lincoln League of Tennessee would eventually grow into the Lincoln League of America.

15. *Western World Reporter,* November 10, 1916; Kelly, "Robert R. Church," 31.

16. Claude Clegg, *Troubled Ground: A Tale of Murder, Lynching, and Reckoning in the New South* (Urbana-Champaign: University of Illinois Press, 2010), xvi.

17. *Memphis Commercial Appeal,* May 5, 1917; Margaret Vandiver, *Lethal Punishment: Lynchings and Lethal Executions in the South* (New Brunswick, NJ: Rutgers University Press, 2005), 121; James Weldon Johnson, *Along This Way* (New York: Penguin Books, 1933), 317; NAACP, "Lynching at Memphis," 185–88; Phillip Dray, *At the Hands of Persons Unknown: The Lynching of Black America* (New York: Modern Library, 2002), 231–34. For additional works on lynchings, see Orlando Patterson, *Rituals of Blood: Consequences of Slavery in Two American Centuries* (Washington, DC: Civitas Counterpoint, 1998); Litwack, *Trouble in Mind;* Stewart E. Tolnay and E. M. Beck, *A Festival of Violence: An Analysis of Southern Lynchings, 1882–1930* (Chicago: University of Illinois Press, 1995).

18. *Memphis Commercial Appeal,* May 5, 1917; Vandiver, *Lethal Punishment,* 121; NAACP, "Memphis May 22 A.D. 1917," supplement to *Crisis,* July 1917, 2.

19. *Memphis Press-Scimitar,* May 7, 1917; NAACP, "Memphis May 22 A.D. 1917," 1–3.

20. *Memphis Commercial Appeal*, May 23, 1917; *Memphis Press-Scimitar*, May 23, 1917; Sweeney, "Trials of Shelby County," 111–13.

21. Ibid.

22. Patterson, *Rituals of Blood*, 173; W. E. B. DuBois, *Black Reconstruction in America, 1860–1880* (1935; reprint, New York: Atheneum, 1962), 678.

23. Litwack, *Trouble in Mind*, 295–96.

24. Grace Elizabeth Hale, *Making Whiteness: The Culture of Segregation in the South* (New York: Vintage Press, 1999), 201.

25. Ibid.; Wood, *Lynching and Spectacle*, 10–11; James Weldon Johnson, "The Practice of Lynching: A Picture, the Problem, and What Shall Be Done about It," *Century Magazine*, November 1927, 65–70.

26. Michael K. Honey, *Southern Labor and Black Civil Rights: Organizing Memphis Workers* (Urbana: University of Illinois Press, 1993), 17–18.

27. Richard Wright, *Black Boy: (American Hunger) A Record of Childhood and Youth* (New York: Harper and Brothers, 1945), 86–87.

28. Jacquelyn Dowd Hall, *Revolt against Chivalry: Jessie Daniel Ames and the Women's Campaign against Lynching* (New York: Columbia University Press, 1993), 141.

29. Goings and Smith, "Duty of the Hour," 240–41.

30. W. Fitzhugh Brundage, *Lynching in the New South: Georgia and Virginia, 1880–1930* (Urbana: University of Illinois, 1993), 272.

31. Hall, *Revolt against Chivalry*, 144–45.

32. Ash, *Massacre in Memphis*, 89, 148; Mary Church Terrell, *A Colored Woman in a White World* (Washington, DC: Randsell, 1940), 31–41.

33. Solvent Savings Bank and Trust Company end-of-year statement, December 31, 1910, box 2, folder 16, Church Family Papers; Church Auditorium rent contract, April 18, 1910, ibid., folder 34; Green Polonius Hamilton, *The Bright Side of Memphis: A Compendium of Information Concerning the Colored People of Memphis, Tennessee* (Memphis: n.p., 1908), 100; Annette E. Church and Roberta Church, *The Robert R. Churches of Memphis* (Memphis, TN: A. E. Church, 1974), 65.

34. Ida B. Wells to Robert Church Jr., September 9, 1912, box XI, folder— Robert Church Jr. Correspondence, Roberta Church Collection, Memphis Room, Memphis Public Library.

35. Wood, *Lynching and Spectacle*, 2; Patterson, *Rituals of Blood*, 179; Goings and Smith, "Duty of the Hour," 238, 241.

36. Johnson, *Along This Way*, 317–18.

37. Copy of *Crisis*, May 22, 1917, box 3, folder 28, Church Family Papers; The NAACP Papers, The Anti-Lynching Campaign, part 7, series A, 1912–1955, reel 17 of 30, Library of Congress microfilm; NAACP, "Lynching at Memphis," 185–88; Patricia Sullivan, *Lift Every Voice: The NAACP and the Making of the Civil Rights Movement* (New York: New Press, 2009), 66.

38. Application for charter, June 26, 1917, box 3, folder 30, Church Family Papers; Church and Church, *The Robert Churches*, 68; Goings and Smith, "Duty of the Hour," 237; Sullivan, *Lift Every Voice*, 66.

39. *Memphis Commercial Appeal*, June 6, 1917; Sweeney, "Trials of Shelby County," 116–17; Adriane Lentz-Smith, *Freedom Struggles: African Americans and World War I* (Cambridge, MA: Harvard University Press, 2011), 42.

40. Untitled newspaper article, no date, box 3, folder 23, Church Family Papers.

41. Ibid.

42. Johnson, *Along This Way*, 320–21; *New York Call*, July 29, 1917.

43. Walter White to Anna Church, December 12, 1918, box 3, folder 31, Church Family Papers.

44. Copy of NAACP branch bulletin, January 1919, box 6, NAACP folder, Roberta Church Papers.

45. Church and Church, *The Robert R. Churches*, 68; Sullivan, *Lift Every Voice*, 66.

46. Robert Church Jr. to James Weldon Johnson, March 19, 1918, box 3, folder 31, Church Family Papers.

47. Robert Church Jr. to James Weldon Johnson, October 24, 1918, box 6, NAACP folder, Roberta Church Papers.

48. Church and Church, *The Robert R. Churches*, 69–70.

Equal Power

Bishop Charles H. Mason and the National Tabernacle Fire

Elton H. Weaver III

Shortly after midnight on Tuesday, December 8, 1936, during the Twenty-Ninth Annual Holy Convocation of the Church of God in Christ (COGIC), a devastating fire destroyed the historic National Tabernacle building located at 958 South Fifth Street in Memphis, Tennessee. For many years the Tabernacle had served as COGIC's national headquarters, convocation center, and meeting place. A fire burst forth while legendary gospel singer and traveling evangelist Elder Utah Smith was leading the regularly scheduled midnight meeting. Smith's well-attended, all-inclusive singing, preaching, and healing services usually lasted until 6:00 a.m.[1] COGIC's early bylaws stated that the yearly convocations were held "to further develop the spiritual and financial uplift of the church."[2] However, the main objective of these historic convocations was, as Bishop Charles H. Mason declared, to "pray the kingdom of God . . . into the hearts of men. That His peace and glory might be the portion of all nations."[3] COGIC's momentous convocations were continuous, round-the-clock revival-style services that lasted for at least twenty-one days. The first three days were always spent fasting and praying for the healing and comfort of all races. Despite the existence of racial segregation, COGIC convocations were interracial and provided black and white delegates safe spaces for social interaction, feasting, and lodging. Mother Isadore Gordon Rainey remembered, "Lots of white people always came to the convocation . . . and some [delegates came] from Africa and Europe, missionaries [and] preachers from foreign countries. "[4] This yearly gathering embodied the three elements of black religion—preaching, singing, and shouting—as defined in W. E. B. DuBois's *The Souls of Black Folk*.[5] COGIC convocations also exemplified novelist James Baldwin's description of the black church experience; he wrote that he had "never seen anything to equal the fire and excitement that sometimes, without warning, fill[s] a [black] church, causing the church to rock."[6] Above all else, COGIC convocations offered black and white Holiness-Pentecostals spiritual empowerment and political revitalization.[7]

On December 8, 1936, moments after Elder Utah Smith's all-night services began, flames and fumes gushed from the basement in volcanic fashion. They quickly soared up to the ceiling and burned the roof. Miraculously, the 2,000 frightened delegates were able to bravely battle their way out before the blazing building was consumed by the inferno.[8] COGIC's National Tabernacle, which had been built around 1924, was worth $25,000. The three-story wooden structure had a spacious balcony and sanctuary, indoor restrooms, a large basement that contained an industrial-size kitchen, and a huge dining hall. The fire also destroyed a one-story wooden building used to house COGIC's out-of-town convocation delegates, situated at 922 South Fifth Street.[9] In the end, the Memphis Fire Department was unable to save the flaming building.

After the firefighters extinguished the flames, fire chief Irby Klinck issued a statement to the *Memphis Press-Scimitar*. According to Klinck, the fire had started in the basement, where an industrial stove used to prepare meals had carelessly been ignored.[10] The *Press-Scimitar* claimed that every person made it out alive, except for an unidentified "Negro found in the ruins." COGIC officials later stated that the deceased person was Elder Anthony "Inkney" Hicks, a COGIC preacher and widower who lived with his seven children in Hattiesburg, Mississippi. Hicks had apparently fallen asleep during the services. When the fire started he was trapped inside, and he ultimately died in the flames.[11] Attempting to satisfy the racial stereotypes of Memphis's white readers, the *Press-Scimitar* ridiculed black COGIC members by first reporting that a Keystone Laboratory truck had been parked outside the Tabernacle to sell members black beauty products, including a hair-straightening formula that supposedly "makes your hair glossy—makes your hair lie down." The article indicted the COGIC delegates for defiling God's house, claiming they were more interested in buying and selling junk food and low-priced beauty products than worshipping God. "Old Negro men sold hot peanuts and candy near the door, where a sign said, no smoking this is holy ground."[12] The *Press-Scimitar* printed the damaging remarks of Elder Frank C. V. Foard to show the public the internal strife and turmoil developing within COGIC's organization. Elder Foard, a native of Mississippi, was evangelizing COGIC churches throughout San Antonio, Texas, at the time. While standing in front of the decimated building, Foard freely expressed his disapproval of COGIC's moneymaking activities. His remarks suggested that God's anger had destroyed the Tabernacle. "I told my friends last night, that something was going to happen. There was too much commercial. Everyone was out for making money, instead of saving souls."[13]

The destruction of the National Tabernacle was a defining moment in the history of COGIC. By the 1930s, this fledgling band of religious migrants had built a politically powerful organization with sufficient autonomy to defy "Boss" Edward H. Crump. After the fire, COGIC withstood a volley of negative press. Indeed, nationwide media coverage of the fire placed this southern-based denomination in the national spotlight, helping to strengthen its image. Bishop Mason's resilience and self-determination brought about the establishment of Mason Temple, COGIC's national headquarters and a rallying place throughout the Memphis civil rights movement. In the end, the devastating fire revealed COGIC's antisegregation stand and persistent commitment to the struggle for racial equality.

In the early twentieth century, Mason's newly established COGIC denomination grew, gained social and political power, and earned a permanent place in Memphis's black religious pantheon. Many of Mason's initial followers were rural migrants who had come to Memphis seeking better employment opportunities. These draymen, common laborers, factory workers, domestic workers, and roustabouts represented Memphis's lower black stratum. But regardless of their previous identities, COGIC members were called "saints" and were encouraged to use customary titles and initials when addressing one another in public, which promoted self-respect and dignity. Many believed that the absorption of spiritual power gave members the ability to overcome sin, intraracial aggression, and racial discrimination. "My life has been threatened by members of my own race. I have been several times struck, and once knocked down by an enemy of right and righteousness. God only gave deliverance," expounded Mason.[14] He sought to revitalize poor people because he believed that no one "is too lowly to receive our attention."[15] Between 1932 and 1934, during the early years of the Great Depression, 30 percent of black Memphians were unemployed, 14 percent lived in dilapidated housing, and 77 percent were renters. Roger Biles described the black community's dilemma: "With a leadership paralyzed by fear and subservient to a paternalistic ruling clique, the black community of Memphis wandered rudderless through the 1930s."[16] By 1936, Mason had achieved social and religious influence. While most Memphians were scarcely making it, Mason was living in a spacious, two-story Victorian home at 1121 Mississippi Avenue. At that time, this former itinerant preacher was transforming his small southern black Holiness sect into an urban phenomenon. "I walked the hills and streets in Memphis and preached in the Methodist and Baptist church[es] and God gave me black and white membership."[17] Mason performed the traditional roles of the black preacher; he was a spiritual and pragmatic leader, liberator, and healer. Mason was an advocate who taught his black congregants how to survive in a segregated world.[18]

The black Holiness-Pentecostal churches were self-governing social centers where black leaders nurtured the spirit of liberation that gave rise to social protest. According to historian Lawrence Levine, while the black mainline churches were seeking "respectability [and] turning their backs on the past, banning the shout, discouraging enthusiastic religion . . . the holiness church constituted a revitalization movement with their emphasis upon healing, gifts of prophecy, speaking in tongues, spirit possession, and religious dance."[19] Historian Leon Litwack suggests that joining Holiness churches helped many blacks endure the age of Jim Crow. "Holiness churches were places of refuge that filled an emptiness in black lives, that raised people out of despair."[20] Mason's contribution was crucial to the African American experience. His religious rituals of praying, praise, and Holiness-Pentecostal rhetoric revitalized the downtrodden. During the Jim Crow era, Mason's southern-based denomination was a safe haven for interracial fellowship and a place where blacks were free to embrace and celebrate their religious cultural roots. The recurring themes in Mason's messages were love, sanctification, social empowerment of the poor and powerless, spiritual and physical renewal, racial equality, and the brotherhood of humanity. Mason taught his followers that preachers had to have "Holy Ghost power," a spiritual weapon that allowed them to stand up to racism and lynching. "Lynching's [*sic*] are being carried on because the preachers are leading the people away from the reproof of God and not to the glory of God," he preached. "They are cowards until they are baptized with Jesus's baptism."[21] Mason hated segregation and believed it was sinful. Consequently, he integrated his church and licensed and ordained white preachers. "There is a curse on us for our segregated sins. Men need to open up and let the love of God come in, that love running out to both black and white: a love without respect of persons."[22]

Although Charles Mason's precise year of birth is not known, he acknowledged September 8, 1866, as his birthday. Born in rural Shelby County, Tennessee, to former slaves, young Mason embraced his parents' Baptist heritage.[23] In 1907 he visited Bishop William J. Seymour's Azusa Street Revival in Los Angeles California, where he witnessed interracial harmony and absorbed the Pentecostal experience, which included spiritual discernment and power, the gift of prophecy, and the ability to speak in tongues.[24]

At COGIC's first convocation, Mason and his new followers organized the Memphis-based COGIC, adopted bylaws, and designated *The Whole Truth* as the denomination's national organ. (By this time, COGIC had ten churches and several hundred members.) Afterward, Mason took the title of chief apostle. In 1911, under the leadership of Elizabeth Woods Robinson (also a former Baptist), COGIC's financially fruitful Women's Department was established. During World War I Mason was arrested several times for his pacifistic teachings; he was charged with obstructing the draft and accepting German money. "I told them not to trust in the power of the United States, England, France or Germany . . . the white people arrest[ed] me and bound me over in jail. I thank God for the persecution," recalled Mason.[25] However, due to sketchy evidence, by the end of the war all the charges had been dropped.

In 1923 COGIC claimed to have about a thousand congregations in

America. By 1936, Mason claimed to be the leader of a religious empire that comprised several hundred thousand followers worldwide. However, the 1936 US Census of Religious Bodies reported that COGIC had only 31,564 followers and 772 churches in America. According to the US Census Bureau, 61.7 percent of all COGIC churches were located in urban America.[26]

At that juncture, COGIC had several million dollars in assets, and Mason was guiding the international denomination from his parish at 672 South Lauderdale Street in Memphis. Mason used a variety of strategies to market COGIC and recruit followers; for instance, he provided discounted railway travel to COGIC's licensed ministers, distributed *The Whole Truth* to COGIC's international membership, aired sermons and gospel musicals on the radio, established interracial partnerships with white clergy, and hosted and accommodated COGIC delegates attending the annual convocation. Both blacks and whites found Mason's style of worship uplifting and empowering. He practiced racial equality in his church. COGIC's earliest racial statement, titled "Equal in Power and Authority," explains Mason's pre–civil rights commitment: "The Church of God in Christ recognizes the fact that all believers are one in Christ Jesus and all its members have equal rights. Its Overseers, both colored and white, have equal power and authority in the church."[27] As David Daniels elucidates, "Here is a public statement in which COGIC intentionally embodied an interracial impulse and understood itself as making a political and moral statement against racism and segregation."[28] COGIC's enduring commitment to racial equality is a neglected chapter in the African American freedom struggle. Contrary to Memphis's segregation policies, blacks and whites were considered equal in Mason's church. Mason's personal progress, black Holiness rhetoric, black cultural religious renewal, religious independence, unauthorized integrated meetings, and belief in racial equality put him in conflict with Memphis's local white establishment, particularly "Boss" Edward H. Crump's anti-integration policy. Crump's position on the status of black Memphians was explicit: Negroes might as well learn their places.[29] Clearly, Mason's rising influence and outspoken white followers caused his church to come under scrutiny. And the fire that destroyed COGIC's historic National Tabernacle was not an accident.

Church of God in Christ bishops A. B. McEwen, Charles H. Mason, and Riley F. Williams. (Courtesy Memphis and Shelby County Room, Memphis Public Library)

After the 1936 fire, COGIC endured a stream of negative publicity. Then the *Press-Scimitar* printed an article titled "Tabernacle Fire Fails to Halt Services of Negroes," which acknowledged the resilience of COGIC's adherents. They did not allow the fire to shatter their faith or stop the convocation, which Mason moved to his Mother Temple parish at 672 South Lauderdale Street. The Mother Temple (originally known as Saint's Home) was the first COGIC church Mason had established upon his arrival in Memphis. The article also depicted the somber yet optimistic, spiritual, bluesy, jazz-like atmosphere of the services. "Black faces [were] lifted upward in an agony of religion. A trombonist blew into his horn. The notes were heavy and sad. The trumpet came in, wild and blatant."[30] The article also quoted the harsh words of Bishop Eddie Morey Page (sometimes spelled Paige), overseer of COGIC's Texas diocese. Bishop Page, who was born in Mississippi, had served as an officer in the African Methodist Episcopal (AME) Church and had worked for the Illinois Central Railroad before becoming a COGIC minister, pas-

tor, and state overseer. Page had come under the influence of Bishop
Mason after hearing him preach on the streets of Memphis. "I heard
Brother Mason preach[ing] on Virginia Avenue," he recalled. "It seemed
like heaven had come down to us. In 1907 the Lord baptized me with
the Holy Ghost and fire."[31] Bishop Page was irritated by the embarrassing
remarks of Elder Frank Foard, who fell under Page's jurisdiction as overseer of Texas. Foard's public outburst was seen as traitorous and as questioning the effectiveness of Page's leadership. Bishop Page felt he had no
choice but to publicly chastise the loose-lipped minister. So, in muckrak-
ing style, the *Press-Scimitar* covered COGIC's battle royal and printed
Page's heated reaction to Foard's comments. The paper reminded the
public that Foard had foretold something bad happening and had warned
his COGIC comrades to stop commercializing God's house. Page challenged the validity of Foard's words and attacked the minister's character.
The bishop claimed he had known Foard for twenty-three years and that
the minister could not be taken seriously because he was "mouthy"—all
talk. "If Foard said anything at all, he must have said it to himself and not
in the pulpit. Foard didn't hang around the Tabernacle much any way,"
countered Page. The article ended by informing the public that white
people were attending the convocation. It delicately implied that unauthorized interracial activity was taking place within this predominantly
black denomination, and it provided proof that Bishop Mason had at
least one white COGIC elder who was from Kansas, Missouri. "There
were a few white men," it reported. "One . . . is an elder in the church
'See.' He proudly displayed his papers."[32]

The *Memphis Commercial Appeal* misidentified the church, stating
that a dreadful fire had obliterated the "Convocation Church of Christ
in God Universal Tabernacle" rather than the Church of God in Christ
National Tabernacle.[33] For some reason, the *Commercial Appeal* falla-
ciously reported that these black "revivalists [were] said to be a branch
group of Father Divine's Heavenly Kingdom in New York City."[34] By
1936, Father Divine's (George Baker's) peace mission movement had
established lucrative East and West Coast branches.[35] Like Mason, Divine
taught the biblical principles found in the scriptures; that life and death
are in the power of the tongue; that as a man thinks, so he is. Divine
taught that mind power plus positive speaking equals action and desired

effects. "It is a privilege to realize that which you surmise, and [so] that which you visualize, can be materialized," instructed Father Divine.[36] At the time of the COGIC Tabernacle fire, Divine's movement was under scrutiny because, in the spring of 1936, its International Righteous Government Committee had forged an alliance with the Communist Party, called for the desegregation of America, and demanded an equal distribution of opportunity. Although Bishop Mason and Father Divine had similarities, no official peace mission branch had been established in Memphis, and the Memphis-based COGIC was not part of Divine's organization. However, some COGIC members may have been curious about Father Divine.

Moreover, the similarities between Mason and Divine were remarkable. For instance, both men were sons of former slaves and had grown up in the South. Both were onetime itinerant preachers who converted to Pentecostalism while attending Bishop William J. Seymour's interracial Azusa Street revival. Both were organizers of annual interracial holy communion banquets and holy convocations, teachers of strict moral codes, and leaders of integrated churches. However, Mason unequivocally rejected Father Divine's celibacy requirement, his doctrine of incarnation, and his belief that he was the black Messiah who had attained oneness with God, was God, and had been sent here to establish heaven on earth.[37] As Divine's popularity increased, Mason denounced his doctrine and divinity and warned Divine's East and West Coast followers that if they joined the peace mission movement they would have to give up their spouses. "The familiar spirit will make one that is led by it call some man God, he himself will say that he is God," cautioned Mason. "There is one man that calls himself Father Divine and his followers angels. Husbands and wives that enter into the kingdom of . . . Father Divine have to give up knowing one another."[38]

In the aftermath of the fire, the black press, in particular the *Atlanta Daily World* and the *Pittsburgh Courier*, printed stories similar to those found in the white press, with several variations. The *Atlanta Daily World* lauded the black and white Memphis undertakers for assisting the out-of-town delegates, especially Thomas Hayes & Sons Funeral Home for sheltering COGIC delegates after the fire.[39] Hayes & Sons had been established in 1902 and truly exemplified its business slogan: "Promptness and Courtesy." Thomas Hayes Sr. was a black community leader, a charter member of Memphis's first NAACP chapter, a mortician, and the founder and president of a prosperous funeral business. Hayes was a member of the historic St. John's Baptist Church, and Mason's wife had grown up at St. John's. Local historian and educator Green P. Hamilton remarked, "Mr. Hayes is a bright example of the place fitting the man and the man fitting the place."[40] In the aftermath of the fire, Hayes and his sons transported carloads of COGIC delegates to the funeral home's chapel, where they were sheltered from the bitter-cold temperatures and freezing rain. Hayes & Sons Funeral Home was situated next door to COGIC's Mother Temple on South Lauderdale Street.

The COGIC property on South Lauderdale had originally been owned by the Reverend Sutton E. Griggs's Tabernacle Baptist Church. Griggs, a black militant who became a conservative Baptist minister, was also an author in the black marginalist tradition. According to Cornel West, this "lifted Griggs above what [he] conceived to be the uncouth, vulgar, unrefined Afro-American folk culture."[41] After the 1929 stock market crash and ensuing economic depression, Griggs lost the church building in 1930, and Mason bought it from Joseph E. Walker's Universal Life Insurance Company in 1931. The two-story brick church was adorned with stained glass windows; it had an indoor pool, gymnasium, 2,000-seat balcony and ample choir seating, office space, and an enormous sanctuary with a seating capacity of 4,500. In 1932 Bishop Mason and COGIC officials, evangelists, and state overseers were photographed in front of the old Tabernacle Baptist Church building. As COGIC's chief apostle, Mason's poised gaze was an indication that he and his fellow black Holiness-Pentecostal leaders understood that they were on the rise. After the fire, and until Mason Temple was completed, the Mother Temple served as COGIC's national headquarters, convocation center, and meeting place.[42]

The *Atlanta Daily World* printed photographs of delegates rummaging through the ashes and rubble for lost belongings. In the days following the incident, observers wondered if COGIC would ever recover.[43] The paper informed the public that the founder of the denomination was in the midst of a terrible "storm" and had recently withstood two major losses. A month before the fire, in early November, Mason's wife Lelia (alternatively spelled Leila or Lela) Washington Mason, the mother of his eight children, had died shortly after suffering a debilitating stroke.[44] Four days after the fire, the *Atlanta Daily World* printed an open letter from the young and industrious Bishop A. B. McEwen titled "Convocation Tabernacle Destroyed"; it appeared under the heading: "Bishop Says Ugly Rumors Are False and Unfounded." Bishop McEwen was born in Oxford, Mississippi, left home at a young age, and took a number of demeaning jobs to work his way through school. "My father and mother did not see me again until I was grown, married, and preaching the gospel. I [had] earned $60 shining shoes to leave home."[45] After relocating to Memphis, McEwen became one of Bishop Mason's most dedicated disciples; over time, he became a pastor and overseer of COGIC's Tennessee diocese, chairman of the Board of Trustees, and bishop of foreign fields. McEwen's letter was intended to counteract the unpleasant and unsubstantiated newspaper stories circulating about COGIC. McEwen explained that the fire had not been COGIC's fault; the building had been inspected and approved by a City of Memphis ordinance, and throughout the convocation, COGIC peace officers and a security team had monitored the entire building around the clock. McEwen ended his letter by imploring black and white Memphians to give COGIC their prayers instead of criticism. "We are thankful more than we can say unto God because we know that he sends the sunshine as well as the rain."[46] In the end, Bishop McEwen's message was explicit: COGIC denied responsibility for the fire. McEwen's letter implied that *someone* was to blame, but for whatever reason, he refused to identify the guilty party.

The *Pittsburgh Courier* falsely reported that Mason's church was the God Universal Tabernacle, the southern branch of Father Divine's peace mission movement. The paper called COGIC members "angels" instead of "saints" and claimed that no one had been injured or trapped inside the burning building. This story infuriated the COGIC leadership; it appeared nearly two weeks after the fire occurred and was circulated nationwide throughout the Associated Negro Press.[47]

In the early spring of 1937, as a form of apology, *Pittsburgh Courier* editor Robert Lee Vann printed a letter written by Elder Richard Page, the son of Bishop E. M. Page. Page requested that the newspaper correct the errors contained in its December 19 article. According to Page, the misinformation "has been very costly to the reputation of this great church, [and the] error has caused undue reflection and criticism upon our church." Page told the editor that COGIC was not connected to a Universal Tabernacle or to one of Father Divine's heavens. In closing, Page informed Vann that Bishop Mason was COGIC's chief apostle and the leader of the denomination.[48]

As the Twenty-Ninth Annual Convocation ended, a white COGIC pastor named James Delk spoke out against segregation and "attack[ed] race prejudice in a scorching manner."[49] In a sermon broadcast on the radio on Sunday, December 6, Delk boldly declared that "there was no segregation in heaven, none in hell, and therefore, should not be any segregation on earth."[50] Reverend Delk was a powerful speaker and an unusual person; he grew up in Pall Mall, Tennessee, and pastored a COGIC church in Missouri. Later, Delk wrote that he had joined COGIC because Bishop Mason embraced integration. "Bear in mind that neither Brother Mason nor myself believe in segregation or Jim Crow but all people . . . do not see this in the same light that Brother Mason and myself see it."[51] After hearing Delk's antisegregation sermon, several white Memphians became outraged and demanded an apology. They charged Reverend Delk and COGIC with violating Tennessee's segregation laws. Since the abolishment of slavery, the state of Tennessee had sanctioned numerous laws that mandated segregated schools, separation on public transportation, separate public recreational facilities, and segregated movie theaters, restrooms, housing, and churches.[52] Delk's message also challenged what Laurie B. Green describes as historic Memphis's unspoken "segregated religious culture."[53] In fact, by joining the predominantly black COGIC, Delk had crossed the color line and entered the forbidden black "segregated realm."[54]

On Monday, December 14, in an effort to resolve the controversy, Los Angeles bishop Eddie R. Driver Sr. (national chairman of COGIC's General Assembly, a graduate of LeMoyne Normal Institute, and a former resident of Memphis) was appointed to clarify COGIC's stance on social equality and explain the meaning of Delk's sermon. As a black man reared in Mississippi, Driver was uncomfortable explaining the thoughts of a white man, even if he was a COGIC minister. Driver's response, however, was straightforward; instead of apologizing for Delk's statements, Driver recalled the history of the post–Civil War and Reconstruction periods to demonstrate that COGIC had not started America's race problems and had not forced whites to follow its tenets. "We [COGIC] have not started social equality—but the gospel we preach will break such social equality up completely. Instead of preaching to Negroes about social equality, talk to these white folks, who are here now: for they are following us."[55]

COGIC's historic National Tabernacle building was destroyed by fire just two days after Delk's antisegregation sermon was broadcast on Memphis radio. This does not prove that the fire was no accident; however, COGIC's response to the fire cast doubt on the media's assertion that COGIC itself was responsible.[56] Furthermore, three days after the conflagration, during a meeting of the General Assembly, a white COGIC preacher, William Dent, strongly advised that COGIC's national headquarters be moved to Chicago. Perhaps Dent thought that relocating COGIC's headquarters to a northern city was the best protective measure. During the course of his appeal, Elder Dent gave "many reasons for this recommendation. The Council received this with great enthusiasm."[57] Subsequently, the committee that supervised the management of the national convocation recommended: "All police supervision of the buildings and grounds be placed under the direct supervision of our appointed Convocation Chief of Police."[58] COGIC's headquarters would remain in Memphis, but the General Assembly was concerned about the safety of its convocation delegates. It therefore established specific convocation procedures; assembled a stronger security team to safeguard the building, especially the kitchen and cafeteria; and pledged to hire only "brothers of trust." The General Assembly also insisted that all convocation employees be approved by the Board of Trustees. The "smoking gun" in the case of the National Tabernacle fire remains a mystery to this day, due, in this writer's opinion, to fear of further acts of arson.

After the convocation ended, Bishop Mason received a letter from the Crump & Trezevant Insurance Agency. Edward Hull Crump, who owned this real estate and insurance agency, also controlled the entire city of Memphis from his office located on the mezzanine floor of the North Memphis Savings Bank building. At that time, Crump was the indisputable boss of Memphis; he ran the city's crooked Democratic machine.

Crump had served twice as Memphis mayor before being ejected in 1916; in 1936, however, he still held an iron grip on Memphis politics and the city's underworld activities. Boss Crump even had a handful of black preachers in his pocket, and black pastors who wanted to succeed in Crump's town had to do business with him. Crump also handpicked Memphis's mayors and other city officials. Historian David M. Tucker maintained that Crump ran "Memphis as his own plantation. If even a mayor revealed a spark of independence, Crump could, and did, replace him as easily as a planter might have fired an overseer."[59]

Mason had failed to do business with Boss Crump and had neglected to insure his buildings. Slighted, Crump's agency now offered Mason $10,000 worth of new insurance policies (beginning December 23, 1936) for the two COGIC buildings that had just been destroyed. The letter read: "We are enclosing Northwestern Policy No. 54185, covering $7,000.00 fire on building situate 958 South Fifth and Policy No. D-125617, covering $3,000.00 fire on dwelling situate 920 South Fifth Street, for three years from December 23rd, 1936."[60] Crump's agency was not giving Mason anything useful. Instead of aiding one of Memphis's leading black religious figures, the agency was offering to sell him $10,000 worth of insurance on ruined buildings. This would not solve Mason's troubles because he needed funds to cover COGIC's $36,000 loss. Believing his church was worthy of support, COGIC's chief apostle decided to ask Boss Crump for help; after all, COGIC was an asset to Crump's city.

Bishop Mason's letter to Crump assured him that COGIC was not affiliated with any cult groups; was a state-chartered and incorporated religious organization; had maintained headquarters in Memphis for twenty-nine years; had 200,000 members worldwide, twenty local churches, and several schools; had purchased the 958 South Fifth Street property for $40,000; and had built the National Tabernacle for $25,000 and the out-of-town saints' quarters for $11,000. For whatever reason, however, Mason had failed to insure the buildings. Mason also let Crump know that "the Tabernacle has stood for religious worship and moral uplift of our people." Mason reminded Crump that his church had provided food for thousands of Memphis's Depression-stricken residents through its freewill offerings and that its convocations brought thousands of people to Memphis every year, contributing $50,000 to the city's economy. Mason warned Crump that business leaders in Chicago, Cleveland, Kansas City, Los Angeles, and even cities in Canada were all bidding to move COGIC's headquarters and yearly convocations to their cities. Finally, Bishop Mason told Boss Crump exactly why he had never asked for his assistance before: "Heretofore we haven't made a call for help because we wanted to be an *asset and not a liability*."[61] Crump's response to Mason has *not* been substantiated. What is clear, however, is that Mason continued with plans to rebuild COGIC's National Tabernacle.

By the fall of 1940, Bishop Mason had secured the necessary funding to lay the foundation and begin rebuilding on the old National Tabernacle grounds. As Mason's superintendent of construction gazed at the building site, he glimpsed the future: "A great building is in the making . . . sturdy walls rising, varying in height. This is . . . what will be the finest building of its kind of any colored group North or South. What I have described to you is not imagination, but reality."[62] During the winter months, however, Memphis experienced a dreadful Reign of Terror, as the Memphis police conducted raids and roundups of allegedly guilty black criminals, claiming they were merely cleaning up the unruly city streets.[63]

Furthermore, on December 5, 1940, a fire of mysterious origins destroyed the female dormitory of COGIC's Saints and Industrial School, located in Lexington, Mississippi. Luckily, none of the students were hurt.[64] Likewise, during the Memphis convocation, a group of thieves interrupted the nonstop services by pulling a fire alarm and yelling "Fire!" This caused many delegates to panic, especially those who remembered the devastating fire that had destroyed the Tabernacle in 1936. In the ensuing chaos, several hundred hysterical delegates stampeded the doors, seeking safety; many of them were robbed, and a number of purses were stolen. "The thieves stole several hundred dollars from the collection plates and escaped with an inestimable number of pocketbooks which were dropped by fleeing delegates."[65] The Memphis police failed to apprehend any of the convocation thieves, who managed to flee the scene before the police arrived. After the robbery, COGIC leaders demanded that Mayor Walter C. Chandler and other city officials end the police terror and lawlessness. "The Convocation and officials asked that the several thousands of delegates and members attending the Convocation be protected from the reign of terror being conducted by Commissioner Joseph Boyle and his police department against Negro citizens."[66] Finally, seeking to calm the racial crisis, Mayor Chandler agreed to deliver a speech at the annual Bishop Mason Day Gospel Feast Service, where Mason's followers celebrated his dedication to the denomination. "Unity" and "good citizenship" were the major themes of Chandler's speech. The mayor told the COGIC clergymen and 6,000 delegates, "We live in a critical period. A community is as good as its citizenship; we in Memphis are proud of our colored citizenship: we couldn't get along without them; Memphis appreciates being the headquarters of a great religious organization as the Churches of God in Christ."[67] The mayor neglected to mention how he planned to protect black Memphians or whether he would use his mayoral powers to break Commissioner Boyle's Reign of Terror. Displeased by the mayor's speech, Bishop W. G. Shipman, overseer of COGIC's western New York diocese, rose and gave COGIC's response: "According to the Bible all men are born equal—being baptized of one blood, we may be unopportuned but not underprivileged and since the Holy Convocation is such an inspiration to the city of Memphis, the city should make a contribution to the cause and give better transportation services. The Negro has never sought social equality, neither does he intend to. All we ask is that justice be meted out to the Negro as well as the White race and be given the same protection."[68] Bishop Shipman's message was clear: talk is cheap. COGIC was not asking for social acceptance; its members wanted justice for black Memphians. They wanted Mayor Chandler and Memphis officials to show respect and appreciation for the headquarters of America's largest black Holiness-Pentecostal denomination and to remember that unity and good citizenship must be mutual.

Mason Temple was finally completed in 1945. The black and white presses declared it the largest black-owned auditorium in America, a monument to the African American race. The building had been designed and constructed by blacks: architect Henry Taylor, building commissioner Riley F. Williams, and superintendent of construction Ulysses E. Miller. The three-story steel building seated 7,500 people; it had three assembly halls, theater-style seating, a worship center, auditoriums, balconies, two large kitchens, two cafeterias, a clinic, beauty and barber shops, a post office, and a baggage room. It cost more than a quarter of a million dollars to build.[69] The *Memphis World* praised Mason Temple, stating, "There are no financial incumbencies except for operating expenses."[70] The *Press-Scimitar* acknowledged Bishop Mason's accomplishment: "Construction of the beautiful Mason Temple with its expansive auditorium and many departments stands as a lasting tribute to Mason's organizing ability and ingenuity."[71] Mason Temple symbolized unity and honored Mason and other COGIC pioneers.

After Bishop Mason died on November 17, 1961, historian Nathaniel D. Williams applauded COGIC for being "possibly the only major religious group in the Christian world which was started by a Negro . . . and not an outgrowth of some white denomination. There are now white members of the denomination. But they joined a sect started by Negroes . . . reversing the traditional pattern of Negroes joining a Christian group initiated by whites."[72] The 1959 edition of *Yearbook of American Churches* claimed that Mason had 380,428 members in America.[73] When Mason died, COGIC reported that it had 1 million members worldwide. While COGIC mourned the loss of its leader, local newspapers covered the funeral and printed stories about Mason's life.[74] COGIC's historical significance should not be miscalculated because, during the pre–civil rights era, Mason's predominantly black institution embodied black aspirations, inspiring social improvement and self-determination. In addition, COGIC refused to imitate the religious methods of the old, established churches; its adherents saw God through their marginalized experiences, preserved black cultural worship, insisted that segregation and discrimination were morally wrong, and used their uniquely black brand of Holiness-Pentecostalism to empower countless people.

Dr. Martin Luther King Jr. spoke at Mason Temple for the first time on July 31, 1959. At that time, segregationists were fighting to keep blacks out of Memphis's city government. After black Republican Dr. B. B. Martin refused to allow black Democratic candidates to hold a political rally in the Martin family's Red Sox baseball stadium, COGIC's Special Executive Commission, consisting of bishops A. B. McEwen, John S. Bailey, Otha M. Kelly, James Oglethorpe Patterson Sr., Ulysses E. Miller, Samuel Crouch, and Ozro T. Jones Sr., permitted the candidates to use Mason Temple as a springboard for their "Freedom Rally Volunteer Ticket Campaign." Russell Sugarmon Jr., the Reverend Benjamin Hooks, A. W. Willis Jr., the Reverend Henry Clay Bunton, and the Reverend Roy Love were the black candidates campaigning on the Volunteer ticket. The candidates claimed they were tired of machine politics and white politicians reneging on promises made to the black community. During the rally, Sugarmon told black voters, "We are bringing a new day to Memphis. Crump is dead. Machine rule is dead and we are going to bury segregation. Rev. Hooks [will] preach the funeral and there [won't] be [any] mourning."[75] Sugarmon was running for public works commissioner, Hooks wanted a juvenile court judgeship, and Bunton and Love were seeking seats on the Memphis School Board. On July 31 at least 5,000 people attended the freedom rally at Mason Temple. After legendary gospel singer Mahalia Jackson performed, some of Memphis's most distinguished black clergymen listened to Dr. Martin Luther King Jr. deliver his first oration in Memphis. King encouraged black Memphians to vote for black candidates. He also explained how the 1954 *Brown v. Board of Education* decision and Montgomery bus boycott were historic milestones for black Americans. "Since 1954 [we] have been standing on the thresh-hold of the most creative period in our history," bellowed King.[76] King reminded the audience that Mason Temple symbolized religious and racial harmony, as he applauded the black Baptists, Methodists, and COGIC clergymen for demonstrating solidarity and collectively supporting the freedom rally. "Working together and rising above denominational lines. This unity is magnificent," concluded King.[77] Although the freedom rally was historically significant, unfortunately, the black candidates could not win the election without white votes.

Nine years after Dr. King first spoke at Mason Temple, COGIC's national shrine became a rallying place for the Memphis civil rights movement. According to historian Michael Honey, during the 1968 Memphis sanitation workers' strike, "At Mason Temple, strikers and their supporters vented intense anger at the police and the white establishment."[78] Dr. King and his Southern Christian Leadership Conference staff returned to Memphis in the spring of 1968 to support the sanitation strike. On the evening of April 3, the eve of his death, King entered Mason Temple and memorably conveyed his final sermon. As he preached, he reminded the crowd of black workers why they were gathered at Mason Temple. "The issue is injustice. The issue is the refusal of Memphis to be fair and honest in its dealings with its public servants, who happen to be sanitation workers."[79] Throughout King's sermon, he encouraged the sanitation workers to continue their fight to earn a living wage. Some of the people who heard King's last oration were the children of the poor black migrants who had helped build Mason's early church. Like Dr. King, Bishop Mason had been concerned about the welfare of the poor and the politically powerless, the people he called God's "little ones." "I will say unto the saints be renewed in the spirit of your mind and be filled with the spirit, for the time of refreshing is come from the presence of the Lord to restore his little ones," predicted Mason.[80] According to Mason, these were the people that God loved the most. Throughout his fifty-four years of ecclesiastical leadership, Mason rejected segregation and integrated his church. Mason envisioned an America where blacks and whites had equal power and authority. King, too, envisioned a truly integrated America, a place where its citizens would be judged by their character and not by the color of their skin.

Notes

1. "Elder Utah Smith Will Hang a Man," *Atlanta Daily World,* April 13, 1938, 2; Lynn Abbott, *Incidents and Anecdotes of the Two-Winged Preacher and Electric Guitar Evangelist Elder Utah Smith* (New York: Case Quarter, 2008), 25–35; *Slide Guitar Gospel (1944–1964),* Document Records, 1995, http://search.alexanderstreet.com/view/work/74669 (accessed May 19, 2015).

2. James Courts, ed., *The History and Life Work of Elder C. H. Mason Chief Apostle and His Co-Laborers* (Memphis, TN: Howe Printing, [1920]), 75; Thomas Oscar Fuller, *The Story of the Church Life among Negroes in Memphis, Tennessee, for Students and Workers, 1900–1938* (Memphis, TN: privately published, [1938]).

3. Charles H. Mason, "Convocation Notice: Object of This Meeting," *Whole Truth,* October 1931, 1.

4. Isadore Gordon Rainey, interview by the author Memphis, February 19, 2005.

5. W. E. B. DuBois, *The Souls of Black Folk* (1903; reprint, New York: Simon and Schuster, 2005), 184–85.

6. James Baldwin, *The Fire Next Time* (New York: Vintage International, 1993), 33; Jesmyn Ward, ed., *The Fire This Time: A New Generation Speaks about Race* (New York: Scribner, 2016).

7. Robin D. G. Kelley, *Race Rebels: Culture, Politics, and the Black Working Class* (New York: Free Press, 1996), 42; Kenneth W. Goings and Gerald L. Smith, "'Unhidden Transcripts': Memphis and African American Agency, 1862–1920," *Journal of Urban History* 21, no. 3 (March 1995): 387–88.

8. "Fire! Terror at Midnight in House of God," *Memphis Press-Scimitar,* December 8, 1936.

9. Eddie R. Driver, chairman, and John E. Bryant, secretary, "Minutes of the Fourteenth Annual COGIC Convocation," Memphis, December 14, 1921, COGIC World Headquarters, 938 Mason Street, Memphis, TN, 38126; "Report on Fire," *Memphis Daily News,* December 9, 1936, 1.

10. "Fire!" *Memphis Press-Scimitar,* December 8, 1936.

11. Death certificate of Anthony Hicks, file 4757, State of Tennessee Department of Health, Division of Vital Statistics; "Negro's Body Found in Tabernacle Ruins," *Memphis Commercial Appeal,* December 9, 1936; Church of God in Christ Minutes of the General Assembly, December 9, 1936, COGIC World Headquarters, 938 Mason Street, Memphis, TN, 38126, 38. The next day, chairman Eddie R. Driver informed the COGIC General Assembly that the remains were those of Elder Anthony "Inkney" Hicks. Hicks pastored a COGIC church in Palmers Crossing, a community in Hattiesburg, Mississippi.

12. "Fire!" *Memphis Press-Scimitar,* December 8, 1936.

13. Ibid.

14. Charles H. Mason, "Horrors," in Courts, *History and Life Work of Elder C. H. Mason,* 33.

15. Forty-Sixth Annual Convocation of the Church of God in Christ, November 25–December 15, 1953, souvenir booklet, 3.

16. Gloria Brown Melton, "Blacks in Memphis, Tennessee, 1920–1955: A Historical Study" (PhD diss., Washington State University, 1982), 131, 159; Roger Biles, *Memphis in the Great Depression* (Knoxville: University of Tennessee Press, 1986), 107, 88–106.

17. Charles H. Mason, "Bishop C. H. Mason Founder: Church of God in Christ Singing, Preaching, Praying," live recording circa 1940s and 1950s, Memphis.

18. C. Eric Lincoln, ed., *The Black Experience in Religion* (New York: Anchor Books, 1974). According to Lincoln, the black preacher's "status did not depend upon formal education or training, but upon his ability to preach the word and to represent his followers before God and before the hostile white world which suffered their earthly existence" (66).

19. Lawrence W. Levine, *Black Culture and Black Consciousness: Afro-American Folk Thought from Slavery to Freedom* (New York: Oxford University Press, 1977), 179–80.

20. Leon F. Litwack, *Trouble in Mind: Black Southerners in the Age of Jim Crow* (New York: Vintage Books, 1998), 395–97.

21. Charles H. Mason, "Message in Part," in Courts, *History and Life Work of Elder C. H. Mason,* 49.

22. Charles H. Mason, "Without Respect of Persons," recorded by Anna Smith, recording secretary, in Minutes of the 26th Annual Convocation of the Church of God in Christ, National Tabernacle, Memphis, 1934.

23. Ithiel C. Clemmons, *Bishop C. H. Mason and the Roots of the Church of God in Christ,* centennial ed. (Bakersfield, CA: Pneuma Life Publishing, 1996), 21; Vinson Synan, *The Holiness-Pentecostal Tradition: Charismatic Movements in the Twentieth Century* (Grand Rapids, MI: Eerdmans, 1997), 70–71; Clarence E. Hardy III, "From Exodus to Exile: Black Pentecostals, Migrating Pilgrims, and Imagined Internationalism," *American Quarterly* 59, no. 3 (September 2007): 743–44.

24. Charles H. Mason, "Tennessee Evangelist Witnesses," *Apostolic Faith,* April 1907, 7; Douglas J. Nelson, "For Such a Time as This: The Story of Bishop William J. Seymour and the Azusa Street Revival" (PhD diss., University of Birmingham, England, 1981), 62–63, 76–77, 213.

25. Mason, "Horrors," 33–34; Theodore Kornweibel Jr., "Bishop C. H. Mason and the Church of God in Christ during World War I: The Perils of Conscientious Objection," *Southern Studies* 26 (Winter 1987): 261–81; Sylvester A. Johnson, *African American Religions, 1500–2000: Colonialism, Democracy, and Freedom* (New York: Cambridge University Press, 2015), 312–20; "German Money to Encourage Negroes to Evade Draft," *Bourbon Daily News,* April 5, 1918; "Pastor Accused of Delivering Pro-German Messages," *Chicago Defender,* April 13, 1918.

26. Courts, *History and Life Work of Elder C. H. Mason,* 98–99; T. F. Murphy, "1936 Church of God in Christ: Statistics, Denominational History, Doctrine, and Organization," in *Religious Bodies, 1936: United States Department of Commerce, Bureau of the Census* (Washington, DC: Government Printing Office, 1941), 1–2.

27. "Equal in Power and Authority," in *A Brief Historical and Doctrinal Statement and Rules for Government of the Church of God in Christ,* ed. William B. Holt (Memphis, TN: n.p., [1917–1918]), 9.

28. David D. Daniels III, "Charles Harrison Mason: The Interracial Impulse of Early Pentecostalism," in *Portraits of a Generation: Early Pentecostal Leaders,* ed. James R. Goff Jr. and Grant Wacker (Fayetteville: University of Arkansas Press, 2002), 255.

29. "Drug Store Policed Six Weeks," *Atlanta Daily World,* December 19, 1940, 6.

30. "Tabernacle Fire Fails to Halt Services of Negroes," *Memphis Press-Scimitar,* December 9, 1936.

31. Eddie M. Page, "My Life and Work," in *The History and Life Work of Bishop C. H. Mason Chief Apostle and His Co-Laborers,* comp. Mary Mason

(Memphis, TN: privately published, 1934), 93–94; Karen Kossie-Chernyshev, "Constructing Good Success: The Church of God in Christ and Social Uplift in East Texas, 1910–1935," in *Blacks in East Texas History: Selections from the* East Texas Historical Journal, 1st ed., ed. Bruce Glasrud and Archie P. McDonald (College Station: Texas A&M University Press, 2008), 111–18.

32. "Tabernacle Fire Fails to Halt Services of Negroes," *Memphis Press-Scimitar,* December 9, 1936.

33. "Negro Tabernacle Swept by Flames: Fire Races through Building Scattering 5,000 Worshippers," *Memphis Commercial Appeal,* December 8, 1936; "Negro's Body Found in Tabernacle Ruins," *Memphis Commercial Appeal,* December 9, 1936.

34. "Negro Tabernacle Swept by Flames."

35. Jill Watts, "This Was the Way: Father Divine's Peace Mission Movement in Los Angeles during the Great Depression," *Pacific Historical Review* 60, no. 4 (November 1991): 496. Watts describes Divine's meteoric rise and explains why his message was so appealing to Depression-era Americans. Besides the appeal of Divine's self-help and antiracist plan, his "syncretic theological" method allowed him to blend Holiness-Pentecostal teachings with New Thought philosophy (positive thinking). Therefore, Divine's "mind power [message] promised that all Americans could become successful and take control of their destiny."

36. Sara Harris, *Father Divine: The Classic Portrait of the Flamboyant Black Messiah* (New York: Macmillan, 1971), xxiii.

37. Watts, "This Was the Way," 477–78, 480, 485, 490–92; Jill Watts, *God, Harlem U.S.A. The Father Divine Story* (Berkeley: University of California Press, 1992), 24–30, 132–44; Henry Louis Gates and Cornel West, *The African-American Century: How Black Americans Have Shaped Our Country,* reprint ed. (New York: Free Press, 2002), 122–25.

38. Charles H. Mason, "Familiar Spirits," in Mason, *History and Life Work of Bishop C. H. Mason,* 90.

39. "Holiness Temple Swept by $25,000 Fire at Midnight Services—1 Dies in Blaze," *Atlanta Daily World,* December 11, 1936.

40. Green P. Hamilton, *The Bright Side of Memphis* (Memphis, TN: privately printed, 1908), 277; Roberta Church, Charles W. Crawford, and Ronald Walter, *Nineteenth Century Memphis Families of Color 1850–1900* (Memphis, TN: Murdock Printing, 1987), 40–41.

41. Randolph M. Walker, *The Metamorphosis of Sutton E. Griggs: The Transition of Black Radical to Conservative, 1913–1933* (Memphis, TN: Walker Publishing, 1991), 61–75; Cornel West, *Prophesy Deliverance: An Afro-American Revolutionary Christianity* (Louisville, KY: Westminster John Knox Press, 2002), 80–81; Finnie D. Coleman, *Sutton E. Griggs and the Struggle against White Supremacy* (Knoxville: University of Tennessee Press, 2007), xii, 130–31.

42. David M. Tucker, *Black Pastors and Leaders: Memphis, 1819–1972*

(Memphis, TN: Memphis State University Press, 1975), 85, 99; Edward A. Cooper, "Temple's Dedication Service," *Whole Truth,* Spring 1932, 6; Fuller, *Story of Church Life among Negroes in Memphis,* 34–35.

43. "Elder Dies in the Flames at Temple: 2000 Saints at Meet Scramble for Safety When Flames Pour In," *Atlanta Daily World,* December 12, 1936.

44. Memorial of Mrs. Lelia Washington Mason, funeral program, November 23, 1936, Tabernacle Church of God in Christ, Memphis; "Lelia Mason Obituary," *Memphis Commercial Appeal,* November 21, 1936, 19; "Mrs. Mason Wife of Holiness Bishop Succumbs to Stroke," *Plaindealer,* November 29, 1936, 8; Eddie R. Driver, national chairman, and Ulysses E. Miller, national secretary, "Resolution Concerning Sister Mason," COGIC General Assembly Minutes, December 11, 1936, 40–41.

45. Thaddeus T. Stokes, "The Man Who Was Never Late for an Appointment," *Memphis World,* February 1, 1958; Bishop C. E. Bennett, "Eulogy of Bishop A. B. McEwen," February 21, 1969, Mason Temple, Memphis, in *Whole Truth,* April 1969; "Bishop McEwen Dead," *Memphis World,* February 22, 1969, 1, 4.

46. A. B. McEwen Sr., "Convocation Tabernacle Destroyed—Bishop Says Ugly Rumors Are False and Unfounded," *Atlanta Daily World,* December 12, 1936.

47. "Fire Threatens 5,000 at Divine's Memphis Heaven," *Pittsburgh Courier,* December 19, 1936.

48. Richard S. Page, "Attention Editor Robert L. Vann: Officer of Church of God in Christ Denies Divine Help," *Pittsburgh Courier,* January 16, 1937.

49. "Race Prejudice Scored as 29th Convocation Closes," *Atlanta Daily World,* December 21, 1936.

50. Ibid.

51. Jams Delk, *He Made Millions of People Happy* (Hopkinsville, KY: privately printed, [1944]), 7.

52. Lester C. Lamon, *Blacks in Tennessee, 1790–1970* (Knoxville: University of Tennessee Press, 1981), 72–73. Lamon suggests that despite Tennessee's segregation laws, black initiative contested "segregation and unequal appropriations" (72).

53. Laurie B. Green, *Battling the Plantation Mentality: Memphis and the Black Freedom Struggle* (Chapel Hill: University of North Carolina Press, 2007), 241–42.

54. Ibid.

55. "Race Prejudice Scored as 29th Convocation Closes," *Atlanta Daily World,* December 21, 1936; Rose Marie McDuff, "The Ethnohistory of Saint's Home Church of God in Christ, Los Angeles, California" (master's thesis, California State University, 1972).

56. "Fire!" *Memphis Press-Scimitar,* December 8, 1936.

57. Eddie R. Driver, national chairman, and Ulysses E. Miller, national secretary, COGIC General Assembly Minutes, December 11, 1936, 41.

58. Eddie R. Driver, national chairman, and Ulysses E. Miller, national secretary, COGIC General Assembly Minutes, December 12, 1938, 51.

59. David M. Tucker, *Lieutenant Lee of Beale Street* (Nashville, TN: Vanderbilt University Press, 1971), 124; G. Wayne Dowdy, *Mayor Crump Don't Like It: Machine Politics in Memphis* (Jackson: University Press of Mississippi, 2006), 13, 49–50.

60. Franklin C. Wilsford, Crump & Trezevant, to Bishop Charles H. Mason, December 24, 1936, E. H. Crump Collection, Memphis and Shelby County Room, Memphis Public Library and Information Center.

61. Bishop Charles H. Mason to Mr. Edward H. Crump, December 28, 1936, ibid.

62. Ulysses E. Miller, "New Tabernacle," *Whole Truth*, September 1940.

63. "Fear Trouble in Memphis, Nineteen on Unholy List: Both Races Reported Disturbed over Insult to Negro Leader," *Atlanta Daily World*, December 18, 1940; Green, *Battling the Plantation Mentality*, 38–41.

64. "Blaze Destroys Church of God School, Bishop Mason to Rebuild," *Atlanta Daily World*, December 6, 1940; Dovie Marie Simmons, Olivia L. Martin, and Louise Dean, *Down behind the Sun: The Story of Arenia Conella Mallory* (Memphis, TN: Riverside Press, 1983), 21.

65. "Fire, Nor Thieves, Nor Satan Himself Can Halt This 20-Day Church Meet," *Chicago Defender*, December 14, 1940.

66. "Nationwide Convocation Appeal for Protection from Police Terror: Churches of God Hold 33rd Annual Convocation at Memphis, Tennessee," *Plaindealer*, December 6, 1940; "Ask Roosevelt to Halt Memphis Police Terror," *Chicago Defender*, December 28, 1940, 1–2.

67. "6,000 Saints Hear Mayor Chandler," *Atlanta Daily World*, December 16, 1940.

68. Ibid.

69. Riley F. Williams and Ulysses E. Miller, *Facts about the Temple: Mason Temple-Memphis, Tennessee* (Bogalusa, LA: Bogalusa News Company, 1945), 19–33.

70. "When the Saints Go Marching In," *Memphis World*, November 30, 1945; Cornelius Range, "Largest Hall Owned by Race: To Shelter the 1945 Church of God in Christ Convocation," *Pittsburgh Courier*, December 1, 1945.

71. "Bishop Mason's Day," *Memphis Press-Scimitar*, December 4, 1949.

72. Nathaniel D. Williams, "Bishop Mason's Obituary Remarks," *Tri-State Defender*, November 25, 1961; "Obituary of the Late Charles Harrison Mason," in official funeral program, November 28, 1961, Mason Temple, Memphis.

73. Benson Landis, *Yearbook of American Churches: Information on all the Faiths of the U.S.A. 1959* (New York: Bureau of Research Publications, 1959), 36–37; "Millions Mourn: A Tribute to Bishop Mason," *Whole Truth*, souvenir ed., 1961.

74. "Bishop Mason Enters Final Rest," *Memphis Press-Scimitar*, November

28, 1961; James L. Hicks, "100,000 Mourn Death of Bishop C. H. Mason: JFK Wires Bishop's Widow," *New York Amsterdam News,* December 2, 1961, 1, 39.

75. "Dr. King Urges Memphians to Elect Negro Candidates," *Memphis World,* August 5, 1959, 6; "Ministers Rap Dr. Martin for Refusing Use of Stadium," *Memphis World,* July 29, 1959, 1.

76. "Dr. King Urges Memphians to Elect Negro Candidates," 1.

77. Ibid.; Sharon D. Wright, *Race, Power, and Political Emergence in Memphis* (New York: Garland Publishing, 2000), 45–50; Michael K. Honey, *Going down Jericho Road: The Memphis Strike, Martin Luther King's Last Campaign* (New York: W. W. Norton, 2007), 29–31, 40.

78. Honey, *Going down Jericho Road,* 210; Stephen B. Oates, *Let the Trumpet Sound: The Life of Martin Luther King, Jr.* (New York: Harper and Row, 1982), 265–93.

79. Martin Luther King Jr., "I've Been to the Mountaintop," April 3, 1968, Mason Temple, in *The Radical King: Martin Luther King, Jr.,* ed. Cornel West (Boston: Beacon Press, 2016), 267–68; Martin Luther King Jr., "I See the Promised Land," April 3, 1968, in *A Testament of Hope: The Essential Writings and Speeches of Martin Luther King Jr.,* ed. James Melvin Washington (San Francisco: HarperCollins, 1986), 279–88; Honey, *Going down Jericho Road,* 415–30.

80. Charles H. Mason, "Times! Times of Refreshing," in Jerry Ramsey, *The Late Apostle C.H. Mason Speaks* (n.p., n.d.), p. 36.

"There Will Be No Discrimination"

Race, Power, and the Memphis Flood of 1937

David Welky

> I'm looking for my mother and my brother; I was wondering where
> can they be.
> Looking for my mother and brother; I was wondering where can they
> be?
> Maybe they're in Memphis; I believe I'll go and see.
> —Big Bill Broonzy, "Terrible Flood Blues" (1937)

In March 1937 the *Memphis Commercial Appeal* published a letter from
P. J. Anderson, principal of the segregated Mildred Jackson Junior High
School in Hughes, Arkansas, a tiny town just a few miles from the Mississippi River. Anderson was one of many African Americans from Hughes
who had sought shelter in Memphis when rising floodwaters forced them
from their homes several weeks earlier. Before heading back to Hughes,
Anderson wanted to thank the people of Memphis for welcoming him
and other black refugees during their moment of extreme peril. "We are
returning to our homes but we would have you know our appreciation
and gratitude," he wrote. "We have been treated very royally by the good
big-hearted people of this town."[1]

Other African Americans joined Anderson in praising the hospitality of Memphians. "One of the most pleasant and hopeful things about
[the flood] has been the impartiality with which flood relief has been
administered with almost no regard to the racial difference of sufferers,"
observed an editorialist in the *Pittsburgh Courier,* a nationally distributed
African American newspaper known for its passionate exposés of racial
injustice. "Deep down in most American people there is not as much
racial antipathy as they often assume for the sake of appearances," the

Courier concluded. When *Crisis* magazine editor Roy Wilkins toured the flooded region in his role as an investigator for the NAACP, he found only "minor discriminations" in the treatment of black refugees in Memphis and elsewhere.[2]

The favorable comments of these African American observers bear the stamp of authenticity. There is no evidence that anyone coerced Anderson into writing his upbeat assessment. Neither Wilkins nor African American newspapers like the *Courier* would have ignored evidence of prejudice or bigotry. These institutions were on the alert for trouble throughout the flood, and during the early days of high water, the NAACP and other civil rights groups, such as the National Urban League, had urged the White House and the Red Cross to prevent discrimination against victims.[3]

Natural catastrophes can disrupt existing social, cultural, and economic patterns, so it is possible that the horrific flood of 1937 might have forced a temporary or even a permanent realignment of racial dynamics in Memphis. Unfortunately, despite the positive assessments of Anderson, Wilkins, and others, it did not. Anyone with even slight knowledge of the civil rights era knows that racial inequality endured in the Bluff City well beyond 1937.

The flood nevertheless provides an interesting glimpse of the city's racial history at a pivotal moment. It offers an opportunity for a kind of status check, a look at the possibilities and limitations experienced by the area's African Americans at that moment. Memphis's handling of the disaster revealed unspoken assumptions regarding African Americans' position in local society. In addition, the flood marked both a beginning and a terminus on the timeline of local history. In some ways it hinted at future progress and an up-and-coming generation of civil rights leaders, while in others it signified the end of a brief era during which black Memphians maneuvered their way into a modicum of power.

In terms of lives affected and damage wrought, the Ohio-Mississippi River flood of January–February 1937 was the worst deluge up to that point in American history, even worse than the better-remembered 1927 disaster. "Only a Dante could describe in verse, or a Wagner in music, the overwhelming character of the flood . . . and the amount of human misery it caused," one survivor recalled. "It's the worst thing that ever happened," Major General John Craig informed the press after flying over the entire 981-mile length of the Ohio River, from Pittsburgh, Pennsylvania, all the way to Cairo, Illinois. "And it is going to get worse."[4]

President Franklin Roosevelt gave his second inaugural address during the early days of the flood, speaking to the crowd through a driving rain that was one small part of an enormous storm system drenching the eastern half of the United States. Two high-pressure fronts, one coming from the Caribbean and one from Canada, had collided over the Ohio River Valley. Frozen in place for nearly a month, the fronts acted as a vacuum that sucked moisture through the trough between them. Around 165 billion tons of precipitation—41.25 quadrillion gallons—hammered the valley during the first month of the new year.

As the Ohio and its tributaries overflowed their banks, a nation still traumatized by the Great Depression and the recurring dust storms that had transformed its breadbasket into a wasteland faced another disaster of unprecedented magnitude. A million people fled from hundreds of farms, towns, and cities. Brackish floodwaters crashed down streets and buried vast fields of fertile soil. More than 200,000 square miles were inundated at the flood's crest, an area five times the size of Tennessee. Nearly the entire populations of Louisville and Paducah, Kentucky, fled as the river exceeded previous records by ten feet or more. Cincinnati suffered from power outages and, ironically, water shortages when the raging Ohio spilled into wells and knocked pumping stations out of commission. Cairo, Illinois, squeezed between the Ohio and Mississippi Rivers, faced extinction if its levees failed.

President Roosevelt quickly repurposed New Deal job-creation agencies into flood-relief agencies. He ordered tens of thousands of Civilian Conservation Corps (CCC) and Works Progress Administration (WPA) enrollees into the fray, along with elements of the army, navy, and coast guard. FDR worked closely with the Red Cross, which organized its largest aid campaign since World War I from its headquarters in Washington and field offices scattered throughout the flood zone.

Memphis, located south of where the Ohio meets the Mississippi, played an important role in the flood saga. January 1937 was a dismal month in the Bluff City. Nearly 8 billion gallons of water—more than 66 billion pounds—pounded the metropolitan area between New Year's Day and Roosevelt's inauguration on January 20. The sun shone on Memphians for a total of 13½ of those 480 hours. With temperatures hovering around the freezing mark, streets iced over and power lines snapped. Mud slides blocked Riverside Drive. Rising waters cut off Highway 51 north of town.[5]

City officials knew trouble would come once floodwater from the Ohio began dumping into the Mississippi, but no one could say exactly how bad things would get. "There are fools, darned fools and those who predict the river," one old-timer muttered. The US Army Corps of Engineers agreed. "With general rains forecast, the crests cannot be predicted," its Memphis district office declared. Every day the water crept higher on the flood gauge marked on the Harahan Bridge. Yellowish waves submerged Mud Island hours before Roosevelt gave his inaugural address. Gangs of black workers (supervised by whites) began removing cotton bales from Front Street warehouses to higher ground. Workers sealed the floodgates on the Wolf River levees and activated machines that pumped out the water infiltrating the north side of the city into the surrounding bayous.[6]

"We are ready," insisted Red Cross regional director George Myer from his temporary command center in the Peabody Hotel. Downtown Memphis was high enough to protect it from any realistic threat of flooding. Instead of preparing for high water, the city was preparing for an inundation of refugees. In 1927, the year of the last great Mississippi River surge, Memphis had hosted 3,700 flooded-out souls. Everyone anticipated a similar number this time around and assumed that most of the refugees would be coming from western Tennessee. American Legionnaires were already stockpiling cots and stoves at the fairgrounds.[7]

By January 23, a slow trickle of exiles was tramping into the city— not from the east, but from eastern Arkansas. Most were sharecroppers fleeing the swollen Black, White, and St. Francis Rivers. First there were 50, then 1,000, then 5,000. City and Red Cross officials scrambled to find more cots, more stoves, more food, more everything. "The highways looked the way you would imagine English highways looked when the black plague struck a section and the people left," one local businessman said. Coughs and wheezes punctuated the shuffling sounds of the poorly shod refugees. Colds, fevers, pneumonia, and influenza stalked the ragged line. Ramshackle cars with chicken coops attached to their roofs rattled by. Flooded-out farmers led cattle and pigs down the road to Memphis. Scam artists told the ignorant refugees that the authorities would confiscate any animals they tried to bring into Memphis, convincing the farmers to sell them their livestock for pennies on the dollar.[8]

Memphis's prosperity depended on a steady flow of cotton from the surrounding rural areas. Now the people, not the products, of these same fields overwhelmed the existing relief setup. "It will be impossible for Memphis to care for all refugees pouring in," warned Mayor Watkins Overton, who had just returned from a truncated honeymoon. Arkansas' brand-new governor, Carl Bailey, promised to redirect his state's refugees away from the Harahan Bridge, but still they came, some 60,000 of them into a city that had planned for 3,700. Memphis faced a public health and humanitarian nightmare.[9]

Authorities stuffed the refugees wherever they could. The fairgrounds, bursting with thousands more people than it could properly accommodate, devolved into a swampy, unhygienic cesspool. Schools, churches, and vacant homes were jammed with exiles. Mayor Overton's emergency flood committee worked with the Red Cross and the WPA to transport people to Chattanooga and Tullahoma, Tennessee; Corinth and Jackson, Mississippi; and any other community that would take them.

On February 10 the floodwaters crested at Memphis at 50.3 feet, more than 15 feet above flood level and almost 4 feet above the previous high-water mark of 46.6 set in 1913. Portions of North and South Memphis were submerged, but the city's commercial, industrial, and cultural centers stayed high and dry, as expected. Roads and schools reopened once the Mississippi began to recede. Workers scoured the fairgrounds clean as the tide of migrants ebbed. Passed in the wake of the catastrophe, the 1937 Flood Control Act appropriated millions of dollars for improved flood walls and levees along Memphis's Wolf and Nonconnah Rivers. Justifiably proud of their role in saving countless lives, Memphians moved on, relegating the great flood of 1937 to a footnote in their city's history.

Memphis's understandable eagerness to forget the flood obscured the fact that blacks and whites experienced the event in different ways. Comments about the lack of racial discrimination during the flood emergency appeared within the context of a social system grounded in discrimination. What Anderson, Wilkins, and the others really meant was that January and February 1937 saw no more discrimination than had occurred before the flood and would probably occur after the flood.

Around 100,000 African Americans lived in Memphis in 1937, accounting for about 40 percent of the population. Most of them lived in the worst parts of town, in ghettos with such evocative names as Slippery Log Bottoms, Queen Bee Bottoms, and Shinertown. Occupying lowlands along the Wolf River and other peripheral districts, these slums were warrens of tumbledown hovels and ramshackle tenements, many of which had communal outdoor toilets rather than indoor plumbing and were health hazards even in normal times. The Depression, amplified by discrimination in employment, made a rough economic situation worse. Unemployment rates for black Memphians hovered around 35 percent throughout the 1930s. African Americans with jobs, most of them involving unskilled labor or domestic work, earned around half as much as employed whites. Even before the flood, then, many local blacks lived precarious existences that left them especially vulnerable to disasters.[10]

Other than a variety of black insurance companies and fraternal organizations, local African Americans endured a profoundly frayed social safety net. The local NAACP chapter was weak and timid. A publicly sponsored Community Welfare League received a mere $2,600 per year from the Memphis Community Fund for antipoverty efforts within black neighborhoods. Local blacks could not even see themselves on movie screens; Lloyd T. Binford, the viciously racist head of the Memphis Censor Board, excised scenes of Louis Armstrong, Lena Horne, and other African Americans from films before clearing them for theaters.[11]

At the same time, black Memphians enjoyed an unusual amount of political power, within carefully prescribed limits. That power would prove critical during the 1937 flood. Unlike in many other places in the South, African Americans in Memphis voted in great numbers, even though they had to pay a poll tax. Often that poll tax was paid by Edward Hull Crump, the brash yet thin-skinned boss of the local Democratic Party, who then held his generosity as leverage over the beneficiaries. Boss Crump began building inroads into the black community in 1909 after almost losing the mayoral election to a candidate who had cornered the African American vote. In exchange for marginally improved city ser-

vices in black districts and a handful of positions within the local Democratic establishment, key black ministers and other power brokers were
willing to round up black votes for Crump's machine-backed candidates.
Crump tightened his grip once Democrat Franklin Roosevelt won the
White House after more than a decade of Republican rule. He used his
Washington connections as a cudgel and ostracized local black Republicans such as Bob Church Jr.[12]

With Democrats firmly in control of local politics, African Americans
found that fealty to the Crump machine paid few dividends. With no
real Republican opposition, however, black voters had few decent alterna-
tives. Segregation remained the law of the land when it came to schools,
amusements, churches, housing, and jobs. Watkins Overton, who had
become mayor a decade before the flood, summed up his support for
the racial status quo in 1927: "We do not favor anything which might
create race friction," he told a campaign audience. "Therefore we are
opposed to Negro police, Negro firemen and general admission to the
white parks." African Americans were expected to be invisible, limiting
themselves to back doors and redlined neighborhoods in the lowlands.
They could vote, but the sad reality was that they had nothing to vote
for.[13]

With resources tight, infrastructure strained, and thousands of
migrants pouring into the city during the 1937 flood, Memphis could
have adopted a "whites-first" attitude toward flood rescue and relief,
guaranteeing white refugees the best of everything while leaving the
scraps for their black counterparts. That this did not occur was due at
least in part to the external oversight of disaster operations. WPA chief
Harry Hopkins disavowed racial prejudice from the moment the waters
began to rise, and Red Cross chairman Cary Grayson, who was close
friends with Roosevelt, vowed that "the Red Cross will assert every effort
to make certain that all phases of the relief work are administered without discrimination." Robert Fechner, director of the CCC, promised the
NAACP that "there will be no discrimination." These men kept their
word, conducting their operations without regard for race and investigat-
ing every report of racial prejudice in the flood zone.[14]

What this really meant was that the Red Cross and the federal government were looking for evidence of discrimination beyond its nor-

mal levels. In fact, the institutionalized racism that had long organized life in Memphis pervaded and even defined flood time in the Bluff City. Authority figures generally ignored unpleasant reminders of systematized inequality. Persistent racism undermined the dominant narrative of a color-blind crisis promoted by Red Cross fund-raisers, Roosevelt administration officials, and Memphis city leaders.

City fathers and political leaders zealously promoted the Bluff City's flood-proof status before, during, and after 1937. Any vulnerability during high water could scare away potential business clients and investors as they imagined their inventories washing downstream. Most of Memphis proper stayed dry at the crest. Inundated areas tended to be on the edges of the city and populated largely by African Americans. On the north side, the Wolf River and Lick Creek, swollen with yellowish backwater from the Mississippi, spilled into the "negro section" near Jackson and Vollentine Avenues, forcing hundreds of families to flee from downscale neighborhoods known as Bear Wallow and Klondike. Street commissioner O. P. William estimated that 98 percent of those evacuees were black. On the south side of town, Nonconnah Creek—really more like Nonconnah River during the weeks of the flood—sent African Americans running from the area around Brooks Avenue (present-day East Brooks Road).[15]

These shantytown districts had been thrown up in the early twentieth century to accommodate migrants pouring into an already overcrowded city. They were built on swampy and unhealthful land that was part of a network of bayous and lowlands that served as natural reservoirs whenever the Mississippi went on a rampage. These areas had flooded before, and there was no reason to doubt that they would flood again. That they primarily housed African Americans reflected the deep, often unspoken socioeconomic inequality permeating the city. Restrictive codes and financial limitations kept black Memphians penned up in a few neighborhoods, most of them undesirable. Neither Roy Wilkins nor anyone else mentioned the skewed racial numbers among local flood victims as evidence of discrimination. Yet the conclusion is inescapable: even if there were few *additional* forms of discrimination during the flood, the disaster exposed inequalities that predated the flood.

"Men, women and children, white and negro, horses, dogs, cows, chickens, hogs, mules—mile after mile . . . they file into the great city," the *Memphis Press-Scimitar* wrote of the incoming migrants. A disproportionate number of that swarm of 60,000 or so people consisted of African Americans who scratched out a meager existence under exploitative sharecropping or tenant farming arrangements with white plantation owners. These systems, which Memphis relied on for its economic well-being, extended class and racial hierarchies across eastern Arkansas. The refugees' material conditions revealed their hardscrabble lives. Many wore rags and had no shoes. Everything they owned could be carried on their backs. They had little if any formal education and were vulnerable to communicable diseases such as pneumonia. "It seemed that all were coughing or running a temperature," one Red Cross official wrote.[16]

Their miserable condition shocked prominent Memphians, who had apparently chosen to remain ignorant of the squalor prevailing just across the state line. "Many of these people who have been gathered into refugee camps are better fed and better cared for than before the floods swept away their homes," Congressman Walter Chandler remarked. George Washington Lee, perhaps the city's most famous civil rights figure, said much the same thing. "It's a peculiar situation," he told the *Chicago Defender.* "Some of the refugees from Arkansas, Mississippi, and other places are living better now than they did at home. We'll have a hard time trying to get them out of Memphis." Lee's comment exposed a city-country division among African Americans. Rather than express outrage at the terrible living conditions in rural areas, he voiced concern that those unwashed bumpkins might never leave.[17]

Plantation owners took steps to ensure that their tenants remained under their control. Investigators found pockets of African American sharecroppers stashed in rented quarters around the city, living in unsanitary conditions under the watchful eyes of white overseers who were wary of handing them over to the Red Cross because, as one plantation owner from near Pritchard, Arkansas, stated, if the sharecroppers got into a refugee camp, "they might not come back." One city worker found 124 "negroes of both sexes" jammed into two rented rooms with only two toilets and washbasins for the entire group. Once again, a white landowner was trying to keep his laborers under his thumb lest they escape into the relative anonymity of the city.[18]

African Americans who entered officially designated refugee camps at the fairgrounds or local schools encountered another form of pervasive yet rarely discussed discrimination: segregation. Neither the Red Cross, the city, the Roosevelt administration, nor the press ever suggested any other option. Formal segregation was so deeply ingrained in the culture of Memphis that no one could even conceive of blacks and whites surviving the crisis together.

All available evidence suggests that black and white refugees received similar food, supplies, and medical care. The flood may have marked one of the few times when "separate but equal" genuinely applied. That does not excuse the inherent inequality of racial segregation. As if by instinct, white and black refugees gathered around separate campfires at the fairgrounds. In a symbolically unfortunate decision, blacks were housed in the cattle barns. Once the fairgrounds became dangerously overcrowded, officials had to find other accommodations for the refugees. Most of those they could not ship out of town were redistributed among the city's segregated hospitals and schools. Hundreds of African Americans were crammed into Porter Elementary School, Booker T. Washington High School, and the aged Shelby County Hospital. Once workers cleaned up the fairgrounds, they built eight new barracks for refugee housing—whites only.

Anyone who praised Memphis for its generous treatment of African Americans during the flood overlooked several realities. Segregation featured prominently in relief efforts. Economic and social inequalities left black residents of the city and surrounding areas especially vulnerable to high water. Outside agencies equalized the distribution of aid as best they could, but they failed to challenge deeper, underlying examples of racism on the grounds that it was not their job or this was not the time for social experimentation.

The clearest and most notorious example of racial disparities in Memphis came as the flood was peaking at the end of January. With the waters climbing and no crest in sight, business leaders whose properties were imperiled by Nonconnah Creek implored Boss Crump to focus the city's efforts on bolstering the rickety levee protecting their plants and factories from certain destruction. Crump, who had sat out the early days of the crisis with a bad cold, sprang into action. After evaluating the situation, he decided the levee needed more workers than the WPA could provide, and fast. Crump ordered 500 inmates from the Shelby County Penal Farm, most of them black, to the barrier. Area planters often used black convicts as forced labor, so Crump was tapping a familiar source of cheap employees.

Crump donned high-laced boots, red and black plaid pants, and a bright green mackinaw so he could personally oversee this ragged army of conscripts. Leg irons clanked as black inmates lugged heavy sandbags to the levee. "Men from the prison camps, pressed into emergency service, worked with revived spirits under his charge," Crump lackey Walter Chandler later crowed from the floor of Congress. Most of the men had been jailed for vagrancy or gambling, minor crimes that were often used to incarcerate blacks who seemed sketchy or uppity.

Conditions on the levee were brutal. High winds sprayed the brackish river water into the men's faces. Everything was heavy and wet. Cold air nipped at their extremities. Trucks piled high with dirt careened through the work gangs. It was lightly organized chaos, and it might not be enough to save the industrial area from serious damage.[19]

More workers were needed, so sometime around February 1, Crump passed the word through the upper ranks of the police department that deputies should send every able-bodied black man they could find to the Nonconnah levees. Anyone who resisted the roundup should be arrested for vagrancy. Paddy wagons patrolled Beale Street, snatching up any black man who dared show his face. Police grabbed sixty-two-year-old Charles Hurse at a billiard parlor and tossed him in a truck with eighteen other kidnapped African Americans. Police verbally abused thirty-nine-year-old Henry Jones after snatching him from Beale Street. African Americans huddled inside movie theaters for days on end rather than expose themselves to the danger outside. "The avenue of glamour, of tragedy, or sorrow, of poem and song, is afraid," reported the *Chicago Defender*'s Dan Burley, who was on the scene.[20]

Conscripts faced additional woes once the trucks deposited them on the levees. National Guardsmen patrolled with rifles. They might not have driven the men plantation style, but their presence intimidated the workers into maximizing their efforts. White levee workers clustered around fires, bracing themselves against the cold drizzle and subfreezing temperature. Authorities pushed away any African American who dared to try to warm his hands. White men shoveled sand into bags. Black men did the more strenuous work of hauling those hundred-pound bags atop the levee.[21]

The "Beale Street roundup" later became a source of white amusement. Local insurance man K. N. Pollard showed no embarrassment when he described the incident at a professional convention in Chicago. "At one time, there was a shortage of labor on [the Nonconnah] levee and the situation was solved by a round-up of negroes from Beale Street, our most famous thoroughfare, about which I am sure you have heard," he explained. Pollard laughed when he recalled victims toiling "in fancy clothes, spats and derbies." He probably lifted that line from an article in the *Memphis Press-Scimitar,* the more liberal of the city's two major newspapers, which had jokingly referred to the "'enlistment' of negroes on Beale Avenue, who worked in their fancy clothes, their spats and derbies." White foremen, the paper claimed, were "still chuckling" over the absurdity of it all.[22]

Weeks after the waters dropped, NAACP executive secretary Walter White filed a "vigorous protest" with Mayor Overton, citing "the shanghaiing of Negro citizens of Memphis by Memphis police." This rebuke changed nothing; Overton was out of town, so White's letter was forwarded to Commissioner of Public Safety Clifford Davis, who ignored it.[23]

It was agitation at the local, not the national, level that stopped the kidnappings and gave Memphis blacks a rare political victory made possible only by the severity of the emergency. The details are as murky as the Mississippi itself, but the turning point appeared to be when African American businessman, activist, and Republican politico George Washington Lee wrangled a conference with Police Commissioner Joseph Boyle. Exactly what was said will never be known, but Lee must have made some threats because conscription soon stopped, and the city turned over the recruitment of black volunteers to a small committee of African Americans.[24]

A group of prominent black leaders met with federal officials at the Civic League on Beale Street—their turf, not the government's. Lee chaired the gathering. Lewis Swingler, editor of the *Memphis World,* acted as secretary. J. B. Martin, a Republican politico who served as Bob Church Jr.'s top lieutenant, was there too. Martin also owned the South

Flood relief. (Courtesy Memphis and Shelby County Room, Memphis Public Library)

Memphis Drugstore and the Memphis Red Sox, a Negro League base-ball team. The list of other attendees read like an honor roll of future Memphis civil rights advocates. The Reverend Samuel A. Owen would become a leader of the 1950s-era Memphis Citizens Committee for the Promotion of Justice. In 1954 he founded Owen Junior College (today, part of LeMoyne-Owen College), which became a hotbed of desegrega-tion activism. Doctor A. N. Kittrelle, another of Church's political associ-ates, helped lead voter registration drives in the early 1950s. Beale Street real estate man Lucien J. Searcy would head the local branch of A. Phil-lip Randolph's March on Washington movement, a militant World War II–era organization dedicated to winning equal employment for blacks. In other words, the flood of 1937 provided an emerging group of civil rights agitators with one of their first major triumphs over the white power structure. It was a lesson not soon forgotten: moments of crisis are opportunities for advancement.[25]

Motivated members of the black middle class won a victory by forcing the federal government to intervene in what had been a local issue. Under an agreement reached at the Beale Street meeting, an emergency committee of respectable, upstanding African American businessmen would funnel black volunteers not to the Memphis police but to the WPA and the Corps of Engineers for employment on the levees. The federal government made another concession when it promised to hire even people who had not previously registered with the WPA and could not prove Tennessee residency. With the Nonconnah levees becoming waterlogged and area businesses imperiled, Boss Crump's men had no choice but to stand aside and cede control of their labor force.[26]

"Members of both races are now conferring together for mutual benefit and cooperation and a spirit of helpfulness is being shown," the *Defender*'s Burley enthused. Searcy exclaimed that the flood marked the first time black Memphians had organized themselves in an emergency. It would not be the last.[27]

The actions of Lee, Martin, and other black leaders hinted at the potential for change over the long term. In the immediate term, however, Memphis showed every sign of maintaining the racial status quo. Anyone who remarked on the lack of discrimination during the flood must not have been reading the newspapers, for clear signs of a racial hierarchy saturated the *Commercial Appeal* and *Press-Scimitar* before, during, and after the flood. Editors divided the pages advertising Sunday sermons into "Churches" and "Colored Churches." Since white churches were the norm, no adjective was necessary. One of the *Commercial Appeal*'s regular features was Hambone, a Sambo-style cartoon character who spouted inanities from his box on the front page. "Drivin my ole cyar roun' dese slip'ry streets, I has to start my stoppin' *early!*" Hambone opined during the flood's early stages.[28]

Memphis's newspapers rendered black refugees invisible, printing no clear photographs of African American flood victims throughout the crisis. This was a white disaster, so far as their illustrations were concerned. Because photos of refugees were often paired with appeals for donations, perhaps editors assumed that people would be less likely to give to the Red Cross if they thought the money would assist African Americans.[29]

In the newspapers, most mentions of black refugees were made in the name of humor. During this grim time, suffering African Americans became an acceptable source of levity for the mainstream press's predominantly white readership. A lively cast of black characters populated the daily papers during the flood. For instance, there was the overweight "mammy" who "waddled" into a refugee center demanding to be "assassinated" against typhoid, or the "old negro" who smuggled a bottle of foul-smelling medicine into the fairgrounds. "That potion is a sho' cure for any ailments," he said. "I mixed it myself." Sometimes they had funny names, such as Refugee Jones or Queen Esther.[30]

The relatively liberal *Press-Scimitar* recorded an exchange between a Red Cross nurse and an African American woman sheltered in a barn on the north side of town. Another relief worker had taken the woman's baby to a hospital. "What is your child's name," the nurse asked, "and where is it now?"

"I declare, I don't know whar dey take de baby," the mother replied.

"Well, what's the baby's name?" asked the nurse.

The mother called over a girl, presumably her daughter. "Leona, what de baby's name?" she asked. Leona didn't know.

"You have to 'scuse me, white folks," she concluded. "I done plumb forgit de baby's name. But I don't never call her by her name nohow. I jest call her de baby."[31]

As exemplified by this anecdote, newspapers often depicted African Americans as countrified stereotypes straight from the most popular novel of the day, *Gone with the Wind*. For white readers, these caricatures negated evidence of black progress in the city and provided reassurance that the days of benevolent paternalism had not ended. The *Press-Scimitar* dubbed 102-year-old Tom Ingram, a refugee from near Dell, Arkansas, the "Uncle Tom of the Flood." The former slave had stayed put as long as he could, watching the waters rise around him until a wagon arrived to take "me and a load of other niggers 'way from Mr. Simmons' place." With no family to support him, he was relying on the Red Cross to be his "new white folks."[32]

As the flood subsided, *Commercial Appeal* columnist Joe Curtis contributed a human-interest story about a group of "negro" refugees riding a steamer back to Bruin's Landing, Arkansas (the half-column article included six reminders that the group was black). A crowd gathered around an "aged negro" singing "Rivah, Stay 'Way from Mah Do'." A "long eared, lean hound" howled plaintively until its owner soothed it. The dog quieted, Curtis said, but kept a close eye on the man "to make sure he was not being sent 'down the river'—like so many negroes were sent down the river many years ago." Elsewhere on the boat, a passenger sighed, "ah sho' is glad to git goin' back home. Ah knows dat ol' groun' jes' waitin' to be tu'ned ovah and planted in cotton." Throw in a broad verandah, a white linen suit, and a cold julep, and the scene could have taken place in 1837 rather than 1937.[33]

"Memphis is safe due to Black men," the *Defender*'s Burley announced in late February. The levees held, the river retreated, and the city issued a collective sigh of relief. Mayor Overton dismissed his emergency flood committee. The Municipal Auditorium's refugee intake center closed after processing some 50,000 people. Traffic on the Harahan Bridge resumed its westerly flow as thousands of Arkansans shuffled back to their threadbare agricultural existence. Patting itself on the back, the *Press-Scimitar* ran a feature on the "Heroes of the Flood," all fifteen of whom were white.[34]

The NAACP, Red Cross, and African American press congratulated themselves for preventing all but the most minor forms of discrimination. "It is stranger than fiction," a *Pittsburgh Courier* editorial remarked. "Perhaps a major catastrophe of this kind banishes jim crowism and lets in the Christian spirit."[35]

Despite the ugly Beale Street roundup, a sense of optimism pervaded African Americans in the area. Thomas Jordan, a ninety-two-year-old blacksmith from Joiner, Arkansas, captured this spirit when a reporter interviewed him at Church Park Auditorium. Born a slave, Jordan had fought in the Union army and survived the floods of 1913 and 1927. This most recent deluge washed away all his possessions, leaving him alone, a refugee in a strange city. Yet he felt good about the future. "I think Negroes will have better times in the South after the flood has gone away," he said. "The white people will learn to be more understanding. This is God's plan."[36]

Jordan's buoyant assessment proved misguided. Memphis soon reestablished the racial *status quo antediluvium*. One well-publicized example of this reversion to form hit the streets when the city staged its annual Cotton Carnival in early May. "In view of the flood disaster and the adverse publicity which Memphis had received over the radio and through the press of the country, [we] should extend full cooperation to officials of the Cotton Carnival Association in the promotion of the 1937 Carnival," the local Chamber of Commerce decreed. Features in *Life* magazine and elsewhere suggested that large sections of Memphis had been swamped. The annual carnival would draw thousands of visitors and a horde of media types with the power to show the world that Memphis was safe, progressive, and open for business.[37]

City leaders considered the event a massive success. Parties, parades, and balls erased lingering memories of the fight with the Mississippi. Lost amidst all the backslapping was the fact that the Cotton Carnival also symbolized the reimposition of a racial hierarchy. African Americans were, for the most part, excluded from the carnival. Instead, they put on a segregated Cotton Makers Jubilee on Beale Street—a black party in a black neighborhood. Local newspapers ran page after page about the carnival while limiting coverage of the jubilee to a few casual mentions of "colored merrymakers."[38]

African Americans were allowed to take small roles in the Cotton Carnival, so long as their participation reinforced the same down-home stereotypes that had pervaded flood coverage. One evening, the crowd enjoyed a chorus of 500 black singers "lifting their voices in spirituals," not unlike the pathetic band that had steamed to Bruin's Landing with dogs howling and dreams of planting cotton.[39]

More dramatic, 200,000 spectators lined the streets on the carnival's final evening for a parade organized around the theme of "King Cotton's Song Book." Organizers promised the floats would present a comprehensive history of music, arranged from the most archaic to the most sophisticated styles. Floats representing high opera and waltzes waited in the rear, while inferior genres passed before the masses. First came a special guest act, a band from Kosciusko, Mississippi, that played "a medley of jungle airs." Next in line was what the *Commercial Appeal* called "a garish float showing a jungle savage beating on his primitive tom-tom."[40]

The hoopla surrounding Memphis's 1937 Cotton Carnival sent a clear message of racial inferiority. Whatever power African Americans had gained during the flood had evaporated. Whites still wrote the city's official racial narrative, and their story concerned a segregated, happy-go-lucky, and profoundly antimodern African American minority who had no business interfering with their social, economic, and cultural betters.

George Washington Lee and other members of the black middle class who had leveraged the crisis into a moment of political opportunity could not translate their victory on the levees into lasting gains. "White people were breathing easier," the *Defender*'s Burley reported, and black Memphians worried that the rebalanced racial power structure would not last. Indeed, a new wave of race-based repression began within months of the river's crest. Incidents of police brutality and harassment against African Americans ticked upward. Police Commissioner Boyle, who had caved in to black demands for better treatment during the flood, put J. B. Martin under surveillance and stood aside when his officers hassled customers at Martin's drugstore.[41]

Smashing victories for Crump-backed candidates in the 1938 elections closed off any possibility for a revival of black fortunes. As long as he needed black votes, Crump had been willing to discuss improving conditions in black neighborhoods and would even distribute a few offices among African Americans. In 1938, however, his machine racked up such large majorities that he deemed African Americans expendable. His coalition no longer required their loyalty. After years of tamping down overt racism, Crump lifted the lid. The machine hounded black Republicans such as Bob Church Jr. into political irrelevance and forced J. B. Martin to relocate to Chicago.[42]

The flood, then, marked a last hurrah for one generation of civil rights leaders, even as it helped inspire others who would carry the torch of racial equality into the 1940s and 1950s. Real change would have to wait for the turbulent 1960s.

"A calamity of the magnitude of the 1937 flood makes all of the victims akin and knits the people into a unity of spirit and purpose, bringing the traditional American trait of neighborliness to the fore," Congressman Walter Chandler told the House of Representatives in June 1937. His words bore some truth. Memphis had fed, clothed, and housed thousands of desperate strangers suffering hard times. But Chandler misrepresented the extent of the Bluff City's neighborliness. Rather than create true unity, the flood revealed the limits of racial toleration in the Depression era. African Americans deserved succor so long as they accepted segregation and cultural inferiority. Economic inequality was so unremarkable that it barely deserved mention, much less recrimination. Power was given grudgingly, and only so long as it served the white majority's interests—in this case, protecting valuable property.[43]

"There will be no discrimination among flood sufferers," the *Pittsburgh Courier* insisted. While true in some ways—and though the even-handedness of the flood relief was certainly noteworthy—the paper's cheerful assessment reflected its blind spots and an unwillingness to connect what was happening in the Ohio-Mississippi River Valley with broader, structural forms of discrimination that influenced every aspect of the human side of the natural disaster.[44]

Notes

1. *Memphis Commercial Appeal,* March 14, 1937.

2. *Pittsburgh Courier,* February 6, 1937; Roy Wilkins to Cary Grayson, March 17, 1937, Papers of the American Red Cross, Record Group (RG) 200, box 1251, folder Cooperation with Other Organizations, National Archives and Records Administration (NARA).

3. Roy Wilkins to Harry Hopkins, January 25, 1937, RG 69, WPA Central Files: General, box 292, NARA.

4. American Red Cross, *The Ohio-Mississippi Valley Flood Disaster of 1937* (Washington, DC: American Red Cross, 1937), 17; *Memphis Commercial Appeal,* January 26, 1937.

5. January 1937 ended up being the second wettest month on record in Memphis, with 17.28 inches of precipitation, second only to the 18.16 inches that fell in June 1877.

6. *Literary Digest,* February 6, 1937, 5; "America's Worst Flood Makes Nearly a Million Refugees," *Life,* February 8, 1937, 22; *Memphis Commercial Appeal,* January 20, 1937.

7. *Memphis Commercial Appeal,* January 23, 1937.

8. K. N. Pollard, "Flood Conditions of 1937," Kenneth McKellar Collection, General Correspondence, box 366, Memphis Public Library.

9. Watkins Overton to Henry Bell, January 28, 1937, Watkins Overton Papers, box 4, folder 35, University of Memphis Special Collections; Carl Bailey to Watkins Overton, January 29, 1937, ibid.

10. Roger Biles, *Memphis in the Great Depression* (Knoxville: University of Tennessee Press, 1986), 88–92; Laurie B. Green, *Battling the Plantation Mentality: Memphis and the Black Freedom Struggle* (Chapel Hill: University of North

Carolina Press, 2007), 20. According to the census, there were 96,550 African Americans in Memphis in 1930, or 38.2 percent of the total population; in 1940 there were 121,536, or 41.4 percent of the total population.

11. *Chicago Defender,* February 20, 1937.

12. Biles, *Memphis in the Great Depression,* 40–44; G. Wayne Dowdy, *Mayor Crump Don't Like It: Machine Politics in Memphis* (Jackson: University Press of Mississippi, 2006), 86–88.

13. Overton quoted in Biles, *Memphis in the Great Depression,* 27.

14. "Report of the Secretary," February 4, 1937, NAACP Papers (microfilm), part 1, reel 6.

15. *Memphis Commercial Appeal,* January 25, February 2, 1937.

16. *Memphis Press-Scimitar,* January 28, 1937; American Red Cross, *Ohio-Mississippi Valley Flood Disaster of 1937,* 105.

17. *Memphis Press-Scimitar,* February 10, 1937; *Chicago Defender,* February 20, 1937.

18. *Memphis Press-Scimitar,* February 11, 1937; E. B. Maynard, "Report on Sanitary and Health Conditions," February 15, 1937, Overton Papers, box 6, folder Flood Disaster (Army).

19. "Speech of Walter Chandler," June 15, 1937, *Congressional Record,* 75th Cong. 1st sess. 3. At Crump's urging, many of the convicts who worked on the levee had their sentences commuted; see *Pittsburgh Courier,* February 20, 1937.

20. *Memphis Press-Scimitar,* February 3, 1937; *Chicago Defender,* February 20, 1937.

21. This segregated division of labor prevailed throughout Memphis's flood emergency; all the maids and kitchen helpers depicted in photographs of the refugee camps, medical centers, and Red Cross checkpoints are black women.

22. Pollard, "Flood Conditions of 1937"; *Memphis Press-Scimitar,* February 8, 10, 1937.

23. Walter White to Watkins Overton, March 5, 1937, Overton Papers, box 4, folder 35.

24. *Chicago Defender,* February 20, 1937.

25. Ibid.; Bobby L. Lovett, *The Civil Rights Movement in Tennessee: A Narrative History* (Knoxville: University of Tennessee Press, 2005), 117, 240; Biles, *Memphis in the Great Depression,* 105; Green, *Battling the Plantation Mentality,* 211, 232; Elizabeth Gritter, *River of Hope: Black Politics and the Memphis Freedom Movement, 1865–1954* (Lexington: University Press of Kentucky, 2014), 190, 290.

26. L. B. Smelser to D. F. Steinbaugh, February 2, 1937, RG 69, WPA Central Files: General, box 293, NARA.

27. *Chicago Defender,* February 20, 1937.

28. *Memphis Commercial Appeal,* January 26, 1937.

29. One unfortunate reality for anyone researching the flood in Memphis is

that no issues of the *World*, the city's African American newspaper, survive from this era.

30. *Memphis Commercial Appeal*, January 29, February 1, 1937; *Memphis Press-Scimitar*, January 28, 1937.

31. *Memphis Press-Scimitar*, February 3, 1937.

32. *Memphis Press-Scimitar*, February 9, 1937.

33. *Memphis Commercial Appeal*, March 4, 1937.

34. *Chicago Defender*, February 20, 1937; *Memphis Press-Scimitar*, February 18, 1937.

35. *Pittsburgh Courier*, February 13, 1937.

36. *Chicago Defender*, February 20, 1937.

37. Minutes, Memphis Chamber of Commerce, February 19, 1937, Overton Papers, box 3, folder Chamber of Commerce.

38. *Memphis Commercial Appeal*, May 9, 1937.

39. *Memphis Commercial Appeal*, May 12, 1937.

40. *Memphis Commercial Appeal*, May 16, 1937.

41. *Chicago Defender*, February 20, 1937; Green, *Battling the Plantation Mentality*, 32, 38–39; Dowdy, *Mayor Crump Don't Like It*, 97.

42. Biles, *Memphis in the Great Depression*, 96–97.

43. "Speech of Walter Chandler," 4.

44. *Pittsburgh Courier*, January 30, 1937.

Taylor-Made

Envisioning Black Memphis at Midcentury

Beverly Greene Bond

> If you can only see what's there—you're not going to see very much
> because in every situation, there's much, much more than what you
> see on the surface.
>
> —Reverend James L. Netters

In 1942 the White Rose Laundry erected a mechanical sign on Linden Avenue in downtown Memphis. The sign depicted an overweight washerwoman bending over a washtub happily scrubbing clothes. It was the classic depiction of the "Mammy," but this caricatured washerwoman's underwear was clearly visible as she bent over her washtub. The Memphis Negro Chamber of Commerce complained that the sign was "a complete effrontery for Negro people," "a subtle although effective ridicule of the race," and an "effort to embarrass Negro citizens of Memphis." The group asserted that "most colored people have to work hard for a living, but we do not believe the many servile tasks that they have to perform should be held up in ridicule and be made a public laughing stock on the highways and streets." When the Negro Chamber of Commerce asked that the sign be removed, the owners of the White Rose Laundry claimed, "We are entirely at [a] loss to understand the cause of any resentment by anybody as certainly no discredit to the negro race was intended. The figure represents the kindly old negro mammy who is loved by people of both races such as the one figured by Aunt Jemima. We are inclined to the belief that the disturbance is being incited by the very small percentage of our negro population who are radical and looking for trouble anyway."[1]

Some white Memphians considered "Mammy" and similar caricatures of "Hambone" or "Uncle Mose" as accurate depictions of African Americans. The *Commercial Appeal*'s "Back to the South Department" used these caricatures in 1923 in response to the migration of thousands of black workers from the Mississippi Delta. "'Sitting on the World'—and Don't Know It!" depicted "Mammy" serving a watermelon to her husband (or son) as he sat at a table atop a "world" of cotton bales.[2] In the 1930s festivities related to the Memphis Cotton Carnival included black men pulling parade floats, just as horses might pull wagons, and black women costumed as mammies sitting with white children, participating in scenes depicting wash day at the plantation, or sitting atop bales of cotton along the carnival's parade route.[3] Black and white Memphians interacted with each other in public and private spaces in the city, but these interactions were shaped by decades of racial assumptions and enforced segregation. By 1920, African Americans accounted for about 40 percent of the city's population, but it was still possible for white Memphians to encounter black Memphians on the streets or in stores, to interact with them in households and workplaces, but not really *see* them as actual human beings. And some white Memphians even believed that black Memphians saw themselves as these caricatures.

The Reverend L. O. Taylor, a black Baptist minister, documented a more authentic version of black life in Memphis. He was a self-taught photographer, moviemaker, and audio recorder; a poet, essayist, musician, and songwriter; and an electrician and candy maker. The Baptist church was the figurative lens through which Taylor interpreted and constructed "community"; in fact, L. O. Taylor was, to some, the essence of his Memphis community. But Taylor also provided the literal lenses through which his community could see themselves or be seen by others. For more than thirty years, Taylor organized or pastored at least four churches in Memphis, trained scores of young ministers in the art of preaching, and taught young men and women to be photographers. He was an empathetic man whose sense of humanity motivated him to reach out to people whose lifestyles might have driven others away. Although he was one of the most prominent ministers in mid-twentieth-century Memphis, many of Taylor's friends remembered that he was "not among the social circle preachers." Instead, Taylor preferred the "fellows out in the street" and spent time with them, hoping they would "go staggering off to church with him."[4] In doing so, Taylor may have won some converts, but his ways of dealing with problems would eventually destroy him.

Like most African American ministers in Memphis in the first half of the twentieth century, L. O. Taylor did not challenge racial norms. The leadership of these ministers centered less on battling systems of oppression than on ministering, educating, and representing those who suffered under these systems. Taylor also encouraged African Americans in his congregations to see themselves as more than "Hambone" or "Mammy." Whether in sermons or photographs, Taylor envisioned African Americans as proud, whole persons. But in his own life, that wholeness was the product of years of struggle and self-reflection.

L. O. Taylor's story, like that of so many other black Memphians, began in the rural Mississippi Delta. His paternal and maternal roots lay in the rural hinterlands of Tennessee, Arkansas, and Mississippi. His father's family came from the rural West Tennessee county of Haywood (about sixty miles east of Memphis); his mother, Nona Brinkley, was a native Mississippian, but her parents, Charley and Malinda Brinkley, were born in Tennessee and Alabama in the decade before the Civil War. As it did for other black southerners, the end of slavery probably provided the catalyst for the Brinkleys' move from one community to another until they finally settled in Mississippi. Records do not indicate when Charley and Malinda met and married, but by 1880, the family was farming land in Tunica County, Mississippi, and all their children may have been born in that state.[5] Four years later, the Brinkleys' nineteen-year-old daughter Nona married Willie Taylor and moved about 100 miles north and west of Tunica County to settle in the small town of Golden Lake in Mississippi County, Arkansas.[6] The Taylors moved from Golden Lake to Monroe to Osceola but remained in Mississippi County, aptly named for its location on the region's main water artery. Like most black workers in Mississippi County, Will and Nona Taylor and their older children worked as sharecroppers, tenant farmers, or day laborers. But the big city—in this case, Memphis—drew the Taylors and thousands of other rural blacks like moths to a flame.

Alonzo Odie Taylor, nicknamed Lonzie, was the third of Willie and Nona's five children and may have been the first to make his way to Memphis.[7] Although few details remain about the Taylors' Arkansas years, the family was apparently nurtured by a strong community base with important ties to the local Baptist church. In fact, the pastor of their church in Monroe, Arkansas, the Reverend Robert Guy, mentored young Lonzie in the early years of his ministry.[8] Guy ordained and licensed Taylor and would become instrumental in Taylor's appointment to his first pastoral position.

The Taylors migrated from rural Arkansas and across the Mississippi to Memphis sometime in the early 1900s. For Lonzie Taylor, this move was motivated in part by his ministerial vocation and the influence of Reverend Guy. Taylor had started preaching at a very young age and was ordained as a teenager. By 1917, he was an itinerant preacher traveling around northern Mississippi. For Nona and Willie Taylor, the move was motivated by economic pressures as well as family issues. Although the exact dates are unclear, it seems that Nona and Willie arrived in Memphis sometime before 1920. But like many migrant women, Nona was drawn back to her household in Scott, Arkansas, by the presence of her young daughter, Grace, whom she may have left in the care of her sons Clarence, Charley, and Jesse. By 1920, Jesse Taylor was married and living near the house occupied by his brothers and sister.[9]

Lonzie Taylor's early life outside of his parents' household was a period of spiritual growth and development as a Baptist minister, but also a period of emotional and personal instability as he tried to adjust to urban life. Lonzie had been "called" to preach as a very young man, most likely while he and his family were still living in Arkansas. The call to preach is an inner feeling or emotion that, according to Andre Johnson, "comes from . . . God or some outer force that pulls, that pushes, that prods a person to accept the role of being first a preacher and then, eventually if that call goes even further, called to pastor." Johnson, a contemporary minister and scholar, has described the process that Taylor probably followed as accepting the call, delivering a trial sermon, and being licensed to preach but not yet formally ordained. As "Minister Taylor," he preached, but he had not yet become "Reverend Taylor."[10]

Taylor later told friends that he first heard the call as a young boy, but those around him would not give him a chance to preach. When he finally had an opportunity to deliver a trial sermon, he was not fully prepared.

He had decided to preach a sermon on "eagles that stir the nest." The church was filled, but Taylor remembered that he had not prayed that evening, and he could not deliver the sermon.[11] He managed to survive this first trial and later developed an effective strategy for delivering his sermons—always praying but never eating beforehand. With the trial sermon behind him, and having honed a more effective preaching strategy, Taylor was "licensed" (by Reverend Guy)—but not yet ordained—and began preaching as an itinerant minister in small communities in northern Mississippi.[12]

In this early period of his ministry, Lonzie Taylor preached at revivals or filled in for vacationing pastors. On one of these occasions, at a small church in rural Coldwater, Mississippi, he met Alice Fisher, who lived with her parents and siblings in Coldwater. Lewis and Sallie Fisher refused to allow their daughter to marry the young itinerant preacher. However, the relationship produced a son, Homer, who was born in June 1918. Taylor may have visited Alice and Homer over the next ten years, but within three months of Homer's birth, the young minister had moved on and either returned to Arkansas or settled in Memphis. Homer was nine years old when his mother died, and he continued to live with her family in the close-knit Fisher household. Although Lonzie Taylor maintained contact with his son, many of his acquaintances were unaware of the boy's existence until the late 1950s, when Homer moved with his wife and children from Coldwater to Memphis.[13]

When Lonzie Taylor arrived in Memphis sometime in 1918 or shortly thereafter, he found a New South city with strong social and economic ties to neighboring rural communities. By the second decade of the twentieth century, African Americans accounted for 37.7 percent of the city's population. Between 1910 and 1920, the number of black homeowners in the city increased by 70 percent.[14] Overall, in the first four decades of the twentieth century, the city's black population more than doubled, but their percentage of the total population dropped from a high of 48.8 percent in 1900 to 41.5 percent by 1940, as an increasing number of whites migrated to the city from surrounding rural areas.[15] The in-migration of both blacks and whites created a continuing atmosphere of rural provincialism in one of the South's largest cities. As historian Gerald Capers observed, "Memphis presented a strange paradox—a city modern in physical aspect but rural in background, rural in prejudice, and rural in habit."[16]

Black migrants like Lonzie Taylor were attracted to Memphis by the abundance of employment, educational, and housing opportunities.[17] The black Memphis that was emerging in the early twentieth century was far from monolithic, and black migrants constituted one of three economic and ideological "communities." By the second decade of the twentieth century, each of these communities responded to racial tension and oppression in a particular manner. Using terms that reflected the classic debate between W. E. B. DuBois and Booker T. Washington, Kenneth Goings and Gerald Smith divided black Memphians into "talented tenth," "accommodationist," and migrant communities. The talented tenth—the educated, economically invested black elite—were in the best position to use the city's political and judicial system to confront white racism. Accommodationists stressed behavior that promoted racial harmony rather that openly challenging segregation and discrimination. Migrants, who had been drawn to the city by expectations of social, political, and economic opportunity, were more militant in their confrontations with racism. Migrants "refused to follow the racial etiquette accepted by older African Americans and others who had become acculturated to urban life."[18]

In his introduction to *The Bright Side of Memphis,* a 1908 directory of African Americans in turn-of-the-century Memphis, Green Polonius Hamilton, an accommodationist and educator in the city's African American schools, described the rich social and cultural institutions in Memphis, as well as the diversity of economic opportunities available to African American residents or those who might consider moving there. Hamilton identified professional and working-class African Americans who were succeeding in the city. His message easily aligned with the boosterism of turn-of-the-century white Memphians. Acknowledging the racial realities of the period, Hamilton, perhaps unconsciously, described the existence of two cities.

Memphis, like many other New South cities, promoted the economic opportunities available to its residents, and Hamilton stressed that black Memphians had access to these opportunities. For white Memphians, the city was "reasonably healthy" and "one of the model cities of the world in point of sanitation," with a pristine water supply, a modern sewage system, and a facility for burning trash and garbage. But in many African American neighborhoods, disease was rampant and mortality rates were high.[19] Although the cost of living was high, the wages for skilled and unskilled workers (including African Americans) were higher than in any other southern city.[20] The city's "complete system of free schools" had to be balanced with the reality that only 30 percent of school-age African American children actually attended the eight elementary schools and one high school in the city's segregated school system. The rosy picture of urban life was also clouded by a serious problem with crime, which Hamilton attributed to "young people of the colored race." Since African Americans were not "instinctively criminal," these criminal tendencies (according to Hamilton) were most likely the result of "a violent and ungovernable temper, which often manifests itself on the slightest provocation," and these fits of temper resulted from the "tropical" climate, poor diet (especially the consumption of too much pork), and the city's reputation as a "wide-open" town.[21]

Like many new arrivals, Lonzie Taylor found it difficult to accommodate to blatant discrimination or to consider the "character-building" goals of the talented tenth as solutions to racial confrontations. Taylor had probably come to the city seeking economic opportunities that were unavailable in small-town Arkansas. According to Goings and Smith, migrants were poorly educated, had little contact with the white community, and experienced daily harassment by the local police. Police officers had "orders to stop all suspicious-looking negroes and search them."[22]

Taylor settled in Memphis sometime after his involvement with Alice Fisher and the birth of their son. Did he come to Memphis seeking the kind of economic opportunity that might convince Alice's father to allow the couple to marry, or did he come to the city to remove himself from the proximity of her angry family? Or had he simply followed his mentor, Robert Guy, to the community where Guy had settled in 1916? In any event, Lonzie's first residence was most likely with his father, Willie. When Lonzie Taylor registered for the draft on September 12, 1918, he listed his occupation as "prisoner workhouse" and his place of employment as "workhouse." He listed Willie Taylor as his relative and his address as 190 Auction Avenue. Although the county workhouse was a detention facility for "criminals convicted in the local courts," there is no information about Taylor's first act of "misbehavior" in the city or what his offense might have been. It may have been a violation of vagrancy laws or some other petty crime, or perhaps he was just a "suspicious-looking Negro" who happened to be in the wrong place at the wrong time. As a prisoner at the Shelby County Penal Farm, Taylor might have been assigned to a private contractor who paid the county 10 cents a day for convict labor to work on roads or railroads, or he could have been assigned to work in the penal farm's laundry or kitchen or on the farm itself.[23]

Lonzie Taylor's second arrest occurred about two years later. The October 15, 1920, edition of a local newspaper reported the arrest of "Lonzi Taylor," a "negro driver" who resided at 180 Auction Avenue. Two police detectives claimed they had watched Taylor, through a hole they had drilled in the floor, take a bill of lading from the office of the Russel-Heckle Feed Company. Taylor admitted stealing money he had collected when delivering feed and then sneaking into the office to destroy the bookkeepers' records of the transactions so there would be no "paper trail."[24] Taylor had allegedly taken $300 over a three-month period. Beyond this brief description of the crime and his arrest, there is no other information on this incident.

After this arrest, Taylor continued to work at several low-wage jobs but became more involved in his ministry. The most important influences in his life from this point on seemed to be his mentor, Robert Guy, and his mother, Nona. Guy had moved to Memphis from Arkansas sometime in 1916 to become the pastor of Pilgrim Rest Baptist Church on North Second and Looney Avenues, a few streets north of the Taylors' Auction Avenue residence. Guy stayed at Pilgrim Rest Baptist for about four years. Nona and Willie Taylor worked as live-in servants at a boardinghouse (at 29 North Bellevue) operated by a widow, Mrs. Nora Richardson. Nona was the cook and Willie was a porter. But as mentioned earlier, records suggest that Nona returned to Arkansas on a regular basis to oversee the care of eleven-year-old Grace, who remained at the family's home in Scott with her brothers. Nona (and perhaps Willie) stayed with Richardson at least until 1924, when Nona moved to a house near Pilgrim Rest and became the church's caretaker. Records are not clear, but it seems that Willie continued to live in the small house on Auction Avenue. Nona's movement back and forth across the Mississippi reflected the strength of family ties as well as the transient nature of migrant life. Nona obviously needed the money she earned working in Richardson's boardinghouse, but she also needed to care for her daughter. Information from the 1920 US census and the 1920 Memphis city directory suggests that she was present in both Memphis and Arkansas sometime during that year.[25]

Lonzie Taylor became more settled in his role as a Baptist minister after 1920. He was the superintendent of Sunday school at Pilgrim Rest while also working at Anderson Tully Box Company. In 1922 a disagreement between Reverend Guy and the Pilgrim Rest congregation led to Guy's resignation and Taylor's first pastoral position. Guy (or the ministerial board) had already ordained Taylor, and he was preaching on an interim or guest basis at Pilgrim Rest and other churches. After Guy stepped down, Taylor accepted the congregation's invitation to take over as pastor. Taylor was settling into his adopted community, and church members were evidently willing to overlook his earlier run-ins with the law, perhaps because these kinds of situations plagued many young black men, especially recent migrants to the city. It is unclear whether the congregation knew about Alice Fisher or Homer. Taylor had joined a mutual aid society (the Supreme Royal Circle of Friends of the World), was running the church's Sunday school, had a job and supported other family members, and was an impressive preacher.[26] However, the congregation decided that Taylor had to make one more move toward "respectability": he had to marry. L. O. Taylor was a "handsome little man" and a sharp dresser who attracted a following of interested young women. He had a reputation as a "fast talker" and "was dating several young women . . . most of them belonged to families that were pretty prominent in that section of Memphis." Longtime friend Lula Adams, who had known Taylor since his early days in Memphis, recalled that church leaders decided they "couldn't have an unmarried man as pastor of the church."[27]

Taylor eventually settled on Marie Porter, and the two married on August 6, 1923. They lived together until January 1927, when, as Taylor stated in his petition for divorce two years later, Marie "willfully or maliciously deserted [him] without a reasonable cause." She moved out of their home without giving notice and never returned. Taylor claimed that in spite of his attempts to make her happy, she "would not live with him."

L. O. and Blanche Taylor. (Courtesy Center for Southern Folklore)

He was granted a divorce in June 1929 and met his second wife, Blanche B. Johnson, at around the same time. The two met on a double date at the Memphis Zoo, married about three months later, and moved into a house on Eldridge Avenue in Memphis. But Blanche Taylor continued to teach in Terrell, Arkansas, for another three years.[28]

Taylor's influence as a Baptist minister grew from the mid-1920s onward. He left Pilgrim Rest Baptist Church to become the seventh pastor of First Baptist Church Broad Avenue (also known as Binghampton First Baptist Church), where he served in some capacity from 1925 to 1940. One writer commented that during these years, Taylor "did more for elevating the prosperity of this church than any other minister to date." This became the pattern at every church he pastored: the membership increased, the physical site expanded, the structure was remodeled, and debts were paid off.[29] Taylor apparently served as pastor of Olivette (or Olivet) Baptist Church during some of his tenure at First Baptist. Olivette was organized in 1924 by forty-seven former members of the historic First Baptist Beale Street Church and moved from a location on Hernando to 270 East Calhoun. Taylor was the congregation's second pastor, serving from 1931 to 1935. He returned to Olivette in 1937, after the sudden death of the church's third pastor, the Reverend F. W. Williams. Taylor was still listed in city directories as pastor at First Baptist Broad in 1938 and 1939, although he was officially at Olivette Baptist, where he remained until 1958.[30]

Whether at First Baptist or Olivette Baptist, L. O. Taylor was hailed for his preaching style, his ability to seek out and minister to people from all walks of life (especially those that other churchgoers considered socially unacceptable), and his administrative skills. Like many black ministers of his day, Taylor was determined to build his churches, and during his forty-plus years of pastoring, he led at least four different Baptist churches in Memphis: Pilgrim Rest Baptist, First Baptist, Olivette Baptist, and Great Hyde Park.[31] The first three were established churches when Taylor became pastor, but Greater Hyde Park began with a small core of members who left Olivette after Taylor resigned (or was removed) as pastor. During his time at Olivette Baptist, Taylor built the church into the largest African American congregation and one of the most influential churches in the city, "based on simple preaching" and simple budgeting.[32] Each member was asked to contribute just 50 cents every Sunday. Olivette had a very large membership, and members simply marked a card to indicate the amount they were contributing. The highest amount listed on the card was $1, but members gave according to their ability—some as little as 25 cents. James L. Netters, a member of Olivette since his youth, noted that "the offerings would be large enough to take care of all of the expenses—salaries, remodel the church, buy pews, and whatever else we needed. The church was debt-free . . . and had $14,000 in the bank when he [Taylor] was terminated."[33]

According to one friend, people traveled "from far and near to hear him preach." Other ministers came to listen to Taylor and learn how to preach; they used his sermons as models that they adapted to their own congregations. Pullman porters, dockworkers, and visitors to Memphis visited Taylor's churches and took his sermons back to the churches in

their hometowns. By the 1930s, Taylor's preaching style and his messages were "migrating," just as the preacher himself had done in the early
1900s.[34] This was a migration of sermons and ideas, of lived and emotional experiences that could be recalled and shared by people with a
common spiritual core.

Alice Taylor Henderson described "minister-students" who visited
her grandfather on Mondays, Tuesdays, and Wednesdays to talk about
what they wanted to preach. For the Reverend P. L. Johnson, these meetings seemed "like a school." Other ministers met with Taylor on Satur-
days, and Taylor tutored special students, including Netters, privately.
The ministers who came to Taylor's classes were usually men who could
not get into seminaries or did not have academic credentials. Some were
from rural churches that met only one or two Sundays a month. When
Taylor met with his students, he asked them what topics or scriptures
they wanted to preach on, and they would then write down or commit
to memory his comments on these topics. Taylor helped the young ministers identify at least three points to focus on and gave them formal or
informal outlines they could use to mold their own sermons. Students
sometimes recorded Taylor's sermons as he preached so that they would
know "how to say what they wanted to say" (or, in some cases, when to
"shout"), or they purchased written sermons. As Henderson recalled,
"Granddaddy never really wrote a sermon for himself; [but] he would
help other people to write sermons."[35] Taylor's goal for his minister-
students and for himself was to deliver sermons that attracted people to
church and made them want to stay. As Reverend Netters pointed out
in his interview:

> The material [Taylor] would share with you had mostly to do
> with sermon building, sermon materials. And, if a minister is able
> to develop a sermon, he can pretty well handle himself other-
> wise. . . . If you can't make the sermon attractive enough to draw
> people, then you're not likely to . . . succeed in much else. . . .
> And, if the minister has any leadership ability at all—if he gets
> enough people around him—he can move up and move out with
> those people because those minds begin to train themselves into
> a direction. The minister will have little to do since the congre-

gation will "lead." But the sermon has to be attractive enough to get people in and hold them.[36]

Taylor instructed his students on how to sit in the pulpit, how to focus on the audience, how to relax before beginning a sermon, and, if their audiences seemed to be drifting away, how to turn things around and regain their interest. Taylor also cautioned his students to recognize when "you've lost your audience, [then] hurry up and sit down. Don't bore them because you can drive people away instead of drawing them to you. . . . [And you need to] know how to end and take your seat, and come back the next time."[37]

To L. O. Taylor, "church" was not just the focus of religious activity; it was the physical and emotional center of community life. For Memphis's growing African American migrant population (of whom Taylor was one example), the church was the major social center where "country folk" brought their old-time religion into an urban setting.[38] In each of the churches Taylor pastored, he worked to create a sense of community. With the exception of his final church, Greater Hyde Park (located at the corner of Mississippi and Alston in South Memphis), Taylor's churches were in the North Memphis–Hollywood–Binghampton area, and even Greater Hyde Park took its name from the North Memphis neighborhood of Hyde Park.[39]

Longtime friend Alberta Fields commented in an interview after Taylor's death that he "loved his churches and he loved his members, and he was very free-hearted." This seemed to be a universal memory among friends, fellow ministers, and acquaintances. He had a gift for interpreting the scriptures in ways that his listeners could understand and apply to their daily lives. Associates who were interviewed after Taylor's death in the 1970s remembered him as a witty, sincere, down-to-earth speaker whose sermons could be understood on many different levels. In one of his most memorable sermons, preached at a funeral, Taylor used a wood pencil with an eraser to reflect on the deceased's history. On another occasion, he used a bundle of sticks tied together to preach a sermon on love, family life, and sticking together.[40]

Bishop P. L. Johnson considered Taylor "one of the most well-known preachers in the city of Memphis" but noted that Taylor was not one of the "social circle preachers. He wasn't interested in socializing. . . . [He felt he had to] get in there where lots of sinners are—you know worldly people . . . [and] bring them to the Lord." Taylor took his ministry into the streets, where he tried to convince alcoholics and prostitutes to visit his church. He would walk, talk, and visit with them, and "they'd go staggering off to church with him . . . straighten themselves out, [and] become his members."[41] Taylor was a minister of the people who seemed more interested in the man on the street than Memphis's black professionals or elites.[42]

Taylor's delivery was just as important as the content of his sermons in terms of reaching his audience. He was a very physical, animated preacher. He paced back and forth—"walking from one side of the pulpit to the other as he talked. . . . And you'd just follow him as he'd go, like you [were] watching a tennis match, and the session became more interesting every time he hit a ball."[43] When "the spirit got really strong in him," Taylor would take off his glasses, put them in his pocket, and start preaching. The congregation could "see the spirit all around him." Gloria Harris Tuggle, whose father was an active layman in the Riverside Association, recalled Taylor preaching at her church, Macedonia–Hyde Park Baptist Church. She described him as a short, feisty, very colorful figure who—like many Baptist ministers in the mid-twentieth century—preached sermons peppered with admonitions about "fire and brimstone, hell and damnation," and the consequences of not living a moral life.[44]

Taylor also nurtured close relationships with the young people in his congregations and his community. As a teenager, Netters looked up to Taylor "as a father" and "became one of the hundreds and thousands around him who loved him." Taylor preached at Netters's graduation from Booker T. Washington High School, officiated at Netters's wedding, was a ministerial role model, and eventually licensed Netters as a Baptist minister.[45]

L. O. Taylor's interest in photography may have started in childhood, but he began photographing his friends, family, and community in the 1930s or 1940s—partly as a hobby, but also as a way to augment his pastoral salary. This helped him maintain a sense of economic and perhaps intellectual independence. Netters recalled that, for Taylor, photography "was a hobby that he had developed into something that would help him to be more independent . . . and he was a very independent person."[46] Taylor may have taught himself the fundamentals of photography, or he may have picked up some of his knowledge from associates at Nolen Picture and Company, where he had most of his early photographs developed and printed.[47] Taylor's photographs and later his films and audio recordings chronicle the external lives and activities of his neighbors, his congregations, and his community. His explorations of African American life and culture in Memphis are not reports on the brutality of oppression or evidence of civil and social inequality. Instead, they are studies in the vitality of community life and personal identity in the segregated urban South. Taylor's photographs were in many ways philosophical reflections on black Memphis that challenged the stereotypical images of "Hambone" and "Mammy." Taylor's photographs were, as one contemporary described them, part of Taylor's efforts to define his community. They opened a window on black life in the 1930s, 1940s, and 1950s—but the photographs were seldom intended for the audience that considered "Mammy" and "Hambone" accurate depictions of African Americans. Taylor's work was produced primarily for his subjects.

When L. O. and Blanche moved from their first home on Eldridge Avenue to a larger one on Hunter Avenue, Taylor set up a small studio on the ground floor and a darkroom in one of the upstairs bedrooms. He used a bedsheet, a window curtain, or a white screen as a backdrop when he photographed clients in either his home or theirs. Taylor photographed individuals, groups, churches, businesses, and schools. His subjects included Tri-State Bank, Dave's Grocery Store, and baptisms in the creek off Lane Avenue near Beale. He also made "funeral" photographs and copied decades-old images that his clients wanted to preserve. Taylor had no preference for particular subjects or sites. According to one friend, "He just loved the camera. . . . Most of the time he had one with him everywhere he would go." He would sometimes take random photographs of people he met on the street, asking them to just "wait a minute, I'm gon' take your picture."[48]

Taylor also taught young people, mostly from schools in his Hunter Avenue neighborhood, how to take photographs. But only a few special students actually worked with him in his studio. Oretha Cannon first met Taylor in 1939, when he preached at a revival in Stanton, Tennessee.

She began working for Taylor in 1946, after she and her sister moved to Memphis and joined Olivette Baptist Church. Cannon remembered first learning how to load film in "a little bitty camera that you use outside . . . something like a Brownie camera," and then how to take the pictures. Most of her work was confined to outside shots; Taylor took the indoor ones that required him to use the network of lights he had mounted around his backdrop.[49]

Taylor made 16mm films and audio disc recordings of people, places, and events in his community, as well as films at the National Baptist Convention. For some of his subjects, these audio recordings were the first time they heard their own voices. People sometimes came to his home to make the recordings, or he visited churches and recorded choirs or soloists performing classics such as "Amazing Grace" or "Hark the Voice of Jesus Calling" or hymns that Taylor may have written himself ("Without the Lord" or "Who Will Go?").[50]

L. O. Taylor started making films in the 1940s or 1950s using a Bolex movie camera. He filmed congregations parading in silent, ordered processions out of churches, travelers arriving at National Baptist Conventions, students at a local business college, and a baptism in a local creek. He purchased a projector and showed his films in churches and schools or at his home. For many viewers, especially those in rural areas, this was their first experience with moving pictures. Taylor also rented movies on a variety of other topics to show to his audiences. These ranged from black history to comedies to a series on "The Church in the Atomic Age," which he rented for a church viewing in September 1945, shortly after the United States dropped atomic bombs on Hiroshima and Nagasaki, Japan.[51] Ticket prices for these movies or to see his slides ranged from 5 to 15 cents, but never more than a quarter; most children paid 10 cents.[52]

Like most African American clergymen in the first half of the twentieth century, L. O. Taylor was a social and political conservative who accommodated to the Crump machine and lagged behind black businessmen and professionals in supporting labor unionism and civil rights. Taylor was not actively involved in politics, preferring to focus on his churches and his community. Perhaps, as Netters observed, Taylor "just didn't have an opportunity . . . to practice being a human being—a full human being. He was rated a second-class citizen [in the segregated society of the period]."[53] But, as suggested by historian Elizabeth Brooks Higginbotham, the churches that Taylor and other black ministers pastored were sources of "psychological resistance," in that they provided "interstitial space in which to critique and contest white America's domination."[54] By the mid-twentieth century, these "interstitial" spaces and the men who led them were moving toward more open opposition to discrimination. When the Crump machine tried to deny labor leader A. Phillip Randolph a venue to deliver a public address in Memphis in 1944, the Reverend George Albert Long sent Crump an open letter challenging his position. Long allowed Randolph to deliver his address to a packed house at his First Baptist Church on Beale Street. He also encouraged black Memphians to speak out and challenge racial discrimination in the city.[55]

But there is little evidence that Taylor supported Long's challenges to the Crump machine or his opposition to segregation and discrimination in the city. Although Taylor encouraged his congregations to vote and to cast their ballots for "what was best for the race," most of his friends and associates agreed that he was not an activist. When he reflected on Taylor's attitude and actions as the civil rights movement took shape in Memphis and surrounding areas, the Reverend P. L. Johnson observed that Taylor "had his own thing (building churches, photographing, recording, and documenting the community) going on," and what he "was doing was important. There was nobody else doing it so why should he leave that and go to civil rights? [Everybody] was doing the civil rights movement [and] it was just a movement. But he had his own thing going."[56]

L. O. Taylor died in 1977, more than half a century after he first came to Memphis as a migrant from the Mississippi Delta. Since his arrival in the city, he had built and pastored four churches and influenced the preaching and administrative skills of countless ministers. Taylor's sermons traveled beyond his pulpits, carried by steamboat workers and Pullman porters, by guests at his churches and congregants at the churches he visited, by fellow pastors and ministerial students, and in his two-volume *Bits of Logic*. He mentored countless young people, teaching them "how to think and how to look at a thing and see more than what's on the surface . . . [and] how to be investigative and searching and look for more than what you actually see because there's more there in almost every situation."[57] Perhaps his most enduring legacy is the treasure trove of photographs and movies he left, images that challenged racist caricatures and envisioned real black Memphis in the mid-twentieth century.

Notes

1. G. Wayne Dowdy, "The White Rose Mammy: Racial Culture and Politics in World War II Memphis," *Journal of Negro History* 85, no. 4 (Autumn 2000): 311–12. Dowdy's article includes the petition sent by the Memphis Negro Chamber of Commerce (and forwarded to Mayor Walter Chandler) and the White Rose Laundry owners' response.

2. *Memphis Commercial Appeal,* June 16, 1923, 12.

3. Cynthia Sadler, "'On Parade': Race, Gender, and Imagery in the Memphis Mardi Gras, Cotton Carnival, and Cotton Makers' Jubilee," in *Tennessee Women, Their Lives and Times,* ed. Beverly Greene Bond and Sarah Wilkerson Freeman, vol. 2 (Athens: University of Georgia Press, 2015), 139–40.

4. Reverend P. L. Johnson, interview by Deborah Bowman (hereafter DB), June 5, 1979, L. O. Taylor Collection, Center for Southern Folklore, Memphis, TN.

5. Nona Brinkley Taylor's birthplace is listed as Mississippi on the 1900 census but as Arkansas on the 1910 census.

6. US Census, 1900.

7. US Census, 1900, 1910, 1920. Another child, Samuel Marshall, was present in the Taylor household in 1900. Samuel, who was identified as Willie's stepson, was most likely Nona's child from a previous relationship. He was no longer in the household in 1910. The names of Nona and Willie's children differed on the 1900, 1910, and 1920 censuses, but they were most likely Charles W. (Willie), Fred J. (Jesse), Alonzo D. (Alonzo O., Lonzie O., or L. O.), Alex (Clarence), and Luvenia (Grace). Taylor did not adopt the initials L. O. until the mid to late 1920s, possibly as a gesture toward the respectability required of ministers.

8. Lula Adams, interview by DB, June 26, 1979, Taylor Collection.

9. US Census, 1920, Scott Township, Mississippi County, Arkansas; Jesse Taylor, US Draft Registration #224, September 12, 1918. Jesse Taylor was living in Joiner, Arkansas (in Mississippi County), farming land owned by Susie McCadden. He listed Will Taylor (190 Auction, Memphis) as his "nearest relative."

10. Dr. Andre Johnson, interview by Beverly Bond (hereafter BB), University of Memphis, July 12, 2016. I would like to thank Andre Johnson for his insight into the process by which Taylor became Minister Taylor and then Reverend Taylor.

11. Daisy Cooper, interview by DB, April 29, 1979, Taylor Collection.

12. Andre Johnson interview.

13. Alice Taylor Henderson (Homer's daughter and L. O. Taylor's only grandchild), interview by BB, March 23, 2009.

14. Campbell Gibson and Kay Jung, "Historical Census Statistics on Population Totals by Race, 1790 to 1990 . . . , for Large Cities and Other Urban Places in the United States," (Working Paper No. 76, Population Division, US Census Bureau, Washington, DC, February 2005), table 43, Tennessee—Race and Hispanic Origin for Selected Cities and Other Places: Earliest Census to 1910; Christopher Silver and John V. Mouser, *The Separate City, Black Communities in the Urban South, 1940–1968* (Lexington: University Press of Kentucky, 2014). Silver and Mouser cite Woofter's assessment of the impact of the growing in-migration of rural blacks to the city; see Thomas J. Woofter, *Negro Problems in Cities* (New York: Doubleday, 1928), 31. Overall, between 1900 and 1940, the city's black population grew from 49,910 to 121,498.

15. Kenneth W. Goings and Gerald L. Smith, "Duty of the Hour: African American Communities in Memphis, 1862–1923," in *Essays in Tennessee's African American History, Trial and Triumph,* ed. Carroll Van West (Knoxville: University of Tennessee Press, 2002), 232; Gibson and Jung, "Historical Census Statistics," table 43; Silver and Mouser, *Separate City,* 21.

16. Gerald Capers, *The Biography of a River Town: Memphis, Its Heroic Age* (Chapel Hill: University of North Carolina Press, 1939), quoted in Goings and Smith, "Duty of the Hour," 232.

17. Goings and Smith, "Duty of the Hour," 232.

18. Ibid., 239. According to Goings and Smith, "The migrants planted the seeds of protest against racial injustice in the city. Yet, unlike the talented tenth and accommodationists, the migrants held the least prestige in Memphis. They were the least educated and had little contact with the white community. They worked in low-paying unskilled jobs, lived in shotgun-style houses, and were despised by the talented tenth and accommodationists for their uninhibited behavior. Additionally, being migrants, they experienced daily harassment from the local police, who were concerned with maintaining control over the growing African American population."

19. Green Polonius Hamilton, *The Bright Side of Memphis* (Memphis, TN: n.p., 1908), 3–4, 6. Hamilton blamed the unhealthiness of black communities on the "lack of education and careful home training," but he felt that African Americans could share in the general healthiness of Memphis if the city government and businessmen would construct larger, well-ventilated housing units, clear the alleys, improve black communities' sanitation, and provide greater access to clean drinking water.

20. Ibid., 5, 11, 12. The employment opportunities Hamilton cited were limited to drugstores, photography studios, tailor shops, feed stores, restaurants, barbershops, undertaking establishments, dental parlors, laundries, shoe shops, ice cream factories, and printing shops. Hamilton acknowledged that black busi-

nessmen faced competition from native-born whites as well as recent immigrants, particularly Italians, but his image of the city was one in which African Americans who were willing to accommodate to segregation could live comfortably.

21. Ibid., 8.

22. Goings and Smith, "Duty of the Hour," 239, 240.

23. Lonzie Otis Taylor, World War I Draft Registration Card #2995, Shelby County, Tennessee, roll 1877693. Although 190 Auction Avenue was the address given on Taylor's draft registration card, Willie Taylor was not listed at that address in the city directory until 1920. See Polk's city directories for 1918, 1919, and 1920.

24. "Bore Hole and Find Identity of Thief," *Memphis Press-Scimitar,* October 15, 1920, 1. Polk's city directories for 1918, 1920, and 1922 show Willie Taylor residing at 180 Auction in 1919 and 1920 and "Lonnie" Taylor "boarding" at that address in 1920. This was most likely the same residence Taylor listed on his draft registration, although it was shown as "190 Auction."

25. US Census, 1920 (Robert W. Guy); Polk's city directories, 1917, 1919, 1920, 1921, 1922 (Nona Taylor, Willie Taylor, Robert W. Guy). The census for the Richardson household was taken on January 10, 1920. But one month later, Nona was back in Scott, Arkansas, when the census was taken on February 16; she was living in the household with her sons Charley and Clarence and her daughter Grace. Sometime after the Arkansas census was taken, she returned to Memphis and continued to work at Richardson's boardinghouse until she moved to the house at 654 North Second and began working at Pilgrim Rest Baptist Church. Adding to the confusion about where Nona and Willie actually resided, Nona described herself as "widowed" on the 1920 Arkansas census, but Willie Taylor's death records indicate that he was very much alive in 1920.

26. Adams interview; Polk's city directories 1922, 1924, 1925–1934. Robert Guy apparently left Pilgrim Rest in 1921 and worked for at least a year at a local car repair shop. In 1922 he became pastor at Olive Grove Baptist—a position he might have held until his death in 1935; see Robert W. Guy, State of Tennessee Certificate of Death No. 2016, August 8, 1935. See *Constitution and By-Laws of Subordinate Circles in the Supreme Royal Circle of Friends of the World,* 1923, 1924, Taylor Collection; receipt for dues, L. O. Taylor, Rising Star Circle No. 3056, Memphis, 1929; Carolyn Yancey Kent, "Supreme Circle of Friends of the World, aka: Royal Circle of Friends," in *The Encyclopedia of Arkansas History and Culture,* www.encyclopediaofarkansas.net (accessed May 28, 2016).

27. Adams interview; Alice Taylor Henderson described her grandfather as "an awesome little minister" who had "a lot of women. . . . He was a fast talker [and] a sweet talker, and women liked him. (Henderson interview).

28. L. O. Taylor and Marie Porter, Shelby County Marriage License; Circuit Court of Shelby County, Tennessee, Decree for Divorce #27704, L. O. Taylor

vs. Marie Taylor, June 12, 1929. Marie Taylor may have left Memphis and moved to Chicago. The 1930 US Census identified a "Marie Taylor" (divorced) born in Tennessee who was about the right age living in a Chicago boardinghouse operated by her aunt and cousin. See wedding announcement—Mrs. Susie Wright of Jericho, Arkansas, for her daughter Blanche B. Johnson and Rev. L. O. Taylor of Memphis, Tennessee, on September 22, 1929, Taylor Collection; Alberta Fields, interview by DB, June 12, 1979, Taylor Collection; Blanche Johnson Taylor, interview by Katie Sandweiss, August 13, 1977; 1910 US Census, Greenville, Mississippi. Blanche Johnson Taylor was born in Mississippi to Johnny and Sarena (Susie) Johnson. Her father died when she was thirteen years old, after which Blanche was raised in Lake Providence, Louisiana, by her mother's half sister, Mattie Davenport. Blanche attended a teachers' training school in Louisiana and taught at a Rosenwald school in Transylvania, Louisiana (near Lake Providence), until her aunt's death in 1922, when she moved to Jericho, Arkansas, to live with her mother and stepfather.

29. Charles Williams, *African American Life and Culture in Orange Mound: Case Study of a Black Community in Memphis, Tennessee, 1890–1980* (Lanham, MD: Lexington Books, 2013), 71.

30. "First Baptist Church Broad—History," www.fbcbroad.org (accessed October 1, 2016). First Baptist Broad and Binghampton First Baptist Church are the same church, but in the 1920s and early 1930s they were listed in city directories as two different institutions. Polk's city directory lists Rev. Lonzie O. Taylor as pastor of either First Baptist Church or Binghampton First Baptist Church during these years. For information on Taylor's tenure and impact at Olivette Baptist Church, see Williams, *African American Life and Culture,* 71. Sorting out the dates of Taylor's tenure at these various churches is difficult. It is possible that he was pastoring more than one church in the 1920s and 1930s, and a small congregation may have met at his home on Eldridge as well.

31. In addition, Taylor may have pastored a small congregation called Calvary Baptist Church from 1925 to 1927, while he was officially the pastor at First Baptist Binghampton (Broad). Alternatively, all three of these churches, though listed in the city directory individually, may have been the same church: First Baptist Binghampton (Broad).

32. Reverend James L. Netters, interview by DB, May 1, 1979, Taylor Collection.

33. Ibid.

34. Henderson interview; Ernest Tatum, interview by DB, June 25, 1979, Taylor Collection. Tatum, one of the ministers trained by Taylor, noted that Olivette was always packed, and "people used to come from out of town to hear L. O. Taylor preach."

35. Henderson interview; P. L. Johnson interview; Netters interview. Reverend Johnson recalled ministers who had studied under Taylor carrying on the

"tradition of Taylor." Taylor's influence was felt through the Minister's Association (Memphis) and the National Baptist Convention.

36. Netters interview.

37. Tatum interview.

38. Samuel H. Randolph Fleming III, "Rural-Urban Migration of Blacks: Changing Social Organization in Memphis" (PhD diss., University of Virginia, 1974), 33–34.

39. Blanche Taylor, interview by DB, June 27, 1978, Taylor Collection.

40. Netters interview. Several of the individuals Bowman interviewed for the Center for Southern Folklore's Taylor Collection mentioned this "pencil" sermon, but Netters provided the most complete description. He also recounted another sermon in which Taylor used the structure of a common broom to reflect on the strength of family relationships. Some of Taylor's poems and topics or themes for sermons are collected in two volumes entitled *Bits of Logic.* Nine of his sermons were published in a volume called *Sermons that Live;* they include "After Really Meeting Jesus," "The Right Man in The Place at the Right Time," "Jesus and the Woman Taken in Adultery," "A Report of a Traveler," and "Brimfulness." The book was sold at the National Baptist Convention in Miami, Florida.

41. P. L. Johnson interview.

42. Netters interview.

43. Ibid.

44. Gloria Harris Tuggle, telephone interview by BB, October 3, 2016.

45. Netters interview.

46. Ibid.

47. Oretha Cannon, interview by DB, April 10, 1979, Taylor Collection.

48. Charles Washburn, interview by DB, June 1, 1979, Taylor Collection.

49. Cannon interview. Taylor also trained James Netters as a photographer and filmmaker (Netters interview).

50. Blanche Taylor, interview by Judy Peiser and Katie Sandweiss, July 27, 1977.

51. Receipt from Ideal Pictures Corporation for rental of "The Church in the Atomic Age," box 1, Taylor Collection.

52. Fields interview; Sylvester Lewis, discussion at Center for Southern Folklore, June 24, 2009; Colleen McDannell, ed., *Religions of the United States in Practice,* vol. 2 (Princeton, NJ: Princeton University Press, 2001), 132–33. McDannell places the movies Taylor made at the National Baptist Convention and others that focus on religious events or themes (e.g., baptisms, church services) in the category of "race movies" because of their themes and the audiences to which they were directed. Most of these movies were black and white, but some friends remembered Taylor doing a few in color.

53. Netters interview. See also Elizabeth Gritter, *River of Hope: Black Politics and the Memphis Reform Movement, 1865–1954* (Lexington: University Press

of Kentucky, 2014), 61; David M. Tucker, *Black Pastors and Preachers* (Memphis, TN: Memphis State University Press, 1975), 67, 102. Tucker cites Ralph Bunche's comments on 1920s and 1930s black preachers in Memphis. In his study *The Political Status of the Negro* (Chicago: University of Chicago Press, 1973), Bunche notes that as a whole, these ministers avoided social questions or comments on discrimination, instead preaching fiery ("fire and brimstone") sermons that aroused the emotions of their congregations. However, by the 1950s, many black clergy were more aggressively addressing these issues.

54. Higginbotham quoted in Kenneth W. Goings and Gerald L. Smith, "'Unhidden' Transcripts: Memphis and African American Agency, 1862–1920," in *The New African American Urban History*, ed. Kenneth W. Goings and Raymond A. Mohl (Thousand Oaks, CA: Sage Publications, 1996), 158–59.

55. Tucker, *Black Pastors and Preachers*, 103–5. Long and his congregation were harassed, and he eventually left the city. The National Baptist Convention, which most of the city's black Baptist churches, including Taylor's Olivette, were affiliated with, did not support Long's actions. The only suggestion that Taylor may have considered supporting Long or anyone else who challenged the system consists of a blank letterhead from the Binghampton Civic Club, found in the Taylor Collection, and a reference to Taylor's presence when two men attacked the Reverend Roy Love and George W. Lee in 1944. See Michael Honey, *Southern Labor and Black Civil Rights: Organizing Memphis Workers* (Urbana: University of Illinois Press, 1993), 206.

56. P. L. Johnson interview; Cooper interview.

57. Netters interview.

"We'll Have No Race Trouble Here"

Racial Politics and Memphis's Reign of Terror

Jason Jordan

In the fall of 1940 black Memphians were subjected to an extensive campaign of police harassment that included searches, seizures, mass arrests, and violence. These actions were carried out under the direction of Police Commissioner Joe Boyle, Mayor Walter Chandler, and longtime political boss Edward Hull Crump in direct response to growing political activism among Memphis's black population. Throughout the 1920s and 1930s the Crump political machine bought its way into political power with the tacit support of Memphis's black elite. Crump used his vast wealth to pay poll taxes for blacks, and in exchange, black community leaders delivered a ready-made voting bloc to Crump's machine candidates. Moreover, those black elites who promoted Crump's policies to the black community were allotted a measure of political access to both Crump and the Memphis government.[1]

Despite this political enfranchisement, the unspoken rules that governed racial politics in Jim Crow Memphis privileged loyalty and obedience to the Crump machine above all else.[2] For a time, black leaders had begrudgingly accepted such edicts, as this was the cost of having a seat at Memphis's political table, however small that seat may have been.[3] By the 1940s, however, many of Memphis's black leaders had begun to see this arrangement as a yoke that circumscribed their political autonomy no less than any unpayable poll tax or violent lynch mob. For all their years of loyalty, black voters had seen very few returns on their investment in the Crump machine. They wanted black police officers. They wanted better schools. They wanted black representation within the city government itself. Instead, they routinely received token gestures and lip service.[4]

Thus, those who constituted the bulk of Memphis's black leadership community—business owners, physicians, educators, clergy, and community activists—began to organize and plot a new course of action. They met in one another's homes, churches, and places of business to debate how to end Crump's multidecade hold on Memphis politics once and for all. Some favored throwing their weight behind Republican candidates to run against Crump's machine-backed Democrats. Others thought their best hope lay with supporting the local Democratic opposition to Crump. Either way, a consensus formed that Crump could not be counted on to further racial progress in Memphis.[5]

Seeing that a full-scale political revolt was on the horizon, Crump and Mayor Chandler directed the Memphis police to begin a campaign that the *Chicago Defender* would dub the Memphis "Reign of Terror." The police occupation of Beale Street and the surrounding black neighborhoods lasted from October to December 1940.[6] During this time, hundreds of black Memphians were stopped, searched, arrested, and often roughed up under the pretense of "cleaning up" Memphis.[7] Such actions, however, had less to do with reducing crime than they did with sending a message to those who opposed the political machine.

Historians of the Jim Crow South have noted the centrality of community and collective efforts in supporting black resistance to disenfranchisement. "Always, there was the sense that no matter how badly off [black] people might be in their own right, they would come together to help others," some have argued.[8] While group solidarity was certainly an asset throughout the black freedom struggle, the concept of mutual aid did not constitute an absolute rule. The draconian actions taken by Memphis's white city government against the black populace showed that in the face of overwhelming persecution, bonds of kinship and community could be twisted and broken. Throughout the Reign of Terror, Memphis's black leaders in particular found themselves at odds with one another over how to respond to the Crump machine's doings. Some acquiesced and abandoned their attempts at political revolt, hoping to earn a small amount of favor for themselves or their constituents. In the process, they also denounced those who continued to protest and fight against the Crump machine's harassment and subjugation.

Electoral politics represents an oft overlooked aspect of the black experience under Jim Crow. To some extent, this lack of acknowledgment makes sense, given that the black vote was so widely restricted throughout the Jim Crow South. Nevertheless, such constraints did not mean that blacks were entirely cut off from the electoral process. This was especially so in the case of Memphis, where black leaders such as Robert Church Jr., the Reverend T. O. Fully, Dr. Joseph Walker, Lieutenant George Lee, Dr. J. B. Martin, and a host of others found ways to sustain a politically active community in black Memphis. Historian Elizabeth Gritter recently explored this topic and shows that even in the face of disenfranchisement, blacks in Memphis carved out a spot for themselves and "formed political clubs, ran for office, engaged in voter registration and education activities, held the balance of power in elections, participated in party politics, used the political arena as a forum for advocating civil rights, and petitioned public officials for better public services and employment opportunities."[9] This political activism was built on the cooperation and unity of local black leaders and was key throughout the Jim Crow era in helping to build a vibrant and flourishing black community in Memphis.

As much as the Reign of Terror was fueled by an increase in black political independence, it also represented a direct assault on these communal bonds. Robert Church Jr., who had been the principal black political figure in Memphis for years, had recently been harassed into leaving town for supporting Republican presidential candidate Wendell Willkie against Crump's Democratic Party.[10] Now the machine set its sights on Church's fellow black activists. The Reign of Terror was meant to sow discord and drive a wedge between Memphis's black leaders, a goal that it ultimately succeeded in doing. The combination of government persecution and internal disputes among black elites over how to respond to such actions derailed and delayed what had been a growing effort to change the status quo of racial politics in Jim Crow Memphis.

The Reign of Terror began October 25, 1940, with a police raid on Dr. John (J. B.) Martin's pharmacy and general store. About 40 white customers and 200 black customers were stopped and searched by Memphis police officers. Despite turning up no evidence of illegal activity at Martin's shop, Police Commissioner Joe Boyle ordered his officers to maintain a presence at the location until further notice. Martin's store was a neighborhood institution, and Martin himself was the newly elected chairman of a Republican political committee. In addition, Martin was president of the American Negro Baseball Association and co-owner of the Memphis Red Sox, the city's Negro League baseball team.[11]

In the Jim Crow era, successful black businesses like those Martin owned stood as points of pride and achievement in black communities. They "suggested the achievements possible for black Americans once they were given a chance to succeed," as one historian notes.[12] Thus, in Martin's case, any one of his accomplishments would have made him a well-known and respected figure in the local black community. All his achievements together, however, made Martin a cornerstone of it. And so the persecution of J. B. Martin symbolically represented an attack on black Memphis as a whole.

When Martin publicly protested that the actions against him and his customers were politically motivated, Boyle went before the local media and declared, "The policing [of Martin's shop] has nothing to do with politics." Instead, he claimed, it was related to allegations of "dope-peddling" on Martin's part by undisclosed sources. Boyle further stated that with the backing of the city government, he was "going to continue policing Martin's place until this nuisance is cleared up . . . I've warned Martin before, and I mean business."[13] To bolster his claim of Martin's ill character, Boyle provided local reporters with records of a dismissed case in which Martin had been accused of buying a stolen shipment of aspirin from two other blacks. Boyle also alleged that, earlier in the year, Martin had intervened to keep a black woman from being taken to court over a speeding ticket, claiming he bribed the police officer who had made the traffic stop. No evidence was provided to support these claims, but as a further dig at Martin's character, Boyle pointed out that the pool hall and restaurant next door to Martin's shop were sites of known drug activity and violence, implying that Martin was either directly connected to these activities or at least knew about them.[14]

It is important to examine the reasons behind the targeted character assassination of Martin. Memphis, as Crump and his machine lieutenants repeatedly pointed out, was not like other southern cities in terms of relations between blacks and whites. The nakedly open violence and intimidation of blacks that occurred in other southern cities such as Little Rock, Atlanta, and Birmingham, to name just a few, were functions of day-to-

J. B. Martin and associates outside his drugstore. (Courtesy Memphis and Shelby County Room, Memphis Public Library)

day life that, by and large, did not occur in Memphis during the Jim Crow era. Crump, Boyle, and others in his regime pointed to this contrast as a sign of supposed racial harmony in Memphis, but in actuality, this could not have been further from the truth.

The outward lack of racial violence in Jim Crow Memphis merely masked a more insidious form of black disenfranchisement. Despite the Crump machine's overtures to blacks, Memphis was not a racially progressive city. However, Crump's desire to shake Memphis's long-standing reputation as a southern backwater and turn it into a city of national importance necessitated a less open form of racial oppression. The horrors of other southern cities would not be tolerated under the national spotlight Crump wanted to shine on Memphis. And yet, Crump and his administration could not abide the idea of equality between the races either.

Boyle, in his role as police commissioner, was the public face of the Reign of Terror, but he had the express backing of the city's political machine. Over the next three months, Boyle, Mayor Chandler, and Boss Crump would justify their actions by various means. Martin was accused of being the operator of a "den of vice" where black outlaws and thugs congregated to take drugs, drink, gamble, and fight. Chandler issued a statement of support declaring unequivocally, "More power to Joe [Boyle]. I believe he is on the right track. . . . Drug addicts cannot hold off long. They have got to have the drug and will come for it sooner or later." Ignoring suggestions of ulterior motives for the raid and occupation and the legal impropriety of those actions based on Martin's political activities, Chandler went on to state, "This is no time for appeasement with law violators and those under suspicion. The man who sells narcotics to the unfortunate victims of the drug habit is entitled to no mercy."[15]

At other times, Martin and his associates were described as "communists" and "race agitators" out to stir up riots. Commissioner Boyle maintained that he had a full list of "undesirables" that were under surveillance, including preachers, doctors, restaurant owners, newspaper reporters, store owners, and even an undertaker. In Boyle's view, it was an "established fact" that "radical labor agitators and subversive agents [had] been working among Southern negroes for a long time." If anyone was to blame for the trouble that fell, it was the blacks themselves who had been out "fanning race hatred."[16]

Boyle pointed out the necessity of his actions by routinely stating that his police force was all that stood between safety and order on the one hand, and all-out racial warfare on the other, the likes of which other southern cities were experiencing. "We are not going to have any trouble with the Negroes in Memphis if it can be avoided," Boyle wrote. "A great many cities in the North and South have had serious race riots with tremendous bloodshed. If careful and stern preparation for the defense of peace will prevent it, it will be prevented in Memphis." Just in case the true intent and meaning of his words had been unclear, Boyle went on to state more explicitly, "I say again this is a white man's country, and always will be and any negro who doesn't agree to this better move on." Boyle claimed that any "intelligent" Negro knew in his or her heart that, "for the safety of all Negroes," a stand had to be taken by their more "reasonable" counterparts.[17]

However transparent such proclamations may have been, they evidently made an impact, as one of the black Memphians who denounced J. B. Martin's political activism was his own brother, William (W. S.) Martin. A local physician and the other co-owner of Memphis's Negro baseball team, W. S. Martin was, like his brother, also involved in local politics. W. S. Martin, however, sought to ward off the type of persecution his brother experienced and essentially threw himself at the mercy of the Crump machine. Only a week after the Reign of Terror began in late October, W. S. Martin wrote a personal letter to Boss Crump, distancing himself from the "serious mistake" of his brother's political activism.

In this letter, W. S. Martin was emphatic that, in contrast to his brother, he was quite grateful for Crump's many years of patronage and benefits, including the construction of new schools and playgrounds and the renovation of three Negro housing projects. Martin took pains to remind Crump of their "30 year-long relationship" and promised to use his position on a local Negro political board to encourage blacks to remain loyal to the Democratic Party from President Roosevelt on down to the Memphis city government. Martin closed his letter by assuring Crump that he "appreciate[d] all you have done for the colored people of Memphis and Shelby county and that I am one hundred percent behind the entire democratic ticket and that I deem it a privilege and an honor in doing so."[18]

Another revealing example of black leaders who prostrated themselves before the Crump machine involved local physician T. O. Fuller. Dr. Fuller had long been a member of Crump's inner circle of black community leaders, and J. B. Martin wrote to Fuller in the hope that he could convince Crump to end the occupation of Martin's pharmacy. In this letter, Martin earnestly pleaded his case, stating that although he was considered one of the more prominent members of Memphis's black community, he was not a wealthy man and could not withstand the loss of business caused by the Memphis Police Department's occupation. Martin wrote, "I have been misunderstood, and I am making this . . . appeal to you to straighten this matter out for me. With all that you have done for the administration, if you can't, no one else can. If you think my activities in politics has anything to do with the matter, I am willing to cease from now on."[19]

It is unclear whether Martin's turnaround represented an actual acquiescence to the machine or simply a desire for his life to return to some semblance of normalcy. There is no record of how Fuller responded to Martin's plea. Based on what is known of Fuller's history, however, one can presume that it did not turn out as Martin hoped. Arguably, Fuller was even more loyal to and more firmly in the pocket of the Crump administration than Martin's brother. Routinely, Crump and Fuller exchanged favors. Crump would donate money to the church that Fuller owned, and Fuller would respond in kind by providing Crump with free passes to see the Martins' baseball team play.[20]

On occasion, Fuller would entreat Crump to write a letter of support to a friend who was hoping to avoid the draft, or he would ask Crump for monetary support to bring a black Baptist convention to Memphis, pledging that this would make valuable inroads with southern Negroes. In time, Fuller tried to persuade Crump of the need to compile lists of loyal members of the black community who could be counted on to pledge their allegiance to Crump in future political endeavors. At Fuller's suggestion, these Negro "Friends of Shelby County" would be organized into constituency blocks by occupation, targeting black business owners, teachers, clergy, general laborers, and so forth. With such close connections to Crump, Fuller's support was far beyond Martin's grasp.[21]

As mentioned previously, Jim Crow Memphis was unlike other southern cities when it came to relations between the city's white ruling class and its black leaders. Up to this point, the two sides had managed to maintain a working relationship in terms of quid pro quo benefits. The black elite kept the broader masses convinced that Crump and his regime were their best hope for political enfranchisement, thus preventing Memphis's black population from causing too much disruption to Crump's agenda. In return, Crump only rarely resorted to the types of heavy-handed racial violence found in other areas of the Deep South, and from time to time he made a token gesture toward addressing one of the many ills plaguing the black community, such as approving the construction of a segregated swimming pool or public park so that blacks had public spaces to congregate that approximated those that white Memphians took for granted.

This relationship, however, was decidedly slanted in Crump's favor. It was something of an open secret in Memphis that dissenters to white authority were taken care of privately and under the cloak of darkness, rather than in the naked daylight of the public watch. Yet, despite the inequality in this relationship, it was still far more beneficial than the racial norms of the Jim Crow South. Thus, even though many of Memphis's black elites were privately none too fond of Crump's paternalism, they felt it was better to make do with his caprices. The sliver of racial equality that existed in Memphis was tenuous at best, and the efforts of J. B. Martin and others threatened to render it nonexistent, ruining it for everyone. In the moment, then, that fear superseded any supposed ideas of racial or even familial solidarity.

The round-the-clock surveillance and policing of Martin's store and customers would continue for weeks with no tangible results in terms of arrests. After the occupation entered its second month, and with the local media beginning to openly question its purpose and efficacy, Boyle ordered his officers to expand their efforts and search not only Martin's customers but also anyone who happened to be in the vicinity and looked like a suspicious character. These searches quickly escalated into mass arrests, the most dramatic of which occurred one night in mid-November when a total of sixty-five blacks were rounded up from various Beale Street establishments and arrested in one fell swoop. Each of them was charged with carrying some type of illegal weapon such as a penknife, a switchblade, or what was known as an "Arkansas toothpick." Five of the arrestees were released the next day because their weapons did not meet the parameters to be considered illegal. The other sixty were fined $50 each. One man, Roy King, protested that the police had no right to search him without probable cause, so he was fined an additional $10 for public intoxication. Police and the local newspapers hailed the mass roundup as a sign that Boyle's occupation was working as intended and pointed to a subsequent decrease in stabbings and in arrests for carrying a weapon as proof.[22]

As dire as the situation was becoming at this point, a few important events offered a bit of hope for a reprieve to the Reign of Terror. The first event of note was the formation of an interracial commission composed of local clergymen and educators who began to speak out against the Crump machine's actions. Fairly diverse in terms of its racial makeup, the commission included not only prominent black ministers, such as George

A. Long of Beale Street Baptist Church, Harry B. Gordon of Centenary Methodist Church, and Howard Perry, but also white clergy who were well known in the city, such as William G. Gerhl of Grace Street Luke's Episcopal Church and Alfred Loaring-Clark of St. John's Episcopal Church. The diversity of this commission was purposeful, insofar as its members wanted to present a racially united front to show the Crump administration that the Reign of Terror affected all Memphians, not just blacks.[23]

For weeks after its formation in November, the commission repeatedly attempted to meet with Boyle, Chandler, or Crump to express their concerns over the harassment, intimidation, and persecution of black Memphians. For just as many weeks, they were repeatedly denied a face-to-face meeting with anyone in charge. Crump's machine had no intention of dignifying the commission's efforts in the public eye, and even granting them a meeting would have meant that their concerns were valid enough to take seriously. Commissioner Boyle went so far as to publicly rebuke the group's efforts, stating that it was dangerously close to promoting full social equality between black and white Memphians, a charge routinely made in the South to impede any racially progressive activism.[24]

The specter of full racial equality touched on deeply rooted fears held by many southern whites. They were afraid that the time would come when they would be compelled to share public spaces with blacks; even worse, they envisioned a future ruled by miscegenation and "tainting" of the white genetic stock. For white southerners, the term "racial equality" had carried these connotations for decades, and Boyle knew exactly how his charges would affect the commission's efforts.

In a sternly worded letter to the group, Boyle wrote, "Lawlessness of this city is our problem, day and night and we suggest you leave it to us. We know what we are doing." Boyle argued that Memphis blacks had absolutely no grounds to complain, given that the taxes they paid totaled only 5 percent of the city's income collection, despite the fact that blacks constituted such a large percentage of the population. "We'll have no race trouble here," Boyle stated plainly. This refrain would become the go-to defense against any and all challenges to white authority in Memphis. The true source of any perceived discontent, according to Boyle, came from "selfish and unprincipled negro paper promoters" who were intent on "conducting themselves as if they lived in Chicago, Pittsburgh and

Philadelphia." Moreover, Boyle charged that the black members of the interracial commission, specifically Reverend Long and Reverend Gibson, were firmly against the notion of "white supremacy," which was the natural order of things in Memphis. Boyle concluded by imploring the white members of the commission to rethink their positions: "Please don't be disturbed—have no misgivings about the negroes here. Much has been done for them. Mayor Walter Chandler, Mr. H. W. Hale and Mr. E. H. Crump have had their interest at heart for many years—long before a majority of the Interracial Commission came to live in Memphis." Never missing a chance to take another shot at J. B. Martin, Boyle also urged the white commission members to be careful of the company they kept, claiming that Martin and his wife, being fair skinned, had once passed for white to attend a Barnum and Bailey Circus and gloated about it afterward. "It is utterly beyond my understanding how you white ministers can get in on a proposition of this kind when you are so poorly informed on what is actually going on."[25]

Knowing the stakes of allowing such charges to stand, the commission strenuously denied Boyle's allegations. Whatever their intentions were in reality, any public admission of advocating for racial equality would have discredited the commission among the majority of Memphis's white population and lost any perception that it was taking the moral high ground. Thus, the united racial front that had begun as an earnest effort to show that the Reign of Terror disrupted the peace of Memphis for all its citizens, not just blacks, had turned into a liability.

Still, many black members of the commission continued to speak out about what they saw as the true reason for the intrusions into black neighborhoods. Reverend Long and other black clergy argued that the search for drug dealers, communists, and other subversives in black neighborhoods was little more than a coded message meant to disguise the political motivations of Crump and Boyle. "The whole thing is over the fact that I was active politically during the recent campaign, but not on the side of the political administration," Long argued in a rebuke to Boyle.[26]

After weeks of refusing to back down, the commission's outspoken protests became, if nothing else, a public relations issue the Crump machine needed to contain. Thus, in early December, the commission was finally granted a two-hour, face-to-face meeting with Commissioner

Boyle and Mayor Chandler. However, only white members of the commission could be in attendance. Thus, the message was clear: despite the commission's efforts to involve blacks in the process of airing their own grievances before the Crump regime, the Reign of Terror would be discussed only on the terms and conditions imposed by the city's white authorities. This was something happening *to* Memphis blacks in the eyes of the machine. It was not something happening *with* them.

With little choice and no room for negotiation, the white members of the commission met with the city leaders. With no black input, however, the results were decidedly mixed. Both sides hailed the meeting as a total success and a landmark moment in the history of race relations in Memphis. Although the details of the meeting and what was discussed were not made public, both sides celebrated and said that any previous tensions had been the result of misunderstandings. The Reverend Alfred Loaring-Clark of St. John's Episcopal Church stated, "We had a very happy conference. . . . From beginning to end, no antagonism was shown and the city stated its intentions of continuing the policy of help and consideration of all negro problems." He went on to describe how "the Interracial Commission stated its objective of better relations between the two races in Memphis. It added that the perfect race relations could better be accomplished by understanding and good will than by force. I think the city agreed in that." The question of social equality between blacks and whites was dismissed with this statement: "No such thing as race equality has ever been mentioned in our meetings. We're all Southerners." The Reverend W. B. Selah of St. John's Methodist Church concurred with Loaring-Clark, saying, "I thought we had a very good meeting and have ironed out any differences that may have existed between city officials and the commission. I believe we will be able to work together." Mayor Chandler was in complete agreement with this assessment: "The ministers who called on us expressed approval of the city's law enforcement program and assured us that their sole desire is to co-operate whenever possible for them to do so. They expressed the feeling that their membership on the commission might enable them to be of good service to the city government in meeting inter-racial problems arising from time to time. Commissioner Boyle and I thanked them and assured them of our appreciation of their good purposes."[27]

Curiously, in the midst of this public celebration, there was no public statement on whether the police occupation of J. B. Martin's store and the surrounding black neighborhoods would end. For all the pomp and circumstance of the meeting, there was nothing tangible to show for it. Perhaps the members of the commission genuinely felt victorious just by virtue of having the opportunity to express their views to those in charge, even if those views had been moderated to an extent. Or, perhaps fearful of the consequences of pushing a more radical agenda, the commission actually bumped up against the limits of what was possible in Jim Crow Memphis in terms of interracial activism.

Although the commission's efforts to end the Reign of Terror ultimately ended with something of a whimper, other ways of addressing the situation were being set in motion. After nearly three solid months of harassment, the news of what was occurring in Memphis eventually filtered out to a national audience, bringing more attention than anyone in the Memphis city government wanted. Ray H. Jenkins, state manager for the Tennessee Republican Party, took note in late November and released a statement that the disenfranchisement of potential Republican voters in Memphis was unconscionable and illegal and needed to be brought to a swift end. In his view, the Reign of Terror "amount[ed] to a confiscation of a person's property," and "that's the most deadly way in the world to put a man out of business." Boyle, in typical blustery fashion, advised Jenkins "to keep [his] hands out of Memphis" and warned him, "When you endeavor to defend J. B. Martin, do you realize you are defending one who is a common fence dealing in stolen property whose police record is notorious in this community and further has been the subject of a narcotic investigation?" As he had told the commission, Boyle went on to write, "you are undertaking to defend practices that no honorable man would countenance."[28]

If Boyle, Chandler, and Crump thought they could avoid an outside investigation into their affairs, they were sorely mistaken. On a national level, there was no institution more dedicated to exposing and ending the machinations in Memphis than the black newspaper the *Chicago Defender*. Martin and other local blacks had reached out to the *Defender* in an effort to draw national attention to their story, in the hope that Crump and Boyle would relent. The *Defender*, having a long-standing national reputation as an advocate of black rights and a long-standing grudge against Boss Crump himself, was more than happy to oblige and ran frequent editorials excoriating the "tyrant" at the head of Memphis politics. Moreover, the paper called on both the Department of Justice and President Roosevelt to do something about the injustices taking place in Memphis.[29]

At the same time, the Justice Department was being pressured by the Southern Conference for Human Welfare (SCHW), an Alabama-based civil rights organization that had been keeping a close watch on events in Memphis. The SCHW sent a letter to the Justice Department damning the Memphis government and citing six specific acts that required federal intervention:

> 1. In retaliation for black community organizing over supporting other presidential candidates than the one Crump preferred, the Memphis police began a systematic campaign designed to drive Martin and other black community leaders out of business "under the guise" of law enforcement. 2. The Memphis police had threatened to "run out of town" "scores" of black Memphians who opposed the Crump regime politically, most notably black newspaper editors and writers. 3. "Scores" of blacks had been arrested solely on a loosely defined charge of "loitering" and nothing else. 4. On segregated streetcars, black Memphians had been routinely provoked to anger by Memphis police in an effort to give the police department "a pretext for wholesale violence." 5. Memphis authorities stockpiled numerous submachine guns in anticipation of their use being necessary in what they saw as the likely event of a full-on race riot. 6. Members of the Interracial Religious Commission had been pressured to cancel a planned conference scheduled for late December because of what police referred to as "reliable evidence" that the conference was meant to be a build-up to a race riot.[30]

Perhaps most pointedly, the SCHW was highly critical of Boss Crump himself, who was trying to stay in the background of Memphis politics but was still the de facto head of the city and responsible for the actions of his subordinates. The letter went on:

These conditions do evidence that a race riot situation is being fanned by the authorities of Memphis, including Ed. H. Crump. As to what reasons lie behind this series of arrests, threats and intimidations, we are not clear. . . . Mr. Crump is apparently fearful that the abolition of the poll tax system in the South will bring a measure of freedom and independence to the citizens of Memphis and make it more difficult for his machine to attempt to herd the voters to the polls to vote for his candidates. He is evidently determined to stamp out any movement for independence in Memphis. By these means, Ed Crump and the city administration of Memphis, which he controls, are seeking to establish an efficient dictatorship which could be used as a pattern to undermine democracy in other parts of the United States, especially in the South. This situation in Memphis calls for the immediate intervention of federal authorities and the Department of Justice to maintain order and elementary American rights in Memphis. We expect that you will use your high authority to intervene in Memphis to maintain order and preserve peace and liberty for the people of Memphis.[31]

Facing such pressure, the Justice Department capitulated and sent a representative, Colonel Amos Woodcock, to Memphis to investigate the situation. After interviewing all the relevant parties, Woodcock reported back to the Justice Department, which issued a report concluding that there was evidence of black intimidation in Memphis. Although the department declined to prosecute anyone for the Reign of Terror, curiously arguing that any charges would not stand up in court, it pointedly reminded Commissioner Boyle and the Memphis city government that harassment of the city's black population violated federal civil rights laws and left the city open to consequences in the future. Even with such a weak denouncement of what was occurring in Memphis, an important point had been made. The normally loquacious Boyle issued a terse statement that read, "We are going to police the store in a different manner." Boyle, Chandler, and Crump refused to comment further on the reasons for their abrupt reversal of position. Thus, after three months of round-the-clock occupation of J. B. Martin's drugstore and the surrounding neighborhood, Boyle finally pulled his police off surveillance duty.[32]

Historians Michael Honey and Laurie Green, among others, have showcased the rigors of daily life under the oppressive rule of Jim Crow. These scholars have revealed in shocking detail the often brutally violent methods employed by those in power to disenfranchise black Memphians both politically and economically. Honey described Memphis during the first half of the twentieth century as a "stronghold of one of the toughest political bosses ever to emerge in the United States, Edward H. Crump."[33] Green described Memphis's pervasive and enduring "plantation mentality" during the Jim Crow era, which she defined as an explicit desire on the part of white Memphians in positions of authority and public influence to hold on to an antebellum way of thinking—in effect, acting as if they were slaveholders without actually owning slaves.[34]

Memphis, as these scholars and others have uncovered, was a gilded city in terms of racial politics. That is, it appeared harmonious to the casual observer, but beneath the veneer of racial cooperation between the city's all-white power structure and its black community laid a bedrock of racial antagonism, violence, and political corruption dependent on the coercion of black voters. That veneer of peaceful relations was the very livelihood of Crump and his political machine for four decades. By working to portray Memphis as a city of racial harmony where blacks were happy with their lot in life, Crump and his regime convinced voters year after year that Memphis was not like other southern cities. It was free from the rioting and urban rebellions that plagued other cities with large black populations. Maintaining this illusion, however, sometimes necessitated drastic action on the part of Crump and his lieutenants. It also required the willingness of some black leaders to look the other way in the face of the machine's oppression.

To a certain extent, the fact that the Crump machine had to resort to open and prolonged harassment was a sign of desperation. In the past, such racially oppressive actions had almost always been done out of the public eye. The Reign of Terror marked a recognition that united black political activism represented a threat to the long-standing racial order in Memphis. For as much as the Reign of Terror was meant to intimidate Memphis's African American population into political submission, it was also an attempt to sow discord and destroy black political unity. And it worked. After the Reign of Terror was over, whenever certain black Memphians opposed the draconian measures of the Crump regime, Crump no longer needed to send in his own troops, as he had in the fall of 1940.

Some of the fiercest opponents of so-called black agitators in Memphis were other black Memphians. Those who had accepted Crump and Boyle's explanation for the Reign of Terror became not only spies but also mouthpieces who could be called on whenever "proof" was needed that black Memphians were content with Crump's policies. For example, in 1943 famed black labor leader A. Phillip Randolph was invited to speak in Memphis by the Reverend George Love of Mt. Nebo Baptist Church. This naturally drew the ire of the Crump machine, which denounced Randolph as a "blatherskite" and "demagogue" intent on "interfer[ing] with the friendly relations between the races that now exists in Memphis."[35] In these sentiments, Crump was backed up by black leaders such as W. S. Martin, George Lee, Blair Hunt, and Ashton Hayes, who all met Randolph at the train station to inform him that he was not welcome in Memphis and would not be allowed to speak as planned.[36] Hunt, who was the principal of all-black Booker T. Washington High School, liked to describe himself as just a "little brown nut in the Crump machine." He even went so far as to pen an editorial in the local press denouncing Randolph and the black pastor who had invited him to town.[37] The *Chicago Defender* called Crump's black allies "the unwilling tools of a Fascist demagogue," while Randolph referred to them as "spineless negro stooges."[38]

Memphis's black leaders had never been monolithic in their political thoughts, but it is undeniable that after the events of the fall of 1940, a new level of separation and vitriol was introduced. To a certain extent, siding with Crump must have seemed like a logical choice. The Crump brand was familiar, and it provided tangible evidence of power and influence. Serving nearly uninterrupted for decades as Memphis's paterfamilias, Crump signified power, order, and stability, whatever the actual merits and qualities of his leadership may have been. To a black community besieged by violence and disruption, this proved to be a powerful lure, even if the source of that violence and disruption was none other than Crump himself. Those who chose to organize against Crump's machine now faced a much more uncertain future as far as black political activism in Memphis went. Creating change in Memphis never would have been easy, but now the challenges of doing so must have seemed nearly insurmountable.

The message of the Reign of Terror had been received and the damage had been done. For months, blacks patronizing J. B. Martin's drugstore had witnessed the spectacle of other blacks being assaulted and hauled off to jail by the dozens each and every day. Martin eventually abandoned Memphis and its racial politics for Chicago, turning over the pharmacy, which had been passed down to him from his father, to his son. Even years after the Reign of Terror ended, T. O. Fuller would continue to report Martin's movements to Crump and Chandler.[39]

The Reign of Terror in some ways represented the last gasp and wild thrashing of a dying regime. Gritter claims that the Reign of Terror revealed Crump's "tenuous" grasp on power at this time. "The extent to which the political boss felt that he had to manipulate black and white votes and crack down on those who threatened his control revealed his own insecurity," she argues.[40] By enacting a systematic repression of black political power, Crump ensured himself a prominent role in shaping the course of Memphis politics for another decade and a half, up until his death in 1954. While he may have come out on top, black Memphians' will to organize and to fight disenfranchisement never went away. The next few decades in Memphis's racial history would be fraught with conflict, both external and internal. The Reign of Terror was only a prologue for things to come.

Notes

1. G. Wayne Dowdy, "E. H. Crump and the Mayors of Memphis," *West Tennessee Historical Society Papers* 53 (1999): 86; G. Wayne Dowdy, *Mayor Crump Don't Like It: Machine Politics in Memphis* (Jackson: University Press of Mississippi), 12–14.

2. Kenneth W. Goings and Gerald L. Smith, "'Unhidden Transcripts': Memphis and African American Agency, 1862–1920," *Journal of Urban History* 21, no. 3 (March 1995): 375–76.

3. Laurie B. Green, *Battling the Plantation Mentality: Memphis and the Black Freedom Struggle* (Chapel Hill: University of North Carolina Press, 2007), 33.

4. Green, *Battling the Plantation Mentality*, 5–6.

5. Ibid., 37–39.

6. "Ask Roosevelt to Halt Memphis Police Terror," *Chicago Defender,* December 28, 1940; "Expect Whitewash of Memphis Terror," *Chicago Defender,* January 18, 1941.

7. "Customers Searched at Negro Business," *Memphis Commercial Appeal,* October 26, 1940; "Boyle Keeps His Eyes on 19 Negroes: They're Fanning Race Feeling in Memphis, Commissioner Believes, Aided by Red Agitators" *Memphis Commercial Appeal,* December 11, 1940; "For Safety of All," *Memphis Commercial Appeal,* December 12, 1940.

8. William H. Chafe, *Remembering Jim Crow: African Americans Tell about Life in the Segregated South* (New York: New Press, 2001), xxx.

9. Elizabeth Gritter, *River of Hope: Black Politics and the Memphis Freedom Movement, 1865–1954* (Lexington: University Press of Kentucky, 2014), 3.

10. Ibid., 140–43.

11. Green, *Battling the Plantation Mentality,* 38–39.

12. Chafe, *Remembering Jim Crow,* xxxii.

13. "Customers Searched at Negro Business," *Memphis Commercial Appeal,* October 26, 1940.

14. "Searchings Continue at Negro Drug Store," *Memphis Commercial Appeal,* October 27, 1940.

15. "Mayor Backs Boyle in Antidrug Crusade," *Memphis Commercial Appeal,* November 1, 1940.

16. "We'll Have No Race Trouble, Says Boyle, Declares Fanning of Hatred Must Come to End, Negroes Get Warning," *Memphis Commercial Appeal,* December 12, 1940; Joe Boyle, "For Safety of All," *Memphis Commercial Appeal,* December 12, 1940; "Boyle Keeps His Eyes on 19 Negroes," *Memphis Commercial Appeal,* December 12, 1940.

17. "The Guest Writer: Reds and Race Prejudice," *Memphis Commercial Appeal,* December 12, 1940; "We'll Have No Race Trouble, Says Boyle," *Memphis Commercial Appeal,* December 12, 1940.

18. W. S. Martin to E. H. Crump, November 1, 1940, E. H. Crump Collection, Memphis Public Library.

19. J. B. Martin to Dr. T. O. Fuller, November 7, 1940, Crump Collection.

20. Dr. T. O. Fuller to E. H. Crump, March 23, March 26, April 16, 1942; baseball ticket from Dr. T. O. Fuller to E. H. Crump, June 27, 1940, Crump Collection.

21. Dr. T. O. Fuller to E. H. Crump, March 23, March 26, April 16, 1942.

22. "Knife-Toting Negroes Fined $3000 in Court," *Memphis Commercial Appeal,* November 15, 1940; "Boyle's Crime Fight Is Showing Results, Theft and Homicide Reports Down 50%," *Memphis Commercial Appeal,* December 20, 1940; "Police Drive Results Reflected in Court, Only Two Fines for Carrying Weapons Levied," *Memphis Commercial Appeal,* December 19, 1940.

23. "Mass Meeting Is Planned by Racial Groups: Whites, Negroes Will Meet to Further Improvement of Relations," *Memphis Press-Scimitar,* January 28,

1941; "Politics, Says Negro Pastor: Referring to Charges Made in Boyle Letter," *Memphis Commercial Appeal,* December 6, 1940; "Boyle Declines to Meet Interracial Commission: Sternly Rebukes Group in Letter Sent to Dr. Howie, Chairman of Organization," *Memphis Press-Scimitar,* December 5, 1940.

24. "Boyle Issues Strong Rebuke to Group for Racial Charges," *Memphis Commercial Appeal,* December 5, 1940.

25. "Boyle Declines to Meet Interracial Commission," *Memphis Press-Scimitar,* December 5, 1940.

26. "Politics, Says Negro Pastor," *Memphis Commercial Appeal,* December 6, 1940.

27. "Racial Commission and City Fathers in Harmony," *Memphis Press-Scimitar,* December 1940.

28. "Boyle Tells Jenkins to Keep 'Hands Out': Nashville Republican Protests Policing of Drug Store," *Memphis Commercial Appeal,* November 29, 1940.

29. "Petition FDR to End Tenn. Police Terror," *Chicago Defender,* February 15, 1941.

30. "U.S. Investigator Reports on Charges that Memphis Negroes Are Intimidated, Col. Woodcock, Here for Four Days, Gives Findings to Attorney General on Charge of Abuse by Police," *Memphis Press-Scimitar,* January 8, 1941.

31. Ibid.

32. "J-Man Reports on Memphis Negro Inquiry—Here's Result: Tells Jackson Evidence that Police Violated Civil Rights Wouldn't Stand in Court—Spoke to Boyle," *Memphis Press-Scimitar,* January 9, 1941; "Police Abandon Store Picketing: Searching of Dr. Martin's Customers Halted," *Memphis Press-Scimitar,* December 1940; "Searching of Dr. Martin's Customers Halted," *Memphis Commercial Appeal,* December 1940.

33. Michael K. Honey, *Southern Labor and Black Civil Rights: Organizing Memphis Workers* (Urbana: University of Illinois Press, 1993), 8.

34. Green, *Battling the Plantation Mentality,* 6, 21.

35. "Crump Says Memphis Can Run Own Affairs," *Memphis Commercial Appeal,* November 13, 1943.

36. "Crump Bans Memphis Rally for Randolph," *Chicago Defender,* November 13, 1943.

37. Enoc P. Waters, "Memphis Forgets Its Blues as War Boom Lifts Negro's Status: He Was Run Out—But He Stayed," *Chicago Defender,* January 23, 1943; "Echoes of Cancelled Meeting Contained in Principal's Letter to Friends and Press," *Memphis World,* November 23, 1943.

38. "Fascism in Memphis," *Chicago Defender,* December 4, 1943; "Randolph Scores Attitude of Memphis Labor Leaders," *Memphis World,* April 4, 1944.

39. Dr. T. O. Fuller to Mayor Walter Chandler, May 4, 1942, Crump Collection; Gritter, *River of Hope,* 149–50.

40. Gritter, *River of Hope,* 173.

Power and Protection

Gender and Black Working-Class Protest Narratives, 1940–1948

Laurie B. Green

In June 1944 twenty-two-year-old Evelyn Bates finally landed a job at Firestone Tire and Rubber Company. Over the past year she had responded to newspaper ads for female defense workers, only to find that employers did not post these openings at the employment office assigned to African Americans.[1] After Firestone's doors finally opened to black women, Bates donned high heels and a full skirt to make her appear larger, passed a written test, and was sent out to the plant, where she was hired. Since graduating from Manassas High School, Bates had cooked in a private household, worked at a whites-only cafeteria as a "salad girl," pressed clothes at a dry cleaners, and spent a few hours trying to lift a sledgehammer to pound springs at National Rose Bedding before walking out. Her journey from domestic servant to factory worker indicates the lengths to which many young black women were willing to go to change the equation of their jobs and identities. Bates had beaten the odds; although thousands of white women worked in Memphis's war industry, most defense contractors refused to hire African American women. Firestone was one of the few to do so, but only late in the war, and only in small numbers. Soon after Bates started there, however, white workers shut down production to protest management's reassignment of a white men's bathroom to black women. And unlike the white female workers, the black women swept floors, cleaned bathrooms, and performed grueling labor such as piling up slabs of rubber or sorting tires in the blazing sun and freezing cold, all while earning less than their white counterparts.[2]

During World War II, African Americans strenuously contested unfair hiring practices, racially coded job classifications, and subpar wages. Their letters to the president, grievances to their unions, and complaints to federal agencies revealed their feelings about language and actions that denigrated and demonized them as women and men, in addition to the tangible inequities they challenged. Federal oversight of the defense economy opened avenues for workers and job applicants to skirt the power of employment authorities, defense contractors, and public officials affiliated with Boss Edward H. Crump's political machine, which intervened in labor matters to an extraordinary degree. Women toiling in industrial laundries, which were classified as essential to defense, complained about sexual intimidation in addition to unfair wages and classifications. In black working men's and women's gendered narratives about these injustices, they represented themselves as skilled workers, astute critics, or potential victims of forced intimacies by white supervisors, characterizations that countered those deployed by employers.

Fourteen months after Bates started at Firestone, just before the United States dropped atomic bombs on Hiroshima and Nagasaki, public outcry erupted in a different, potentially more lethal realm of everyday black life—the urban space outside the workplace. This time, the protest was triggered when two young black women who worked the late shift at a café were raped by police officers. These assaults were not isolated incidents; Bates, in fact, had quit her first job as a domestic servant partly because she had to wait alone at the bus stop on nights when her employer kept her late to help with the parties she hosted. The vulnerability of young black working women had become acute during the war, when anti-vice and anti–venereal disease policies gave patrolmen blanket authority to arrest women on the streets. Parents of other young women who had been sexually abused had muffled their distress because they feared reprisals. This time, the two mothers' indignation at the police chief's concoction of a story that cast their daughters as syphilitic prostitutes led them to publicly voice their own narratives and feelings in an interview for a front-page story in a daily newspaper. The intensity of protest among blacks angered by police brutality and cover-ups, as well as by white moderates intent on exposing the Crump machine's corruption, persuaded Shelby County's attorney general, a Crump confidant, to take this case to court—the first involving assaults on black women by white men.

These two vigorous movements for racial justice—one about rac-ist labor practices, the other about police brutality and sexual assault—addressed different realms of everyday life. When analyzed together, they reveal much about broader ferment in wartime and early postwar Mem-phis. Increasingly, historians of the black freedom movement in the urban South do not restrict their research to legal battles over voting rights and segregation, nor to middle-class leaders; they search out the grass-roots history of working-class African Americans who energized or forged new movements for racial justice. We still need to do more, however, to explore why black men and women emboldened by union struggles did not shed their activist identities when they passed through the factory gates. They added thousands of members to the NAACP roster, joined civic clubs, registered to vote, attended mass meetings, and contributed to legal funds to expose cover-ups of police violence that might have involved neighbors, church members, or even relatives. When police bru-tality became a flash point for working-class protest at the end of the war, it augmented labor organizing.

Working-class African American women and men articulated their understandings of racial justice as they organized against labor inequities and police violence in the urban South. This essay pays close attention to personal and political narratives these women and men conveyed about their treatment as workers in letters to the president, grievances, com-plaints, and oral histories. Their appeals for support cited occurrences of supervisors insisting that they restricted African Americans to unskilled job classifications because they were incapable of completing the work that whites performed, and these black workers posited their own coun-ternarratives. This essay likewise examines petitions, affidavits, reports, and newspaper articles that illuminate the meanings of protests against police brutality and rape among working-class black Memphians who attended mass meetings, jammed the courthouse gallery, and contrib-uted to legal funds. The black community denounced the police chief's portrayal of the patrolmen who committed acts of violence as morally superior to black survivors, whom he described in terms of male bestiality or female sexual aggression. Black narratives related the stories of these assaults from the opposite perspective, well aware that bringing justice in these cases rested directly on which narrative won out. The emotions expressed in their narratives, in addition to their content, illuminate what was at stake for those demanding racial justice on the cusp of the postwar era.

Intangible Inequities

The racially coded and gendered distinctions in hiring, classification, and wage structures imposed by Memphis's defense contractors during World War II were not merely extensions of entrenched racist practices. Federal oversight of the defense economy had destabilized unwritten laws that had long subordinated blacks to whites in Memphis industry. In 1941 President Roosevelt unleashed both new expectations and animosities when, in a last-ditch effort to head off a planned March on Washington by up to 100,000 African Americans, he issued Executive Order 8802, which banned discrimination in the defense industry, unions, and federal agencies on the basis of "race, creed, color, or national origin."[3] The Fair Employment Practices Commission (FEPC) he created could investigate charges of discrimination and hold hearings, but it lacked enforcement power; nonetheless, black Memphians who perceived the war as a fight against fascism abroad and racism at home flooded the office with complaints in the hope of enlisting the FEPC's help in challenging their employers, who had the backing of Boss Crump's political machine. Because the federal directive stated that labor disputes in the defense industry must be settled by mediation, not strikes, the National War Labor Board (NWLB) and US Conciliation Service served as arbiters in unfair labor practices cases. This restructuring forced defense contractors and Crump officials to justify discriminatory practices. As black women and men described in complaints to Roosevelt, to the FEPC, and to union leaders, white bosses discriminated, in part, by maligning their intelligence, capability, or morality, not as personal qualities but in terms of race and gender.

Soaring employment and Roosevelt's executive order created both new expectations and frustrations for Memphis's black workers. From September 1942 to September 1943, nonagricultural employment in the city nearly doubled from 27,269 workers to 48,857. Ford began manufacturing airplane engines; Fisher Body became Fisher Aircraft, a subassembly plant for B-25s and B-29s; Firestone produced rafts, army vehicle tires, and gas masks; Continental Can turned out shell cases; and Kimberly-Clark and Quaker Oats opened new facilities. Procter & Gamble's Buckeye Cotton Oil Company, Chickasaw Ordnance, and National Fireworks contributed to the nation's ammunition supply, and new military supply depots and hospitals became major employers.[4] Longtime residents and migrants from the surrounding cotton region responded by lining up at the Memphis offices of the US Employment Service (USES), determined to secure better jobs; however, African Americans encountered exclusionary practices when it came to obtaining jobs in these manufacturing plants and military facilities. Men found themselves restricted to common laborer classifications and wages, while women had a hard time locating any defense work at all outside of laundries. Susie Brister, a resident of South Memphis, wrote to President Roosevelt in July 1942 to express her bitterness at receiving no referrals for job openings other than as a maid. There was "a fence around the jobs here against Colored people," she declared, and he needed to "tear [it] down."[5]

At the USES, managers' efforts to appear nondiscriminatory while upholding segregation created aggravating experiences for black applicants, convincing many of them to write letters to federal officials as a means of protest. Southern USES managers divided their offices into "white" and "colored" areas, but FEPC investigators learned that Memphis and other Tennessee cities maintained these offices in two entirely different locations. That arrangement allowed the local USES to post work orders slated for whites at one office and those for African Americans at the other, without any explicit reference to race.[6] Black female applicants became exasperated with what Margaret Jackson described as "a long hot tramp of trying to get work," only to be refused entry at the office listed in an ad.[7] Ella Rose Dotson, who appealed to Roosevelt for help from October 1942 until February 1944, described visiting the employment office on South Second near Beale Street, where she found no postings for defense jobs, then traipsing to the downtown office on Union, only to be sent back to South Second, where "they didn't give me any work, only said they could give me white lady day work in their homes which they have always gave me but that is not defence work to help my country."[8] Jackson's and Dotson's letters asked Roosevelt to see

Firestone Tire and Rubber Company. (Courtesy Memphis and Shelby County Room, Memphis Public Library)

them as real women—exhausted, frustrated, offended by their treatment by a federal agency, and deserving of the same opportunities as white women.

Women sought support and respect by infusing their stories with feelings and analysis. Dotson's quest for defense work ended in 1944 at a small Memphis plant, after the FEPC found the USES in violation of a federal guideline requiring duplicate job postings in "colored" and "white" offices. However, her refusal to accept the first defense job she was offered, as a charwoman (factory maid) in Knoxville, prompted FEPC regional official A. Bruce Hunt to reassert that she was only qualified to be a maid. In a letter to Hunt, Dotson pressed him to consider her feelings: "Mr. Hunt, you will find me to state the truth about things if it hurt me, because it is the only way in life." Dotson's extraordinary persistence won her a job, but not until the war was nearly over.

Almost universally, black Memphians who labored in defense plants, military hospitals, and industrial laundries confronted dual wage structures and contradictory job classifications that devalued their labor in relation to that of white workers. The lower wage rates could cause severe economic hardship. At an NWLB hearing in June 1942, federal mediator John Green, speaking for the union's position, explained that because of Procter & Gamble's wage system in its southern Buckeye plants, workers "are unable to purchase sufficient food and other necessities without falling into debt. Consequently, an increasing number of men are being garnished every pay day." This "untenable practice" could "not be condoned by the fact that it is the custom in the area," he argued, rebutting the company's stance.[9]

If "southern tradition" alone could not justify wage disparities, job classifications could. As a result, the two issues became entangled as black workers pushed their unions and the federal government to redress their restriction to unskilled classifications with lower pay than that received by whites with higher classifications who performed similar tasks. At Fisher Aircraft, where white workers dominated one of the city's largest workforces—6,687 workers by 1943—black workers held officers' feet to the fire at United Auto Workers Local 988 when it came to these issues. At Buckeye Cotton Oil, with a significant black majority, they formed the militant core of organizing within Local 19 of the radical-led United Cannery, Agricultural, and Packinghouse Workers of America. Workers also reached out to black community activists and FEPC officials when they grew frustrated with stalling tactics by their unions or the NWLB.

Formal grievance procedures, however, did not fully capture their outrage at managers' denigration of their characters, particularly claims that they were incapable of performing complex jobs because they lacked the requisite mental capacity. Black workers interpreted such psychological abuse as attempts to rationalize their classifications. In 1944, for instance, some black workers at Fisher Aircraft complained to the FEPC that their foreman had restricted them to the most basic manual labor—loading products into ovens—and lowered their classification. As described by Fisher employee Osie King, "The white man with [me] would relieve me of all tabulating and chart reading" and rise to a higher classification.[10]

This disparagement of black employees' intelligence and capabilities sometimes extended beyond the factory floor, as occurred in another Fisher case that went to the US Conciliation Service. In October 1943 Lawrence Matlock and his coworkers complained to the union and the FEPC that they had been hired as file-burr workers (to file down sharp metal edges) but were classified and paid as common laborers. Matlock wrote: "During my employ at Fishers, many whites have been employed as riveters with nothing more than the training experience in a government sponsored school as I had," yet no blacks held such positions. After the case stalled at the US Conciliation Service, the frustrated men consulted outspoken Memphis Urban League director Benjamin Bell, who negotiated their transfer to bench assembly, a semiskilled job that included riveting. This shift did not stanch their complaints after the men learned that whites performing the same tasks were classified and paid at a higher level.[11] They were likely unaware that Memphis mayor Walter Chandler had surreptitiously intervened after the president of the Chamber of Commerce contacted him. Chandler coached Memphis's congressman Clifford Davis on how to approach US Conciliation Service chief John Steelman to ensure that nothing changed at Fisher. "Naturally, if wage differentials which have existed in the South because of the superior mental ability of the white worker are to be destroyed, I fear for the negro's welfare here," he wrote. If black workers competed with whites, they would lose their jobs when the economy weakened and "become a charge on the public." This would "destroy the negro's own advancement and cause him to lose the gains that he has made." According to Davis, Steelman assured him that the case would not see the light of day anytime soon.[12]

Like at Fisher, workers at Buckeye utilized their own powers of analysis. Buckeye's Hollywood plant, which ran the world's largest cottonseed-crushing operation, employed a workforce of 250, 90 percent of it African American; at the Jackson Avenue plant in the Binghampton neighborhood, a workforce of 750 to 950, 70 percent of it African American, produced cotton linters for smokeless gunpowder.[13] Since Procter & Gamble opened its first cottonseed-processing facility in Mississippi in 1901, the workforces at is southern Buckeye operations had resembled those on plantations.[14] In 1942, according to Lucius Jones and Charles Burton, their foreman informed them that they would be replaced by "men with more intelligence" after new expeller machinery was installed. This change was implemented in May, and the white workers were paid 90 to 95 cents an hour; months later, black men were put back on the job at a rate of 60.6 cents an hour. In a parallel case heard by the Regional War Labor Board (RWLB) in 1943, a supervisor had replaced black wash tank operators with white workers because, he said, they were inefficient, even though the blacks workers had taught their replacements how to run the tanks. He reassigned them as bleach tank operators, a classification that required them to perform the same tasks for less pay. Sixteen men walked off their jobs and demanded a review in June after the RWLB ruled in favor of Buckeye.[15]

Black men who assembled and disassembled machines and did general repair work repeatedly filed grievances and FEPC complaints against classifications that cast them as servile by nature. The wartime context enabled them to collectively organize against their designation as "helpers" and that of newly hired whites as "apprentices" or "learners." The "helper" title had no logical connection to their experience, skills, or actual responsibilities and had entrapped some workers for years. Eldridge Westbrooks, an employee since the 1920s, asserted that he did "everything a millwright does" but remained a "millwright's helper," and Harry Owens asserted that he still labored as a mechanic's helper for 50 cents an hour—more than 10 cents less than apprentices earned. Unlike the "helpers" who trained them, apprentices and learners advanced over time into increasingly higher classifications.[16]

Although a majority of black women remained domestic workers in private households, thousands entered defense work through laundries and dry cleaners in either military facilities or commercial establishments that were reclassified as essential to the war effort. White women also worked in laundries, but many pursued factory work as jobs opened up.[17] Even laundry workers who made the lowest wages took home more than maids and cooks, and they relished leaving the isolation and personal control of household service. However, they endured steamy conditions, slippery floors, and unsanitary workrooms without chairs, drinking fountains, or adequate restrooms. African American women, who typically operated the hot, heavy pressing machines—as did Evelyn Bates at Herbert Cleaners—averaged only 20 to 28 cents per hour, and those who were paid by the piece might press up to 500 shirts a day.[18] Black laundry workers in industrial laundries, whether in military hospitals or civilian businesses that cleaned the uniforms of servicemen, protested racist pay differentials and job classifications, poor working conditions, practices that gave white women power over black women, and sexual harassment. They took particular umbrage at opposing racial constructions of black and white women that pit them against each other.

Coverage in local newspapers helped turn laundry workers' protests into community issues. The *Memphis World,* a black publication, allotted space to women's stories of supervisors' abuse of power, economic subterfuge, and disrespect. Employees at several of Memphis's fourteen commercial establishments joined the Laundry Workers International Union, and there were strikes for union recognition at Crescent Laundry, Model Laundry-Cleaners, and Kraus Cleaners, each of which employed hundreds of workers. In the first strike since Loeb's Laundry opened in 1887, roughly 200 employees walked out in August 1945. Such conflicts came under the aegis of the US Conciliation Service, the War Labor Board, and the FEPC after 1943.[19] Loeb's Laundry workers told a *World* reporter that management refused to tell them how much they had earned before actually distributing their pay—a practice that must have struck a chord for those who had come from plantations. And a 1943 article about a mass rally in support of a strike at Kraus quoted a worker who "resented the fact that Kraus officials practiced the habit of searching their personal pocketbooks, as if they were deceitful."[20] Her statement about this unwarranted intrusion resonated with complaints about other, more intimate violations elsewhere.

Laundry workers at Kennedy General Hospital had no right to unionize because the facility, opened in 1942, was under military command, but they complained to the FEPC about wages, classifications, and their treatment by laundry manager Albert Hattendorf. In December 1943 thirty-eight workers signed a petition demanding a pay raise to rectify the inequity between white and black women's wages. Gertrude Carter, who had initiated the petition along with Katie Hall, learned from white coworkers the following April that Hattendorf had raised the white women's wages. According to their complaints, Carter and Hall monitored the presses and kept track of finished items, which involved expertise and responsibility. But Hattendorf classified them as press operators, while categorizing white women who performed the same duties at a higher level. FEPC investigator John Hope later reported that not one of Hattendorf's classifications applied to both black and white workers. The women he interviewed described the manager's contempt; he refused to raise their wages, and "if they didn't like it they could get out" because he could replace them with German prisoners "for ten cents an hour." Even more significant, the women decried his rule that black women had to ask permission to use the restroom from white women with higher classifications. This requirement constructed an intimate power relation within an industrial workplace, forcing black women's subjugation to white women who had the power to either accommodate or humiliate them.[21]

In 1942 the Negro Chamber of Commerce and Housewives League circulated their own petition—not about real laundry workers but about white sexualization and romanticization of the iconic laundry worker. The petition, signed by hundreds, condemned White Rose Laundry's new "mechanical sign" displaying a "Negro washer-woman" laundering underwear. According to the petition, the owners should honor the "poor Negro mothers" who "humbly supported their children and educated them to be worthy and respectable citizens of a great country." This language removed any hint of sexuality from this symbolic figure, yet it contrasted with the idealized "Mammy" figure that sacrificed for whites, which White Rose claimed to honor. The petition universalized this disrespect as "a complete effrontery to Negro people" who performed "many servile tasks."[22]

Actual African American laundry workers at the Veterans' Hospital appealed to the FEPC in the spring of 1945 regarding the most serious type of forced intimacy: sexual coercion by a white male supervisor.[23] Three women—former Kennedy General employee Gertrude Carter, along with Dovie McManius, and Mammie Holloway—expressed desperation after being dismissed from their badly needed jobs. They claimed they had been fired not because of their poor performance, as the plant manager maintained, but because they had refused to "date" newly hired supervisor Albert Miller. Before that, they argued, they had received "very good" or "excellent" ratings. Holloway added that plant manager

Dr. H. C. Dodge had fired her for reporting his actions, and Carter stated that Miller had asked her what she "would charge him for a date." At another point he lay a blanket in the dressing room and "got angry because [she] would not go in there with him." Finally, the women claimed that women who had sex with Miller were allowed to evaluate black coworkers who did not.

Carter, McManius, and Holloway presented this sexual abuse as extreme racist behavior and thus illegal; however, none of the federal officials who reviewed the case supported that characterization, despite sharply divergent opinions about how to proceed. Veterans' Administration personnel director G. H. Sweet backed the laundry manager's statement that he had fired the women because of their poor performance and dismissed their complaints as unfounded "allegations." The director of the Fifth Civil Service Region, O. E. Myers, concluded that the actions did "not constitute racial discrimination." FEPC regional director Witherspoon Dodge, a southern Congregational minister and former union organizer, retorted that even if Miller's behavior could not be defined as racial discrimination, some agency should "afford job protection for decent people of all races against . . . personally immoral and socially economic depredations." The case file ended in October 1945, as the FEPC was being shuttered.

Black men and women who organized inside and outside of unions collectively strove to eliminate injustices in hiring, classification, and wage structures. Ostensibly, federal oversight of the nation's defense economy should have enforced objective standards, but often it did not. In Memphis, however, that federal intervention opened routes whereby working-class African Americans could press for equity outside of channels controlled by the Crump machine—even though the FEPC ultimately had only limited power, and Memphis officials found ways to interfere behind closed doors. Those who wrote letters, filled out complaint forms, filed grievances, and gave interviews brought critical physical and emotional dimensions to stories about their subordination as black women and men—about enduring "long hot tramps" that ended with "day work" instead of war work, being classified as "helpers" instead of "learners," or performance ratings that were tied to forced intimacy. Their language in these formal communications may have differed from the language they used at home, but their passionate critiques of the maligning of men's intelligence and women's moral character carried over into struggles in a different sphere of everyday life after the war.

Protest Narratives: Vulnerability and the Politics of Protection

As Carter, Hall, and McManius pressed the FEPC for help, public outcry erupted over the rapes of two young African American women and a police cover-up that cast not the perpetrators but the young women themselves as threats to society. On August 3, 1945, at 1:30 a.m., two police officers accosted the women at a bus stop in midtown just after they left work at a café.[24] Unlike the sexual abuse of the Veterans' Hospital laundry workers, these assaults did not take place on the job; however, young working-class women—especially African Americans—who worked late shifts far from their neighborhoods faced serious risks. Ferment over incidents of police sexual abuse of women had mounted during the war; now it sparked community activism and a rare public challenge to language that depicted these women as licentious and infectious. The Crump machine's notoriety for police brutality—from the "Reign of Terror" against union organizers and black migrants in 1940 to beatings of black servicemen and veterans, labor activists, and others during the war—had imbued police violence with powerful symbolism as the face of public authority in Memphis.

Rumor was the primary means by which news of these sexual assaults circulated. In contrast, this case sparked public statements, mass meetings, and financial contributions across class lines from African Americans and white moderates who represented the young women as vulnerable and innocent.[25] The *Press-Scimitar* described the rapes as "so revolting that [they] shocked even newspapermen." The *World* called them "wantonly and bestially criminal assaults on two young, poor, and defenseless Negro working girls." The Shelby County attorney general took the unprecedented step of prosecuting the policemen.[26]

For working-class black women, nighttime thoroughfares represented both routes home and potential danger as late-shift patrolmen trolled these same avenues for prostitutes. Alice Wright, age seventeen, and Annie Mae Williams, age twenty, had left their jobs as dishwasher and cook at Fred's Café near Poplar and Cleveland and were heading home to their Binghampton neighborhood, a few miles to the east. Each was supporting a son—Wright a fourteen-month-old, and Williams a three-year-old. As they waited for the bus, patrolmen J. W. Torrey and B. J. Lewis drove up and accused them of loitering, implying that they were prostitutes. The women insisted that they had just left work, so the officers demanded to see their health cards, invoking Tennessee's requirement that food service workers certify that they were syphilis free. As all four knew, however, the law mandated that workplaces retain the cards.

In 1939 the Memphis Health Department had used federal funds made available by the National Venereal Disease Control Act of 1938 to open treatment facilities. It encouraged patrolmen to order syphilis tests for women they arrested, and it gave judges the option of quarantining those who tested positive.[27] In 1941 Congress passed the May Act, which expanded federal power to police civilian life in regions with military bases, and twenty-seven Tennessee counties approved local policies designed to "protect soldiers against venereal disease." In the first year, the police arrested 189 women, 70 percent them black, yet blacks and whites had the same rate of syphilis infection.[28] Three years later, escalating pressure from African Americans about abuse of power by the police convinced Lieutenant Colonel A. F. Brand, director of the Venereal Disease Department, to dispel "confusion" by explaining that patrolmen could arrest women only for the "violation of some law," that Tennessee required health cards to ensure that food workers did not spread syphilis, and that the city health department administered examinations solely "for the information of employers of domestic help"—a reference to exams performed to appease white women's fears that their maids could give them syphilis through contact with household items such as ashtrays and dishes.[29]

On the night of August 3, the two patrolmen forced Wright and Williams into their squad car and drove north on Cleveland, then east on Jackson Avenue. Amidst vulgar taunts, one of the men ordered Williams to empty the change purse she was clutching, then demanded to know why she had a slip from the ear, nose, and throat clinic, insinuating that she had syphilis. In tears, Williams ripped up the clinic slip; later, police investigators would find the pieces, confirming that the women had not fabricated the story. The circuitous, hour-long drive ended at a secluded, wooded site a mile southeast of the women's homes, off Union Avenue Extended. According to the young women, one officer remarked, "Ain't a S. B. out here. I thought [it] would be full," an indication that Torrey and Lewis were not the only ones who brought women there. Torrey pulled Williams from the car and raped her, while Lewis forced Wright to perform fellatio, threatening to blackjack her when she resisted. The women's statements emphasized that they had fought back, perhaps anticipating that their characters would be smeared. Lewis warned Wright that if she told anyone what had happened he would "put in a claim and it will fall on [you]," referring to charges of prostitution.

Protest originated with their mothers, Viola Wright and Hazel Byrd, immediately after their daughters returned home at 3:00 a.m. and poured out their stories. Domestic workers with several children to support, the two mothers—one separated from her husband, the other a widow— lived next door to each other on Broad Avenue, near the Paradise Grill and the Early Grove Baptist Church (which the Wrights attended) and south of a Buckeye plant. Byrd and her daughter Annie Mae, who was separated from her husband, had moved to Memphis only eight months earlier from Fayette County, a plantation region east of Memphis.[30]

Beginning early Friday morning, narratives emerged that portrayed Alice Wright and Annie Mae Williams from opposing viewpoints. Viola Wright and Hazel Byrd, on one side, and Police Chief Carroll Seabrook, on the other, articulated competing ideas about who needed protection and who should do the protecting. Both narratives impacted public reactions and the subsequent legal proceedings. Throughout the case, the mothers' interviews, affidavits, and court testimony drew on critical and emotional language that transposed typical racist depictions of black men and women with images of white police bestiality and their daughters' vulnerability. According to the mothers' affidavits, after their daughters described being picked up and sexually brutalized, all four of them, along with Alice's sister, discussed what to do for the rest of the night. At 8:00 a.m., Viola Wright and Hazel Byrd rode the bus to the café to inform Fred Dudzick that their daughters were quitting their jobs, to ensure their safety. "Mr. Fred," a white Mississippi native in his late thirties who boarded at a house nearby, urged them to report the assaults and offered to accompany them to the police station. Dudzick was likely appalled at this abuse of police power and felt a sense of paternalistic responsibility.[31]

The two mothers took an extraordinary risk by escorting their daughters to the police station and reporting the assaults directly to the police chief. Seabrook spurned their explanations. Instead of seeing their daughters as trauma victims, he labeled them threats to the patrolmen and to the general population he was sworn to protect. According to the mothers' affidavits, Seabrook initially indicated that he would detain Wright and Williams until the next day, but when they returned on Saturday to pick them up, he informed them that he was holding their daughters until Monday and refused to allow them access until then. By Monday, Seabrook had accumulated enough evidence to discredit them. He had arranged a police lineup, for example, but when the young women identified Torrey and Lewis, he threatened to send them to the penal farm, causing them to back off from making a positive identification. Seabrook had also subjected Wright and Williams to blood tests for venereal disease, which found that Wright was healthy but Williams was in the early, contagious stage of syphilis, a claim that contradicted the information on her health card. In order to "keep little children from getting [syphilis]," Seabrook ordered that Williams be remanded to the West Tennessee Medical Center for an eleven-day quarantine. He told Viola Wright to take Alice home and not discuss what had happened. Williams, as it turned out, had grounds to file rape charges, but Wright did not because state law defined rape as forced vaginal intercourse. Meanwhile, police investigators had recovered evidence corroborating the young women's account, including the fragments of the clinic slip and a handkerchief soiled by Torrey. Public Safety Commissioner Joe Boyle, Seabrook's superior, fired the officers but did not arrest them or issue a statement.

Outraged, the mothers defied Seabrook's "gag order" and agreed to an interview with a *Press-Scimitar* reporter. The article politicized the cover-up as evidence of the Crump machine's unbridled corruption, critiquing officials for "trying to cloak in silence a crime committed by two uniformed officers." It portrayed the mothers as humble supporters of their large families and quoted Wright as saying that Seabrook had ordered her to "take [her] daughter, go home, and keep [her] mouth shut."[32] The story used the race and class identities of the beleaguered mothers to dramatize the gross imbalance of power between the women and the police chief, adding fuel to editor Edward Meeman's message about Memphis politics. Earlier, the reporter had sent a confidential letter to H. L. Mitchell, the white cofounder of the Southern Tenant Farmers' Union, headquartered in Memphis. Mitchell forwarded it to black sociologist Charles S. Johnson at Fisk University, who sent it to the national NAACP office. The reporter stated that, on the pretext of checking for health cards, a "number of other young Negro girls have been assaulted by policemen in Memphis but have been fearful to bring their complaints into the open." It also described leading Catholics' response to an incident involving a fifteen-year-old Catholic girl who had been "picked up and held in the city jail for 48 hours." The reporter believed that Shelby County's attorney general might prosecute Torrey and Lewis if enough pressure were brought to bear on him. From New York, Roy Wilkins exhorted the executive secretary of the Memphis branch of the NAACP, railroad postal worker Utillus Phillips, to "make an effort to get justice," despite the climate of terror. The organization's special counsel Thurgood Marshall interlaced local, regional, and national concerns in his own letter: "There has been too much of this type of discriminatory action by policemen in the South, and it is our job to break it down."[33]

The *Memphis World* aimed its coverage at black leaders whose modus operandi had been to cooperate with Crump officials. On August 10 a letter on the front page blasted "an apparently totally demoralized, disorganized, program-less, fearful, 'back gate' talking, 'front page' whispering, bewildered, and supine Negro leadership." The writer held black leaders responsible for not addressing "police brutality, police rapine and coercion of defenseless Negro women and girls, police intimidation of Negro soldiers and defense workers . . . [and] police coercion of an entire segment of the local population under the convenient cloak of disease eradication." He called for a Memphis version of the international conference that had launched the United Nations a few months earlier, in order to "chart a current as well as a post-war program for the civic welfare of the Negroes of Memphis." Four days later, the front page of the *World* featured a reprint of the *Press-Scimitar* article beside an editorial titled "We Must Act on This!" that echoed the earlier piece's caustic tone: "The whole city has had about two weeks now," it declared, "to quiver, shake heads, bemoan, deplore, wax indignant, express disgust, and otherwise castigate a system" in which such an assault could take place; nonetheless, a "creeping moral paralysis" prevailed. Protest snowballed in mid-August as leaders from several quarters took public positions. Crump's allies remained quiet, but the church-based Deacons and Trustees Union issued a statement declaring that "to make Memphis safe," it would face "this challenge like men." Ministerial alliances, civic clubs, and welfare organizations condemned the "bestial outrage," rhetorically assuming the historically dangerous mantle of protecting black women.[34]

Significantly, most who attended mass meetings and made contributions were working-class African Americans, many of them labor activists. Firestone workers had struck in June, and the Loeb's Laundry strike commenced in August; the *World* reported the latter alongside coverage of the campaign to obtain justice for Wright and Williams. The heavily working-class Early Grove Baptist Church in Binghampton became a pillar of the support movement, as did the newly energized NAACP.[35] Branch membership had soared from 400 in 1939 to 1,500 by 1943. It would reach 3,600 by 1946, transforming the NAACP from a moribund organization into a vibrant one dominated by working-class people determined to pursue civil rights on multiple fronts. Combined local and national pressure convinced Memphis NAACP leader Phillips to push for the patrolmen's prosecution by coordinating a defense fund to defray costs for an attorney and assist "the distitute [*sic*] mother of eight children, who is the mother of one of the outraged girls."[36]

In early September, Shelby County's attorney general Will Gerber announced that he would personally prosecute the patrolmen, an unprecedented step in a case involving a white man accused of raping a black woman. A grand jury finally indicted Torrey for rape, a capital offense, and it indicted Lewis for aiding and abetting a capital offense. City leaders, well aware of race riots in other cities and the political condemnation of white moderates, seized the opportunity to display a commitment to justice. Simultaneously, however, Gerber denounced contributors to the NAACP fund and others who censured him for not acting earlier—a tactic that rekindled criticism. African Methodist Episcopal (AME) minister Dwight Kyle, a recent Memphis arrival who now chaired the NAACP

Executive Committee, defended the branch's decision to hire its own attorney to investigate the case.[37]

When the trial opened at the county criminal court in November, Gerber dramatically asked every potential juror—fifty white men—whether he could "give a Negro justice in a case involving a white man" and rejected all who responded negatively. When the court reconvened in late January for the three-day trial, Gerber called Wright and Williams to the stand, along with a series of other witnesses, including police investigators, who corroborated the women's stories. In equally dramatic closing remarks, he exhorted the jurors not to hinge their decisions on "the color question" but to employ "reason, justice and common sense" in order to reach a conclusion "as a family man, citizen, and officer of the State."[38]

If Gerber presented Wright and Williams as truthful and respectable, the defense lawyers followed Seabrook's lead. Attorney Weinstein taunted Annie Mae Williams as "the syphillectice [*sic*] stiff" and Alice Wright as "the mother of the bastard baby." His partner Scruggs tendered his own version of that night's events: "Now isn't the truth of this matter that you . . . went to town on a whoopee party and that your mothers upbraided you for getting home so late and you two made up this 'cock and bull' story?"[39] The outcome hinged on the women's character and chastity, but Weinstein and Scruggs added stereotypes of black women to convince jurors that if sex had occurred, no force was necessary. Weinstein and Scruggs's references to carousing, unwed motherhood, and syphilis overrode Gerber's evidence. The jurors reached a not-guilty verdict in less than an hour.[40]

African Americans made their disapproval of Weinstein and Scruggs known from the segregated gallery, jam-packed on both sides, with more African Americans out in the corridor. When Weinstein accused the women of bringing charges because of NAACP pressure, his reference to the "League for the Protection of Colored People" prompted several black spectators to nudge one another and giggle audibly. Weinstein berated them, and Judge Kinkle sent the jury out of the room before singling out Benjamin Bell for special reproach; Bell's outspokenness as the Urban League executive secretary had led to his dismissal in 1943.[41] Their laughter was in fact political commentary, making them participants instead of passive observers.

The January 24 acquittals of Torrey and Lewis fanned the flames of black opposition. From the point of view of the national legal team led by Thurgood Marshall, a victory had been won just by bringing the case to trial, which would send a warning to southern police officers. Locally, however, the acquittals appalled African Americans, whose voices were now joined by those of returning veterans. In Binghampton, the unpunished rapes of young neighborhood women struck a deep chord, as police intimidation and brutality continued. With anger swelling, the Reverend A. J. Campbell, pastor at Early Grove and an NAACP member, braved potential reprisals to write to Marshall. "I am staking my life for justice!" he proclaimed, confiding his fear that if the NAACP failed to act, members would abandon the organization. An article in the nationally circulated *Afro American* reflected this urgency, reporting that "the verdict has been described as 'the greatest miscarriage of justice.'"[42]

This turmoil over justice reflected more than the acquittals in this case. Within the week, news broke about a mentally impaired sixteen-year-old African American boy, Fred Jackson, who had been indicted for raping a white woman, killing her infant sons, and setting her house on fire. The trial opened in mid-February, before the private investigator hired by the NAACP could present proof that the police had coerced Jackson into confessing and that the real killers had framed him. Emotions ran strong, tapping into deep-seated concerns about potent portrayals of black men as threats to white women that had been used historically to justify lynching and, more recently, the death penalty. This time, Gerber did not query prospective jurors about their fairness toward African Americans. He pronounced the crime "the most heinous ever committed in this country" and demanded the death penalty. He was joined in this opinion by the public defender, leaving Jackson, who had the mental capacity of a child, to defend himself. Within minutes, the jury found him guilty and sentenced him to death, even though he was a minor. Claiming that their son was incapable of orchestrating such a crime, Young and Mary Jackson, aided by the *World,* established a legal fund to hire defense attorneys and an investigator. They garnered such extensive support that in April 1947, even Crump's black allies appeared at a mass fund-raising meeting in the cavernous Mason Temple. Nevertheless, Tennessee's Supreme Court upheld the conviction, and the US Supreme

Court rejected a review. Mary Jackson visited Governor Jim McCord and pleaded, unsuccessfully, that he stay the execution. Thousands lined up outside the funeral home to view Fred's body in August.[43]

Police brutality, sexual assault, forced confessions, and convictions built on racist representations continued to spur working-class protest, with assaults of young women and veterans being most salient. A 1948 petition signed by 1,500 members of the East Memphis Citizens Club asserted that patrolmen continued to "molest . . . our young girls and women, making indecent approaches."[44] Because fear of reprisal persisted, the largest responses coalesced around those events that occurred in full view of witnesses, such as the August 1947 beating of Adelaide Hudson, a young, pregnant domestic worker who lived at Foote Homes public housing, by patrolmen who became incensed when she failed to call them "Sir." Witnesses echoed her vulnerability; the officers had sexual motivations, they insisted, noting that Hudson had been scantily clad on that hot afternoon when the police burst into her home in pursuit of her nephew.[45]

Black Memphians mobilized around racist structures in employment offices and workplaces during the war, and they challenged union leaders and federal officials who hindered rather than enabled their battles against racist practices. They now used their energies to organize against police brutality and rape. This nexus was apparent in August 1948 following the shooting death of twenty-three-year-old veteran and sanitation worker James Mosby in his front yard in Binghampton. Members of the NAACP, Memphis CIO, ministerial alliances, civic clubs, student groups, and social organizations signed petitions, contributed funds, and attended mass meetings at churches such as First Baptist in Binghampton and Avery Chapel AME in South Memphis. The petition circulated by the East Memphis Citizens Club condemned the depiction of Mosby as a rabid beast who had been shot after supposedly assaulting an officer and biting his arm; it referred to the police as the real savages. It defended Mosby as "a young World II veteran who served his country as a soldier both in the States and Overseas"; he was "a father of two infant children, and an employee of the City"; he was the son of "property owners in Binghampton, and devout Church Communicants"—identities that commanded honor and respect.[46]

The growing opposition had concrete consequences. First, it invigorated voter registration drives leading up to the August 1948 Democratic primaries and impacted the outcome of the elections, dealing Crump his first blows at the ballot box since the 1910s. African Americans and white moderates combined to influence not only local contests but also state elections, defeating Governor Jim Nance McCord (who had rejected Mary Jackson's plea) and sending Crump opponent Estes Kefauver to the Senate.[47] These results look more stunning if we consider that in July, southern Democrats had reacted to Truman's civil rights platform by organizing the States' Rights Party. Second, the groundswell of protest and delivery of petitions after Mosby's death convinced Mayor James Pleasants to approve the hiring of Memphis's first black police officers since the beginning of the twentieth century, in spite of his earlier refusal. In petitioning Pleasants, the East Memphis Citizens Club invoked the memory of the rapes of "two Binghampton girls" by white police officers three years earlier, which still served as the most potent indicator of vulnerability and injustice.[48]

The hiring of black police officers has long since been cemented into the historical memory of Memphis's civil rights movement, as have the severe limitations Seabrook imposed when he barred the black officers from carrying weapons or arresting whites. This history usually starts with the appointments in 1948, rather than the activism against racist labor practices and police rape out of which they were born. From this vantage point, the civil rights movement in Memphis appears straightforward; it fits accounts from other southern cities that appointed black officers in the same period and maintains an emphasis on desegregation. Analyzing the movement from the perspective of this more complicated activism related to two spheres of everyday life, and taking into account the deep-rooted sentiments about black and white manhood and womanhood that accompanied it, forces questions about the meanings of the civil rights movement to local working-class people after World War II.

Notes

This essay is based on chapters 2 and 3 in Laurie B. Green, *Battling the Plantation Mentality: Memphis and the Black Freedom Struggle* (Chapel Hill: University of North Carolina Press, 2007), 47–111.

1. All material on Evelyn Bates is from an interview with the author, Memphis, August 9, 1995.

2. White women held 16.6 percent of Memphis's manufacturing jobs in September 1942 and 33.8 percent one year later. The Firestone percentages were slightly higher. War Manpower Commission, Labor Market Development Report for August 15, 1943, box 14, folder Labor—1943, Walter Chandler Papers, Memphis and Shelby County Room, Memphis Public Library and Information Center, Memphis, TN.

3. Clarence W. Smith to War Manpower Administration director Paul V. McNutt, May 3, 1943, reel 25, file Complaints Not against Particular Companies, Office of Budget and Administration, Region VII, Selected Documents from Records of the Committee on Fair Employment Practice (hereafter FEPC Records), Record Group (RG) 228, National Archives microfilm (Glen Rock, NJ: Microfilming Corporation of America, 1970); Executive Order 8802, https://www.ourdocuments.gov/doc.php?flash=true&doc=72 (accessed June 15, 2016).

4. War Manpower Commission, Labor Market Development Report for August 15, 1943; correspondence, box 13, folder Housing Authority, 1943, Chandler Papers; correspondence, box 5, folders Fisher Body Company and Ford Plant, ibid.; Labor Market Report for Memphis, November 15 to December 15, 1942, box 8, folder Labor, ibid.; field report by John Beecher, [May 1942], reel 77, Office Files of John Beecher, file Memphis, Tennessee, FEPC Records; Michael Honey, *Southern Labor and Black Civil Rights: Organizing Memphis Workers* (Urbana: University of Illinois Press, 1993), 178; Robert A. Sigafoos, *Cotton Row to Beale Street: A Business History of Memphis* (Memphis, TN: Memphis State University Press, 1979), 207. For more information on Fisher during World War II, see http://usautoindustryworldwartwo.com/Fisher%20Body/fisherbodymemphis.htm (accessed June 14, 2016).

5. Susie Brister to President Roosevelt, July 2, 1942, reel 27, file Complaints against a Particular Company, Office of Budget and Administration, Region VII, FEPC Records.

6. Memorandum from A. Bruce Hunt, Director, Region VII, to Will Maslow, Director of Field Operations, June 21, 1944, reel 52, Central Files, Office of Budget and Administration, file Weekly Reports by Region, Region VII, October 1943–June 1944, FEPC Records; Annual Report, memorandum from John Hope II to John A. Davis, Director, file Office Files of Eugene Davidson, FEPC Asst. Director, October 1941–April 1946, Division of Review and Analysis, FEPC Records; Benjamin F. Bell Jr. to Paul V. McNutt, July 28, 1943, RG 228, box 7, Closed Cases T–U, folder USES, 7-GR-60, 61, 82, 110, 113, National Archives and Records Administration (NARA).

7. Margaret Jackson to President Roosevelt, June 5, 1942, reel 27, file Complaints against a Particular Company, Office of Budget and Administration, Region VII, FEPC Records.

8. Ella Rose Dotson to President Roosevelt, January 7, 1943, and larger correspondence involving Dotson in RG 228, box 7, Closed Cases T–U, folder USES 7-GR-1, 3, 4, 9, FEPC—Region II.

9. Mediators' Report, NWLB, June 18, 1942, Case No. 59, Mediation and Conciliation Service File 196-8955, RG 280, NARA.

10. Newspaper clipping, n.d., reel 76, Tensions Files, file Tennessee, Memphis, FEPC Records.

11. Correspondence and complaints, RG 228, box 4, Closed Cases D–J, folder Fisher Memphis Aircraft (Division of GMC), 7-BR-109, 7-BR-130, 7-BR-287, FEPC—Region VII.

12. Mayor Walter Chandler to Honorable Clifford Davis, November 13, 1943, and Davis to Chandler, December 1, 1943, box 15, folder Labor—1944, Chandler Papers; minutes, Committee for Economic Development, July 1, 1943, box 12, folder Economic Development, Committee for, 1943, ibid.

13. Bureau of Labor Statistics, US Department of Labor, "Appraisal of Wages in the Memphis, Tennessee, Plants of the Buckeye Cotton Oil Company," unpublished reports to the wage investigator of the National War Labor Board, May 1, 1942, reel 76, Division of Field Operations, Office Files of Will Maslow, September 1943–January 1945, FEPC Records.

14. On Buckeye, see http://www.referenceforbusiness.com/history2/58/Buckeye-Technologies-Inc.html and http://pubs.acs.org/doi/abs/10.1021/cen-v020n007.p438a (accessed June 18, 2016).

15. Reuel Stanfield, United Cannery, Agricultural, and Packinghouse Workers of America (UCAPWA) Local 19 business agent, to A. Bruce Hunt, May 5, 1944, RG 228, box 3, Closed Cases B–D, folder Buckeye Cotton Oil, 7-BR-292, FEPC—Region VII; Arbitration Decision in the Matter of the Buckeye Cotton Oil Company and UCAPWA, May 28, 1943, ibid.; Mediation and Conciliation Service File 300-6436, RG 280, NARA.

16. John Hope II to A. Bruce Hunt, [circa April 27, 1944], RG 228, box 3, Closed Cases B–D, folder Buckeye Cotton Oil, 7-BR-292, FEPC—Region VII.

17. Wartime labor statistics had categories for "Negroes" and "Women" but not for black women. Honey, *Southern Labor and Black Civil Rights*, 197, cites Negro Chamber of Commerce estimates for 1941: 20,251 total black women workers, which included 12,000 domestic servants and 4,500 laundry workers.

18. D. K. Jones, Commissioner of Conciliation, Progress Report re Model Laundry, July 24, 1942, Mediation and Conciliation Service Files 209-3424, RG 280, NARA; Bates interview.

19. From the *Memphis World:* "Laundry Workers Being Organized," July 2, 1943; "Laundry Workers Meet Wed. Night," July 6, 1943; "Laundry Workers Essential to War," July 9, 1943; "Kraus Employees on Strike, Backed by Laundry Union," July 23, 1943; and "Loeb's Laundry Workers Strike," August 21, 1945;

Mediation and Conciliation Service Files 209-3424 on Model Laundry and 199-7432 on Crescent Laundry, RG 280, NARA.

20. From the *Memphis World*, see: "Loeb's Laundry Workers Strike," August 21, 1945; "Laundry Workers Being Organized," July 2, 1943; Laundry Workers Meet Wed. Night," July 6, 1943; "Kraus Employees on Strike, Backed by Laundry Union," July 23, 1943; and "Second Week of Kraus' Strike," July 30, 1943.

21. Kennedy General Hospital, Memphis, Tennessee, 7-GR-485–487, RG 228, box 1, Active Cases A–S, FEPC—Region VII.

22. Memphis Negro Chamber of Commerce and Housewives League to White Rose Laundry Cleaners, October 5, 1942, box 9, folder Negroes—1942, Chandler Papers.

23. The following account is based on FEPC file, May 5–October 9, 1945, reel 80, file Veterans' Hospital, Memphis, Division of Field Operations—Active Cases, June 1943–April 1946, Region VII, FEPC Records.

24. Except where noted, this account of the assaults and the immediate aftermath is based on sworn affidavits obtained on August 15, 1945, by attorney Drury B. Crawley for the Memphis NAACP. NAACP Papers (microfilm), part 8, series B, 25:00309–00310, 00312–00316, 00328–00333, 00334–00335, 00336–00338 (Bethesda, MD: University Publications of America, 1988). Because of their nature, many of the details are not included here.

25. See also Laurie B. Green, "Challenging the Civil Rights Narrative: Women, Gender and the 'Politics of Protection,'" in *Civil Rights History from the Ground Up: Local Studies, a National Movement,* ed. Emilye Crosby (Athens: University of Georgia Press, 2011), 52–80.

26. "Press-Scimitar's Account of Police Attack Charges," reprint, *Memphis World,* August 14, 1945; "We Must Act on This!" *Memphis World,* August 14, 1945; "Grand Jury Indicts Two Ex-Policemen," *Memphis World,* September 7, 1945.

27. Allan M. Brandt, *No Magic Bullet: A Social History of Venereal Disease in the United States Since 1880* (New York: Oxford University Press, 1987), 146–47; L. M. Graves, MD, Superintendent of Health, to Chandler, March 11, 1941, June 12, 1942, box 8, folder Health Department, 1941, Chandler Papers; Chandler to Clifford Davis, June 13, 1942, ibid.; Chandler to Hon. Kenneth McKellar, June 13, 1942, ibid.

28. Brandt, *No Magic Bullet,* 161–70; "War on Prostitution Called All-Out Here," *Memphis Commercial Appeal,* June 9, 1942.

29. Lt. Col. A. F. Brand, "Venereal Disease Control Office Issues Statement Regarding Health Cards," *Memphis World,* June 22, 1945.

30. I am using pseudonyms in place of the four women's real names.

31. US Census Bureau, Memphis, Shelby County, Tennessee, 1940, 98–107, http://www.archives.com/GA.aspx?_act=ImageViewCensus1940&FirstName=Fred&LastName=Dudzick&Location=TN&UniqueId=132621884&type=census&folderImageSeq= (accessed July 8, 2016).

32. "Press-Scimitar's Account of Police Attack Charges," *Memphis World*, August 14, 1945.

33. "Report from Memphis," NAACP Papers, part 8 series B, 25:00318; Charles S. Johnson to Roy Wilkins, August 15, 1945, ibid., 25:00327; Roy Wilkins to Utillus R. Phillips, August 18, 1945, ibid., 25:00317; Thurgood Marshall to Utillus Phillips, September 5 and 26, 1945, ibid., 25:00339–00340, 25:00342.

34. Edward Smith, "Writer Stresses Need to Consider State of the City for Negroes," *Memphis World*, August 10, 1945; "Press-Scimitar's Account," "We Must Act on This!" and "Plans for Prosecution of Rape Case Outlined by Many Civic Groups," *Memphis World*, August 21, 1945.

35. "Loeb's Laundry Workers Strike," *Memphis World*, August 21, 1945; Honey, *Southern Labor and Black Civil Rights*, 200, 327n46; Rev. A. J. Campbell to Thurgood Marshall, February 13, 1946, NAACP Papers, part 8, series B, 25:00366, 25:00369.

36. "Plans for Prosecution of Rape Case," *Memphis World*, August 21, 1945; Utillus Phillips to Walter White, July 28, 1943, and Utillus Phillips to Ella Baker, May 13, 1946, box C185, group II, series C, NAACP Papers, Manuscript Division, Library of Congress, Washington, DC.

37. "Grand Jury Indicts Two Ex-Policemen," *Memphis World*, September 7, 1945, 1.

38. *State of Tennessee v. J. W. Torrey and B. J. Lewis* (Criminal Court, Division I, Shelby County, Tennessee, 1946); "Attitudes toward Negroes in Police Rape Case Balk Jury Selection—New Panel," *Memphis World*, November 9, 1945.

39. *Tennessee v. Torrey and Lewis*.

40. Robert Tillman to NAACP, NAACP Papers, part 8, series B, 25:00356.

41. *Tennessee v. Torrey and Lewis*.

42. Marshall to Phillips, February 6, 1946, NAACP Papers, part 8, series B, 25:00366, 25:00369; Rev. A. J. Campbell to Marshall, February 13, 1946, ibid., 25:00366367–69; "Ex-Cops Freed of Attack Charge," *Afro American*, February 9, 1946.

43. From the *Memphis World*, see: "Jury Gives Death Verdict to 16-Year-Old Boy in Goss Case," March 1, 1946; "Fred Jackson's Parents Seek Funds to Save Youth from Chair Feb. 28," January 24, 1947; "Willing Workers Club Aids Fred Jackson Fund," March 7, 1947; "Fundraising Mass Meet for Fred Jackson at Mason's Temple April 27," April 22, 1947; "Fred Jackson Nears Doom—Governor Is Asked to Save Him," August 1, 1947.

44. Petition from East Memphis Citizens Club to Mayor James Pleasants Jr., n.d., box 6b, folder Police Department, 1948, James Pleasants Jr. Papers, Memphis and Shelby County Room, Memphis Public Library and Information Center, Memphis, TN.

45. "Testimony of Eyewitnesses Refute Police Denials of Beating Expectant Mother," *Memphis World*, August 8, 1947.

46. From the *Memphis Worlds,* see: "Young Overseas Vet Shot to Death by Police Officers in His Yard—Binghampton Citizens Are Aroused," August 24, 1948; "Mayor's Office Gets Petition Seeking Race Police," September 7, 1948; and "Donors to Mosby Fund," September 14, 1948; petition from East Memphis Citizens Club to Mayor James Pleasants Jr.

47. "Negro Voters Join with Liberal Whites to Lift 'Iron Curtain' as Browning, Kefauver Win Posts," *Memphis World*, August 19, 1948; "Crump Beaten in Election," *St. Louis Argus,* reprint, *Memphis World*, August 17, 1948; "The People of Tennessee Take Back the Power," *Memphis Press-Scimitar,* reprint, *Memphis World*, August 19, 1948. These articles are reacting to the August Democratic primaries, the key elections in the state.

48. Harry Woodbury, "Use of Negro Police to Be Given Trial; Applications Sought," *Memphis Commercial Appeal*, September 10, 1948; petition from East Memphis Citizens Club to Mayor James Pleasants Jr.

Black Memphians and New Frontiers

The Shelby County Democratic Club, the Kennedy Administration, and the Quest for Black Political Power, 1959–1964

Elizabeth Gritter

In 1959 African Americans in Memphis made an unprecedented effort at the polls. Four black men ran for public office as a unity slate called the Volunteer Ticket. More than a political campaign, it was a crusade for freedom as they and other black Memphians pressed for civil rights, political power, and human rights. Daisy Bates of Little Rock Nine fame and Dr. Martin Luther King Jr. both traveled to Memphis to speak on their behalf. Although the black office seekers all came in second, candidate Russell B. Sugarmon Jr. said, "We won everything but the election." Their campaign galvanized the black freedom struggle in Memphis, leading to the gaining of power by the Shelby County Democratic Club (SCDC), a black political organization encompassing the city and county that became one of the most powerful civil rights organizations in Memphis. Sugarmon served as its executive director, and it represented the power of the black vote at a time when most black southerners were disenfranchised. Indeed, not until the Voting Rights Act of 1965 were most eligible African Americans in the South able to vote. Yet in 1960, 28 percent of black southerners could vote, an underrecognized figure in scholarship on civil rights and southern politics. The story of Sugarmon and the SCDC reveals how a portion of these African American voters used politics as leverage for civil rights before passage of the Voting Rights Act. Exploring their relationship to John F. Kennedy's presidential campaign and administration also puts a spotlight on how local black leaders and groups interacted with the Kennedys, whereas much of the scholarship has focused on interactions between the Kennedys and well-known leaders such as Martin Luther King Jr.[1]

African Americans in Memphis were able to vote because of the dominance of the Edward H. Crump machine, skilled black political leadership, the mobilization of ordinary black Memphians, and state political conditions. The Crump machine, which dominated Memphis political life from 1909 until Crump's death in 1954, incorporated black Memphians into its arsenal for maintaining control. The common perception is, as Memphian Benjamin L. Hooks said, "We didn't vote, we were voted." Although this statement contains an element of truth, the presence of skilled black leaders such as Robert R. Church Jr. and George W. Lee, who engaged in voter registration campaigns in the 1910s through 1950s, attests to the fact that black leaders and ordinary black civilians marshaled their forces into a black voting presence. A two-way street existed between black Memphians and the Crump machine, and the former could use their political leverage for better public service and economic and other opportunities. Still, despite the call for civil rights by some black leaders, African Americans were always relegated to second-rate citizenship; never did the Crump machine call for the end of segregation, which would have been most uncommon among southern white politicians of the time. Moreover, African Americans did not face the white primary in Memphis and were subject to a poll tax, which the Crump machine sometimes paid to ensure the African American vote.[2]

After Crump's death in 1954, there was no successor to take his place. Memphis politics was in disarray and had no clear leader, even though holdovers from the Crump machine were still in place. This fracturing of Memphis politics opened the door for a new group of black Memphians—not those who had negotiated with and accommodated to Crump—to rise up as leaders. Russell B. Sugarmon Jr. and his wife Laurie, A. W. Willis Jr., Jesse H. Turner, H. T. Lockard, future national NAACP leader Benjamin L. Hooks, and Vasco and Maxine Smith were among those who broke new ground in the black freedom struggle in Memphis. Building on the efforts of those who came before them, they were mainly northern educated and Memphis natives. Sugarmon, for instance, had been educated at Morehouse, Rutgers, Boston University, and Harvard Law School. The University of Tennessee Law School had paid his admission to and expenses at Harvard because he was African American. Dedicated to civil rights, Sugarmon had returned to Memphis because he did not like conditions for African Americans there and wanted to improve them. In the 1950s these leaders largely engaged in a two-pronged strategy for civil rights: they used political and legal means, and they used protest. They utilized the network of existing civic clubs, the Bluff City and Shelby County Civic Club Council, to boycott the *Commercial Appeal* for not using courtesy titles for African Americans and for engaging in other discriminatory coverage. Maxine Smith and Laurie Sugarmon tried to integrate Memphis State College but were denied admission because of their race; they subsequently became the only two women to serve on the board of the local branch of the NAACP. In fact, all these leaders got involved in the city's NAACP chapter, which became the most dominant civil rights organization in Memphis and the largest branch in the South by 1961. By 1964, it boasted 7,000 members.[3]

"This was pre-sit-in movement; we saw the ballot as the voice of the people," recalled Maxine Smith. Voter registration among black Memphians grew tremendously during the 1950s—from 19,614 in 1951 to 62,606 in 1960, a 219.2 percentage point increase; most registered in 1955 and later. After becoming involved in the NAACP branch, Smith became a full-time volunteer and membership chair, as well as the coordinator of voter registration. With help from national NAACP leader W. C. Patton, she spearheaded the branch's voter registration efforts. Other drives taking place to increase voter registration included that of the Citizens Nonpartisan Voter Registration Committee, which involved representatives of the NAACP, church groups, and labor organizations. George W. Lee headed the Lincoln League, the leading black Republican group in the 1950s. Its membership was older, representing the older generation's allegiance to the Republican Party. The Shelby County Democratic Club was largely a "vestpocket" organization in the 1950s, according to its former president H. T. Lockard. But that would change with the 1959 campaign, when the Lincoln League and the SCDC came together to support the four black candidates. The club attracted a younger, more energetic membership than the Lincoln League.[4]

The 1959 campaign utilized a ward and precinct structure to aid the black office seekers. After the election, Russell Sugarmon and others reorganized the Shelby County Democratic Club into a permanent ward and precinct structure, enabling it to become a more significant and powerful political force. According to Sugarmon, "There were about twelve or fifteen hundred, maybe two thousand, people who were ready to keep going after that campaign." He recalled:

> We came up with an article of the bylaws which stated that we had joined to achieve certain goals. The club would be organized by precinct. Anybody who lived in a particular precinct who wished to join could have meetings in their precinct and invite interested people from the precinct to come and find out what it was about and what we planned to do. This would achieve some political power. And then, hold an election and elect a chairman, a secretary, and so forth. If there were ten people, the chairman and the secretary would be on our central committee. If there were more than ten, the chairman, the secretary, and one other person would be on the central committee. The central committee would be responsible for electing county-wide officers of the club, and the central committee would be responsible for determining what issues should be raised in elections and screen candidates to decide and endorse who we supported by vote. That's what we set up.[5]

In addition to a written constitution governing the operations of the Shelby County Democratic Club, each branch had its own constitution. The executive committee's purpose was to "manage the affairs of the club, set policy, adopt programs, elect officers, and generally direct the affairs of the club."[6]

Another key development in the civil rights struggle in Memphis occurred in March 1960 when LeMoyne and Owen College students staged sit-ins at a downtown variety store and then at the local public library. The black library branch lacked resources, and no integration had occurred despite Jesse Turner's 1957 lawsuit against the library system's discriminatory practices. "The sit-in demonstrations settled everything," Lockard later said. "It was like somebody threw a light on material that had been soaked with some kind of inflammable matter because it really

Benjamin Hooks, Martin Luther King, Russell Sugarmon, Henry Buntyn, and Eliehue Stanback in 1959. (Courtesy Memphis and Shelby County Room, Memphis Public Library)

spread like mad," recalled Sugarmon. Even though lawsuits had previously been filed regarding the library as well as the bus system and other public accommodations, it took the sit-ins to desegregate these public facilities and lead to better employment opportunities. In fact, many of the students involved in the sit-ins had participated in the 1959 electoral effort. Their initial sit-in at the library led to a twenty-month direct action movement in downtown Memphis in 1960 and 1961, coordinated by Maxine Smith at the NAACP office. It targeted every public facility, in addition to demanding better employment opportunities. In the meantime, Smith became executive secretary of the NAACP's Memphis branch.[7]

The ward and precinct network of the Shelby County Democratic Club was used to organize the sit-ins and communicate during them. Membership and leadership of the NAACP and the SCDC overlapped, and issues related to desegregation were discussed at both places. For instance, Lorene Thomas, wife of internationally known entertainer

Rufus Thomas, was a member of the NAACP and assistant corresponding secretary for the SCDC. Leaders and members worked through the
NAACP branch on a nonpartisan basis, but politically, they were SCDC
participants. The leaders of both groups tended to be middle class, and
most could not be considered wealthy; the membership consisted of the
black working class, with many at the bottom end of the working-class
scale. To be sure, there were class differences as well as generational differences. Some black Memphians resented working under Sugarmon and
Willis, claiming they had been born with "silver spoons" in their mouths,
given that both men's parents were black professionals. Precinct leaders
tried to smooth over these differences, as well as those related to sexism;
many precinct leaders were women, and some clubs included men who
found it difficult to take orders from a woman. In addition, some of the
students wanted the adults to take more aggressive actions concerning
civil rights.[8]

Nevertheless, the black community developed amazing unity in its
political efforts during the early 1960s. This was especially apparent in its
role in John F. Kennedy's presidential campaign in 1960. The local election that year brought some successes for black Memphians. Vestiges of
the old Crump machine, used to negotiating for the black vote, got black
voters' support by promising to take "For Colored" and "For White"
signs down from county office buildings and to hire the first black deputy sheriffs. Both these promises were carried out before Election Day so
black voters would not have to worry about being double-crossed. Previously, the black vote had not been considered desirable by some white
politicians in these post-Crump days; now it was openly courted, which
signified the strength of black voters and was an achievement in itself. In
fact, when Sugarmon and Democratic Club leaders met with Crump politician David Harsh, he had on his desk a pamphlet printed by the Democratic Club that explained the organization, including who manned the
offices and who the precinct leaders were. Harsh told them, "I looked at
this thing, and anybody who can put this kind of organization together is
going to be hard to stop in this town."[9]

Nationally, Memphis's black voters were recruited by the Kennedy
campaign. John L. Seigenthaler, a campaign aide and former *Tennessean*
reporter, knew about the political work of Sugarmon and Willis through

their efforts in Fayette and Haywood Counties (Willis had been campaign manager for the Volunteer Ticket and was heavily involved in the Democratic Club). The Eisenhower administration had sent investigators to examine the denial of voting rights in these Black Belt counties near Memphis. Many African Americans had been evicted from their homes for trying to vote, leading to the formation of a tent city. The Memphis NAACP branch assisted these residents by providing them with food and other necessities. Seigenthaler knew about the 1959 campaign and remembered what a courageous effort it had been for Sugarmon and the other black candidates to even register to vote.[10]

Sugarmon and Willis, who were business, law, and political partners, formed a partnership with Seigenthaler during the 1960 presidential campaign. Seigenthaler told Robert F. Kennedy, who was his brother's campaign manager, that these two men would do more to help their cause than anyone else in Memphis. Seigenthaler proceeded to develop a better political relationship with them than with leading white politicians in Memphis, and Sugarmon would call Seigenthaler with any questions or concerns. Seigenthaler recalled that part of the reason for their camaraderie was that they were all around the same age.[11]

More broadly, the Kennedys' interest in black Memphians stemmed from the existence of a civil rights division in the Kennedy campaign, which operated as part of the Democratic National Committee and worked with other campaign divisions and staff. Its director, Marjorie Lawson, had some contact with Sugarmon. The division's activities included disseminating campaign flyers and brochures promoting John Kennedy's record of commitment to civil rights and contact with African Americans, advising campaign manager Robert Kennedy and other campaign staff on civil rights, working with black leaders in the South and North on behalf of Kennedy, collecting statistics on the black vote and promoting black voter registration, working with the black press to generate positive coverage of Kennedy's stance on civil rights, and publicizing endorsements by celebrities such as singer-actor Harry Belafonte and distinguished intellectuals such as historian John Hope Franklin. The division was also responsible for the "Kennedy Airlift," which transported black entertainment, sports, and political figures, such as baseball star Hank Aaron, to different cities to campaign for Kennedy.[12]

At the request of Robert Kennedy, Willis and Sugarmon traveled to St. Louis to meet with campaign staff. That was where Sugarmon met the candidate's brother for the first time, and he was impressed with Robert Kennedy's directness. Sugarmon recalled that he and Willis were the only attendees from Memphis at that meeting. They also traveled to Washington, DC, to meet with members of the Kennedy campaign. Seigenthaler later recalled, "You couldn't have asked for two fellows with more potential for leadership than these two. They understood the business of politics and both of them looked upon it as an honorable profession." According to Seigenthaler, they embodied the Kennedy spirit. "It was not a cliché in those days, the New Frontier. I mean I think those of us who were in it felt it. Certainly Russell and A. W. thought it meant something more than just a trite phrase. . . . They were part of the New Frontier in their own minds and in that campaign and were actively involved in it." Because of these meetings, Tennessee governor Buford Ellington appointed an African American to the five-member Tennessee campaign committee. Unlike in previous years, almost all campaign committees were integrated in Memphis, with apparently no objections from white Democratic leaders. The Republicans had integrated many years earlier. Sugarmon also helped the Kennedy campaign link up with black churches to spread its message to black voters. In addition, Seigenthaler recalled that Sugarmon and Willis had "lovely, effective wives" who were involved in the political campaign, so working with them was like getting two for one.[13]

Sugarmon and Jesse Turner directed the black Democratic campaign for Kennedy and relied on extensive advertising, personal door-to-door contact, and small meetings where questions could be asked, as opposed to mass rallies. The main issue was how to convince African Americans that Kennedy was stronger than Nixon on civil rights. The Democratic Party was seen as the party of Jim Crowism, so they had to overcome black dislike for Democrats; however, because the Democratic Party had young black leaders, it was more appealing to young black voters than the Republican Party. Although Kennedy's Catholicism was a national controversy, his religion made little difference to local black voters. Meanwhile, the black Republican campaign, directed mainly by George W. Lee, held big rallies and focused on past benefits the Republicans had given African Americans, such as federal jobs. The Shelby County Democratic

Club released a flyer featuring photographs of leading black Memphians and what they had to say about civil rights; for instance, they pointed out that the Democratic platform endorsed the 1954 *Brown* decision. They stressed, in the words of Sugarmon, a "new frontier for Memphis Negroes" and that African Americans had "to have guts and not let anti-Negro Southern Democrats force them out of the Democratic party." The local black newspaper, the *Tri-State Defender,* endorsed Kennedy, carried advertising for the Democrats, and published an eight-page section filled with photographs of Kennedy with various African Americans. The paper also printed endorsements of Kennedy by prominent African Americans such as Cab Calloway, Mahalia Jackson, and Harry Belafonte. Moreover, the "Kennedy Airlift" concentrated its efforts on Memphis.[14]

Another key factor in getting support among African Americans was John Kennedy's efforts on behalf of a jailed Martin Luther King Jr., which helped turn many black voters throughout the South to Kennedy. King had been jailed in Atlanta because of his participation in the sit-in movement there. John Kennedy called Coretta Scott King to express his concern and offer his help, and Robert Kennedy interceded with the judge to have King released. Word of these developments spread throughout the black community, partly because the Kennedy campaign disseminated a pamphlet to black churches on the Sunday before Election Day, publicizing the Kennedys' actions. In this flyer, the Reverend Martin Luther King Sr. was quoted as saying that he had a suitcase full of votes and was going to "dump them in [Kennedy's] lap."[15]

That campaign season led to the first integrated political event for women in the city. Josephine Burson, a white Jewish woman, was part of the planning committee for the visit of the vice presidential candidate's wife, Lady Bird Johnson. Burson would not agree to the committee's suggestion to set up separate affairs for white women and black women, saying that it negated everything she stood for. She told them, "I'm not going to have two separate affairs. Either we meet together or we don't meet." She won, and the meeting was held at the city auditorium. It was a stand-up affair, as the committee members were afraid that if chairs were set up, the women might segregate themselves.[16]

John F. Kennedy actually spoke in Memphis during the campaign. Members of the Memphis NAACP Youth Council managed to work their way to the front of his downtown campaign appearance, where he stood with his back facing the river. They unrolled a twenty-five-foot-long sign in front of the platform that just said, "Help." Sugarmon recalled that the people on the platform, including Kennedy, covered their mouths to hide their laughter. He noted that it was a clever, slick way to get the candidate's attention concerning civil rights. In his speech, Kennedy said they stood at a "New Frontier" and claimed the "Democratic Party has always looked forward."[17]

The night of the election, Robert Kennedy called the Democratic Party headquarters of Shelby County from Hyannis Port, seeking the returns of the black precincts. He had a list of every black precinct in town, and he thanked Sugarmon for his efforts during the campaign. According to assistant precinct leader Jennie Betts, the Democratic Club was a key reason why, after decades of voting Republican in national elections, black Memphians turned to the Democratic Party. Seventy-three percent of African Americans in Memphis and Shelby County voted for Kennedy, whereas 57 percent had voted for Eisenhower in 1956. Even so, Tennessee as a whole voted for Richard Nixon. One apparently key factor was Kennedy's support of a $1.25 minimum wage. Tennessee whites probably turned to Nixon because of anti-Catholic feelings in some rural areas, the large Republican vote in East Tennessee, and the switching of party identification by some whites based on economic issues and civil rights. On November 14 Sugarmon wrote to SCDC members to pass along congratulations from the president-elect's national headquarters, state headquarters, and local headquarters for a job well done. The "campaign you conducted represents the finest effort to date by a Negro political organization in our city," he wrote. He said he was proud of them and added his personal congratulations. When Robert Kennedy asked what could be done to show appreciation for the black precincts' work, Sugarmon suggested that all the precinct leaders be invited to the inauguration, and Seigenthaler made it happen. Around ninety precinct leaders were invited, and they traveled by bus to Washington for the occasion; some even attended an inaugural ball. Sugarmon did not make the trip to DC because of family obligations. One of the precinct leaders was Druzy Anderson, an upbeat woman who lived in the Foote Homes housing project and had only one leg. Anderson headed the tenant association there, which raised the funds to send her to the inauguration.[18]

Even though Kennedy lost Tennessee, the initiative to attract the black vote paid off in the end. Many factors led to Kennedy's victory in this extremely close election, but one key factor was the black vote. The southern and national black vote went for Kennedy, and it proved to be the deciding factor in the four key states of New Jersey, Michigan, Illinois, and South Carolina. As the *New Republic* reported, "If the Negro voters of America hadn't shifted last Tuesday to John Kennedy, Vice President Nixon would now be holding press conferences as President-elect." African Americans had been shifting to the Democratic Party since the days of Franklin D. Roosevelt and his New Deal programs that benefited them, but their turn to the Democratic Party in the 1960 election was unprecedented. The *New Republic* noted that this shift was "more dramatic than [that of] most" other groups and that "the magnitude of the shift" was greater in the South.[19]

Sugarmon and Willis continued their relationship with Seigenthaler during his tenure as administrative assistant to Robert F. Kennedy, who became the attorney general; they maintained a relationship with the Kennedy administration as well. Sugarmon and Seigenthaler became life-long friends. Seigenthaler depended on Sugarmon's political insights and used him as a point person whenever he wanted to know what was going on in Memphis. According to Seigenthaler, Robert Kennedy thought highly of Sugarmon and Willis—calling them "bright lights"—and he would have welcomed them as lawyers in the Justice Department. Seigenthaler recalled, "I never really met anybody that was as attractive and tough-minded, well-spoken, astute as Russell. He was clearly an intellectual with a street sense and a great sense of humor and could laugh at himself."[20]

The relationship between black Memphians and the Kennedy administration was better than that between white politicians and the Kennedy administration, Seigenthaler remembered. This was evidenced by Mayor Henry Loeb's disapproval of the hearings held by the US Commission on Civil Rights in Memphis in 1962 and remarks he scrawled on a telegram in which the US attorney general's office praised the city for its desegregation of public facilities. He wrote, "They are not sincere," "City Commission not involved," "Wire does not help in any way," and "My advice has been and is 'keep your nose out of our affairs.'"[21]

Black Memphians used their support of John F. Kennedy to press for civil rights. In a *Commercial Appeal* advertisement based on Jonathan Swift's *A Modest Proposal,* the Memphis branch of the NAACP published a memo to President John F. Kennedy and "loyal American citizens everywhere" that was titled "A Modest Proposal for the Annexation of the City of Memphis, Shelby County, Tennessee." "Tragically, while you call us to launch out on the 'New Frontier' of life, we here in Memphis are engulfed with unsolved problems of the old frontier," it observed, pointing out that black citizens in Memphis faced much racial discrimination, including the denial of job opportunities, separate and therefore inferior education, and "White Only" signs on publicly supported facilities. They vowed to resist "these evils" by exercising the right to vote, taking legal action, and engaging in economic boycotts, picketing, and sit-ins. They petitioned President Kennedy for the annexation of Memphis to the United States "so that all citizens may participate in the challenge of democracy as we are taught through the principles so beautifully expressed in such documents as the Declaration of Independence, the Constitution of the United States, Lincoln's Gettysburg Address, The Emancipation Proclamation, the Supreme Court's 1954 Decision, and your magnificent inaugural address."[22]

Political appointments and other perks were obtained as a result of the special relationship between black Memphians and the Kennedy administration. Sugarmon received and accepted a special invitation to attend the independence ceremony in Trinidad and Tobago as a representative of the president. He was offered and turned down a position as assistant federal district attorney. Thanks to pressure by Sugarmon and the Shelby County Democratic Club, Odell Horton, a member of the Memphis NAACP's legal staff, was appointed an assistant US attorney; he later became a judge. Horton was appointed even though Mayor Loeb was upset about it. Roberta Church, daughter of the late political giant Robert R. Church Jr., was appointed a consultant in the Department of Health, Education, and Welfare for the vocational rehabilitation of aged and disabled people. Sugarmon and Willis also shook hands with President Kennedy at a Lincoln's birthday celebration in Washington that was connected to civil rights; they were among 800 top officials and civil rights leaders invited to the event. In addition, they met with Robert Kennedy in DC to discuss federal legislation for voting rights—so that blacks could vote in federal elections—and according to Sugarmon, Kennedy had no conception of the obstacles. Kennedy told them, "What you need to do is go home and get your people up off their asses and get them registered to vote."[23]

When James Meredith integrated the University of Mississippi in 1962, the Kennedy administration used its connections with black Memphians to make it happen. Meredith stayed with Maxine and Vasco Smith; they were supposed to keep him hidden but took him dancing instead. Government agents picked him up at Willis and Sugarmon's law office on Vance Avenue, put him in a car with FBI agents, and escorted him to Ole Miss. Willis also served as a lawyer for Meredith.[24]

The Kennedy administration monitored the civil rights situation in Memphis. Both John and Robert Kennedy praised the city for its peaceful desegregation of public schools. In 1962 the US Civil Rights Commission held a hearing in Memphis about the state of civil rights there, consulting with NAACP officials and members, among others. Seigenthaler visited with Mayor Loeb as part of his tour of the South on behalf of the administration's efforts toward school desegregation. In a wire to Loeb on February 6, 1962, a Justice Department official congratulated the city commission and Memphis citizens for peacefully and cooperatively desegregating the eating facilities of major stores in the city (the mayor's adverse reaction to this wire was mentioned earlier). In 1963 the Supreme Court ruled in *Watson v. Memphis* that the city's gradual park desegregation plan was unconstitutional; the US government filed a friend of the court brief on behalf of the plaintiff calling for speedier desegregation.[25]

In the meantime, Sugarmon remained executive director of the Shelby County Democratic Club, charged with managing its affairs as approved by the executive committee. Willis served as its secretary and vice president. These two men were key figures in the organization, which had its office in their law office at 588 Vance Avenue; its campaign headquarters was located at 333 Beale Street. Sugarmon was witty, brilliant, soft spoken, and a key political strategist; he could talk effectively one on one with anyone from a judge to a street person. Willis was small of stature, of medium build, a fast and voluble talker, and an organizational genius; he liked to deal with figures and projections, and according to Sugarmon, Willis conceived the precinct organization of the SCDC. A. Maceo Walker, millionaire son of J. E. Walker, the leading black Democrat in Memphis before his death in 1958, served as president of the club, as did chauffeur Frank Kilpatrick, the Reverend Alexander Gladney, and Vasco Smith in the 1960s. Fred Davis, later one of the first black City Council members, helped with the SCDC's reorganization in 1959 and served as its treasurer in the mid-1960s. The club represented a cross section of the black population, and its membership included professors, union activists, youths, businesspersons, civic club members, NAACP members, and women. Labor leader George Holloway, for instance, was involved with both the SCDC and the local NAACP branch. Very few whites joined the club; some, however, worked as volunteers or contributed financially. Sugarmon estimated that the SCDC started out with about 35 or 40 precincts after its restructuring in 1959 and exceeded 100—its high mark—in 1964. During the 1960s there was a backbone of about 60 strong clubs; the rest had varying degrees of continuity. In 1961, 65 precinct clubs existed, with some having as many as 100 members. By 1962, the group claimed 3,000 members. Clubs existed in most black precincts. The SCDC had various committees, including a ward and precinct organization committee, an entertainment committee, and a program and screening committee. The screening committee interviewed candidates for public office and selected which ones the SCDC would endorse.[26]

The SCDC operated democratically and in unison with the local NAACP branch; both groups were primarily concerned with achieving civil rights. They had overlapping leadership and membership, and both groups met monthly. Sugarmon recalled, "Any issue that affected the black vote or the black community we discussed [in] both places. So what it gave us was a cadre, citywide and countywide, of people who had some sophisticated insight about issues and probably how it affected our folk." Although the SCDC board set the agenda and recommended candidates to endorse, precinct club members could raise issues, and they always had a voice in these matters. Board members sometimes called precinct leaders before club meetings to pass along their ideas, allowing the precinct clubs to discuss these matters in their own meetings. Block clubs existed within precinct clubs, and block captains were responsible for working their blocks in support of the club as a whole.[27]

Precinct club members were the "troopers" of the organization, as Vasco Smith termed them. Precinct leaders and workers, including street or block captains, would walk routes in their neighborhoods, based on canvassing maps, in an effort to educate voters, urge them to register to vote and support SCDC candidates, and recruit new members of the club. They carried volunteer cards designed to record the availability of those living in their precincts to work in the campaign. They left campaign materials at black establishments such as barbershops and asked people to place signs in their yards. They obtained lists of registered voters and called on those people to urge them to vote. They also invited SCDC-endorsed candidates to lawn and Coke (Coca-Cola) parties and other neighborhood gatherings. Lillie Wheeler, a precinct club leader, raised money for the club by selling lemonade and tickets to children's dances. During the Kennedy campaign, she took children door-to-door with her, and they knew just as much about the candidate as she did. Wheeler believed that everyone has influence over at least five or ten individuals, so she urged people to tell others about the Democratic Club. Fred Davis was another club member who was actively involved in organizing precincts. At the time, he was a debit insurance agent and went door-to-door collecting insurance premiums; he organized his policyholders in each precinct and turned them into a political force. He recalled, "I had them to the point that I could make five phone calls and contact everybody on every street in the neighborhood because we had block captains and precinct captains and all that. I called the five people who headed the precincts, and they would take it from there." Precinct leaders and members worked on Election Day, and given their working-class status, the club paid many of them to do so. Maxine Smith said the club did a "terrific" job of getting black Memphians to understand that they could control their own political destinies. Vasco Smith recalled that he and his political counterpart Frank Kilpatrick would "ride together, sometimes making three and four different precinct meetings where we would make talks to get people enthused into the whole business of voter registration, voter education, and voter participation. . . . That group . . . just had a sort of religious zeal for doing these things."[28]

A key line of communication to the black voter was the church, and the Shelby County Democratic Club utilized it. The club and the Memphis NAACP branch met at the same place: Mount Olive Christian Methodist Episcopal Church, at the intersection of Linden and Lauderdale. SCDC meetings opened with a prayer in an attempt to cultivate a relationship with its churchgoing members. Some ministers endorsed the club and spoke during campaigns. But assistant precinct leader Jennie Betts remembered that the club asked ministers not to announce their endorsements in church because doing so could hurt their tax status; rather, they asked ministers just to announce that there was an election and who was running. However, Lillie Wheeler recalled that some churches collected offerings for candidates; she also recalled praying for the success of the office seekers. Furthermore, it was common knowledge that some ministers took money from candidates or others who were trying to buy their support for one candidate or another. At election time the SCDC also put out its ballot in the black churches. The Reverend C. F. Williams served as chaplain of the organization.[29]

White politicians considered the SCDC a powerful organization that made its presence known at election time. The club sent office seekers questionnaires about the issues, and local candidates, regardless of party affiliation, made presentations to the club and were interviewed by precinct leaders. The precinct leaders would then nominate the candidates they considered worthy of club endorsement, have a debate, and take a vote. At times, according to Betts, it was hard to decide who to endorse, because somebody might have tried to influence club leaders to support a particular candidate, bespeaking to the club's influence. Politicians knew that the SCDC could deliver votes. If the SCDC endorsed you, white politician Hunter Lane recalled, you were supposed to help with campaign expenses. The club distributed sample ballots among the black community for local, state, and national candidates, including African American candidates. If not for that sample ballot, H. T. Lockard believes he might not have been elected; in 1964 he became the first local black county commissioner in the twentieth century. And the club kept office seekers accountable by throwing its support behind candidates who kept their promises to the black community. Club leaders called elected officials, pressing them to make gains for African Americans and asking them for jobs or employment opportunities. SCDC workers manned tables on Election Day, where they had card files of all the Democrats registered to vote in each precinct. As voters left the polling place, they went to the SCDC table so that their names could be checked off as having voted. In midafternoon the poll workers took note of who had not voted yet and went to remind them to vote, a process that generally worked. Precinct workers also knocked on doors to get folks out to vote. Precinct worker Johnnie Mae Peters ran a babysitting service at her house, where teenage girls watched voters' children while they went to the polls. Poll or precinct watchers monitored the polls for any irregularities in Election Day procedures; this included inspecting the voting machines. They also passed out the SCDC sample ballot and literature on behalf of candidates endorsed by the club.[30]

Capitalizing on the success of the Shelby County Democratic Club, Sugarmon and other black leaders formed the Tennessee Voters Council (TVC) in 1962 in order to organize black communities throughout the state and coordinate the black vote in statewide elections. Willis served as secretary of the council, and Sugarmon acted as its general chairman. Back in 1958, Sugarmon had observed that the black vote had canceled itself out in the governor's race, with black voters splitting between the white candidates. He realized that this was an ineffective way to marshal black support. Recognizing the influence and presence of black Masons, he got the Reverend Charles F. Williams, the Prince Hall Masonic leader of Tennessee, to serve as first chair of the council. Williams sent letters to Masons statewide urging them to join the Tennessee Voters Council; he sent letters to the Eastern Stars, the women's division, as well. Meanwhile, Willis took the lead in obtaining lists of all the black barbers and beauticians in the state, as well as any other black groups he could locate. These individuals, along with other African Americans who had been recruited, met in Park Johnson Hall at Fisk University and formed the TVC; representatives from Tennessee's fifty-two counties attended the meeting. Like the SCDC, the TVC formulated questionnaires for candidates, some of whom spoke to representatives of the council. The TVC was not without dissension, however. For instance, two members, labor leader James

Walker and his wife and political activist Willa McWilliams, walked out of a 1962 meeting and resigned from the organization because they rejected its endorsement of Frank Clement for governor. Splinter groups formed because of disagreements over the endorsements.[31]

Nevertheless, the Shelby County Democratic Club, the local branch of the Tennessee Voters Council, remained a dominant presence in Memphis elections. The group's twenty-month direct action movement ended in February 1962 with the desegregation of public facilities and eating places at downtown department stores, as well as better employment opportunities for African Americans. Although no African American held political office, blacks wielded the balance of power in elections. Some political milestones had occurred, however. In 1960 Jesse H. Turner received *New York Times* coverage after being elected a member of the Shelby County Democratic Executive Committee. By 1964, African Americans had received at least forty political appointments, up from a mere two in the 1950s. But as Maxine Smith commented, the most aggressive civil rights leaders were not chosen for these appointments.[32]

The high-water mark of the Shelby County Democratic Club occurred in 1964, when it encompassed 101 clubs and 7,000 members. In 1963 and 1964 seventy-eight persons served on its executive committee, including thirty-six women. Although other black political clubs existed, the SCDC was the strongest and the only countywide group. In Shelby County, black voter registration was approximately 95,000 out of a potential 119,000. The year 1964 also marked the peak of influence of the Tennessee Voters Council. In the wake of the assassination of John F. Kennedy, Lyndon B. Johnson was running for the presidency, with Republican Barry Goldwater as his opponent. In Tennessee state elections, Ross Bass was running for the Senate against Governor Frank Clement. Clement made the mistake of stating that he would not have supported the Civil Rights Act of 1964, so African Americans turned against him, ensuring Bass's victory. The SCDC and TVC were victorious in other ways as well: some 99 percent of African Americans threw their support behind Democratic Party candidates in general; their votes helped elect Democrats to the presidency and the Senate, as well as an all-Democratic delegation in the state legislature. They followed the SCDC's sample ballot that urged them to vote for all Democratic candidates. Representing another victory for civil rights was the fact that A. W. Willis Jr. became the first African American elected to the Tennessee General Assembly since the late nineteenth century. Similarly, H. T. Lockard won election to the Shelby County Quarterly Court, also known as the County Commission, becoming the first African American to hold local office in decades.[33]

In the meantime, local black Republicans experienced a decline in power. A "new guard" of white Republicans became prominent in Memphis, and they were determined to diminish George W. Lee's power and the local Republicans' moderate, civil rights–oriented leadership. Their rise was in line with the ascension of Barry Goldwater nationally—the conservative candidate for president in 1964 who espoused states' rights and rigid anticommunism. Many African Americans rallied behind Lee, but he was defeated in 1962 in a bid for reelection to the Republican State Executive Committee, losing to two white Republicans; in 1964 he was denied a seat as delegate to the Republican National Convention after decades of faithful service to the party. That year, African Americans and organized labor accounted for most of the votes for Johnson, whereas many white Memphians voted for Goldwater.[34]

The Johnson administration went on to pass the second of its two milestone civil rights laws with the Voting Rights Act of 1965, which enabled most eligible African Americans in the South to vote. But the Shelby County Democratic Club's influence waned as its success bred failure. Instead of remaining largely united, black members fractured into separate black political clubs; some wanted to be leaders rather than followers, and others had personal agendas that did not encompass the welfare of the black community. This fracturing led to some political success, however. For instance, H. T. Lockard formed his own political league, and his advocacy on behalf of victorious gubernatorial candidate Buford Ellington in 1966 led to his appointment as the first black cabinet member in Tennessee history. But the heyday of the SCDC was over. The assassination of Martin Luther King Jr. in Memphis struck another blow against the black community; it was like a "heart attack" for them, Sugarmon recalled. Jennie Betts saw a decline in political interest when members of the black community started to move away from one another.[35]

In conclusion, the story of Russell B. Sugarmon Jr. and the Shelby

County Democratic Club demonstrates the remarkable political aptitude of black Memphians at a time when most black southerners were disenfranchised. The fact that they had a better relationship with the Kennedy administration than did white officials in Memphis shows their political skill and acumen. In a few short years, they went from running for public office to winning public office while holding the balance of power in elections. In all their affairs, they fought for civil rights and displayed an important vision for politics, one in which the promises of freedom and equality held true for all people.

Notes

1. Sugarmon quoted in L. F. Palmer Jr., "We Won Everything but the Election," *Tri-State Defender,* August 29 1959, 9. Voter statistics are from Donald R. Matthews and James W. Prothro, *Negroes and the New Southern Politics* (New York: Harcourt, Brace and World, 1966), 18. Works on the 1959 election include Christopher Silver and John V. Moeser, *The Separate City: Black Communities in the Urban South, 1940–1960* (Lexington: University Press of Kentucky, 1995); William E. Wright, *Memphis Politics: A Study in Racial Bloc Voting,* Eagleton Institute Cases in Practical Politics no. 27 (New York: McGraw-Hill, 1962); J. Morgan Kousser, *Colorblind Injustice: Minority Voting Rights and the Undoing of the Second Reconstruction* (Chapel Hill: University of North Carolina Press, 1999); James B. Jalenak, "Beale Street Politics" (senior honors thesis, Yale University, 1961); Elizabeth Gritter, "'Women Did Everything Except Run': Black Women's Participation in the 1959 Volunteer Ticket Campaign in Memphis, Tennessee," in *Entering the Fray: Gender, Politics, and Culture in the New South,* ed. Jonathan D. Wells and Sheila R. Phipps (Columbia: University of Missouri Press, 2010); Elizabeth Gritter, "'This Is a Crusade for Freedom': The Volunteer Ticket Campaign in the 1959 City Election in Memphis, Tennessee" (master's thesis, University of North Carolina, 2005).

2. Elizabeth Gritter, *River of Hope: Black Politics and the Memphis Freedom Movement, 1865–1954* (Lexington: University Press of Kentucky, 2014); Benjamin L. Hooks, telephone interview by the author, October 11, 2000, handwritten notes in author's possession.

3. Benjamin Muse, *Memphis* (Atlanta: Southern Regional Council, 1964), 23; Sherry L. Hoppe and Bruce W. Speck, *Maxine Smith's Unwilling Pupils: Lessons Learned in Memphis's Civil Rights Classroom* (Knoxville: University of Tennessee Press, 2007); Lucille Black to Maxine Smith, May 19, 1960, NAACP Papers, group III, box C186, folder Memphis NAACP 1960, Manuscript Division, Library of Congress, Washington, DC; Russell B. Sugarmon Jr., interview

by the author, Memphis, October 12, 2000, Southern Oral History Program (SOHP), University of North Carolina at Chapel Hill, transcript, 4–5, 18 (copies of the SOHP interviews are also available in the Everett Cook Collection of the Memphis–Shelby County Room of the Memphis and Shelby County Public Library and Information Center); Maxine Smith, interview by the author, Memphis, October 9, 2000, SOHP, transcript, 5–6, 34–35; Citizens Improvement Committee (Sugarmon was the author but is not listed as such), "Why the People Support the Crusade against the Commercial Appeal," n.d., Russell B. Sugarmon Jr., personal papers, Memphis, copy in author's possession.

4. Maxine Smith interview, 2000, 8–9; H. T. Lockard, interview by the author, Memphis, July 19, 2004, typed notes in author's possession; Maxine Smith interview, 2000, 6–7; Jennie M. Betts, interview by the author, Memphis, June 28, 2004, SOHP, transcript, 36; Lillie J. Wheeler, interview by the author, Memphis, June 28, 2004, SOHP, transcript, 15, 21–22; Jalenak, "Beale Street Politics," 29–30, 55.

5. Sugarmon interview, 2000, 14.

6. Fred L. Davis, interview by the author, Memphis, October 11, 2000, SOHP, transcript, 1–2; Jalenak, "Beale Street Politics," 54.

7. H. T. Lockard, interview by the author, Memphis, October 10, 2000, SOHP, transcript, 40; Sugarmon interview, 2000, 7; Betts interview, 37, 49; Maxine Smith interview, 2000, 16; Elizabeth Gritter, "Local Leaders and Community Soldiers: The Memphis Desegregation Movement, 1955–1961" (senior honors thesis, American University, 2001); Laurie B. Green, *Battling the Plantation Mentality: Memphis and the Black Freedom Struggle* (Chapel Hill: University of North Carolina Press, 2007), 221, 232–41; Gloster B. Current to Jesse H. Turner, June 14, 1961, NAACP Papers, group III, box C146, folder 1961–1962.

8. "Sugarmon Leads Democratic Club," *Memphis World,* December 15, 1962, 1; Jalenak, "Beale Street Politics," 47–48; Sugarmon interview, 2000, 16–17; Maxine Smith interview, 2000, 9–10; Betts interview, 1, 21–24; Wheeler interview, 8–9; Russell B. Sugarmon Jr., interview by the author, Memphis, July 30, 2004, transcript (in author's possession), 13, 54; H. T. Lockard, interview by the author, Memphis, July 29, 2004, SOHP, transcript, 20.

9. Harsh quoted in Sugarmon interview, July 2004, 36; Sugarmon interview, 2000, 28–31; Clark Porteous, "17 Endorsed by Negro Demo Club," *Memphis Press-Scimitar,* August 1, 1960, A. W. Willis Papers, box 3, folder 18, Memphis–Shelby County Room, Memphis and Shelby County Public Library and Information Center; Richard Connelly, "Negro Vote Deal Called 'Shocking,'" *Memphis Commercial Appeal,* July 22, 1960, 23.

10. Seigenthaler was an assistant to campaign manager Robert F. Kennedy. John L. Seigenthaler, interview by the author, Nashville, July 29, 2013, transcript (copy in author's possession); "Chairmen's Office," n.d., Robert F. Kennedy Pre-Administration Papers, box 133, folder Campaign Coordinators, Lists

of 8/22–9/27/60 and Undated, John F. Kennedy Library and Museum (hereafter JFK), Boston; John L. Seigenthaler, telephone interview by the author, October 4, 2004, typed notes in author's possession; Green, *Battling the Plantation Mentality*, 228–29.

11. Seigenthaler interview, 2004; John L. Seigenthaler, telephone interview by the author, October 7, 2007, typed notes in author's possession; Seigenthaler interview, 2013; Barbara Gamarekian to Russell Sugarmon, October 10, 1960, Robert F. Kennedy Pre-Administration Papers, Correspondence Series, box 29, folder Su–Suk, JFK; A. W. Willis Jr. to John Seigenthaler, ibid., box 32, folder Will–Wilm.

12. This analysis is based on my exploration of the Civil Rights Division Papers, boxes 140–150, Democratic National Committee Papers, JFK. On the airlift, see "Hank Aaron and Bill Bruton Tour for Kennedy," October 29, 1960, news release, Democratic National Committee Papers, box 150, folder Press Releases, Final 10/7/60–11/3/60, JFK; "Kennedy Airlift," n.d., ibid., folder Schedules 9/15/60–11/4/60 and Undated; Marjorie Lawson to R. B. Sugarmon, September 10 and August 30, 1960, ibid., box 142, folder S 8/15/60–9/27/60.

13. Seigenthaler interview, 2013, 11, 26; Russell B. Sugarmon Jr., interview by the author, Memphis, June 13, 2007, transcript, 11–12 (copy in author's possession); Jalenak, "Beale Street Politics," 148; Seigenthaler interview, 2013, 7–8, 23–24.

14. Jalenak, "Beale Street Politics," 150–57 (Sugarmon quoted on 156); "Carvan Itenerary [*sic*]" and "Itinerary for Hank Aaron–Bill Bruton Tour," n.d., Democratic National Committee Papers, box 150, folder Schedules 9/15/60–11/4/60 and Undated, JFK; Shelby County Democratic Club, "Clearing the Way for J. F. K. in Tennessee," [1960], copy in author's possession.

15. Officially, this pamphlet was sponsored by the Freedom Crusade Committee, but it was instigated by the Kennedy campaign. "'No Comment' Nixon versus a Candidate with a Heart, Senator Kennedy: The Case of Martin Luther King," November 1960, Democratic National Committee Papers, box 140, folder Campaign Materials 9/21/60–11/4/60, JFK. For the back story, see Taylor Branch, *Parting the Waters: America in the King Years, 1954–63*, paperback ed. (New York: Simon and Schuster, 1989), 351–70. Also see Seigenthaler interview, 2004.

16. Josephine Burson, interview by the author, Memphis, July 28, 2004, transcript, 7–8 (copy in author's possession).

17. Excerpts from remarks of Senator John F. Kennedy, September 22, 1960, press release, Democratic National Committee, John F. Kennedy Pre-Presidential Papers, series 12.1, box 911, folder Riverside Drive Rally, Memphis, Tennessee, 9/21/60, JFK; Sugarmon interview, 2007, 13.

18. Sugarmon to Democratic Party Headquarters, November 14, 1960,

Russell B. Sugarmon Jr. Papers, box 2, folder 4, University of Memphis Special Collections; Jalenak, "Beale Street Politics," 143, 158; Sugarmon interview, 2000, 24–25; Jay Hall, "Big Negro Vote Given Kennedy," *Memphis Commercial Appeal,* November 9, 1960, 5B; Betts interview, 36; Seigenthaler interview, 2013, 15–16.

19. Richard M. Scammon, "How the Negroes Voted," *New Republic,* November 21, 1960, 8–9, Democratic National Committee Papers, box 149, folder Post-Election Analysis 11/10/60–11/21/60 and Undated, JFK.

20. The "bright lights" quote is from Seigenthaler interview, 2007, and the other is from the 2004 interview. The general information in this paragraph is from those interviews and from Seigenthaler interview, 2013.

21. Burke Marshall to Henry Loeb, February 6, 1962, Henry Loeb Papers, series 1, box 3, folder 32, Memphis–Shelby County Room, Memphis and Shelby County Public Library and Information Center; Commission on Civil Rights, "Transcript of Proceedings," June 24 and 25, 1962, p. 10, Berl Bernhard Papers, box 10, folder Proceedings, Jun. 24, 25, 1962, JFK.

22. Memphis Branch, NAACP, "Re: A Modest Proposal for the Annexation of the City of Memphis, Shelby County, Tennessee," *Memphis Commercial Appeal,* February 22, 1961; John A. Morsell to Jesse H. Turner, February 24, 1961; Roy Wilkins to Jesse H. Turner, February 27, 1961, all in NAACP Papers, group III, box C146, folder 1961–1962.

23. Sugarmon interview, 2007, 15, 28–29; Russell B. Sugarmon Jr., interview by the author, Memphis, June 19, 2004, typed notes in author's possession; Jalenak, "Beale Street Politics," 158–59; Lyndon B. Johnson to Ethyl B. Venson, July 30, 1963, Venson Papers, box 2, folder 4, Memphis and Shelby County Public Library and Information Center; Associated Press, "Kennedy, Too, Honoring Abe," n.d., scrapbook, Sugarmon personal papers; Lyndon B. Johnson to Russell Sugarmon Jr., July 15, 1963, ibid.; Henry Loeb to Tom Robinson, March 24, 1962, Loeb Papers, series 1, box 3, folder 3; Dean Rusk to Russell B. Sugarmon Jr., August 29, 1962, Sugarmon personal papers; "Members of the U.S. Delegation," n.d., Sugarmon Papers, box 2, folder 13, University of Memphis Special Collections; Joseph M. LaRocca to OVR Central Office and Regional Office Staff, June 21, 1961, Roberta Church Papers, box 1, folder 20, Memphis and Shelby County Public Library and Information Center; "Ex-Memphian Gets Rehabilitation Job," *Memphis Commercial Appeal,* July 8, 1961, copy in ibid., box 2, folder 7.

24. Sugarmon interview, 2007, 18; Vasco Smith, interviews by the author, Memphis, October 9, 10, 12, 2000, SOHP, transcript, 61–62.

25. White House diary, October 5, 1961, JFK, http://www.jfklibrary.org/white%20house%20diary/1961/October/5 (accessed February 24, 2007); Robert F. Kennedy to Henry Loeb, October 19, 1961, Loeb Papers, series 1, box 3, folder 32; The Supreme Court of the United States, October Term, 1962,

I. A. Watson Jr., et al., Petitioners v. City of Memphis, et al., brief of the United States as amicus curiae, filed February 7, 1963, Library of Congress Law Library, copy in author's possession; US Commission on Civil Rights, press memo, July 12, 1963, Erwin Griswold Papers, box 3, folder 4, Harvard University Archives, Cambridge, MA.

26. Vasco Smith interviews, 2000, 91–93; Vasco Smith, interview by the author, Memphis, July 12, 2004, SOHP, transcript, 2–3; Sugarmon interview, 2000, 14, 36; Sugarmon, interview, July 2004, 20, 25–26, 34; Davis interview, 1, 3; Jalenak, "Beale Street Politics," 53–54; Russell B. Sugarmon Jr., "Report of Special Committees," n.d., Sugarmon personal papers; H. A. Gilliam to R. B. Sugarmon Jr., May 3, 1962, ibid.; R. B. Sugarmon to J. Lewis Taliaferro, May 22, 1962, Sugarmon Papers, box 1, folder 3, University of Memphis Special Collections; David N. Harsh to Russell B. Sugarmon, May 31, 1962, Sugarmon personal papers; "Backing of Pritchard by Dem Club Victory for Sugarmon, Willis!" *Memphis World,* June 16, 1962, Sugarmon Papers, box 2, folder 4, University of Memphis Special Collections; "Walker Heads Farris-Davis Committee," *Memphis World,* July 14, 1962, ibid.; Neal Gregory, "Shelby County Negro Voters Split on Major Contests," undated newspaper clipping, ibid.; "Gladney, Holloway, Stokes, Sugarmon, Turner in Race," undated newspaper clipping, ibid.; R. B. Sugarmon Jr. to Treasurer of Shelby County Democratic Club, July 16, 1962, Sugarmon personal papers; "Sugarmon Leads Democratic Club," *Memphis World,* December 15, 1962, 1; Michael C. Lydon, "When the Negroes Get the Vote—IV: Memphis Taste of Victory," newspaper clipping, May 12, 1965, Sugarmon Papers, box 2, folder 4, University of Memphis Special Collections; Jalenak, "Beale Street Politics," 53–55; "Nine Candidates Interviewed by Negro Democratic Club," *Memphis Commercial Appeal,* July 9, 1960, M. A. Hinds Papers, box 1127, University of Memphis Special Collections.

27. Sugarmon interview, 2000, 17; Jalenak, "Beale Street Politics," 49, 58; Sugarmon interview, July 2004, 41; Wheeler interview, 36–37, 39–40; Betts interview, 44, 54; Johnnie Mae Peters, interview by author, Memphis, June 29, 2004, SOHP, transcript, 25–26.

28. Vasco Smith interview, 2004, 6, 9; Betts interview, 13; Davis interview, 4; Maxine Smith, interview by the author, Memphis, July 26, 2004, SOHP, transcript, 10–11; Sugarmon interview, July 2004, 3, 13, 48; Wheeler interview, 3, 12, 14, 16; Betts interview, 13–14, 43; Davis interview, 3–4; Peters interview, 23–24; "Precinct Coordinator's Guide," Sugarmon personal papers. Also see "Area Team," 1962; "Tally Sheet for Watchers and Precinct Leaders," 1962; "Instruction Sheet for Street Leaders," 1962; "Instructions for Canvassers," August 2, 1962; "Instructions for Precinct Leaders," 1962; and "Instructions to Car Drivers," 1962, all in Sugarmon Papers, box 1, folder 3, University of Memphis Special Collections.

29. Sugarmon interview, July 2004, 4; Betts interview, 24–26; Wheeler

interview, 13; Alexander Gladney, "Dear Reverend" form letter, July 9, 1962, Sugarmon Papers, box 1, folder 3, University of Memphis Special Collections; "Sugarmon Leads Democratic Club," *Memphis World,* December 15, 1962, 1; Jalenak, "Beale Street Politics," 107; Agenda of the Shelby County Democratic Club, April 21, 1960, Sugarmon personal papers.

30. Peters interview, 27; James Hunter Lane, interview by the author, Memphis, June 15, July 14, 2004, SOHP, transcript, 3–4; William Morris, interview by the author, Memphis, June 24, 2004, SOHP, transcript, 21–22; Thomas E. "Pete" Sisson, interview by the author, Memphis, June 22, 2004, SOHP, transcript, 19–20; Vasco Smith interview, 2004, 4–5; Sugarmon interview, July 2004, 47; Peters interview, 13, 25–26; Betts interview, 23, 29, 47; Lockard interview, July 29, 2004, 19; "Poll Check-off List," n.d., Willis Papers, box 3, folder 18; Russell B. Sugarmon Jr. to "Dear Fellow Memphian," July 28, 1962, Sugarmon Papers, box 1, folder 3, University of Memphis Special Collections; "Proposed Questions for County Commissioner," "Proposed Questions for Congressional Candidates," and "Proposed Questions for Gubernatorial Candidates," 1962, ibid., box 1, folder 13; Shelby County Democratic Club, "Instructions for Precinct Watchers," 1962, ibid., box 1, folder 3; "Sample Ballot: Vote the Shelby County Democratic Club Ticket," 1962, ibid.; Shelby County Democratic Club, "Instructions for Poll Workers on Election Day," 1962, ibid.

31. Sugarmon interview, 2000, 14–16, 39; Sugarmon interview, July 2004, 15–16, 41–42; "Farris Gives Frank Answers," *Memphis World,* June 16, 1962, Sugarmon Papers, box 2, folder 4, University of Memphis Special Collections; "2 Walk out after Tenn. Vote Group Selects Clement!" *Memphis World,* June 16, 1962, ibid.; "Negroes Won't All Vote One Way—That's Good," *Memphis Press-Scimitar,* July 17, 1962, ibid.; Neal Gregory, "Shelby County Negro Voters Split on Major Contests," undated newspaper clipping, ibid.; "Proposed Bylaws for State-Wide Voters Council," ibid., box 3, folder 9; Frank G. Clement to C. F. Williams and A. W. Willis Jr., June 2, 1962, ibid., box 1, folder 5; "Proposed Questions for Gubernatorial Candidates," 1962, ibid.; "About the Tennessee Voters Council," 1964, ibid., box 3, folder 9.

32. The other candidates for the Shelby County Democratic Executive Committee were A. Maceo Walker, Willa McWilliams Walker, and Alexander Gladney. Gloster B. Current to Henry Lee Moon, "Memphis Boycott Successful," February 6, 1962, NAACP Papers, group III, box C146, folder 1961–1962; Maxine Smith interview, 2004, 14–15; Jalenak, "Beale Street Politics," 77; Muse, *Memphis,* 9–10; Lydon, "When the Negroes Get the Vote"; Stanley S. Scott, "Jesse Turner Wins Nomination to Democratic Executive Post," *Tri-State Defender,* August 6, 1960, 1; "Memphis Democrats Elect Negro," *New York Times,* August 6, 1960, 8; Wilma Dykeman and James Stokely, "The Big Cure for Segregation," *New York Times Magazine,* September 24, 1961, 30; Gritter, *River of Hope,* 215.

33. Sugarmon interview, July 2004, 25; Sugarmon interview, 2000, 16;

Shelby County Democratic Club, Executive Committee Mailing List, 1963–64, Sugarmon Papers, box 3, folder 2, University of Memphis Special Collections; Listing of Name, Address, and Telephone Number of Chairman, [1964], ibid., box 2, folder 1; Shelby County Democratic Club, "Pull One Big Democratic Lever for Freedom," 1964, ibid., box 1, folder 7; "Tennessee Voters Council Analysis and Proposed Budget for November 3, 1964, Election," 1964, ibid.; Muse, *Memphis,* 2.

  34. G. Wayne Dowdy, *Crusades for Freedom: Memphis and the Political Transformation of the American South* (Jackson: University Press of Mississippi, 2010), 90–92, 99–101, 106.

  35. Sugarmon interview, June 2004; Betts interview, 14–15, 42; Lockard interview, July 29, 2004, 10, 18, 21–22; Maxine Smith interview, 2004, 47; Davis interview, 17; Vasco Smith interview, 2004, 57; Wheeler interview, 18–19; Peters interview, 28–29.

"Since I Was a Citizen, I Had the Right to Attend the Library"

The Key Role of the Public Library in the Civil Rights Movement in Memphis

Steven A. Knowlton

Memphian Jesse Turner, an African American, wanted his wife to be able to use the library. Throughout the winter of 1949 Allegra Turner was in mourning for a younger brother who had been killed in a railroad accident. Looking for a diversion, Jesse Turner suggested that a visit to the library might help Mrs. Turner "become engrossed in both fun and facts."[1] Mr. Turner, an officer at the Tri-State Bank located just a few blocks from the Cossitt Library on Front Street, had used the Memphis Public Library's main branch (named for its benefactor, Frederick Cossitt) in the past. Crucially, he had never sat down or tried to borrow a book. Due to a quirk in the rules of segregation, Jesse Turner had been allowed to stand in the reference section while he looked up a few facts in a book. Had he attempted to use the full range of the library's facilities, he would have known better than to suggest that Mrs. Turner would be welcome at the Cossitt Library downtown.

Her travails that day encapsulate the everyday realities of African American life in segregated Memphis. Allegra Turner, who was familiar with the workings of libraries from her days as a student and instructor at Southern University and the University of Chicago, entered the library and made straight for the card catalog. Almost immediately, a white library employee redirected her to a "small, white picket-fenced area" to wait while library staff bustled about deciding "what should be done." In the end, Mrs. Turner was instructed to leave Cossitt Library and visit the Vance Avenue branch library, reserved for the use of African Americans.[2] She proceeded out to Main Street to find a telephone, intending to call her husband and have him pick her up—but the only establishments open at that hour were restricted to whites. So she caught a bus and, sitting in the rear, rode all the way out to her apartment in the Binghampton neighborhood, several miles away.[3]

Eight years later, Jesse Turner would surprise his wife when he appeared on the television news in a report about "a well-dressed Negro man [who] entered the front door of the main library at Peabody and McLean and requested a library card to borrow books."[4] Turner's actions on June 17, 1957, were among the earliest in a swirl of antisegregation activism that African American Memphians and their allies would engage in until the city's public facilities were open to all. The libraries were the locus of legal action and direct action, and Jesse Turner would become one of the foremost spokespeople for civil rights in Memphis. All this became possible in the eight years between Mrs. Turner's ejection from Cossitt Library and Mr. Turner's formal application to use the facility. Memphis and its libraries—and the United States—had changed, but not always in ways that made life easier for African Americans.

In a way, the struggle to desegregate the public libraries of Memphis is a microcosm of the larger civil rights struggle in the Bluff City. While the white leaders of the city did not encourage the violence seen in other southern cities toward civil rights protesters, they were slow and reluctant to open the library to readers of all races—and the library was the first public institution to be desegregated. The libraries of Memphis loomed large in the minds of Jesse Turner and others as symbolic spaces from which the city government barred them.

The concept of libraries as communal sanctuaries is vital. As Wayne Wiegand describes it, the library is a place where "the act of reading becomes dependably pleasurable, empowering, intellectually stimulating, and socially bonding" because it occurs in the presence of others who also value reading.[5] For African American readers, the segregation of the Memphis Public Library was doubly damaging: the only branch open to African Americans suffered from an inferior collection and poor service, and they were excluded from the community of readers who found their intellectual home in the Central Library.

In the end, the desegregation of the libraries met less resistance than did the efforts to open up schools. Michael Fultz offers the perspective that, compared with other public facilities, libraries provide less of an occasion for the dreaded "social equality" (which, according to Whitney Strub, translates as whites and African Americans forming intimate relationships). Library service is a transactional enterprise, more akin to shopping than to sharing a schoolroom.[6] The director of the Memphis Public Library during the desegregation lawsuit, C. Lamar Wallis, concurred: "I told [the library board] that . . . there would be no violence. . . . Reading in a library is a fairly private affair, you do not mingle with the people around the table with you."[7] Nonetheless, Turner's victory in the courts—which was spurred by direct action, including some of the first sit-ins in the city—proved to be a key moment that led to many other legal breakthroughs in the desegregation of public facilities in Memphis.

While victories in the courts—notably *Brown v. Board of Education* in 1954—broke down some legal barriers to integration (de jure if not de facto), they also led to "massive resistance" by whites, who chose to close schools rather than allow their children to attend classes with blacks. Efforts to desegregate libraries also met with massive resistance.[8] But just as school closures quickly eroded white citizens' will to resist desegregation by sacrificing their own services, so did library closures and vertical integration—in most cases, library service was restored, with full access to African Americans, within a few days.

Massive resistance had little support in Tennessee. Rather, white authorities responded to court rulings that ordered desegregation with foot-dragging.[9] Memphis authorities kept mum throughout the period, and in fact, they continued to build segregated schools even after *Brown*.[10]

The hostile atmosphere of mid-1950s Memphis brought about bold actions by African Americans to end legal segregation, including lawsuits to open Memphis State University to students of all races and to desegregate city buses.[11] A forty-five-day boycott of the city's largest newspaper, the *Commercial Appeal*, demonstrated the economic clout of the African American community and succeeded in forcing the largest white-oriented newspaper in Memphis to agree to use "titles of respect before the names of Negroes" and otherwise engage in fair reporting about African American activities.[12]

It was in this atmosphere of African American activism and white backlash that Jesse Turner made his move to desegregate the library.

In 1955 the Board of Directors had opened the new Central Library at McLean and Peabody and officially changed its name to the Memphis Public Library; the old Cossitt Library downtown had been transformed into a reference-only branch. As was the case throughout the establishment in Memphis, library leaders apparently chose to ignore the question of desegregation and simply moved forward in administering the city's segregated libraries. In response to frequent petitions from African American citizens, the library board began construction of a second branch for African American readers, but it would not open until after all the libraries had been desegregated.

Before the library board could make any headway on building another branch for blacks, it was confronted with an immediate demand for service by an African American patron at the Central Library. On a sunny Monday, June 17, 1957, Jesse Turner left home for work. During a break from his duties at Tri-State Bank, he ventured to the Central Library and "requested of Mr. Jesse L. Cunningham the necessary cards and/or permission for him and his children to use the facilities of the main library."[13] Library director Cunningham denied him such permission and told reporters, "I was acting on the custom that prevails in this community and the South." The librarian referred Turner to the Vance Avenue branch. The library's Board of Directors "sustained [his] action, unanimously."[14]

Turner's audacious request generated headlines in the white-owned *Memphis Press-Scimitar*. When a reporter pressed Cunningham to provide a legal justification for denying Turner library services, the director admitted, "There is no law, city, county, or state, that I know of that would have prevented" issuing a library card to Turner, and the board had never adopted a policy "in writing" against serving African Americans at the main library. He asserted, however, that the library on Vance Avenue served African Americans, and although it did not have the same holdings as the Central Library, "the library assistant there, if she knew what the borrower wanted and that he was a person really trying to do something and not trying to make a scene, would get the book and have it for the borrower."[15]

Once his personal visit failed, Turner formally appealed for access to the library. Via his attorney H. T. Lockard—president of the Memphis branch of the NAACP and the litigator handling the bus lawsuit as well—

Turner asked for a library card and noted that a denial based on race was "unlawful as well as discriminatory."[16] After months of stalling, on October 2 the board voted unanimously to deny Turner's application to use the Central Library.[17] In his formal response to Lockard, board president Wassell Randolph wrote:

> It will be contended that Negro readers are not permitted to have joint use of reading rooms with White readers, and it has been and is the unanimous opinion of the Directors that this is not advisable, nor is it conducive to harmonious relations among the people of our City. Forcing people to associate together against their will is the antithesis of freedom. . . . Sadly, recent events have opened wounds which we thought were healed forever, and have destroyed friendships developed among the people of the two races for the welfare, principally of our Negro citizens and for their general advancement; and the Library Directors on their own part, are unwilling to increase the tension or widen the breach now so painfully apparent.[18]

Turner and Lockard persisted, corresponding with the library board throughout the first half of 1958, but they were repeatedly rebuffed. However, other parties were also pressuring the library to desegregate. The most forceful protest was launched by a group that made its case on June 20. Rowland Hill, a white professor at the still-segregated Memphis State University, had gathered signatures from students and faculty at his institution and other colleges in the city and presented an impassioned plea to the Board of Directors.[19] The library did not change its policies, but Hill and his colleague Lawrence Edwards were "ousted" by university president J. Millard Smith.[20] Several signatories later corresponded with Cunningham to rescind their support of desegregation.

Within a fortnight, the African American–owned *Memphis World* was speculating whether Lockard would file suit against the library on Turner's behalf. The report quoted Turner:

> When I go to the library, I am not looking for a particular book. I want to look in some periodical for statistics and facts, in mate-

rial which can not be found at the Negro branch. I feel that I have the right to go [to] any library I choose, for my tax money also goes to support the libraries. It was pretty insulting to be told by Mr. Jesse Cunningham that I was "too intelligent" to want to go to the main library. It would seem to me that "the more intelligent you are the less you need a library" is going backwards.

Turner admitted he had not used and "would never" use the Vance Avenue branch, despite its proximity to his home.[21]

Despite recent setbacks in the other desegregation cases proceeding in Memphis, Lockard and Turner moved forward with legal action. Working with fellow attorneys A. W. Willis Jr. and Russell Sugarmon Jr., Lockard filed suit in federal court on August 15, with the support of the national NAACP.[22] Turner, "on behalf of himself and others similarly situated," sued all the members of the Board of Directors of the Memphis Public Library, as well as Cunningham. For ease of reference, the case was called *Turner v. Randolph*. Turner asked the court to adjudicate the question of whether segregated libraries in Memphis are permissible, to issue an injunction forbidding segregation in the libraries, and to grant him his court costs.[23] Turner sued under laws arising from Reconstruction-era legislation to preserve the rights of freed people under the Fourteenth and Fifteenth Amendments.[24] Although they had been "dead letters" for many years, these laws were still on the books and had formed the basis for much important litigation since the late 1930s.

Despite evidence that desegregation must come—the federal government had made it clear in Little Rock in 1957 that it would support school desegregation, and the Tennessee Board of Education had approved the desegregation of Memphis State University—the whites in charge of the library were steadfast in their maintenance of the color line. Even before the board had a chance to meet and discuss Turner's lawsuit, Cunningham was confidently reporting that "the Library Board is definitely committed to the continuance of our policy."[25]

The City Commission was firmly behind segregation at the library. Commissioners Stanley Dillard, John T. Dwyer, Henry Loeb, and Claude Armour all affirmed that they were "strongly opposed to integration of the Memphis public libraries and will fight any lawsuit that seeks to force it." Loeb repeated Cunningham's assurance that "we have separate but equal facilities. Anyone from one branch can call for a book from any other branch. I don't know how you could make it more equal."[26] In the midst of all this action, Cunningham retired as library director and was replaced by C. Lamar Wallis beginning December 1.[27]

The suit would linger many months in court, as Judge Marion Boyd allowed delays to obstruct any decision. Even after the case was reassigned to William E. Miller of the Middle District of Tennessee, there was no movement on the library lawsuit until the spring of 1960.[28]

This did not mean the library escaped the attention of African Americans in Memphis. On the evening of September 22, 1958, four young people followed Turner's lead and approached the Central Library for service. The first student was told he must go to the Vance Avenue branch, request his book, and wait another day for it to be sent there. He then proceeded to ask librarian Mary Haley if he could listen to records in the library's music room. "You know that you cannot use the music room," she replied. He asked if he could borrow a record but was told this was impossible because "none of the Branches may borrow records, since the Record Collection is set up for borrowers who come to this branch." The other students were also denied access to the books they requested.[29] Cunningham was convinced that these young people had been "sent to the library [and] coached and rehearsed for the definite purpose of being witnesses in our case when it comes to trial." If so, their interaction with Haley provided plenty of proof that the treatment of African Americans at the Central Library was discriminatory and unequal.[30]

A similar incident occurred on December 15 when a black woman was directed to the registration desk to get a library card, and the registration desk directed her to Vance Avenue.[31] Whether Cunningham's suspicions were well-founded is unknown. There is no record of any coordinated activity to create a pool of witnesses for the lawsuit.

There was no direct action at the library throughout 1959, but other events that year were of concern to African American library patrons. The winner of that year's mayoral race was Henry Loeb, the former city commissioner and a strong supporter of segregation at the library. In his campaign, Loeb pledged to "fight any integration order all the way."

However, he maintained that a Loeb administration would provide services that were "separate but equal, but I mean equal in all fairness."[32]

By the beginning of Loeb's term in January 1960, Turner was still waiting for his lawsuit to have its first hearing. With one delay after another, Memphis had managed to avoid both desegregation and the violence that accompanied it in other cities. The exceptions were the peaceful matriculation of eight black students at Memphis State in the fall of 1959 and compliance with federal regulations at the interstate bus terminal.[33]

The desegregation movement continued despite Loeb's election. Turner filed another lawsuit to desegregate the airport.[34] A mass meeting was held to organize a boycott of local car dealers after a segregated auto show was held in the city auditorium.[35] And on March 19, 1960, African Americans took their place in the Memphis Public Library, regardless of policy. The sit-in was not a novel form of protest; back in 1939, several African American youths had entered the library in Alexandria, Virginia, and read quietly until they were arrested. As a result of their protest, the city built a branch for African Americans.[36] Even so, the wave of sit-ins that swept the South in early 1960 took most observers by surprise. From a single sit-in at a Greensboro, North Carolina, Woolworth's on February 1, the idea spread to Raleigh, Nashville, Montgomery, and other locales across the South.[37] The students of Memphis were ready, and one of their first targets was the Central Library.

Marion Barry, a graduate of LeMoyne College who was attending graduate school at Fisk University in Nashville, had participated in sit-ins at the state capital. He returned to his hometown and spread enthusiasm for protest among his acquaintances.[38] The leaders of Memphis civil rights organizations were caught by surprise when a group of students from LeMoyne College and Owen Junior College staged the first sit-in at the lunch counter of McLellan's Variety Store on March 18. The protesters left the lunch counter as police arrived, and no one was arrested. The students had brought along a photographer from the African American–owned *Tri-State Defender* but had apparently neglected to inform anyone at the NAACP of their plans.[39] Years later, many key figures in the NAACP such as Willis, Sugarmon, and Maxine Smith had no recollection of the lunch counter being the site of the first sit-in.

The next day's protest would have a far different outcome. More than three dozen students staged simultaneous sit-ins at the Central Library and the Cossitt Reference Library. The reason for choosing the libraries over other segregated facilities remains unclear. But one protester, Jennie Betts, recalled having a strong grievance against the libraries: "There wasn't nothing in [the Vance Avenue branch]. . . . I was in college and you just couldn't find anything in the black library that we needed. . . . The one I sit in, everything I wanted."[40] In court hearings, protesters Gwendolyn Townsend, a LeMoyne student, and Clyde Battle, a student at Owen Junior College, testified that a group of students had been discussing their term papers, and a common complaint was that their college libraries lacked the materials they needed for research, so "they decided to go to the main branch to get the books we needed."[41]

On Saturday, March 19, a little after noon, twenty-two young African Americans entered the Central Library and, saying little, began to use the library's card catalog and read at the tables provided. A white librarian observed, "They just came in and scattered around and sat at the tables." Even hostile witnesses admitted that they were "courteous and not loud or boisterous." Fourteen others entered the Cossitt Reference Library and sat in the section reserved for white patrons. At both locations, white librarians advised the African American patrons of the rules regarding segregation and asked them to leave. When the protesters remained in the library, the librarians called police. They admitted that "the reasons they had the students arrested was that they were Negroes."[42]

Within minutes of the protesters' arrival, police had arrested thirty-six of them. Also arrested were five reporters and photographers from the *Memphis World* and *Tri-State Defender*. This was the first time members of the press had been arrested during a sit-in protest. The students and newspapermen were charged with disorderly conduct, loitering, and threat of breach of peace.[43]

The charges were serious enough that the accused were required to post bond, and they spent many hours in jail until they were able to do so. To pass the time, the protesters sang spirituals and prayed with Baptist ministers.[44] The students put on a brave face, commenting that the only hardship they suffered was "sitting on those hard benches they have in the jail."[45] The arrested newsmen—and African American public opinion—were less sanguine. The *Memphis World* noted that the young

LeMoyne College students arrested after Cossitt Library sit-in, March 19, 1960. (Courtesy Special Collections Department, University of Memphis)

men had been "dumped into jail cells with drunks and other socially undesirables."[46] Burleigh Himes, the arrested city editor of the *Tri-State Defender*, recalled his experience with "disgust. . . . Offensive to the physical, moral, or aesthetic taste, and you can throw in all the synonyms such as loathsome, sickening (you should have seen the food they offered us in that jail), repulsive, revolting and nauseous for a good measure of the treatment."[47] L. F. Palmer, the *Defender*'s editor, recounted being "forced to line up against the wall, frisked (searched) and ordered into a small bull pen. . . . Made to accommodate about 15 or 16 . . . shortly our bull pen was holding 41 men . . . back to back or belly to belly."[48]

The "gutsy, wonderful kids . . . threatening the status quo by fighting peacefully for first class citizenship" galvanized the Memphis civil rights community.[49] Maxine Smith recalled that the executive board of the local NAACP branch was meeting to discuss plans for a Memphis sit-in movement when it received the call to come bail out the library protesters.[50] Lawyers Russell Sugarmon and A. W. Willis were quickly dispatched to the jail to arrange for the protesters' release.[51] The proceedings lasted several hours. Judge Beverly Bouche set the bond at $352 for each protester, totaling $14,432 for the group.

In the meantime, a hastily arranged mass meeting on Saturday evening at the Mount Olive Christian Methodist Episcopal Church drew ministers from numerous churches, and they promised to call on their congregants to contribute money for the sit-in movement.[52] The meeting also resulted in the adoption of a statement for the press, which read: "The Memphis Branch of the NAACP . . . wishes to declare its wholehearted support of these students, their objectives and their non-violent demonstrations. This branch further pledges its moral, financial and legal resources to assist them in achieving these goals."[53] By the time the bond hearings began at 10:30 p.m., the NAACP had rounded up $5,270 in cash and put up corporate bonds for the remainder.[54] The police entered the church at around 1:15 a.m., nightsticks in hand, to clear out the building, threatening to "lock you up for loitering on the streets at 1:30 a.m."[55]

The library protesters, released in groups of fifteen or so, were greeted outside the jailhouse by a jubilant crowd of about a hundred people and escorted to a gathering in a residence at 519 Vance Avenue—right next door to the Negro branch of the library.[56] As they were released, most of the protesters declined to comment for the press, although Ed Young served notice that "We have just begun to fight."[57] When asked why she was at the library, Gwendolyn Townsend told a reporter, "I felt that since I was a citizen, I had the right to attend the library."[58]

The arrests were not inconsequential. The *Tri-State Defender* ceased publication for a week until its staff could file their reports.[59] A number of students were fired from their part-time jobs or domestic work.[60] Despite the approbation they received in the press, not all the students' families were pleased. Marion Barry recalled that his mother's first reaction to the sit-ins in Nashville had been to reprimand him: "Boy, what are you doing in jail?"[61] The long-term fate of most of the Memphis protesters has not been tracked, but Fred Jones, one of the Greensboro sit-in pioneers, was blackballed from employment after his graduation.[62]

The Sunday following the first sit-ins, African American churches were filled with sermons urging support for the protesters. Herbert Brewster noted that the students "were merely applying Gandhi and Nehru's tactic of passive resistance to compel the white race to live up to its own political and religious philosophy," and he claimed that "even the old, discarded Supreme Court doctrine of 'equal but separate' education facilities is not being lived up to." He told his congregants that phonograph records could be checked out only at the Central Library, and when library director Wallis was asked for a response, he claimed that "so far as he knows no Negro has asked to take out records."[63]

The protesters appeared in court before Judge Bouche on Monday, March 21. In addition to the crowd (including parents of the protesters) that filled the courtroom gallery to capacity, around 250 African American supporters quietly rallied outside the Central Police Station, which also housed the City Court, for the duration of the hours-long hearing. A line of police blocked every entrance to the building, fire hoses at the ready to disperse the crowd.[64] The team of lawyers from the NAACP (described as "every single Negro attorney in Memphis") defended the protesters.[65] Benjamin Hooks claimed that the charge of disturbing the peace should have been pinned on the police rather than the students who were quietly using the library: "If the city policemen would have not arrested these defendants, this hearing would not have been necessary. This mass disturbance was brought on by the police department." The city attorney, James F. A. Shea, pressed the argument that the students had conspired to create a disturbance. Lockard took offense, saying, "There cannot be a conspiracy as long as you are acting within law, within your constitutional rights. These students were within their rights to enter a public library and use its facilities in an orderly manner."[66]

Despite Judge Bouche's admission that the defense lawyers had "done pretty good," he found the protesters guilty of disorderly conduct; the charges of loitering and disturbing the peace were dropped. Bouche, in the end, agreed with the prosecutor's argument that the protesters' actions were a "threat to disorder." Bouche declared that the sit-ins were a "mass demonstration that breeds contempt for the law, an open invitation to mob rule, to violence. I don't care whose mob rule or whose violence, I am not going to stand for it."[67]

The journalists' fates were different. Bouche agreed with their defense that they had merely been performing their normal duties associated with reporting and dismissed the charges against most of the newspaper staff. L. F. Palmer, however, was fined $50 for "talking above a whisper while covering a story in the Front Street Library."[68]

In addition to the 250 standing vigil outside the courtroom, 2,000 African American Memphians gathered that evening at Mount Olive Church to await news of the hearing. Another $3,000 in cash was raised for the students' defense, and "feeling for the cause of the Negro students and their fight ran high through the two-hour meeting." The library sit-ins had stirred the African American community of Memphis to take mass action. Vasco Smith "said the day has finally arrived. 'People are shedding tears; tears of joy.'" In addition to the cash raised, the Mount Olive meeting resulted in a proposal to stay away from (but not "boycott") downtown businesses on Thursdays and Mondays. The NAACP garnered 115 new members that night.[69]

The promised mass action started the very next day. On Tuesday, March 22, there were sit-ins at the Cossitt Reference Library as well as at the Brooks Memorial Art Gallery. Thirteen protesters entered the Brooks Gallery, and ten entered Cossitt, "selected books and began reading."[70] Prosecutors proffered charges of loitering, disorderly conduct, and disturbing the peace, and the Tuesday protesters spent the entire day in jail before being bailed out after midnight.[71]

The fervor throughout the African American community carried forward into the spring. On March 29 a crowd of 4,500 met at Mount Olive Church and pledged $6,700 in cash and a commitment to continue to "struggle as long as it is necessary for us to obtain full citizenship."[72] On the morning of April 4 police arrested four students at the Cossitt branch, and four more students were arrested that afternoon at the Central Library.[73]

The library sit-ins sparked a mass movement in Memphis. Sit-ins occurred over the next seven months at lunch counters, bus stations, and churches, resulting in 318 arrests and the eventual desegregation of most public accommodations in the city.

Reactions in the white community varied. The Memphis Committee on Community Relations (MCCR), a body of "moderate" whites whose main aim, according to Laurie Green, was "avoiding civil strife," attempted to arrange meetings with new mayor Loeb and the City Commission.[74] On March 28 the mayor and the City Commission held a conference, closed to the public, with the attorneys representing the protesters. In defiance of the MCCR's hope for moderation, the attorneys requested that "this honorable body desegregate forthwith all public facilities." City commissioner William Farris commented, "I was elected by the citizens of Memphis on a platform to maintain racial segregation and I am going to do just that."[75] No compromise was reached.

The lack of progress was unsurprising. Loeb had recently called the protests an "attempt to take the law and customs of generations into their own hands in groups."[76] Faced with the city government's intransigence, protesters continued their sit-ins and other direct action—but they also ramped up their legal activity. In early May, Willis and Sugarmon announced plans to sue for desegregation of the city's tennis courts, the Brooks Art Gallery, the Pink Palace Museum, and Ellis Auditorium.[77]

As these sit-ins and boycotts pressured the segregated establishments of Memphis, lawyers for Jesse Turner finally got their day in court. On June 29 Judge Miller ruled against Lockard's motion for summary judgment—meaning that both parties agreed to the set of facts presented, and the judge would be required to rule only on the question of how the law applied.[78] Depositions occurred through the summer. Among the facts revealed were the budgets for the different libraries, with vastly different sums appropriated to the Vance Avenue branch and the branches serving white patrons.

A swift turn in the mayor's attitude was noted at the end of the summer. Loeb and the city commissioners met with the library board to reconsider the "long standing policy" of keeping facilities segregated. The library board voted unanimously to defer to the City Commission in determining whether to change the policy.[79]

Loeb was under pressure to desegregate from a number of directions. The federal Justice Department was urging him to desegregate, and he thought that doing so in the libraries would bolster the city's defense in a lawsuit against the public school system. It would show that the city was acting in good faith to move with "all deliberate speed" to desegregate public facilities.[80] Although Loeb never admitted it, the continual disruption caused by the sit-ins and picketing must have influenced his decision. He frequently announced publicly, "I am a segregationist . . . but not a professional segregationist." His personal inclination toward segregation was tempered by a strong sense of duty to enforce the law and maintain order.[81] In addition, his own lawyers advised him that the lawsuit would probably be decided in favor of Turner.[82]

The first step in Loeb's desegregation program was the announcement on September 19, 1960, that bus riders "will not be asked to change seats because of their race."[83] Meanwhile, the City Commission had met on September 15 and agreed to desegregate the libraries. The library board agreed to "abide by that decision."[84] On October 13 the City Commission announced the new policy: "The City Commission has decided the facilities of the public libraries shall be made available to all citizens of the city." Loeb added, "The libraries were open to all citizens this morning, period. That's all there is to it."[85] Later that day he explained, "We have opened the libraries. I'm a segregationist and I'm going to do everything I can to hold on to what we've got. But I'm going to do it legally. We will not go beyond the law."[86]

Despite Loeb's statement "That's all there is to it," there was, in fact, more to the case. During a hearing on November 9 regarding a consent decree governing the desegregation of the libraries, an unexpected issue arose. Randolph, the library board president, observed that the board had agreed to desegregate only the library—not the restrooms. "There was no discussion about desegregation of the restrooms, and I understand that there is a city ordinance which prohibits this," he testified.[87]

Because the libraries had been built without separate restrooms, African American patrons were required to use the janitor's bathroom in the basement of the Central Library. It was a single toilet for both sexes, cramped and difficult to access.[88] Loeb and the City Commission agreed with Randolph that the desegregation order did not cover the restrooms. They authorized their lawyers to amend the proposed consent decree to clarify that the restrooms would remain segregated, even though the library was not.[89]

At a hearing on December 9, attorneys for the library board argued that the ordinance requiring segregated bathrooms was part of the building code. It required separate restrooms for whites and African Americans and that each be labeled as such. Turner's lawyers demanded that the order include language desegregating "all facilities within the library" and that the case not be dismissed until enough time had passed to assess the success of desegregation.[90]

Judge Miller ruled in favor of both sides. His order of January 4, 1961, confirmed that all library units, "excepting restrooms and toilet and lavatory facilities," were to be operated without racial discrimination. However, he agreed to hear the new defense and rule on the constitutionality of the city ordinance.[91] The case was continued until May.

In the meantime, the North Branch—planned as a second segregated library for African Americans—was completed and officially dedicated on March 26, 1961. The library's information pamphlet about the new branch stated, "It will be open to all residents of both Memphis and Shelby County."[92]

At the May 3 hearing, the defense argued that, based on an earlier decision out of Norfolk, Virginia, "separate but equal" was still constitutional with regard to restrooms. They also introduced evidence that, in Memphis, "venereal diseases among negroes are 27 times greater than among whites," making public health a justification for maintaining separate restrooms.[93] Lockard called the last point "a flagrant subterfuge aimed at cutting off one segment of the population from public places."[94]

Miller's ruling came on July 22, 1961. He found that the "separate but equal" doctrine "has been generally swept away" and that segregated restrooms violated the equal protection clause of the Fourteenth Amendment. As to the issue of venereal disease, Miller found that "in the absence of proof, one would be led to believe that venereal disease would not be expected to occur to any appreciable extent among that segment of the population, whether white or negro, using the . . . public libraries of the city." Furthermore, toilets are not a significant vector for venereal disease.[95] Miller's order stated that "all public restrooms, lavatories, toilets and other public facilities in all public library units . . . shall hereafter be maintained and operated by them without discrimination."[96]

Although Loeb wanted to "fight the restroom case to the final limit," all parties recognized that the law was on Turner's side, and the board agreed to drop the suit. After the final order was filed on August 19, Wallis had his staff "remove the 'white' and 'colored' signs from the restrooms quietly and with as little publicity as possible."[97] The public libraries in Memphis were no longer segregated by law.

In contrast to the great publicity surrounding the inauguration of the library sit-in movement, the successful conclusion of Jesse Turner's lawsuit garnered little attention. The *Press-Scimitar* and the *Commercial Appeal* each gave it three or four column inches. The *World* made it front-page (but not headline) news, and the *Tri-State Defender* ignored it completely.[98] The final ruling on the restrooms got a two-sentence write-up in the *World*.[99]

The lack of press coverage was proportionate to the lack of drama at the library after desegregation. In the first week, fewer than 200 African American patrons registered for library cards at the formerly all-white branches.[100] Among them were Allegra Turner and her three sons.[101] Two African Americans attended a book talk on October 20, and their presence caused no disturbance.[102]

Although the number of African American patrons at formerly all-white branches increased over the next few months to more than 2,000, African Americans' library use lagged behind white use at least through 1967. A report commissioned by the library that year found that only 35 percent of African Americans surveyed had library cards (compared with 48 percent of whites), and that only 18 percent had visited a public library in the previous year (versus 41 percent of whites). The Memphis Public Library's long history of segregation, underfunding, and poor service to African American patrons had lasting effects. One African American respondent reported that she didn't use the library because "we used to couldn't go for so long and I never worried about it then."[103] Some may have been put off by the attitudes of people like Wallis, who wrote that the African American patrons he encountered were "polite, courteous, and understanding, and the older students have shown a surprising knowledge of the card catalog."[104] Others, deterred by the distance of the Vance Avenue branch from their homes, never picked up the habit of visiting the library once branches were opened closer to them. And, of course, reading requires both literacy and leisure time, both of which were more common among whites than among African Americans in the 1960s.

Allegra Turner called the day of Miller's desegregation order "bittersweet." Her oldest child was already ten, well past the age when she would have liked to introduce him to the pleasures of the library and instill a lifelong habit of patronizing it.[105] And the library's resistance to desegregation left ill will in the community. In 1967 the Youth Council of the Memphis NAACP sent a petition to the library board accusing it of hiring "Negroes for your Negro branches only." It reminded the board, "Your record of service to this large segment of our community is disgusting. We have not forgotten that it was you who, when forced to integrate, continued to maintain segregated restrooms and then attempted to justify your action in court by arguing that you were protecting your white patrons from the venereal disease infested Negroes. No, we have not forgotten."[106]

Perhaps the lack of jubilation over the library's desegregation was simply due to a shift of focus, as African Americans in Memphis had moved on to new lawsuits, new protests, and new threats. The library sit-ins kicked off an energetic embrace of protest by black Memphians that lasted for years and had profound effects. Boycotts and pickets of downtown businesses absorbed the energies not only of students but also of many adults working with the NAACP and other civil rights organizations. By 1963, movie theaters, buses, the zoo, the Brooks Memorial Art Gallery, and three golf courses were desegregated. Schools were desegregated by law in 1961 but remained largely segregated in practice until at least 2016, despite the implementation of a busing plan in the 1970s. Parks remained segregated through 1963.[107]

Doris Mulhearn notes that the library desegregation suit had "tremendous symbolic meaning in the struggle for civil rights in Memphis."[108] It was one of the first of many victories. Yet, even as Judge Miller was ordering the restrooms desegregated, Mayor Loeb was outlining what the rest of the decade would hold in a speech at the Rotary Club:

> I know, as does every intelligent Negro citizen of Memphis, that full citizenship never comes to any minority group through the hands of politicians attempting to use the minority group. It does not come from always asking and never giving. It does not come from continuously pushing and not pulling in the whole community's interest. It does not come from political chicanery of shrewd leaders of Negroes whose talents could be better used in leading their constituents down the road of responsibility. Full citizenship comes from the toil of the level-headed people of common sense and moderation. . . . It comes finally—and this had not been done and this is the challenge—with an assumption of responsibility by the Negro community meeting the white community half way on what is best for all of us.[109]

Even as Loeb was conceding defeat, he was making it clear that he would continue to resist the inclusion of African Americans in the civic life of Memphis. Loeb's intransigence would have tragic repercussions in 1968, when his hard line against striking sanitation workers caused Martin Luther King to visit Memphis to support the protesters—and encounter an assassin's bullet.

The legacy of Jim Crow library operations was not resolved overnight. In fact, allegations of racism in hiring and promotions persisted into the 1980s.[110] But by 2005, the library system showed that, in Wanda Rushing's words, "Memphis is not the place it was" when it named its main branch after Benjamin Hooks (who had gone on to have a long career as a judge, federal communications commissioner, and executive director of the national NAACP), thereby creating "a powerful symbolic resource in civic space for establishing a community of memory and retelling the constitutive narrative of the city."[111] Today, visitors to the Benjamin L. Hooks Central Library will find African Americans well represented among its patrons and, to a lesser extent, among the staff. In another show of change, the widow of Jesse Turner, the man who sued to force the library's desegregation, was appointed to its Board of Directors in 1990 and served for twelve years.[112]

Notes

1. Allegra W. Turner with Jini M. Kilgore, *Except by Grace: The Life of Jesse H. Turner* (Jonesboro, AR: Four-G Publishers, 2004), 119.

2. For a history of the founding of the Cossitt Library and its segregated branches, see Rheba Palmer Hoffman, "A History of Public Library Service to Negroes in Memphis, Tennessee" (MA thesis, Atlanta University, 1955); Steven A. Knowlton, "Memphis Public Library Service to African Americans, 1903–1961: A History of Its Inauguration, Progress, and Desegregation" (MA thesis, University of Memphis, 2015).

3. Turner, *Except by Grace,* 110, 120.

4. Ibid., 111.

5. Wayne A. Wiegand, *Main Street Public Library: Community Places and Reading Spaces in the Rural Heartland, 1876–1956* (Iowa City: University of Iowa Press, 2011), 6.

6. Michael Fultz, "Black Public Libraries in the South in the Era of De Jure Segregation," *Libraries and the Cultural Record* 41, no. 3 (2006): 348–49; Whitney Strub, "Black and White and Banned All Over: Censorship and Obscenity in Postwar Memphis," *Journal of Social History* 40, no. 3 (2007): 685–715.

7. C. Lamar Wallis, interview by JoAnn A. Lynn, November 28, 1984, transcript, Mississippi Valley Collection, University of Memphis Libraries.

8. The cities of Danville and Petersburg, Virginia, and Greenville, South Carolina, closed their libraries rather than desegregate. See David M. Battles, *The History of Public Library Access for African Americans in the South, or, Leaving behind the Plow* (Lanham, MD: Scarecrow Press, 2009), 119–20; Stephen Cresswell, "The Last Days of Jim Crow in Southern Libraries," *Libraries & Culture* 31, no. 3/4 (1996): 559–61.

9. Martha Barret Morrow, "The Reaction in Tennessee to the Supreme Court Desegregation Decision of 1954: From May, 1954, through December, 1957" (MA thesis, Memphis State University, 1964).

10. Beverly Bond and Janann Sherman, *Memphis in Black and White* (Charleston, SC: Arcadia Publishing, 2003), 135.

11. Bobby L. Lovett, *The Civil Rights Movement in Tennessee: A Narrative*

History (Knoxville: University of Tennessee Press, 2005), 345; G. Wayne Dowdy, *Crusades for Freedom: Memphis and the Political Transformation of the American South* (Jackson: University Press of Mississippi, 2010), 59–61.

12. Thomas J. Hrach, "Insults for Sale: The 1957 Memphis Newspaper Boycott," *Tennessee Historical Quarterly* 72, no. 1 (2013): 44.

13. H. T. Lockard to Wassell Randolph, July 15, 1957, Library History Collection, Memphis and Shelby County Public Library and Information Center, Memphis (hereafter cited as LHC).

14. John Spence, "Negro Asks to Borrow Books from Library," *Memphis Press-Scimitar,* June 28, 1957.

15. Ibid.

16. Lockard to Randolph, July 15, 1957, LHC.

17. Minutes of the Board of Directors of Memphis Public Library, October 2, 1957, LHC.

18. Wassell Randolph to H. T. Lockard, October 3, 1957, LHC.

19. The other colleges included Memphis State University, Christian Brothers College, Southwestern College at Memphis, and the University of Tennessee College of Medicine. Today, these institutions are known as, respectively, University of Memphis, Christian Brothers University, Rhodes College, and the University of Tennessee Health Sciences Center.

20. "Advocate of Integration Resigns from MSU," *Memphis Press-Scimitar,* July 19, 1958; "Prof. Hill Quits MSU; Gets Top Post at Tenn. Wesleyan College," *Tri-State Defender,* July 26, 1958; "Smith Moves to Prevent Fall Integration at MSU," *Memphis World,* August 13, 1958.

21. "Lockard Expected to Take Library Ruling to Court," *Memphis World,* July 5, 1958.

22. "Negro Use of Libraries Is the Object of Suit," *Memphis Press-Scimitar,* August 15, 1958; "Hearing Is Urged on Negroes' Suit," *Memphis Commercial Appeal,* August 16, 1958.

23. *Turner v. Randolph,* complaint, LHC.

24. Mark Wahlgren Summers, *The Ordeal of the Reunion: A New History of Reconstruction* (Chapel Hill: University of North Carolina Press, 2014), 270–71.

25. Jesse Cunningham to E. M. Hall, August 19, 1958, LHC.

26. "Four Officials Are in Accord to Fight Integration of City Libraries," *Memphis Commercial Appeal,* undated clipping from summer 1958, LHC.

27. C. Lamar Wallis to Wassell Randolph, August, 25, 1958, LHC; Minutes of Board of Directors, October 16, 1958.

28. Richard Connelly, "Integration Suit Put on Docket," *Memphis Commercial Appeal,* June 29, 1960.

29. Mary T. Haley, memorandum, September 29, 1958, LHC.

30. Jesse Cunningham to Walter Chandler, September 30, 1958, LHC.

31. Mrs. Langley, report, December 15, 1958, LHC.

32. Dowdy, *Crusades for Freedom,* 68.

33. "Memphis U. Quietly Integrates Classes," *Memphis World,* September 16, 1959; "Jim Crow Signs Take Another Tumble Here," *Memphis World,* October 24, 1959.

34. "City Officials in Segregation Case," *Memphis Press-Scimitar,* January 8, 1960.

35. "Shift Gears in Freedom Fight," *Tri-State Defender,* January 30, 1960.

36. Battles, *History of Public Library Access,* 82–83.

37. Taylor Branch, *Parting the Waters: America in the King Years, 1954–1963* (New York: Simon and Schuster, 1988), 271–84.

38. Russell B. Sugarmon Jr., interview by Elizabeth Gritter, October 13, 2000, transcript, Everett R. Cook Oral History Collection, Memphis and Shelby County Public Library and Information Center.

39. Wesley Pruden Jr., "Dozen Negroes Stage Sit-in: McLellan's on Main Closes," *Memphis Commercial Appeal,* March 19, 1960.

40. Jennie Mary Betts, interview by Elizabeth Gritter, June 28, 2004, transcript, Cook Oral History Collection.

41. "Attorneys Appeal Fines of 'Sit-in' Students," *Memphis World,* March 26, 1960.

42. Jay Hall, "Judge Sets Bond for Negroes Held after Two Sit-ins," *Memphis Commercial Appeal,* March 20, 1960; "Attorneys Appeal Fine of 'Sit-In' Students"; "Sit-in Bailout Is Large Order for 41 Negroes," *Memphis Commercial Appeal* March 20, 1960.

43. Hall, "Judge Sets Bond."

44. "Protesting Students and Newsmen Jailed," *Memphis World,* March, 23, 1960; "Sit-in Bailout Is Large Order"; L. F. Palmer, "Story from Inside Jail," *Tri-State Defender,* March 26, 1960.

45. "Protesting Students and Newsmen Jailed."

46. "Truce in 'Sit-ins' Denied by Attorneys," *Memphis World,* March 26, 1960.

47. Burleigh Himes, "Disgusting Is the Word for It," *Tri-State Defender,* March 26, 1960.

48. Palmer, "Story from Inside Jail."

49. Himes, "Disgusting Is the Word."

50. Maxine Smith, interview by Elizabeth Gritter, October 9, 2000, transcript, Cook Oral History Collection.

51. "Memphis NAACP Pledges All-Out Support to 'Sitters,'" *Memphis Commercial Appeal,* March 20, 1960.

52. "Protesting Students and Newsmen Jailed."

53. "Memphis NAACP Pledges All-Out Support."

54. "Sit-in Bailout Is Large Order."

55. Markham Stansbury, "Memphians Rally, Help Arrested in Sit-Downs," *Tri-State Defender,* March 26, 1960.

56. "Protesting Students and Newsmen Jailed."

57. "Sit-in Bailout Is Large Order."

58. Gwendolyn Townsend quoted in Dowdy, *Crusades for Freedom*, 78.

59. "40 Arrested in Memphis," *New York Times*, March 20, 1960.

60. "LeMoyne 'Sit-in' Students Ousted from Part-Time Jobs," *Memphis World*, March 30, 1960.

61. Marion Barry Jr. and Omar Tyree, *Mayor for Life: The Incredible Story of Marion Barry Jr.* (New York: Strebor, 2014), 60.

62. "'First' Sit-in Student Here," *Tri-State Defender*, January 14, 1961.

63. Charles Edmundson, "Negro Pastors Rally Forces for Sit-in Trial of 42 Today," *Memphis Commercial Appeal*, March 21, 1960.

64. "37 Negroes Fined in Memphis Case," *New York Times*, March 22, 1960; "Negroes at Fever Pitch, Vow All-Out Support of Students," *Tri-State Defender*, March 26, 1960.

65. "'Sit-ins' Created Drama Equal to '10 Commandments,'" *Memphis World*, March 26, 1960; "Editor Palmer, 36 Others Fined," *Tri-State Defender*, March 26, 1960.

66. "'Sit-ins' Created Drama Equal to '10 Commandments.'"

67. "37 Negroes Fined in Memphis Case."

68. Ibid.

69. "Negroes at Fever Pitch."

70. "Memphis Stops 2 New Sitdowns," *New York Times*, March 23, 1960.

71. "Truce in 'Sit-ins' Denied by Attorneys."

72. "Citizens Vote to Continue Rights Quest," *Memphis World*, April 2, 1960.

73. "More Sit-in Arrests Made," *Tri-State Defender*, April 9, 1960.

74. Laurie B. Green, *Battling the Plantation Mentality: Memphis and the Black Freedom Struggle* (Chapel Hill: University of North Carolina Press, 2007), 220.

75. "Mayor, City Commissioners Meet with Race Attorneys," *Memphis World*, April 2, 1960.

76. "Open Letter to Mayor Loeb," *Tri-State Defender*, April 9, 1960.

77. "Suits to Be Filed against Pink Palace, Tennis Court, Art Gallery," *Memphis World*, May 7, 1960; "Sue to End Segregation at Ellis Auditorium," *Memphis World*, May 21, 1960.

78. Steven H. Gifis, *Dictionary of Legal Terms: A Simplified Guide to the Language of Law* (Hauppauge, NY: Barron's Educational Series, 1998), 481.

79. Minutes of Board of Directors, September 9, 1960.

80. Mantri Sivananda, "Controversial Memphis Mayor Henry Loeb III, 1920–1992: A Biographical Study" (PhD diss., University of Memphis, 2002), 115; Minutes of Board of Directors, October 20, 1960.

81. Henry G. Loeb Jr., interview by Elizabeth Gritter, June 21, 2004, transcript, Cook Oral History Collection.

82. "Desegregation at Libraries," *Memphis Press-Scimitar,* October 14, 1960.

83. "Ends J' Crow Policy," *Memphis World,* September 19, 1960.

84. Minutes of Board of Directors, September 15, 1960.

85. "Desegregation at Libraries."

86. "City Commissioners Integrate Libraries," *Memphis World,* October 19, 1960.

87. "Library Hearing Hits a Snag," *Memphis Press-Scimitar,* November 9, 1960.

88. Wayne Dowdy, discussion with the author, September 2014.

89. Minutes of Board of Directors, November 21, 1960.

90. "Library Trustees Ask U.S. Ruling," *Memphis Press-Scimitar,* December 9, 1960.

91. *Turner v. Randolph,* order, January 4, 1961.

92. "Dedication of the North Branch," pamphlet, March 26, 1961, LHC.

93. *Turner v. Randolph,* memorandum brief on behalf of the defendants, June 20, 1961.

94. "Segregation in All Public Restrooms May Be Challenged," *Memphis World,* May 15, 1961.

95. *Turner v. Randolph,* opinion, July 22, 1961.

96. *Turner v. Randolph,* order, September 5, 1961.

97. Minutes of Board of Directors, July 31, 1961.

98. "Desegregation at Libraries"; "Library Branches Are Desegregated," *Memphis Commercial Appeal,* October 14, 1960; "City Commissioners Integrate Libraries."

99. "Lavatories in Memphis Public Libraries," *Memphis World,* August 19, 1961.

100. "Less than 200 Negroes Ask for Library Cards," *Memphis Press-Scimitar,* October 21, 1960.

101. Turner, *Except by Grace,* 122.

102. "Less than 200 Negroes Ask for Library Cards."

103. Lila Leatherwood and Dorothy Stover, "Research Project to Assess Attitudes of Habitual Readers and Non-Readers Toward the Library" (Memphis, TN: TRENDS, July 1967), LHC.

104. C. Lamar Wallis to John Wakeman, February 27, 1961, LHC.

105. Turner, *Except by Grace,* 122.

106. Memphis NAACP Youth Council to Memphis Public Library Board, June 16, 1967, LHC.

107. Dowdy, *Crusades for Freedom,* 80–85.

108. Doris Ann Youngblood Mulhearn, "Southern Graces: Women, Faith, and the Quest of Social Justice, Memphis, Tennessee, 1950–1969" (PhD diss., University of Memphis, 2012), 96.

109. "Text of Mayor Loeb's Address before Club," *Tri-State Defender,* August 12, 1961.

110. Memorandum from Maxine A. Smith (executive secretary, Memphis branch, NAACP) to Memphis and Shelby County Public Library and Information Center board members, "Charges, Findings, Questions, and Recommendations for the Memphis and Shelby County Public Library and Information Center," September 4, 1986, LHC.

111. Wanda Rushing, *Memphis and the Paradox of Place: Globalization in the American South* (Chapel Hill: University of North Carolina Press, 2009), 61.

112. Turner, *Except by Grace,* 122–23.

"You Pay One Hell of a Price to Be Black"

Rufus Thomas and the Racial Politics of Memphis Music

Charles L. Hughes

In December 2001 Rufus Thomas died in Memphis at the age of eighty-four. At his funeral, he was feted by friends, colleagues, and admirers who remembered his many accomplishments and asserted his importance in shaping the history of world culture. Thomas deserved the praise. During a career that began in the 1920s, Thomas influenced nearly every major development in Memphis musical culture in the twentieth century, from Mississippi minstrel shows to Beale Street blues to Black Power soul. He recorded the first hits on both Stax and Sun Records, the city's two most famous record labels. He performed on Beale Street in its early-twentieth-century heyday and remained associated with its culture long enough to be called an "ambassador" for the street and its music scene when it became a popular tourist destination at the end of the century. And he promoted the city's black musicians (and community) through his long tenure at radio station WDIA, where he provided some of the first on-air exposure to the city's blues and R&B artists. In Memphis's storied musical history, Rufus Thomas was one of its most consistent and significant players.

But some eulogizers of Thomas went even further. Tennessee governor Don Sundquist remembered Thomas as an "ambassador of unity" who "taught us not to see the world in black or white but in shades of blues."[1] These romantic words echoed the predominant narrative of Memphis's musical history. To this day, the public understanding of Memphis music is one of racial cooperation and breakthrough. In both popular and scholarly understandings, Memphis is positioned as a place where black and white came together through sound and transcended the boundaries of racism and racial segregation. Many of the specific components used to support this assertion—blues, rock 'n' roll, soul music, Beale Street, and even WDIA—were directly and significantly shaped by Rufus Thomas. And as Sundquist's words suggest, Thomas himself was a well-known figure in these narratives, particularly through his pivotal work at Sun and Stax.

This romanticism greatly distorts the racial politics of Memphis music. It obscures the history of racial tensions that shaped Memphis music, erases the active labor of musicians in negotiating these complexities through their musical work, and overestimates the role of white musicians in pioneering these interracial blends and embodying racial progress.[2] More troubling, though, is the fact that this myth masks a crucial theme in Thomas's life and silences a critique he leveled throughout his career. Thomas consistently challenged music's racial disparities, raising sustained and significant objections to the practices that limited the careers of black musicians and afforded disproportionate opportunities to their white colleagues. In the final decades of his life, Thomas took particular umbrage at the myth of color-blind progressivism and its accompanying devotion to white heroes. While Thomas recognized the crucial role played by musicians (including himself) in exposing the maliciousness of white supremacy, he also pointed out the limitations of music's capability to erase such tenacious barriers. The fact that Thomas became a figure of this supposed racelessness reflects a deep misunderstanding of the artist's career and the larger erasure of racial conflict and black accomplishment in the story of Memphis music. A repositioning of Thomas, and greater attention to his own words, creates a counternarrative of Memphis music around a central player within that history.

"I was born in the country, but I was raised in town."[3] Rufus Thomas was born in 1917 in Cayce, Mississippi, which he described as "a little town about as wide [as] the back of my hand."[4] At age two, Thomas moved with his sharecropper parents to South Memphis, where he would remain for the rest of his life. Thomas's journey reflected a well-worn path for Mississippi Delta blacks in the early twentieth century. Memphis had been a site of opportunity for African Americans since the end of the Civil War, when thousands moved to the city to escape the Delta's economic privations and brutal racial politics. The city boasted one of the South's largest and most successful black populations. Even as legalized white supremacy reasserted itself through Jim Crow segregation and state-sanctioned violence at the turn of the twentieth century, Memphis's black citizens organized into vibrant communities that built economic wealth, developed cultural institutions, and resisted white supremacy at the ballot box and through direct action.

This process also fueled Memphis's growing reputation as a center for African American music. Although often associated with rural traditions, Memphis's black music was the soundtrack of urban progress as new black migrants mixed rural traditions with sonic innovations. Just after Thomas's family arrived, a fellow migrant named W. C. Handy contributed to this process by writing a series of anthems such as "Memphis Blues" and "Beale Street Blues" that made the city and its entertainers internationally famous and paved the way for jazz and modern blues. Just like Thomas, Memphis's black sounds were "born in the country" but "raised in town," and although Thomas was too young to participate in the earliest stages of this process, his personal journey followed this larger trajectory.

Once in Memphis, Thomas's parents instilled a love of music, respect for labor, and commitment to progress in their young son. His father worked a series of jobs and provided Rufus with some of his first lessons as a performer.[5] "His father evidently loved music," remembered Rufus's daughter Carla, "because he said they used to stand outside and he'd teach them how to tap and he played Jew's harp."[6] Rufus's mother—whom he described as "a great church woman" with "the kind of deep-seated intelligence that you don't get out of books"—also provided crucial inspiration for her young son.[7] "She was pushing me to do it. She knew I loved entertainment. She said, 'Son, if this is what you want, do it. Do it but always respect the feelings of other people.' And I did."[8] Thomas ultimately attended Booker T. Washington (BTW) High School, a center for self-improvement and community empowerment during the Jim Crow era.

A bright and enthusiastic student, Thomas was particularly inspired by one of the school's most prominent teachers, a history instructor named

Nat D. Williams. "He was sort of my mentor," Thomas told John Floyd. "He had a mind like nobody I'd ever met. He used to take me around to adult functions. I'd be the only kid in there. I guess he just wanted to show me how the other side worked."[9] Williams's mentorship took place inside the classroom as well, where he taught African American history and insisted that his students recognize their own position in a rich legacy of resistance and reinvention. Thomas praised Williams as "one of the finest minds of any person I know," "a *black* mind" who inspired students to intellectual growth and social engagement.[10]

Williams also encouraged Thomas to participate in the "Ballet," a variety show featuring performances by BTW students designed to raise money to correct the funding disparities in a segregated educational system. As Louis Cantor notes, "The Board of Education never provided equal funds for the black schools in Memphis, [so] some of the BTW faculty decided to do something about it."[11] Preparing for the Ballet was a schoolwide affair; there were classes devoted to creating costumes, and teachers recruited talent from among the student body. Under Williams's leadership, the Ballet became a "major star-studded production" that attracted large local crowds to Ellis Auditorium. "Even though only BTW students were used," Cantor writes, "the Ballet soon became the major black talent show in the city."[12] Williams urged Thomas—who had first performed on Beale Street at age six, playing a frog in a theatrical production—to take part.

The Ballet gave Thomas his first sustained opportunity to perform in front of a live audience, but also his earliest education into the way music could simultaneously represent advancement and restriction for African Americans. Thomas—a dark-skinned "kid from the slums"—valued Williams's insistence that the Ballet break from its earlier colorism in casting and its adherence to what Thomas called the "upper-crust" music that had characterized the first shows.[13] But Williams's innovations included the addition of a minstrel show, which seems contradictory to the Ballet's aspirations. However, minstrel-style performances remained common in black entertainment through the 1940s and often represented one of the only spotlights for black entertainers.

Thomas eventually resisted minstrelsy's most obvious racial marker. Like many African Americans in this period, Thomas initially "blacked up" to exaggerate the racialized caricatures of minstrel-era performances. "I did that for maybe two years, the blackface," he remembered. "Then one day I woke up and looked in the mirror, and what did I see? I saw me . . . I thought, 'I don't have to put this stuff on my face. My skin's already black, so why am I doing this?' And immediately I stopped using that stuff."[14] Thomas's decision paralleled a decline in the practice (among both blacks and whites) throughout the early twentieth century, but minstrelsy remained a powerful force in his early career.

Most directly, he joined the famed Rabbit Foot Minstrel Show and toured the rural South during the summer months. The Rabbit Foot Minstrels, a formerly all-white (and blackfaced) ensemble, had recently expanded to include a segment featuring black entertainers. Thomas had previously performed exclusively in Memphis, but the minstrel show took him to rural Arkansas and Mississippi. "During the day at the parade, you'd have maybe fifty or a hundred people," he told Peter Guralnick, "but at night it just look like they come out of the cotton bolls, out of the woodworks, man!"[15] He also witnessed the firm color lines that divided the audience: "We'd work under a big tent, looked like a circus tent. Blacks on one side, whites on the other. You'd have an aisle that ran down the middle—that separation thing."[16] The musicians witnessed that same "separation thing" when they traveled between shows. "We traveled by bus and when we'd get in town we'd get a room in some people's house because there were no hotels or anything like that for black people. We'd get a room for 50 cents a night. I think tops was 75 cents when you'd get into a plush house. That's how we survived out there, by living in people's houses."[17]

Thomas faced an equally segregated environment when he returned to Memphis and performed at home. Each summer he took part in performances by the Royal American Show during the Cotton Carnival, a whites-only celebration of Memphis's cotton history held on the banks of the Mississippi River. A central feature of the Cotton Carnival was what Laurie Green terms "mythic historical reenactments of plantation life" in which "African Americans' participation was limited to the few who played the slaves, mules and horses." In protest, black Memphians created a counterpart called the Cotton Makers' Jubilee that took place on Beale Street and "showcased local talent."[18] First held in 1936, the Cotton Makers' Jubilee defied the physical and ideological restrictions of the whites-only celebration.

As part of the Royal American Show, Thomas was at the heart of this tension. "We did a midnight show [on Beale Street] after we left from down on the riverfront . . . because blacks were not supposed to be on the midway at all down on the riverfront." In fact, Thomas recalled, the segregation was even more rigid than it had been when he worked with the Rabbit Foot show. Rather than having a rope separating blacks from whites under the same tent, Memphis authorities refused to allow any blacks into the Cotton Carnival at all. "I felt out of place and I've always felt out of place [when] I'm working for whites . . . and my people couldn't come see me."[19]

Despite Thomas's distaste for performing in segregated spaces, his popularity meant that he spent a great deal of time entertaining white audiences at venues such as Curry's Club Tropicana and the Cottage Inn. Even as he won the applause of white crowds, Thomas found that his budding stardom offered him no immunity from either the physical or the figurative indignities of segregation. "That was during the time that we had to come in through the back; we didn't come in through the front—there was no such thing as fraternizing, and if you had to go to the bathroom, you went out in the back, because there were no facilities for you."[20] The color lines were policed inside the venues as well; Thomas recalled that the Cotton Club's bouncer prevented white women—but not men—from approaching the bandstand to speak with the black musicians. "There was no contact, hardly any contact at all."[21] At these shows, Thomas—backed by such Memphis musical luminaries as drummer Al Jackson Sr. and his band—learned to balance the imperative to entertain with a deep personal resentment. "You worked according to the conditions that surrounded you in the environment and I lived through it and I didn't like white folks at all for these kinds of things, at all. But I grew."[22]

The "separation thing" extended even further. Even absent the literal minstrel mask or the physical segregation of audiences, Thomas recognized that audiences structured their musical expectations around seemingly fixed categories of racial difference.[23] Even into the jazz and R&B era, black music "still wasn't regarded as pop. No pop—if there was a black voice, it automatically came under the heading of rhythm and blues."[24] The sonic manifestation of Jim Crow segregation—what Karl Hagstrom Miller calls "the musical color line"—had significant commercial implications for black artists like Thomas, who recognized that—regardless of their sound—black musicians had far less access to the more lucrative pop market than their white counterparts.[25] Although Thomas soon realized that his gruff voice made him better suited for bluesy material, he consistently performed a wide repertoire that linked the comedy and novelty numbers of his minstrel beginnings with the rapidly expanding range of pop, blues, and R&B sounds that excited black audiences in the 1940s and 1950s.

Thomas's increasingly skeptical view of music as a vehicle for racial liberation was also nurtured by a different kind of painful encounter: as a youth, Thomas was beaten by a Memphis policeman.[26] This type of brutality was a common experience for black Memphians in this period, as the Memphis Police Department routinely targeted African Americans for harassment and assault.[27] For Thomas, this incident reaffirmed his suspicion of whites and his determination to succeed despite the humiliating demands of life and labor in Jim Crow Memphis. "For years and years, I didn't like white folk at all. But I knew that I had to survive. I knew that I had to live. I had to work, and that's how I had to make my living. And I made it."[28]

His survival required the development of black-controlled musical spaces. Thomas remained a fixture in the theaters, juke joints, and nightclubs that dotted the city. Most important were the gigs on Beale Street, both for seasoned pros like Thomas and for upstarts who hoped to gain a foothold in the city's busy music scene. One key opportunity for those upstarts was Amateur Night at the Palace Theater, which Thomas started hosting in 1940. Thomas oversaw some of the earliest performances by the deep pool of talent that would revolutionize Memphis's music, including Bobby "Blue" Bland and B. B. King, who both gave their first performances at Amateur Nights that Thomas hosted.[29] As he noted, "They called it amateur, but Memphis amateurs are the world's professionals."[30]

During this time, Thomas married Lorene Taylor, whom he had met in high school. The couple moved into a home on Edith Avenue. "When I first married," Rufus remembered, "I was living in a house where there was no lights, no inside plumbing, all on the outside. Outside toilet, we got water from the outside in a bucket. . . . We had lamplight, outside plumbing, but we kept that place clean."[31] Thomas's plight was common among black Memphians; as Green notes, a federally funded study in the 1930s found that "77 percent of [African Americans in the city] lived in shacks that inspectors deemed substandard and lacking indoor plumbing."[32] The city's solution to this problem was to build new housing projects like Foote Homes, a complex located just south of Beale Street. The Thomases moved there following the births of their children Carla and Marvell. "Thank heaven," Rufus recalled, "we got light, inside plumbing, and all of these things."[33]

Despite his reputation, show business did not provide Rufus Thomas with a sufficient or consistent income, so he took a job at a textile mill called the American Finishing Company. The industrial sector provided an important jolt to Memphis's postwar economy and to the black freedom movement, due to the influx of new black migrants and the shop-floor resistance among black workers.[34] Although there is no evidence that Thomas participated in any direct action, he witnessed how racial power influenced the activities of his fellow workers. "I never sat down and talked to my boss the entire twenty-two years I was at American Finishing Company," Thomas recalled. He also remembered a minor confrontation that signaled the deeper tensions that would soon boil over into widespread resistance.[35] Initially, he said, "white folks had the same shift [as black workers], and during those days, whites not only got the front of the streetcar, they got the front of the line waiting for it." After African Americans began to jostle for position with their white counterparts, the company ended the shifts of Thomas and other black workers half an hour early to "avoid a confrontation between blacks and whites when they lined up for a streetcar."[36]

Starting in 1951, Thomas went directly from his shift at the factory to another job as a host on the pioneering all-black radio station WDIA.[37] "When I first started at WDIA, . . . no black voice had ever been on radio. Everything was white," he said.[38] In fact, Thomas's former mentor, Nat D. Williams, had been hired as the station's first black host in 1948. Faced with a lack of listeners and sponsors, the station crafted a slate of programs and personalities that would appeal to the black community in Memphis and across the Mid-South. Given his decades of experience,

Thomas was the perfect choice as an on-air personality. He hosted several shows that spotlighted the talents of Memphis musicians and the eclectic tastes of the black audience. He mixed local stars such as Little Milton and Junior Parker with national blues and rock 'n' roll stars like Little Richard and Muddy Waters. According to Cantor, "He also liked to play a totally unknown singer or group," one who was "still struggling to get the name recognition that Rufus knew only WDIA could provide."[39] Thomas thus helped establish the sound and personnel for a new generation of black Memphis music that bridged the early Beale Street days with the coming revolutions in rock 'n' roll and R&B.

Thomas and others also created what Green terms a new "black public sphere" on WDIA, "a kind of free space where identities need not be defined by the parameters of Crump's Memphis."[40] WDIA deejays were encouraged to speak directly to the local black audience, through both their patter and their on-air voices. The station also hosted several programs devoted to community affairs and conversation, making WDIA one of the only places where black political and social issues were publicly debated.

Additionally, Thomas and other WDIA personalities became well known for their charitable activities, which—like the Washington High School Ballet—linked the goals of community uplift and political independence.[41] For instance, Thomas hosted a 1953 talent show designed to fund scholarships for local black students; it was organized by the Klondyke Civic Club, a neighborhood-based group that "linked concerns about home, family, schools, and community to collective political action and involved large numbers of women."[42] Most prominent were the WDIA Goodwill and Starlight Revues, designed to raise money for the education of disabled black children in Memphis. Although disability limited the educational opportunities of all children, African American children faced particular difficulties due to Jim Crow resource restrictions. "They didn't have any way of getting to school, no way of even trying to get an education," Thomas recalled. "If you were handicapped, you were just there. No teachers to teach you."[43] In response, WDIA planned yearly charity concerts featuring performances by local and national stars and hosted by WDIA personalities, including Thomas. Like the on-air programming, the Revues featured performers representing jazz, blues, gospel, and pop.[44]

Even as WDIA offered a more liberated environment for its personalities and its listeners, it maintained some of segregation's restrictions. When Thomas first arrived, for example, he could not use the toilet facilities inside the studio building. He recalled, "I did like I used to do in the white nightclubs that I used to work—go outside in the back." But eventually Thomas rebelled, saying that he was "a part of this institution now" and had earned the right to "use the facility."[45] The restroom controversy paralleled a larger racialized division of labor.[46] "During that time," Thomas remembered, "we weren't permitted to turn the knobs or push the switches" in the radio control room, which was separate from the black on-air personalities. "We worked on the side of a big plate-glass window. We sat at a table; we did the commercials from over there, and there was a white fellow sitting at the controls."[47] Thomas grew weary of this divide. "I didn't like white folk at all because of what was happening," since "they thought at this time that we couldn't get our things together with twisting knobs." Thomas taught himself how to work the controls when the white engineer was absent from the studio. "I'm not going to be a part of anything that I don't know anything about. Nothing."[48]

Thomas's success at WDIA did not allow him to quit his day job, but it did give him enough cachet to make records for the first time in his career.[49] Record companies often sought to release songs by radio personalities, given their built-in audience and the desire to cement good relationships with the powerful disc jockeys who could make or break records commercially by playing them (or not) on their shows. Thomas recorded his first single, "I'll Be a Good Boy" and "I'm So Worried," in 1950 for the Dallas-based label Star Talent.[50] Cut live at Curry's Club Tropicana with a group of local pros, "I'll Be a Good Boy" was an energetic jump blues, while "I'm So Worried" featured a slow-dragging groove and an emotive vocal by Thomas. (Thomas's single was released as part of Star Talent's Folk Series and Blues & Rhythm Series, which illustrates the racialized separation from pop that Thomas recognized in live performance.)[51] The next year Thomas recorded under the pseudonym "Mr. Swing" for the Bullet label in Nashville, and in 1952 he cut several sides for the powerful Chess Records in Chicago. Though commercially unsuccessful, these early singles documented a transitional moment when a new

Rufus Thomas working at the American Finishing Company. (Courtesy Willy Bearden and Robert Gordon)

generation of black musicians mapped the terrain between early jazz and blues and the rock 'n' roll and R&B to come.

The engineer on most of these early singles was Sam Phillips, a young white Alabamian who had recently moved to Memphis to work in radio and recording. Phillips had a particular interest in black music, scouting the bands on Beale Street and listening to the shows on WDIA in the hope of finding local talent. Given his talent and connections, Rufus Thomas was a perfect collaborator. When Phillips launched his Sun Records label in 1953, many of his artists—including Roscoe Gordon and B. B. King—had direct relationships with Thomas, who had popularized their work through Amateur Nights and WDIA. Even though Phillips is credited with "inventing" the powerful Memphis sound and "discovering" this pivotal generation of black artists, the young producer needed the support and skill of key gateway figures like Thomas.[52]

It was fitting, then, that Sun's first major hit was a Rufus Thomas recording. As indicated by its title, "Bear Cat (The Answer to Hound Dog)" was clearly a rewrite of Big Mama Thornton's earlier hit, and in fact, it later provoked legal action from Thornton's record label. Despite the similarities, "Bear Cat" demonstrated Thomas's unique talent as a vocalist—from the yelping meows to the easy conversationalism of the verses—and the rolling rumble that defined the Sun sound. As the record climbed to number three on the national R&B charts, Thomas formed a touring group called the Bear Cats that performed around the Mid-South and included numerous notable members of Memphis's black music scene. The following year he released a follow-up single, "Tiger Man," which failed to reach the heights of its predecessor but further sharpened Thomas's playful approach.

Despite his accomplishments, Thomas was soon released from Sun Records, as were all the black artists who helped Phillips achieve his early success. In the aftermath of Elvis Presley's arrival in 1954, Phillips shifted Sun's focus to white artists who could blend black musical traditions (and the direct influence of artists like Rufus Thomas) with sounds from country and white pop. While this musical blend seemed to signal a breakdown of racial segregation at the dawn of the civil rights era and presaged the romanticism of Governor Sundquist's comments at Thomas's funeral, the immediate effect on Thomas and the other black musicians at Sun was decidedly negative. "Sam discarded all of the black artists that were there, including me," Thomas told John Floyd. He wondered whether Phillips thought "that maybe blacks and whites couldn't do it together. Maybe he thought that way, and if he did, he found out that was incorrect. Not right."[53] Although the dominant narrative still positions Sun Records as a vehicle for racial progress and its founder as a progressive boundary-buster, Thomas repeatedly derided what he saw as Phillips's mistreatment of black artists.[54] "He was a rat . . . Sam stepped on a lot of people."[55] Thomas's anger at Phillips was based on both a personal loss of opportunity and a broader betrayal of the black artists Thomas had championed for decades before Phillips arrived. Returning to his factory job and WDIA shifts, Thomas awaited his next opportunity.

In 1961 Thomas heard about a new local record label, Stax, located in South Memphis not far from Foote Homes. Founded by white bankers Jim Stewart (a fiddle player) and his sister Estelle Axton, the label started out recording country and rockabilly artists, but its lack of early hits led to a shift toward R&B and black artists. Upon hearing of the new label, Thomas brought demo recordings of himself and his daughter Carla to Stax in the hope of being signed.[56] Axton and Stewart recognized the family's talent and Thomas's radio connections, and they signed both Rufus and Carla to contracts. "We launched both companies," Thomas claimed. "I launched [Sun], and my daughter and I launched [Stax]."[57]

Thomas's hyperbole was justified. Both creatively and economically, the success of Rufus and Carla Thomas shaped Stax Records into the entity that made the soulful Memphis sound internationally recognizable in the 1960s and 1970s. Creatively, Rufus's recordings helped map the spare funk that characterized the label's trademark sound. Commercially, Carla's "Gee Whiz" became the label's first major national hit, and the father-daughter duet "Cause I Love You" attracted the interest of powerful Atlantic Records producer Jerry Wexler. He licensed the single for national release and signed a broader distribution agreement with Stax that propelled the label's ascent. Wexler, who knew Rufus from WDIA, which had helped make hits of many Atlantic recordings, was attracted not only by the commercial possibilities of the Thomases' singles but also by Stax's interracial workforce. A racial liberal, Wexler viewed Stax, with its white leadership marketing black records produced by an integrated studio staff, as a potential model for southern and American progress. Excited, Wexler traveled to Memphis to seal the deal.

Unfortunately, even this breakthrough was tinged with racial discrimination. Wexler invited Stewart and the Thomases to seal the deal in his suite at Memphis's famed (and segregated) Peabody Hotel. (Wexler told Peter Guralnick that he chose the Peabody in part because Jim Stewart "was not yet ready to invite Negroes into his home.")[58] "I'm sharp, I got on my good clothes, and I'm cleaner than nineteen yards of chitlins," Rufus recalled, but the hotel's security would not allow the Thomas party to enter through the hotel's front door. Instead, they were told to use the rear entrance and the service elevator. Initially, Thomas refused: "I told them, 'Hell no, I ain't riding no service elevator. . . . See, I can go back right in the street where I was and forget you people. I am *not* riding that elevator!'"[59] Eventually, Lorene Thomas convinced her husband to climb through the trash-strewn alley—assuring him that a deal with Atlantic would mean they would "never have to do it again"—and the family sealed the deal with Wexler in his Peabody suite.[60] Wexler recalled that, "on the way up, Rufus said, 'Same old story, back walking through the garbage.'"[61]

Lorene Thomas was a crucial participant in the Memphis civil rights community at the moment her husband launched Memphis soul. "She was just on top of everything," remembered NAACP president H. T. Lockard. "She was such an advocate of what the branch stood for . . . and of course everybody listened when she got up to speak."[62] She served as the NAACP's correspondence secretary throughout the 1950s and 1960s, during the organization's period of greatest expansion. Under the leadership of executive secretary Maxine Smith, the Memphis chapter gained in size and militancy. "Anything, everything, Lorene was there," Smith remembered. "She gave so much of herself to so many people without ever expecting any kind of return."[63] Thomas focused much of her attention on voter registration; in the Forty-Eighth Ward where she lived, for example, she recalled increasing the rolls "from 200 registered voters . . . to 2,200 when I left there."[64] She also participated in pickets and other direct action campaigns that forced the city to desegregate.[65] Her children were involved in the cause as well. "All of them used to march . . . during that time," Rufus remembered. "I didn't," he added.[66]

As Lorene Thomas pushed for justice in the streets and at the ballot box, her husband's star rose thanks to a series of hits at Stax. In 1963 he recorded his biggest hit to date, "Walking the Dog," which married the boasting rhymes of black jump-rope traditions to the latest dance innovation among black youth. (He wrote the lyrics to "Walking the Dog" while bent over a boiler at American Finishing Company, where he continued to work during the early years of his success with Stax.) But Thomas chafed against the disparity in the racial power structure at Stax. Although he valued his white colleagues and praised Jim Stewart for not switching to white artists once the label became successful (as Phillips had done), Thomas's recollections puncture Stax's reputation as a progressive or even a color-blind space.

Thomas was most discontented with what he perceived to be a lack of proper credit. Although Thomas long claimed to play an important role in producing his sessions—giving parts to musicians, directing the arrangements, and even encouraging the musicians to do a "professional job" rather than fooling around in the studio—he never received producer credit when the record was released. Thomas not only lost compensation as a producer but also saw it as a denial of his creative agency. "I been doing that since *way* back, I mean since I was quite young, putting things together," he noted. "But I never got credit for it."[67]

Steve Cropper, a white Stax guitarist, received cowriting and production credit on many of the label's classic recordings. Cropper developed his reputation as a key member of the Stax cadre in the 1960s and gained symbolic power as a white participant in the integrated Memphis sound. But Thomas was unconvinced. "Steve Cropper was a guitar player and that's all Steve Cropper was . . . some of the songs that Steve Cropper's name appeared on as producer and all of that . . . had no business at all on there."[68] Thomas's opinions about Cropper's disproportionate credit have been echoed by other black musicians at Stax.[69] Thomas also resented what he saw as the guitarist's unwillingness to cede control over studio operations or the creative direction of Stax's artists. He was unambiguous about the reasons behind this: "Steve Cropper had that *white* thing that said because you're black, you're supposed to do exactly what this white man says." Thomas's complaints were some of the most prominent examples of the underappreciated history of racial discontent at Stax, particularly among black musicians who felt they lost opportunities because of their race; some also recalled moments of racial conflict during sessions.[70] As Thomas summed it up: "Steve Cropper . . . just turned out to be fat lousy. In plain, everyday English, a rip-off."[71] When Thomas's career stalled in the mid-1960s, he blamed it in part on Cropper's control. He observed, "After Steve Cropper eventually left . . . I started doing the records without Steve and the records came along very well without him."[72]

There were many reasons for Thomas's drop-off in popularity, but it is true that his commercial resurgence began in 1970, after Cropper had left Stax and Thomas began to work with a different producer. Beginning with 1970's top-ten hit "Do the Funky Chicken," Thomas returned to the charts with a string of hits that updated his signature comical dance numbers for the burgeoning funk era. With their bubbling rhythms and thick arrangements, these playful records contributed to Stax's expansive black soundscape by offering a jubilant, blues-rooted counterpoint to the gospel politics of the Staple Singers or the jazz-influenced symphonies of Isaac Hayes. Marketed as both an elder statesmen (one press release called him the "Soul Grandfather") and the "world's oldest teenager," Thomas and his music recalled deeper traditions and pointed toward the musical future.[73] Funk hits like "Funky Chicken" and "Do the Push and Pull" made him one of Stax's most successful artists in the 1970s.[74]

Thomas also remarked that the racial politics at Stax improved because "when you got black people into the organization it helped a lot."[75] Most prominent was Al Bell, who became its president in 1968. A former disc jockey and civil rights activist, Bell shifted Stax toward the politics of Black Power and amplified the sounds and images of the black freedom struggle on Stax recordings. He signed artists who had direct connection to the movement, including the Staple Singers. Bell sought to associate Stax and its personnel with the politics of black freedom on a local, national, and even international level.

In 1968, after the assassination of Martin Luther King, Memphis officials turned to Stax artists, hoping they could quell local tensions and reassure outsiders that the city remained peaceful. "People in high places," remembered Stax publicity director Deanie Parker, "really didn't think much of what we were doing at [Stax], until they needed someone . . . whom they thought they could call to appeal to the people who they thought were going to burn this city down," at which point "we were invited into the halls of the mayor's office."[76] Rufus Thomas—whose continuing presence on WDIA made him an even more crucial spokesman— was one of those approached by Memphis leaders. Despite the fact that Mayor Henry Loeb and others had actively fought the campaigns waged by Lorene Thomas and others in the NAACP, they now hoped that Rufus Thomas would serve as peacemaker. "Some of the white officials that knew me came to my home and asked me to see if I could quiet down . . . the unrest that was in the neighborhood," Thomas remembered. "I was able to do a little something in there, ask the fellows in the neighborhood that, that was about to create some problem, in their own neighborhood."[77]

Three years later, Thomas was again called on to address a local crisis. In October 1971 four Memphis police officers beat a seventeen-year-old African American named Elton Hayes to death following a traffic stop. Uprisings and disturbances spread throughout Memphis's black neighborhoods, and Loeb met with leaders from the black community in an effort to quiet the disturbances. Among the group were several Stax representatives, including Rufus Thomas, who met with the white leaders to advocate for better and more just policing in the African American community. Although they failed to achieve any significant change in the relationship between black Memphis and the police department, the group convinced Loeb to lift the mandatory curfew imposed after Hayes's death. In March 1972 Rufus Thomas was recognized by the Memphis City Council for "outstanding contributions to the city" and received the key to the city from Mayor Loeb. Around the same time, the state of Tennessee honored the Thomas family for their musical accomplishments.[78]

But Thomas's role as ambassador to Memphis's white community was matched by his involvement in Stax's Black Power politicization. He appeared at the company's spotlight events at the Black Expo, a convention organized by Jesse Jackson's Operation Breadbasket.[79] He appeared at a benefit for the reelection of Mayor Richard Hatcher in Gary, Indiana, and performed at a benefit for sickle-cell anemia with Muhammad Ali and Nina Simone.[80] In 1975 Ali and Thomas raised money for a Muslim community center in Cleveland.[81] Thomas even performed in Liberia in 1972 at the request of President William Tubman. Such performances were commonplace in the 1970s as a demonstration of the cultural linkages between the African diaspora and the worldwide significance of soul culture. Thomas's successful shows affirmed his personal popularity and Stax's relevance to the Pan-African arts movement. "I had a distorted impression of what Africa was really like," he remarked upon his return. "I was certainly relieved that Africa wasn't like what most of us are used to seeing on television and movies."[82]

It was also in 1972 that Thomas appeared at the Wattstax festival at the Los Angeles Memorial Coliseum—a day-long event commemorating the 1965 Watts rebellion and celebrating the power of Memphis soul music in the Black Power era. A crowd of more than 100,000 black people enjoyed performances by Isaac Hayes, the Staple Singers, and others, along with appearances by the Reverend Jesse Jackson (who delivered his famous "I Am Somebody" speech to open the concert) and Melvin Van Peebles that cemented the event's connection to the continuing struggle for black freedom and equality.

Thomas's appearance came near the end of the day. As the sun set, he lit up the hot Los Angeles afternoon with the joyous polyrhythms of his recent hits "Do the Funky Chicken" and "The Breakdown." Thomas then encouraged the jubilant crowd to leave the bleachers and dance with him on the football field. Thousands streamed onto the grass, joining Thomas in a spontaneous party that reaffirmed Wattstax's goal of community love through soul music and demonstrated the middle-aged performer's continuing relevance to the Soul Power generation. Unfortunately, Stax had agreed to leave the field untouched as part of its agreement with the coliseum. So Thomas's group dance not only endangered the label's insurance deposit but also risked tainting the trouble-free concert with an image of supposedly unruly and destructive black patrons. The concert's producers told Thomas that he needed to get the people off the field and back to their seats as quickly as possible. "Power to the people, now let's go to the stands!" Thomas implored the crowd, turning a call for order into a winking affirmation of the day's liberatory energies. The gambit worked, and the concert—and perhaps Stax's financial security—was saved.

His Wattstax appearance was only the most prominent example of Thomas's deep connection to Black Power. Although he lacked the political fire of the Staple Singers or the evocative "Black Moses" image of Isaac Hayes, Thomas remained a key figure when Black Power politics and Memphis soul carried Stax to its greatest commercial success and cultural prominence. As a reporter noted in the black *Chicago Metro News*, "Rufus Thomas was right. We were doing the breakdown, and what was crumbling in that breakdown was the old nigger—for these were new Black people."[83]

Just three years after the triumph of Wattstax, Stax Records closed amid financial troubles and internal unrest. The Thomas family moved to a new home on Joanne Street, in the Cherokee neighborhood, where they were among the first black residents. "As soon as the blacks started moving in," Lorene Thomas told interviewers in 1977, then you saw all of the 'for sale' signs going up."[84] "When blacks move in, the whites move out," Rufus added. "It makes no difference what stature you have, if you're a lawyer, a teacher, a congressman, whatever. They just didn't want any part of that."[85] Similar patterns of "white flight" emerged throughout Memphis (and the United States) during the 1970s, as white residents moved to the suburbs to avoid new black neighbors and racially integrated public schools.[86] "It is said that . . . when blacks move into the neighborhood the value of the property goes down," said Thomas. "That's a lot of bull, you know."[87] Nonetheless, this narrative gained power as a supposed explanation for urban decline in the 1970s.

Even Beale Street fell victim, bulldozed in the early 1970s as part of an urban-renewal project to stimulate the city's beleaguered downtown by encouraging new investment and development. By the 1980s, Beale Street was under the control of private developers and was being repurposed as a tourist district to capitalize on Memphis's musical history. Central to that, of course, were the many developments in which Rufus Thomas had played such a central role.

Late in life, Thomas came to be known as the "Ambassador of Beale Street." He appeared in a number of documentaries devoted to the street's history and culture and made a memorable appearance in Jim Jarmusch's acclaimed 1989 film *Mystery Train*. He was honored with a historical plaque and the only official parking place on Beale. He continued to perform in Memphis and elsewhere, and he remained on the airwaves at WDIA. In the last decades of his life, Thomas became a celebrated elder statesman and living embodiment of Memphis's musical history.

Thomas relished this role. Still, he demanded that black musicians play a greater part in the solidifying narrative of Memphis music that defined public memory and even civic policy. For example, when the city erected a statue of Elvis Presley on Beale Street in 1980, Thomas pointed out, "Elvis Presley is not synonymous to Beale Street at all. I've always resented the fact that he's there." Instead, Thomas suggested honoring the street's black heroes. "I would prefer a statue like Lieutenant [George W.] Lee, who was a prominent black man here in the city, or a person like Nat Williams, or a person like Maceo Walker, who was one of the top businessmen in the city, all black."[88] More broadly, Thomas refuted the popular notion that Presley transgressed racial boundaries during his early career. "I never saw Elvis in a club. Never saw him on Beale Street. I'm not saying he wasn't there, but I never saw him there."[89] Thomas also questioned the common narrative that Presley collaborated with black musicians. "I never did see Elvis during those times that people were saying that he was hanging around with different black musicians," he recalled.[90]

Thomas linked this historical misinterpretation to an erasure of his own significance, along with the wider challenges faced by African American artists. He was furious that Sam Phillips refused to acknowledge his role in the early history of Sun Records: "They'd put us on panels together and he never did mention it. But I'd always come back and say, 'Sam didn't tell you that I made the first record.' He was an arrogant bastard. He is today. Back then he had a big car, it was maybe a foreign car, a Bentley, and he'd boast about the money he made that got him this car. I said, 'Yeah, but if it hadn't been for me, he wouldn't have had that car.'"[91] Asked by an interviewer why Memphis had not progressed as far as other music cities had, Thomas replied that it was because "the masses of the musicians and entertainers here in the city are black. Think about what I'm saying."[92] And he still regretted his lost opportunities. "With all the hit records I've had, if I'd been a white boy, I would have made it," he lamented. "People know about me . . . but I still have not gotten the recognition that I deserve."[93]

Even when death brought him a new round of recognition, Thomas's consistent work to promote Memphis's black community in the face of a discriminatory city and music industry has been lost amidst the reassuring rhetoric of healing and inclusivity. More than that, Thomas himself has been reduced to a jolly figure whose smiling face and jubilant music seemingly symbolized what Guralnick described as "a bottomless appreciation for the human comedy that left little room for the drab or dreary in his presence."[94] But these connected distortions are refuted by Thomas's own words and actions throughout his long career.[95] In numerous interviews he advanced a recurring thesis that music (in Memphis and elsewhere) possessed the same structural and personal impediments to African American advancement as any other aspect of American society. He struggled to overcome these limitations in a career that brought him great success but also left him unconvinced that he had reached his full potential. Thomas's work certainly demonstrates the possibilities of music as a tool for racial progress, but it also demonstrates that mystified notions of music as a colorless utopia can do a significant disservice to the musicians and listeners who give that music its meaning as both art and commodity. Rufus Thomas articulated that paradox throughout his life, from the way he understood the skin-color politics of minstrelsy to his complex relationship with his colleagues at Stax Records. For Thomas, this paradox defined him.

In 1992 the Smithsonian Institution interviewed Thomas for a project documenting the history of Memphis music. In an extended conversation marked by his characteristic eloquence and humor, Thomas spoke of his great accomplishments, from Washington High School to WDIA to soul stardom to his Beale Street "ambassadorship." He reiterated his criticisms of Sam Phillips, his complex appraisal of Stax, and his disdain for the false racial separation of pop and R&B. He praised his wife and children, honored his colleagues, and celebrated his city. At the end, he was asked to summarize his career and his hoped-for legacy. "You pay one hell of a price to be black," he told the interviewers. "But I am not going to die from it. I'm going to survive, and I'm going to live. And I'm going to do something recognizable, so when I pass off this land of the living . . . I will be remembered for what I have done—what I have done for the community, what I have done for my people, what I have done for the whole universe."[96] What Rufus Thomas did—and what it meant—deserves that consideration.

Notes

1. Bill Ellis, "'Heaven's Youngest Teenager': Friends, Fans Pay Respects to Rufus Thomas," *Memphis Commercial Appeal,* December 21, 2001, A1.

2. I explore these dynamics in Charles Hughes, *Country Soul: Making Music and Making Race in the American South* (Chapel Hill: University of North Carolina Press, 2015).

3. Rufus Thomas, interview by David Less and Robert Palmer, Memphis, 1976, Civil Rights History Project Audio Collections, series 4, Mississippi Valley Collection, Preservation and Special Collections, University of Memphis (hereafter cited as Rufus Thomas, MVC interview).

4. Louis Cantor, *Wheelin' on Beale: The Story of the Nation's First All-Black Radio Station* (New York: Pharos Books, 1992), 93.

5. Thomas later said that his father "worked at Bluff City Coal and Ice Company, Broadway Coal and Ice Company and other various jobs and night-watchman and that kind of thing." Rufus Thomas, interview by Margaret McKee and Fred Chisenhall, Memphis, October 9, 1973, 1, Everett R. Cook Oral History Collection, Memphis and Shelby County Public Library and Information Center, Memphis (hereafter cited as Rufus Thomas interview, Cook Collection).

6. Carla Thomas, interview by Portia Maultsby, Memphis, September 5, 1984, 2, SC 18, Portia K. Maultsby Collection, Archives of African American Music and Culture, Indiana University, Bloomington, IN.

7. Peter Guralnick, *Lost Highway: Journeys and Arrivals of American Musicians* (Boston: Little, Brown, 1999), 58.

8. Rufus Thomas, interview by Ray Ann Kremer and Pat Faudree, n.d., 23–24, Cook Oral History Collection.

9. John Floyd, *Sun Records: An Oral History* (Memphis, TN: DeFault-Graves Publishing, 2015), 27.

10. Rufus Thomas, interview by Portia Maultsby, Memphis, September 6, 1984, 2, Maultsby Collection.

11. Cantor, *Wheelin' on Beale*, 38.

12. Ibid., 39.

13. Rufus Thomas, Maultsby interview, 4.

14. Floyd, *Sun Records*, 28. Elsewhere, Thomas suggested that his motivation for giving up blackface was medical. "My doctor told me I had what they call hypersensitive skin. . . . It would break me out in big splotches and I had to stop." Rufus Thomas interview, Cook Collection, 3.

15. Guralnick, *Lost Highway*, 60.

16. Floyd, *Sun Records*, 31.

17. Ibid.

18. Laurie Green, *Battling the Plantation Mentality: Memphis and the Black Freedom Struggle* (Chapel Hill: University of North Carolina Press, 2007), 242.

19. Rufus Thomas interview, Cook Collection, 3–4.

20. Rufus Thomas, Maultsby interview, 9.

21. Rufus Thomas interview, Cook Collection, 7.

22. Ibid.

23. In fact, some scholars have argued that the decline of blackface fueled the belief in inherent sonic differences and racial categorization. See, for example, David Walker Gilbert, *The Product of Our Souls: Ragtime, Race and the Birth of the Manhattan Musical Marketplace* (Chapel Hill: University of North Carolina Press, 2015); Karl Hagstrom Miller, *Segregating Sound: Inventing Folk and Pop Music in the Age of Jim Crow* (Durham, NC: Duke University Press, 2013).

24. Rufus Thomas, MVC interview. Thomas also noted that this dichotomy flattened distinctions between types of black music.

25. See Miller, *Segregating Sound*, 3 and throughout.

26. Rufus Thomas, interview by Pete Daniel, David Less, and Charles McGovern, Memphis, August 5, 1992, 18, Rock 'n' Soul Video History Project Collection, Interviews, series 4, box 9, National Museum of American History, Archives Center, Smithsonian Institution, Washington, DC (hereafter cited as Rufus Thomas, NMAH interview).

27. See Green, *Battling the Plantation Mentality*, 81–112.

28. Rufus Thomas, NMAH interview, 18–19.

29. Charles Farley, *Soul of the Man: Bobby 'Blue' Bland* (Jackson: University of Mississippi Press, 2011), 24. Farley later notes, "If there was one other special person, besides his mother and B. B. King, who had encouraged Bobby from the start and continued as a friend throughout the years, it was Memphis music legend Rufus Thomas" (242).

30. "40 Years of Memphis Soul," Stax press release, January 1971.

31. Rufus Thomas interview, Cook Collection, 22–23.

32. Green, *Battling the Plantation Mentality*, 31.

33. Rufus Thomas interview, Cook Collection, 23.

34. For more information on the frequency of these strikes and their political impact, see Green, *Battling the Plantation Mentality*, 28–31.

35. Cantor, *Wheelin' on Beale*, 95–96.

36. Ibid., 96. This incident reflects a pre–civil rights generation tradition of what Robin Kelley terms "infrapolitics," in which battles over public space played a central role in acts of resistance that were not recognized as organized movement activity but were nonetheless crucial to the eventual success of movement campaigns. See Robin D. G. Kelley, "We Are Not What We Seem: Rethinking Black Working-Class Opposition in the Jim Crow South," *Journal of American History* 80, no. 1 (June 1993): 75–112.

37. Many of the station's personalities lived in Foote Homes, reinforcing the project's reputation as an important site of black community formation during the pre–civil rights generation.

38. Rufus Thomas, NMAH interview, 19.

39. Cantor, *Wheelin' on Beale*, 125.

40. Green, *Battling the Plantation Mentality*, 181.

41. The station also formed the WDIA Teen Town Singers, a group of high school students who performed at fund-raisers around the city. Both Carla and Marvell Thomas performed in this ensemble.

42. Green, *Battling the Plantation Mentality*, 201. At this event, the Klondyke Civic Club "received assistance from the North Memphis Civic Club, the Belmont Park Civic Club, the Hyde Park Civic Club, the Hollywood Civic Club, and the Fifth Ward Civic Club," indicating the importance of this kind of event to Memphis's black community.

43. Floyd, *Sun Records*, 71.

44. For more on the variety of artists featured at these revues, see Cantor,

Wheelin' on Beale, 204–6. For a striking collection of photographs of the revues, see Ernest Withers with Daniel Wolff, *The Memphis Blues Again: Six Decades of Memphis Music Photographs* (New York: Viking, 2001).

45. Rufus Thomas, NMAH interview, 19.

46. See Green, *Battling the Plantation Mentality,* 181.

47. Rufus Thomas, NMAH interview, 19–20.

48. Rufus Thomas interview, Cook Collection, 8.

49. It is perhaps no surprise that labor—and particularly the night shift—would be a recurring theme in Thomas's music. One of his earliest singles, "Night Workin' Blues," lamented the mistreatment he experienced both on the job and at home, while his Stax release "All Night Worker" used the image as a metaphor for sexual skill.

50. For more information on these early sessions, see http://www .706unionavenue.nl/70661165. See also Miller, *Segregating Sound.*

51. Both songs featured prominent saxophone parts by Evelyn Green, a pioneering female musician and later a member of B. B. King's band.

52. This narrative is forcefully asserted by Peter Guralnick in his biography *Sam Phillips: The Man Who Invented Rock & Roll* (New York: Little, Brown, 2014). Guralnick devotes attention to Thomas and correctly identifies him as predating Phillips's involvement, but he both explicitly and implicitly credits Phillips with galvanizing the music and its personnel in a way that obscures the work of Thomas and others.

53. Floyd, *Sun Records,* 34. Guralnick suggests that Thomas may have wanted to leave Sun because of a planned WDIA label called Starmaker. Guralnick, *Sam Phillips,* 193–94.

54. Thomas was not the only one. As documented by John Floyd, Peter Guralnick, and others, other black Sun musicians—including Roscoe Gordon and Ike Turner—lodged similar complaints against Phillips. See Floyd, *Sun Records;* Guralnick, *Sam Phillips.*

55. Rufus Thomas interview, Cook Collection, 32.

56. Thomas also shopped Carla's first recordings to Vee-Jay Records in Chicago, reflecting the national sweep of his celebrity on WDIA.

57. Rufus Thomas, NMAH interview, 13.

58. Peter Guralnick, *Sweet Soul Music: Rhythm and Blues and the Southern Dream of Freedom* (New York: Little, Brown, 2012), 106.

59. Robert Gordon, *Respect Yourself: Stax Records and the Soul Explosion* (New York: Bloomsbury, 2015), 45–46.

60. Ibid.

61. Rob Bowman, *Soulsville USA: The Story of Stax Records* (London: Omnibus Press, 2011), 15.

62. Michael Erskine, "Mrs. Thomas Was in the Wings on the Civil Rights Stage," *Memphis Commercial Appeal,* February 9, 2000, A14.

63. Ibid.

64. Lorene Thomas, interview by Ray Ann Kremer and Pat Faudree, n.d. [1977], 22, Cook Oral History Collection.

65. She was even captured by photographer Ernest Withers protesting outside a segregated grocery store during a boycott. See http://memphislibrary. contentdm.oclc.org/cdm/singleitem/collection/p13039c0112/id/22/rec/1.

66. Rufus Thomas interview, Cook Collection, 26.

67. Rufus Thomas, MVC interview.

68. Rufus Thomas, Maultsby interview, 19.

69. Other musicians included Carla Thomas and Sam Moore. See Carla Thomas, Maultsby interview; Sam Moore, interview by Portia Maultsby, New York, NY, February 24, 1983, Maultsby Collection.

70. See Hughes, *Country Soul.*

71. Rufus Thomas, MVC interview.

72. Ibid.

73. The name "Soul Grandfather" came from "King of Canines (Rufus Thomas) Meets King of Liberia," Stax press release, August 1971. Stax's January 1971 press release for "Funky Chicken" was titled "40 Years of Memphis Soul" and offered a summary of Thomas's many accomplishments.

74. Beyond his role as a funk pioneer, some of Thomas's final hits for Stax were considered potential winners in the emerging disco market. In the September 9, 1974, issue of *Radio and Record Mirror,* an anonymous reviewer said that Thomas's "Funky Bird" has "a great disco sound" and that both it and its flip side will "get continued club play."

75. Rufus Thomas, MVC interview.

76. Deanie Parker, interview by David Less, Memphis, November 7, 1999.

77. Rufus Thomas interview, "Rock and Roll; Renegades; Interview with Rufus Thomas," part 4 of 4, WGBH Media Library and Archives.

78. For information on Hayes, see Gordon, *Respect Yourself,* 242–44. See also "Stax's Artists Rufus Thomas and Isaac Hayes Receive 'Recognition Awards,'" Stax press release, April 1, 1972.

79. Black Expo ad, *Jet,* September 30, 1971, 59.

80. "Rufus Thomas Headlines Benefit for Mayor Hatcher," Stax press release, November 1, 1971; James Cortese, "From the Music Capitals of the World: Memphis," *Billboard,* February 26, 1972, 18.

81. "Rufus Thomas to Join Champ for Cleveland Temple Opening," Stax press release, May 1975.

82. "King of Canines (Rufus Thomas) Meets King of Liberia." In 1977 Thomas traveled to South Africa, provoking the ire of a group of local antiapartheid activists who urged him not to appear. "I was told that I shouldn't go to South Africa because of their polices. Well, I'm living with that same type of thing so why shouldn't I go. I had a Snack and Rap session at Memphis State and the

students told me I shouldn't go. I said, 'If I lived through the era which I had to come up through this point and I made it through that then I can make it through South Africa or any other part of the country.' I went. I had a beautiful time." Rufus Thomas interview, Cook Collection, 18.

83. "A New Birth," *Chicago Metro News,* March 10, 1973, 17.

84. Lorene Thomas interview, 1.

85. Rufus Thomas interview, Cook Collection, 16.

86. Although Thomas's children were adults by the time of Memphis's busing crisis, he offered his opinion on the topic in a 1977 interview: "My wife used to have to walk three miles to school every day and a bus for the white kids used to pass her every day going to Whitehaven School . . . [S]o now if it comes to busing, the black kids are being bused along with the white kids, so you make a fuss about it when the white kids have been bused all the time and the black kids are walking. Why should you raise all that hell about it when you've been bused all the time[?]" Rufus Thomas interview, Cook Collection, 48.

87. Ibid., 22.

88. Rufus Thomas, NMAH interview, 49.

89. Floyd, *Sun Records,* 71.

90. Rufus Thomas, MVC interview.

91. Floyd, *Sun Records,* 34.

92. Rufus Thomas interview, Cook Collection, 42. During the same conversation, interviewer Ray Ann Kremer noted that Elvis and other prominent whites had emerged from Memphis, to which Thomas responded, "The masses are black, baby." And later, when Kremer suggested that "entertainment is probably the one area where I don't think [race] matters," Thomas responded firmly, "But it does."

93. Ibid., 44.

94. Peter Guralnick, http://memphismusichalloffame.com/inductee/rufusthomas/.

95. Guralnick has been particularly insistent in suggesting that—despite the long trail of evidence—Thomas's resentment was either short-lived or can be dismissed as the complaints of a proud man. In his piece on the Memphis Music Hall of Fame (see note 94), Guralnick suggests that Thomas's discarding by Sam Phillips "left him embittered—but not for long." Guralnick's recent biography of Phillips, which contains extensive material about Thomas, frames the complaints of Thomas and others as unfortunate detours in Phillips's career, rather than serious complications to the narrative of racial progressivism that Guralnick attributes to both Phillips and Sun.

96. Rufus Thomas, NMAH interview, 26.

"If the March Cannot Be Here, Then Where?"

Memphis and the Meredith March

Aram Goudsouzian

On June 8, 1966, the congregation at Metropolitan Baptist Church in South Memphis was angry. Three days earlier, James Meredith, the courageous icon who had integrated the University of Mississippi in 1962, had started walking from downtown Memphis, heading south on Highway 51 to Jackson, Mississippi, to encourage voter registration and the defiance of white intimidation. The next day, just south of Hernando, a white man from Memphis shot and wounded Meredith. The day after that, practically every major figure in the civil rights movement descended upon Memphis, determined to carry on Meredith's march. That morning, Meredith had been discharged from his room at Bowld Hospital, stirring accusations of racist treatment of the civil rights martyr.

With Martin Luther King sitting behind him, the Reverend Bill Smith stepped to the pulpit and articulated the sadness, frustration, and rage surrounding the attack on Meredith. Cries of affirmation rang through the packed church. Then, while preachers Fred Shuttlesworth and King continued to stir the audience, Smith stepped into the church's back room, where he worked with white authorities to plan a protest march to Bowld Hospital. Inspector C. E. Swan was on the phone with police headquarters, and Smith stood behind him. "If you're going to march down the sidewalk, you'll have to define your terms," relayed Swan. "Will it be in two or three or what? You don't want to obstruct the sidewalk. If you do, I'm not sure I can get the go-ahead on this." Smith thought for a moment, rocking back on his heels. They could march in rows of three, he said. The terms were acceptable.[1]

The day before, Mississippi highway patrolmen had bullied and jostled civil rights leaders who were continuing Meredith's walk. But on this evening in Memphis, the police supervised a tidy, silent, two-mile nighttime march to the hospital with a carefully selected group of about fifty protesters, who then returned home without incident. "Those Mississippi cops could learn a lot if they crossed the border," remarked one reporter.[2]

This understated incident captured a particular dynamic of racial politics in Memphis in the midst of the civil rights movement. On the one hand, black Memphians shared the racial burdens and discontent that plagued their neighbors in Mississippi. On the other hand, the city had established patterns of accommodation that both fostered and fettered black protests for freedom. This duality was on display during June 1966, as the Meredith March passed from Memphis to Jackson.

The Meredith March—also known as the March against Fear—was the last great march of the civil rights movement. Occurring at a moment of transition within the black freedom struggle, it nevertheless brought together civil rights leaders and activists of disparate ideologies, uniting them for three weeks over the shared goals of black freedom. It featured such dramatic events as the shooting of James Meredith; a mob attack during a march through Philadelphia, Mississippi; and a brutal tear gas attack by the Mississippi Highway Patrol in the town of Canton. It is most famous for its stop in the Mississippi Delta town of Greenwood, where Stokely Carmichael of the Student Nonviolent Coordinating Committee (SNCC) unveiled the slogan "Black Power," which would define a generation of black protest.[3]

The march lasted for twenty-two days, and twenty-one of them were spent moving through Mississippi. Yet Memphis played a critical role in this mass civil rights demonstration that stoked national attention. James Meredith began his journey there, which framed the early public understanding of his endeavor. His attacker, Aubrey Norvell, hailed from the suburb of Bartlett, which shaped narratives of racial violence among both integrationists and segregationists. And in the aftermath of the shooting, Memphis hosted important events that not only determined the character and success of the march but also influenced the course of the struggle for black freedom. Titans of the civil rights movement orated from the pulpits of Memphis churches. Those same leaders, along with activists from

Memphis and Mississippi, engaged in contentious debates in the rooms of the Lorraine Motel. Even as the march continued south through Mississippi, its headquarters remained at Centenary Methodist Church in Memphis.

The Meredith March also revealed the successes, frustrations, and tensions of black politics in 1966 Memphis. The city's whites exhibited both hostility and accommodation toward black protesters, demonstrating both connections to and distinctions from the racial patterns of Mississippi. For the vibrant local branch of the NAACP, the demonstration presented an opportunity to assert its historic strength, even as the march highlighted the complicated dynamics among distinct local branches and the national office. For the Reverend James Lawson, the march challenged the NAACP's top-down approach, as Centenary Methodist Church achieved his vision of an activist church driven by grassroots pressure and militant nonviolence. For many more citizens of the Bluff City, their personal participation in the Meredith March against Fear shaped their lives and ideologies, which ranged across the spectrum of black politics, guiding the future of the Memphis movement.

"That's James Meredith," a black woman told her friend. "He's marching to Mississippi."

On the Sunday that Meredith began his journey, onlookers in the neighborhood just south of Beale Street were leaning out windows, gazing from porches, and spilling onto sidewalks. A curious caravan followed Meredith, the hero of the 1962 Ole Miss crisis. Four men, two black and two white, planned to accompany him on his 220-mile trek from Memphis to Jackson. Reporters, policemen, and a few FBI agents observed the proceedings. Members of the Memphis branch of the NAACP lent their support by joining this first leg of the journey. Some local black women walked a few blocks, and a group of neighborhood children joined in, lending the procession a merry air.[4]

Meredith was disappointed, however, that most of those cheering him were women and children. "Negro men are afraid to be men down here," he grumbled. The two announced aims of his walk were to encourage black voter registration and to defy the South's culture of racial fear. But he also wanted to demonstrate the strength of black men. Instead of

Claude Sterrett, James Meredith, and Vasco Smith on the first day of the March against Fear. (Courtesy Memphis and Shelby County Room, Memphis Public Library)

a mass march that imposed on local communities and endangered women and children, he sought proud, independent men to join his quest.[5]

Of Meredith's four original companions, two were from New York:

record executive Claude Sterrett and minister Robert Weeks. The third was Sherwood Ross, a Washington, DC, radio reporter who served as a press agent. The fourth marcher was Joseph Crittenden, a native of Rolling Fork, Mississippi, whose family had moved to Memphis in 1940. Crittenden made a good living by fixing farm and construction equipment and operating a gas station and convenience store in North Memphis. A member of the NAACP, he had marched in Washington in 1963 and had gone to Selma in 1965. Crittenden had decided to walk with Meredith that very day while driving home from church.[6]

Meredith's trek was front-page news in the *New York Times,* but the *Memphis Commercial Appeal* did not even report on it that first day. When Meredith left from the downtown Peabody Hotel, about eight or ten whites watched with curiosity, while a single man protested by waving a small Confederate battle flag. Only as they continued down Highway 51 into more rural environs did they face more serious hostility. Cars buzzed close to the road's gravel siding, trying to scare the marchers. Whites hollered racial slurs. Two men on horseback wearing ten-gallon hats waved massive Confederate flags and shrieked rebel yells.[7]

The next day, Meredith and his companions crossed into Mississippi. Just south of Hernando, the northernmost town on Highway 51, Crittenden noticed a portly, middle-aged white man drive off the road into the thick pine woods. Soon after, the white man emerged from a gully and shot at Meredith three times, wounding him with many pellets of bird shot. Because of this violence, the city of Memphis once again figured in the demonstration.[8]

Crittenden was among the small group that rode back to Memphis in the ambulance with Meredith. The young white ambulance driver was going too slowly, so Sherwood Ross threatened that unless they rushed back to Memphis, he would tell the world that the ambulance driver was responsible for the death of James Meredith. Only then did he flip on the siren. The ambulance took Meredith to the emergency room at John Gaston Hospital, where Crittenden was sure they would treat a black patient.[9]

After receiving emergency care, Meredith was transferred to a private room at William Bowld Hospital. That hospital became the site of a whirl of political activity. C. L. Dinkins, president of Owen College and a board member of the City of Memphis Hospitals, rushed to the hospital to make arrangements, as did Maxine and Vasco Smith of the Memphis NAACP. FBI agents and Memphis policemen occupied the hospital rooms flanking Meredith's. At 3:00 that morning, comedian-activist Dick Gregory arrived from Chicago. The next morning he protested the violence by launching a one-day "reverse walk," trudging from Hernando to Memphis accompanied by his wife Lillian and a few other companions, their grim demeanors reflecting a larger black bitterness over this naked attack.[10]

As civil rights organizations vowed to carry on the march in Meredith's name, major political figures flocked to Memphis and visited his bedside. They included Representative John Conyers and seven other members of Congress who had been traveling to Mississippi to observe primary elections; John Hooker, Democratic candidate for Tennessee governor; and John Doar of the Justice Department. Black leaders arrived as well, including Martin Luther King of the Southern Christian Leadership Conference (SCLC), Floyd McKissick of the Congress of Racial Equality (CORE), Stokely Carmichael of SNCC; Whitney Young of the National Urban League, and Roy Wilkins of the NAACP. With three blasts from a shotgun, Meredith's walk had transformed into a mass march with national significance.[11]

On the afternoon of Tuesday, June 7, a small group that included King and Carmichael took up the march from the spot where Meredith had fallen. That evening, everyone was back in Memphis for a mass meeting at Centenary Methodist Church. Samuel "Billy" Kyles, the pastor from Monumental Baptist Church, served as master of ceremonies, and as he recalled, the major civil rights leaders were jockeying for position: "There was a lot of discussion on who was going to speak first, and who was going to speak last." The meeting started about an hour late. More than 600 people jammed into the church, with a large overflow crowd spilling into nearby First Baptist Church. At a moment when the civil rights movement was approaching a crossroads, this mass meeting offered a chance to define not only the march's purpose but also the goals and tactics of the movement itself.[12]

Roy Wilkins spoke first. The NAACP prized order, legal process, and political relations. While decrying the shooting of Meredith, he warned against militant tactics; instead, he encouraged the audience to channel their rage and frustration into political action. "Now you can't go home and get your gun, God forbid, but you can support the [civil rights] bill that is before Congress," he pleaded. Whitney Young of the Urban League called for order and unity but warned against those who wanted a "segregated black nationalist society."[13]

Floyd McKissick and Stokely Carmichael advocated a more militant approach. McKissick, the new director of CORE, called the Statue of Liberty a hypocrite. "We ought to break that young lady's leg and throw her in the Mississippi," he exclaimed. Carmichael, the charismatic new chairman of SNCC, added, "I'm just a poor black boy who's not going to beg for what I want. I'm gonna take it." They captured both a mood and an idea. A generation of black activists had endured enormous sacrifice, and despite the passage of the Civil Rights Act of 1964 and the Voting Rights Act of 1965, many African Americans remained frustrated with second-class citizenship and a society that demeaned black culture and black humanity. "The only way we're gonna have justice in this country is when we organize and take it," thundered Carmichael. "We need power!"[14]

Martin Luther King charted a middle course, acknowledging the rage and frustration that drove so many black Americans, but funneling those emotions into disciplined, nonviolent action that created political pressure from the grass roots. From the pulpit, he celebrated the courage of James Meredith and the gains of the civil rights movement. Black Americans still lacked genuine freedom, though. "Freedom is not some lavish dish that the white man will pass out on a silver platter while the Negro merely furnished the appetite," he warned. "If we are going to be free we are going to have to suffer for that freedom, we are going to have to sacrifice for it, we will have to march the highways of the nation for it, and I am still convinced that there is nothing so powerful to dramatize an injustice than the tramp, tramp, tramp of marching feet." Recalling past triumphs such as the Birmingham campaign of 1963, he sought to place the Meredith March of 1966 in that same nonviolent tradition.[15]

Later that night, these debates continued at the Lorraine Motel on Mulberry Street, just south of downtown Memphis. In an era when it was difficult to find respectable lodging in black districts, the Lorraine was clean and modern. Black entertainers such as Louis Armstrong, Cab Calloway, and Lionel Hampton stayed at the Lorraine when they performed in Memphis. "They felt they was at home," recalled motel owner Walter Bailey. "They would come back in the kitchen. They would pick their own room to stay in." They were allowed to ignore check-in and check-out times, and they could even negotiate room rates. Now, as civil rights leaders and activists arrived in Memphis, they filled the Lorraine Motel. King, a regular guest, was in room 307.[16]

Into the wee hours of the morning, representatives from the major civil rights organizations, along with activists from Memphis and Mississippi, packed into King's room to debate the meaning of this hastily improvised mass demonstration. Wilkins wanted a quick, organized march with significant white participation, hoping it would serve as a lobbying tool for the civil rights bill in Congress. But his aims were thwarted. Mississippi activists affiliated with organizations such as the Mississippi Freedom Democratic Party and the Delta Ministry wanted to register more voters and empower local black people. The Deacons for Defense and Justice, a relatively new group with roots in Louisiana, sought to provide armed protection for the marchers. SNCC and CORE supported these proposals. Frustrated with mass marches designed for the public consumption of white liberals, they wanted political activity that helped black people on the ground. They believed that blacks needed to steer their own movement and that nonviolence had outlived its utility as a tactic. SNCC developed a statement that called for slowing down the march and diverting its path into the black-majority Mississippi Delta, where SNCC had a long organizing history.[17]

During this meeting, the more militant forces drove the NAACP and the Urban League out of any official participation in the march. Carmichael insulted Wilkins and Young by insinuating that they were "lackeys of the white power structure." The more venerable leaders saw no way to work with the young upstarts, so they packed up their briefcases and left. King insisted that the march be open to all races and that it remain nonviolent, but he also abstained from defending Wilkins and Young. The end result of the Lorraine Motel meeting was that King and the SCLC were left to harness the radical energies of SNCC, CORE, and grassroots activists as the march moved south through Mississippi.[18]

The next morning, Memphis still had a starring role in the drama. James Meredith was proud, quirky, and independent. He was affiliated with no civil rights organizations and was a critic of nonviolence. Now a contentious, nonviolent mass demonstration was being carried out in his name, and he was unhappy. So before starting the next stage of the march in Coldwater, King, McKissick, and Memphis attorney A. W. Willis went to Meredith's bedside to seek his blessing. After a frank discussion, they gained his consent. At 10:55 a.m., Bowld Hospital administrator David Hoxie arrived at Meredith's room with discharge papers (regular checkout time was 11:00 a.m.). King and McKissick objected that Meredith was still recuperating and deserved better treatment. Meredith huffily signed the papers and told Hoxie to "get the hell out of my room."[19]

Willis called the incident "tantamount to eviction," and King promised a reaction of "righteous indignation." As indicated by the mass meeting at Metropolitan Baptist Church that evening, many black Memphians saw this as another example of second-class treatment based on racial prejudice. (Louis Britt, the attending physician, later recalled that when Meredith was transferred to Bowld, another doctor initially planned to put him in the prison ward—common practice for a black man with a gunshot wound.) If nothing else, Meredith's presence was putting a strain on the hospital, with police and reporters taking over nearby rooms. Hospital administrators defended the discharge, but they also undermined the march leaders' calls for unity by dishing about their debates with Meredith.[20]

As he left the hospital, Meredith provided the controversy with a strange coda. He had barely slept because of his painful pellet wounds, and he was frustrated with both the march leaders and the hospital. He donned a suit and tie and called a press conference. Early that afternoon, he softly and impassively read his statement, then stopped as tears ran down his face. He slumped into a chaise lounge, nearly fainting from the stress and the hot television lights. He left Bowld Hospital in a wheelchair and flew home to New York City that evening.[21]

Meanwhile, Meredith's attacker gained attention. Forty-year-old Aubrey James Norvell lived with his wife in the Memphis suburb of Bartlett. After he shot Meredith, most people assumed he was a violent white supremacist in the vein of the Ku Klux Klan. But as the press investigated him, a more mysterious portrait emerged. He had no known connection to any segregationist group. Though recently laid off from his job as a hardware clerk, he was not poor. A graduate of Tech High School, he had served in the army during World War II, and he and his father had once owned their own hardware store. His acquaintances described him as quiet, helpful, and friendly. His family professed complete shock at his action. "He never mentioned civil rights one way or the other," said a neighbor.[22]

Throughout his hearing and bond posting, Norvell never revealed a motive. His silence allowed both sides to charge conspiracy. Meredith's fellow marchers, other civil rights activists, the NAACP Legal Defense Fund, and a variety of liberal northern congressmen all questioned how the Mississippi police and the FBI could have allowed Norvell to shoot Meredith three times. They suggested that Norvell was in cahoots with racist authorities.[23]

More remarkably, segregationist politicians and other white southerners claimed that Norvell was involved in a conspiracy against Mississippi whites. They charged that integrationists had orchestrated Norvell's shooting of Meredith to create a crisis, inviting reporters and federal officials to upset southern mores. An officer from the Mississippi State Sovereignty Commission—a state-funded organization designed to preserve racial segregation—investigated this possibility; he even authorized a bribe to Norvell's attorney for information that confirmed it was "a hired put-up job." One of their justifications was that Norvell had used bird shot, ensuring that he would merely wound Meredith. They also argued that Norvell was not a real southerner but rather an "outside agitator"— he was, after all, from Memphis.[24]

There was a joke that went like this: A black minister in Chicago received a call to preach in Mississippi. He fell to his knees, praying for God to go with him. "Well," replied God, "I'll go as far as Memphis."[25]

Memphis and Mississippi were connected in the black imagination. Memphis was a gateway, a crossroads, both of the Deep South and distinct from it. With so many migrants from Mississippi, black and white, settling in Memphis, the connections were strong. When a reporter asked Meredith why he started his march from the Peabody Hotel in downtown Memphis, he replied: "Well, you know that Memphis is considered the northern capital of Mississippi, and that is why I am starting here."[26]

Yet when Roy Wilkins was orating at Centenary Methodist Church, he drew a sharp distinction between Memphis and Mississippi: "It is hard for you to remember that just a few miles south of here there is another country. We are going to show the people of Mississippi that they are part of the 50 states." Indeed, Mississippi was still primarily rural, with a plantation-based economy; it had the South's lowest rates of registered black voters and a long history of racial brutality. In Memphis, by contrast, almost three-fourths of eligible blacks were registered to vote, a legacy of the political machine run by "Boss" E. H. Crump. The city had no crude white demagogues in the vein of Ross Barnett or Bull Connor. Prominent whites such as former mayor Edmund Orgill, attorney Lucius Burch, and *Memphis Press-Scimitar* editor Edward Meeman served alongside black leaders such as Maxine and Vasco Smith, Billy Kyles, and LeMoyne College president Hollis Price on the Memphis Committee on Community Relations (MCCR), which fostered the peaceful integration of many public facilities in advance of the 1964 Civil Rights Act.[27]

As one reflection of liberal whites' image of race in Memphis, the Memphis Area Chamber of Commerce sent James Meredith a public telegram that condemned the attack on him. It also portrayed Memphis as an oasis of racial peace: "We trust that you, in fairness to the community that has labored long and with unparalleled success to effect racial harmony second to no city in America, will experience in your heart and mind that there are 1,200,000 Memphis area citizens who lament what one person has done to you." The message celebrated the city's "well-deserved reputation as a peaceful and progressive community where goodwill and brotherhood take precedence over lawlessness and deprivation of the rights of any individual." In Mississippi, there were no parallel reactions to Meredith's shooting or to the subsequent march.[28]

Yet the city's white mainstream did not support the Meredith March. A column by Nat D. Williams in the *Tri-State Defender* chronicled all the ways that Memphis whites were grumbling about the march. Some said it was useless because blacks were already making progress. Others thought it stoked white resentment of black people, like the 1965 Watts riot. Still others argued it was an artificial attempt to revive a flagging civil rights movement.[29]

The *Commercial Appeal,* the most prominent newspaper in Memphis, reflected a larger racial closed-mindedness. Editor Frank Ahlgren had a reputation for being fair and liberal, but in the opinion of James Lawson, he had no sense of the black community's discontent and was "a racist through and through." Indeed, the newspaper's position was openly hostile toward the march. "The rag-tag march moves on toward Jackson," fumed one editorial. "Let those who might be inclined to follow the leadership of the bitter, arrogant and vindictive individuals be warned that they will have only themselves to blame for the consequences that will flow from any shedding of blood precipitated under these circumstances." It was accompanied by a cartoon showing a giant man representing "Responsible Negro Leadership" trying to stop the black masses from marching. Another editorial praised the "sovereign state of Mississippi" and labeled the Meredith March pointless. In July the newspaper published the complete text of a harangue on the floor of the House of Representatives by Mississippi congressman Thomas Abernathy, who blamed the national media and the federal government for violating the rights of white Mississippians in favor of radicals, including "goateed riffraff and just plain junks and punks from all over the nation."[30]

On June 19, 1966, the *Commercial Appeal* ran a special letters-to-the-editor section focusing on the Meredith March. Of the sixteen letters, only two were somewhat sympathetic to Meredith—and one of those condemned him as "news-hungry." The other letters assailed the communist influence in the black freedom movement, bewailed the media's bias against the South, chided outspoken activists such as Dick Gregory, and characterized King and Meredith as professional troublemakers who inflated minor incidents. One Mississippi woman wrote that whites would let blacks vote "if they would do it in the right way." A correspondent from Memphis said that Meredith's "blatant exhibitionism" should have been quelled by the NAACP. A Memphis man echoed white Mississippians' conspiracy theory that civil rights sympathizers had arranged the Meredith shooting: "The whole event was a hoax from the beginning."[31]

Law enforcement officials shared that hostility. One of the police officers guarding Meredith's room at Bowld Hospital growled that "he was a damn fool. He was just asking to get shot." According to an investigator from the Mississippi State Sovereignty Commission, an FBI agent based in Memphis was working on the assumption that civil rights advocates had coordinated the shooting of Meredith. The investigator met with Inspector N. E. Zachary, chief of the Memphis Police Department's Homicide Squad, who related that although the case was outside his jurisdiction, "it was general consensus among all with whom he had talked that the shooting looked like a planned affair." In other words, the same department that tried to cooperate with black protesters in Memphis also believed the far-fetched conspiracy theories that animated die-hard white supremacists in Mississippi.[32]

Memphis was an NAACP town. Many politically active ministers were also members of Martin Luther King's SCLC, but they saw no need to establish a branch of that organization because the NAACP was so strong. There was no real SNCC presence. One tough critic of the NAACP named O. Z. Evers started a local branch of CORE, but it lacked staying power. By contrast, the Memphis NAACP had more than 1,500 members by 1966. Its educated, middle-class leaders included a number of married couples committed to the movement, such as Vasco and Maxine Smith, Jesse and Allegra Turner, Ben and Frances Hooks, A. W. and Anne Willis, and Russell and Laurie Sugarmon. Maxine Smith, the branch's executive secretary, was fearless and dynamic; Roy Wilkins called her "a woman of inexhaustible energy and leadership." She constantly challenged the slow pace of school integration, attracted new members, started voter registration campaigns, and organized public demonstrations for racial justice.[33]

The Memphis NAACP followed a top-down model: its leaders formulated plans to present to rank-and-file members, endorsed candidates for political office, and negotiated behind the scenes with white leaders to integrate public facilities. In advance of passage of the 1964 Civil Rights Act, the NAACP helped achieve the desegregation of public institutions such as the library, the zoo, museums, parks, golf courses, theaters, and assorted restaurants. Sit-ins and picket lines were often steered by the NAACP rather than by grassroots insurgency.[34]

The Memphis NAACP leadership knew James Meredith. A. W. Willis had served as Meredith's attorney of record during his 1962 court challenge to integrate the University of Mississippi; Meredith admired Willis's practical, hard-driving approach. Prior to the riot at Ole Miss that fall, Meredith had stayed in relative seclusion in Memphis with Maxine and Vasco Smith. (However, they did go dancing one night, leading to a famous photograph. As Maxine recalled, "I was supposed to be hiding him, and we ended up doing the Twist!") So in 1966, the NAACP's Maxine and Vasco Smith and Lorene Osborne were among those who accompanied Meredith on the first day of his march. As Maxine stated, "He deserved a flock of people. . . . There's no way I couldn't be a part of that march."[35]

Maxine Smith spoke at the June 7 mass meeting at Centenary Methodist Church. NAACP leaders attended the planning sessions at the Lorraine Motel, and NAACP members housed and fed visiting volunteers, worked at march headquarters, provided rides, and donated money. Members from the adult, college, and youth divisions all marched through Mississippi. The branch's association with the march was a point of pride as well as a recruiting tool. "Not far from our own city limits, James Meredith was cowardly shot down. Mississippi law enforcement have abused our fellow Freedom Fighters with vile language, billy clubs, and tear gas," read one appeal for new members. "This suffering will not be in vain if it will only serve to awaken many of us, who seem to believe we are free, from our apathy and lack of concern."[36]

The march also revealed an interesting dynamic between the national NAACP office and its local branches. Roy Wilkins removed the national NAACP from official participation in the march, since he was unwilling to work with radical groups such as SNCC and CORE. But the march was national news, and NAACP members were flocking to Mississippi. So in its official press releases, the national office both criticized the march leadership and celebrated its branch members' contributions to racial justice, including those of the Memphis leaders who originally walked with Meredith.[37]

The Memphis branch had an excellent relationship with Wilkins. But as the march moved south, the Memphis NAACP got embroiled in a dispute between the national office and the branch in Philadelphia, Pennsylvania. Cecil Moore, head of the Philadelphia branch, annoyed the national leadership with his brash, militant appeals to the black working class. In 1966 the NAACP proposed to split Moore's kingdom into five separate branches, weakening his power. Amidst this controversy, Moore headed south to march through Mississippi, stopping first in Memphis for a mass meeting on June 12 at the Pentecostal Temple of the Church of God. But he did not speak there and accused Jesse Turner of keeping him off the podium. "He knew that I am not in agreement with national NAACP officials, and he wanted to stay on their good side," charged Moore. He said that Wilkins and Turner were "languishing in Uncle Tomism."[38]

This incident highlighted both the power and the limitations of a Memphis movement led by the NAACP. The branch had a practical, moderate philosophy and a track record of desegregating institutions and building political power. But deeper issues that intertwined race and class—from police brutality to limited job opportunities to inferior schools—still plagued the black majority. The myth of Memphis as a site of racial harmony obscured these problems. A "plantation mentality" still infected the city's race relations. Critics of the NAACP style sought a wider base for black politics. The Meredith March provided one opportunity to build that base.[39]

The marchers faced a huge logistical challenge. They would be going 220 miles over three weeks, much longer than a typical civil rights march. Without any advance planning, march leaders had to invite, house, and feed volunteers from across the country. They needed big tents, portable toilets, and transportation between Memphis and the march site. They had to plan routes, schedule rallies, connect with local leaders, and negotiate with law enforcement. They needed lawyers, phone lines, and financial contributions. Much of this burden fell on black leaders from Memphis, including ministers with organizing experience and national contacts, such as Benjamin Hooks, Harold Middlebrook, Billy Kyles, Ralph Jackson, and James Lawson. They may have been skeptical of Meredith's initial walk, but once he was shot, they helped transform the march into a successful mass protest for black freedom.[40]

When Martin Luther King first learned of the attack on Highway 51, he called Lawson, who tried to contact Meredith. The police had already cordoned off Bowld Hospital, and the fire department soon responded to a bomb threat there. Lawson tried to deliver to Meredith a hastily scribbled note on a piece of torn, yellow-lined paper: "M. L. King has just called me—sends a message to you. Wants me to call him back this evening." Meredith refused to accept the note, but Lawson touched base with A. W. Willis, who got Lawson into Meredith's hospital room that night, smoothing the path for King's visit the next morning.[41]

Lawson's pastorate, Centenary Methodist Church, served as headquarters. Planners took over a classroom and the library, where King worked the phone lines, exploiting his clout with liberals who could deliver marchers and money. Middle-aged NAACP types and bearded SNCC militants gathered outside the church in the broiling heat, ready to take up the march. A group that included King piled into Lawson's station wagon. After a pit stop at a Jack Pirtle's restaurant shack for fried chicken and orange Ne-Hi soda, they headed down Highway 51. Joseph Crittenden showed them the exact spot where Meredith had been shot, and they recommenced the march from there.[42]

In the coming days, King and others put out calls for marchers, instructing them to check in at Centenary. They accommodated all individuals who made their way to the church, registered, and agreed to adhere to nonviolence. Over the next few weeks, an estimated 2,000 volunteers arrived. SCLC's Hosea Williams oversaw operations; SNCC's Bob Smith coordinated transportation; Don Smith of CORE ran the press room, while Herb Callender and Stoney Cooks handled other logistics. The church's lower level housed areas for registering new marchers, serving food, answering phones, and overseeing press relations. A bulletin board relayed messages to volunteers, and a big map on the wall traced the march's progress.[43]

Perhaps because Aubrey Norvell hailed from Memphis, a surprising number of white Memphians showed hospitality to the participants. "This is the first time I've ever been in a southern community where so many whites offered their homes to house civil rights workers," marveled Cooks. But the black community in particular rallied behind the effort. Gladys Carpenter of the Memphis NAACP, who headed the housing committee, said, "People are constantly coming in, offering food and homes. I know things were pretty good in Memphis, but I must admit I'm amazed."[44]

"People came from everywhere to here," recalled activist David Acey. "Memphis was the pivotal point. Everybody came to Memphis." Volunteers picked up marchers from the airport or the bus station and ferried them from the church to Mississippi. Others typed forms or answered phones. Black-owned restaurants such as Culpepper's Barbecue delivered food. Memphians fixed meals for the marchers in their own kitchens, or they donated bedding or office supplies. They might not have marched through Mississippi or wielded a picket sign, noted Harold Middlebrook, but "this was their contribution to the movement."[45]

"My concept of the church is as a movement of people who are so called, by God, in the Kingdom, that they develop then a passionate concern for the life of the world and for the welfare of the neighbor," stated Lawson. He had led the nonviolent workshops in Nashville that laid the foundation for that city's 1960 sit-in movement. Upon being assigned to Memphis in 1962, he found a church with a long tradition of activism and an economically diverse congregation, but it "had become in-grown and comfortable." He criticized how the NAACP orchestrated black protests in Memphis, because the organization served as a buffer between the black masses and white-dominated institutions. "The NAACP leadership thought primarily in terms of influencing legislation and court action," he recalled. The Memphis sit-ins in the early 1960s helped desegregate public facilities, he argued, but they did not mobilize black Memphis to fight for broader types of justice. Lawson envisioned a movement that engaged in sustained, militant, nonviolent confrontation that forced the entire city to recognize racial inequality.[46]

During his speech at Centenary, Martin Luther King had told the audience that as the march moved toward Jackson, "everybody under the sound of my voice should make witness in some way." The subsequent organization of black Memphians realized the hopes of King and Lawson and other architects of nonviolent direct action. The effort pulled together a wide array of black citizens to challenge white supremacy in Memphis and beyond. At first, a few church members feared the consequences of all this political activity, but only one person voted against the motion to make Centenary the official march headquarters. "I can't think of a better thing for the church to be doing," said one member. Another asked, "If the March cannot be here, then where?"[47]

As the march continued south, Memphians stayed involved. Coby Smith marched the whole way to Jackson, and his experience captured not only a host of dramatic moments but also the march's impact on a generation of activists. Smith was one of two young men who had integrated Southwestern College. He was smart and charismatic, and a group of liberal white attorneys had helped pay his tuition. He became active in Memphis politics through his parents, who were members of the Shelby County Democratic Club, and in 1965 he joined the interracial Southern Student Organizing Committee. Smith attended the mass meeting at Centenary, where he met King and suggested that they recruit volunteers from Memphis colleges and high schools. He then quit his summer job and started marching.[48]

Smith loved the day-to-day experience of marching. He met civil rights legends, sang folk songs around a campfire, flirted with girls, and debated political philosophy. He grew to revere Stokely Carmichael, calling him "the most charismatic guy you ever met." Carmichael had a confrontational style and politics that appealed to black youth. Smith joined advance teams that went into black communities, stoking their excitement about the arrival of the march.[49]

Smith marched into Greenwood, where Carmichael unveiled the famous "Black Power" slogan, a call for black unity, pride, and independence that many whites feared as a repudiation of the movement's old principles. He marched into Canton, where the Mississippi Highway Patrol launched a brutal tear gas attack on hundreds of marchers. And he marched into Jackson, where thousands piled into the streets on that triumphant final day after three weeks of what King had called "the tramp, tramp, tramp of marching feet." After the march, Smith moved to Atlanta, joined SNCC, and then returned to Memphis to cofound the Black Organizing Project and the Invaders, two related Black Power organizations that gained prominence during the 1968 sanitation strike.[50]

Not every marcher was like Coby Smith. Every marcher had a political commitment to black freedom, but that commitment took many forms. As Chris Drags, a native white southerner and graduate student at Memphis State University, marched through Como, he pleaded with a reporter to "please, please go and tell people outside Mississippi that very few of us are like Norvell. There are a lot here who feel that all Negroes should get all civil rights and that's why I'm here." A few days later, a *Detroit Free Press* column told the story of two people marching together through Sardis. One was a white businessman whose conscience had moved him to fly down and march for a day. The other was an old black domestic worker from Memphis who, in response to the businessman's story, just remarked, "Bless you."[51]

Joseph Crittenden kept marching after the shooting of Meredith. Because he had to take care of his mother and his business, he drove home every night in his truck, labeled "Crittenden and Son" on the side. One night he was driving north on Route 3, passing through the town of Banks, when some whites recognized the name on his truck; three cars chased him down gravel roads before he escaped. Similarly, Jesse Turner and three white Catholic priests were driving on Route 16 through rural Leake County, where the Ku Klux Klan had burned down St. Joachim Catholic School for Negroes that very morning. Two cars of white thugs saw them and gave chase for ten miles at high speeds, almost causing a vehicular disaster.[52]

Elaine Lee was a twenty-one-year-old NAACP Youth Council member and recent graduate of LeMoyne-Owen College. Throughout those three weeks of the march from Memphis to Jackson, she drove down in the mornings with one of her brothers (she was the seventh of fourteen children in a politically active family), and after a day of walking and demonstrating, they headed back to Memphis. She appreciated "the groundswell in the towns, the people, the expressions on their faces. They could see that we were doing something for them." She did not characterize herself as radical, but she admired Stokely Carmichael and his call for Black Power. The quest for black independence and pride made sense: "The only thing we had experienced was White Power."[53]

David Acey considered himself a militant, but the Meredith March broadened his perspective. A military veteran in his late twenties, he had been active in the NAACP Youth Council, participated in the sit-in movement, and helped found the Black Student Association at Memphis State University. He, too, admired Carmichael, and he was skeptical of King's nonviolence; if the Klan attacked, he vowed to fight back with his switchblade. But on the march through Mississippi, he recalled, "I learned to appreciate King. King gave us a spiritual, in-depth insight. He could see further in this thing than we could." King would chat with young black men like Acey and ask them, Is the Klan sick? Yes, they would answer. King would counsel that if you are a doctor, you do not jump in bed with the patient. "With Martin Luther King, you really had to walk with him to understand him," said Acey. "The more you walked with King, the more you could do it."[54]

James Lawson, like King, advocated for nonviolent direct action as he marched toward Jackson. As an early mentor to many SNCC activists, he was a close observer of the organization and its evolution, and he encouraged its young militants to consider the problems of armed self-defense in the context of a mass demonstration that included women and children. But he did not call for nonviolence out of passivity or to appease white people. He celebrated how the march helped black Mississippians fight segregation and register to vote. But, he reflected, "my major quarrel with the March is that in spite of all the talk about 'black power' and militancy, the leaders did not push toward turning the demonstration into radical direct action." He advocated campaigns of civil disobedience that would immobilize the white power structure, that pressed the demands of the larger black community. "Somewhere along the line the civil rights movement will have to become revolutionary," he stated.[55]

These varied experiences indicate that as Memphis shaped the Meredith March, the march also shaped Memphis and its people. The 1968 sanitation strike and the assassination of Martin Luther King would overshadow the city's longer history in the civil rights movement. Yet two years earlier, Memphis had been the early epicenter of a mass demonstration of enormous significance with profound effects on the nation, the movement, the city, and the people who participated in it.

Notes

1. *Boston Globe,* June 9, 1966, evening edition.

2. *Louisville Courier-Journal,* June 9, 1966; *Boston Globe,* June 9, 1966, evening edition.

3. See Aram Goudsouzian, *Down to the Crossroads: Civil Rights, Black Power, and the Meredith March against Fear* (New York: Farrar, Straus, and Giroux, 2014). This essay is based primarily on sources originally used to research *Down to the Crossroads.* On the Meredith March, see also Taylor Branch, *At Canaan's Edge: America in the King Years 1965–68* (New York: Simon and Schuster, 2006), 476–95; John Dittmer, *Local People: The Struggle for Civil Rights in Mississippi* (Urbana: University of Illinois Press, 1994), 389–402; David Garrow, *Bearing the Cross: Martin Luther King, Jr. and the Southern Christian Leader-*

ship Conference (New York: William Morrow, 1986), 473–89; Peniel E. Joseph, *Waiting 'til the Midnight Hour: A Narrative History of the Black Power Movement* (New York: Owl Books, 2006), 132–46; Peniel E. Joseph, *Stokely: A Life* (New York: Basic Civitas, 2014), 101–23.

4. *Baltimore Sun,* June 6, 1966; *New York Times,* June 6, 1966; *Nashville Tennessean,* June 6, 1966.

5. *Washington Star,* June 7, 1966; "Statement: My Walk from Memphis to Jackson," May 31, 1966, box 14, folder 2, James Howard Meredith Collection, Special Collections, University of Mississippi.

6. Joseph Crittenden, interview with the author, Memphis, February 13, 2010; *Washington Post,* June 7, 1966.

7. *New York Times,* June 6, 1966; *Memphis Commercial Appeal,* June 6, 1966; *Washington Star,* June 7, 1966; Sherwood Ross, telephone interview with the author, January 27, 2010.

8. Crittenden interview; *Atlanta Constitution,* June 7, 1966.

9. *Washington Post,* June 7, 1966; Crittenden interview; Ross interview.

10. *Tri-State Defender,* June 11, 1966; *Memphis Press-Scimitar,* June 7, 8, 1966.

11. *Boston Globe,* June 7, 1966; *Memphis Commercial Appeal,* June 8, 1966; John Doar, telephone interview with the author, March 17, 2010; James Meredith, "Big Changes Are Coming," *Saturday Evening Post,* August 13, 1966, 25.

12. Samuel "Billy" Kyles, interview with the author, Memphis, March 23, 2010; *Nashville Tennessean,* June 8, 1966; *Memphis Press-Scimitar,* June 8, 1966.

13. *Memphis Commercial Appeal,* June 8, 1966; *Louisville Courier-Journal,* June 8, 1966; *Christian Science Monitor,* June 9, 1966.

14. *Christian Science Monitor,* June 9, 1966; "The March Meredith Began," *Newsweek,* June 20, 1966, 29–30.

15. Martin Luther King speech, June 7, 1966, series 3, box 11, Papers of Martin Luther King, King Library and Archive, Atlanta; *Memphis Press-Scimitar,* June 8, 1966. The written speech in the King archives says the "tramp tramp of marching feet," while press accounts quote it as "the tramp, tramp, tramp of marching feet."

16. Walter Bailey oral history, container 20, folder 11, Sanitation Strike Oral History Collection, Special Collections, University of Memphis.

17. Roy Wilkins with Tom Mathews, *Standing Fast: The Autobiography of Roy Wilkins* (1982; reprint, New York: Da Capo Press, 1994), 315–16; Owen Brooks, interview with the author, Jackson, MS, May 25, 2010; Jesse Harris, telephone interview with the author, April 5, 2010; Lawrence Guyot, telephone interview with the author, March 31, 2010; Lance Hill, *The Deacons for Defense: Armed Resistance in the Civil Rights Movement* (Chapel Hill: University of North Carolina Press, 2004), 246–47; Cleveland Sellers, telephone interview with the

author, July 27, 2011; "Ideas for Proposed Statement," reel 38, Papers of the Student Nonviolent Coordinating Committee, microfilm collection.

18. Stokely Carmichael interview, November 7, 1988, box 7, folder 3, Southern Regional Council, "Will the Circle Be Unbroken?" transcripts, Special Collections, Emory University, Atlanta; Sellers interview; Stokely Carmichael with Ekweume Michael Thelwell, *Ready for Revolution: The Life and Struggles of Stokely Carmichael (Kwame Ture)* (New York: Scribner, 2003), 494–99.

19. *Memphis Press-Scimitar,* June 8, 1966; *Los Angeles Times,* June 9, 1966. On Meredith, see Charles W. Eagles, *The Price of Defiance: James Meredith and the Integration of Ole Miss* (Chapel Hill: University of North Carolina Press, 2009), 201–20; Aram Goudsouzian, "Three Weeks in Mississippi: James Meredith, Aubrey Norvell, and the Politics of Bird Shot," *Journal of the Historical Society* 11, no. 1 (March 2011): 23–58.

20. *Washington Post,* June 9, 1966; *New York Times,* June 9, 1966; Maurice Elliott, "The Racial Integration of the Memphis Medical Center," January 17, 2007, 12, manuscript in author's possession; *Chicago Daily News,* June 8, 1966; *Memphis Commercial Appeal,* June 9, 1966.

21. *Memphis Press-Scimitar,* June 8, 1966; *Washington Post,* June 9, 1966; *New York Post,* June 8, 1966.

22. *New York Post,* June 8, 1966; *Memphis Press-Scimitar,* June 7, 1966; *Newsday,* June 8, 1966; *Memphis Commercial Appeal,* June 7, 1966.

23. *Nashville Tennessean,* June 7, 1966; *Memphis Press-Scimitar,* June 17, 1966; *New York Amsterdam News,* June 11, 1966; *Bergen (NJ) Record,* June 8, 1966; *Baltimore Afro-American,* June 18, 1966; *Congressional Record—Appendix,* June 13, 1966, A3165–A3166; *Delta Democrat-Times,* June 7, 1966; *Cleveland Call and Post,* June 18, 1966; *Washington Post,* June 21, 1966.

24. *Jackson Daily News,* June 7, 1966; *Jackson Clarion-Ledger,* June 10, 13, 16, 24, 1966; Frank Boykin to James Eastland, June 10, 1966, file series 1, subseries 18, box 1, folder 52, James O. Eastland Collection, University of Mississippi; *Congressional Record,* June 8, 1966, 11999; Tom Scarbrough to Erle Johnston, June 20, 1966, Mississippi State Sovereignty Commission Files, SCR ID# 1-67-4-145-2-1-1, http://mdah.state.ms.us/arrec/digital_archives/sovcom/.

25. Karl Fleming, *Son of the Rough South: An Uncivil Memoir* (New York: PublicAffairs, 2006), 269.

26. *Tri-State Defender,* June 11, 1966. David Cohn famously wrote that "the Mississippi Delta begins in the lobby of the Peabody Hotel in Memphis and ends on Catfish Row in Vicksburg." David Cohn, *Where I Was Born and Raised* (Cambridge, MA: Riverside, 1948), 12. On migrating musicians and Memphis, see Robert Palmer, *Deep Blues: A Musical and Cultural History of the Mississippi Delta* (New York: Penguin Books, 1982), 204–47.

27. *Memphis Commercial Appeal,* June 8, 1966; Russell and Gina Sugarmon oral history, May 29, 1968, container 24, folder 238, Sanitation Strike Oral His-

tory Collection, Special Collections, University of Memphis; Jesse Turner oral history, ibid.

28. *Memphis Commercial Appeal*, June 8, 1966.

29. *Tri-State Defender*, June 18, 1966.

30. James Lawson oral history, box 46, folder Oral History Transcript—James M. Lawson—September 24, 1969, Special Collections, Vanderbilt University, Nashville; Lucius Burch oral history, box 46, Folder Oral History Transcript—Lucius Burch—September 3, 1968, ibid.; *Memphis Commercial Appeal*, June 21, 28, July 26, 1966.

31. *Memphis Commercial Appeal*, June 19, 1966.

32. *New York Post*, June 7, 1966; Tom Scarbrough to Erle Johnston, June 20, 1966, Mississippi State Sovereignty Commission Files, SCR ID# 1-67-4-146-1-1-1, http://mdah.state.ms.us/arrec/digital_archives/sovcom/. Pete Hamill's column in the *New York Post* quotes the police officer as saying, "He was just askin' t' get shot."

33. Miriam DeCosta-Willis, interview with the author, Memphis, March 5, 2010; Kyles interview; Miriam DeCosta-Willis, *Notable Black Memphians* (New York: Cambria Press, 2008), 116–17; Membership Report for Memphis Branch, box 4, folder 11, Maxine A. Smith NAACP Collection, Memphis and Shelby County Room, Benjamin L. Hooks Central Library, Memphis; Roy Wilkins oral history, April 18, 1973, container 24, folder 250, Sanitation Strike Oral History Collection, Special Collections, University of Memphis; Sherry L. Hoppe and Bruce W. Speck, *Maxine Smith's Unwilling Pupils: Lessons Learned in Memphis's Civil Rights Classroom* (Knoxville: University of Tennessee Press, 2007), 18, 30–65. On the NAACP's activity around the time of the Meredith March, see Report of Executive Secretary, May 4, 1966–June 26, 1966, box 1, folder 6, and Personal Correspondence Notebook, April 26, 1966–June 6, 1966, box 10, both in Maxine A. Smith NAACP Collection. On documents related to Memphis's CORE branch, see reel 42, Papers of the Congress of Racial Equality.

34. Bobby L. Lovett, *The Civil Rights Movement in Tennessee: A Narrative History* (Knoxville: University of Tennessee Press, 2005), 192–200; Sharon D. Wright, *Race, Power, and Political Emergence in Memphis* (New York: Garland, 2000), 55–60; Hoppe and Speck, *Maxine Smith's Unwilling Pupils*, 61–91.

35. James H. Meredith, *Three Years in Mississippi* (1966; reprint, Jackson, MS: Meredith Publishing, 1996), 176; Hoppe and Speck, *Maxine Smith's Unwilling Pupils*, 39; press release, June 11, 1966, group IV, box A56, folder Meredith, James 1966, National Association for the Advancement of Colored People Collection, Manuscript Division, Library of Congress, Washington, DC; Maxine Smith, interview with the author, Memphis, July 22, 2011.

36. Report of Executive Secretary, May 4, 1966–June 26, 1966; Personal Correspondence Notebook, June 6, 1966–August 28, 1966, box 10, Maxine A. Smith NAACP Collection.

37. Press releases, June 10, 11, 1966, group IV, box A56, folder Meredith, James 1966, NAACP Collection, Library of Congress.

38. Matthew Countryman, *Up South: Civil Rights and Black Power in Philadelphia* (Philadelphia: University of Pennsylvania Press, 2006), 120–79, 230–31; *Memphis Press-Scimitar,* June 13, 1966.

39. See Laurie Green, *Battling the Plantation Mentality: Memphis and the Black Freedom Struggle* (Chapel Hill: University of North Carolina Press, 2007), 253–54; Michael K. Honey, *Going Down Jericho Road: The Memphis Strike, Martin Luther King's Last Campaign* (New York: W. W. Norton, 2007), 11, 44–45.

40. Harold Middlebrook, telephone interview with the author, March 31, 2010; James Lawson oral history, box 46, folder Oral History Transcript—James M. Lawson—August 21, 1969, Special Collections, Vanderbilt University; Charles Morgan Jr., *One Man, One Voice* (New York: Holt, Rinehart and Winston, 1979), 72; Harold Middlebrook oral history, July 21, 1968, container 23, series 2, folder 1, Sanitation Strike Oral History Collection, Special Collections, University of Memphis.

41. Handwritten note from James Lawson, box 43, folder James Meredith March—Clippings—1966, James M. Lawson Papers, Special Collections, Vanderbilt University; James M. Lawson, "The Meredith March . . . and Tomorrow," *Concern,* July 15, 1966, 4.

42. Lawson, "Meredith March . . . and Tomorrow," 4; Morgan, *One Man, One Voice,* 72–73; *New York Post,* June 8, 1966; Crittenden interview.

43. SCLC fund-raising letter signed by Martin Luther King and Hosea Williams, undated, box 19, folder 1, Northern Student Movement Collection, Schomburg Center for Research in Black Culture, New York City; press release and flyer, June 15, 1966, reel 13, Papers of the Congress of Racial Equality—Addendum; *Memphis Press-Scimitar,* June 16, 1966; *Memphis World,* June 18, 1966.

44. *Baltimore Afro-American,* June 18, 1966; Joel Bernard to Jacqueline Bernard, June 13, 1966, box 1, folder 1, Jacqueline Barnard Papers, Wisconsin Historical Society.

45. David Acey, interview with the author, March 23, 2011; press release and radio station advertisement, June 15, 1966, reel 13, Papers of the Congress of Racial Equality—Addendum; Middlebrook interview.

46. Lawson oral history, box 46, folder Oral History Transcript—James M. Lawson—August 21, 1969, Special Collections, Vanderbilt University. See also Honey, *Going down Jericho Road,* 81–82; David M. Tucker, *Black Pastors and Leaders: Memphis, 1819–1972* (Memphis, TN: Memphis State University Press, 1975), 113–28; David Halberstam, *The Children* (New York: Random House, 1996), 471–76.

47. Martin Luther King speech, June 7, 1966, series 3, box 11, King Papers; Lawson, "Meredith March . . . and Tomorrow," 5. On Lawson's status in Memphis at the time of the march, see also *Tri-State Defender,* June 18, 1966.

48. Michael Cody, interview with the author, Memphis, January 14, 2016; Coby Smith, unpublished memoir in the author's possession.

49. Coby Smith, interview with the author, February 9, 2010.

50. Ibid.; Smith, unpublished memoir; Shirletta J. Kinchen, *Black Power in the Bluff City: African American Youth and Student Activism in Memphis, 1965–1975* (Knoxville: University of Tennessee Press, 2015), 39–69.

51. *Washington Daily News,* June 10, 1966; *Detroit Free Press,* June 11, 1966.

52. Crittenden interview; *Jackson Clarion Ledger,* June 25, 1966; "Holy Child Jesus Mission and 'The March,'" series 20, box 2, folder 10, National Catholic Center for Interracial Justice Records, Marquette University, Milwaukee; *Washington Star,* June 25, 1966.

53. Elaine Lee Turner, interview with the author, Memphis, January 21, 2016.

54. David Acey, interview with the author, Memphis, March 23, 2011.

55. Lawson oral history, box 46, folder Oral History Transcript—James M. Lawson, August 21, 1969, Special Collections, Vanderbilt University; Lawson, "Meredith March . . . and Tomorrow," 5.

Nonviolence, Black Power, and the Surveillance State in Memphis's War on Poverty

Anthony C. Siracusa

Around 8:30 p.m. on the night of Thursday, August 10, 1967, the doors to Centenary Methodist Church on East McLemore Avenue in South Memphis burst open. "We came to tell these people what we want," a young man exclaimed to the closed meeting of the Memphis Area Project–South (MAP-South) advisory committee. "We want to show our support," he said, demanding that the two antipoverty workers recently fired by Memphis's War on Poverty Committee be immediately reinstated.[1] "We had several of the other brothers call up and rumor that there was going to be some trouble if something wasn't done about this illegal dismissal," Black Power advocate Calvin Taylor later remembered.[2] Urging the young man to leave the church and "calling for quiet," the senior pastor at Centenary—the Reverend James M. Lawson Jr.—addressed the firing of Coby Smith and Charles Cabbage by asking the group gathered outside a question: "Who hired Coby?" he asked rhetorically. "I did," he answered, "and I hired Cabbage. As long as I'm in there, you know the battle's being fought."

Known internationally as an expert on nonviolence, Lawson had called the closed-door meeting to give the two fired Black Power advocates a fair hearing. He implored the MAP-South leadership to overturn the two men's dismissal—which it did—but for the youths gathered at Centenary on that summer night, poverty was only part of the problem. Squad cars roved back and forth in front of the historic black church, surveilling the scene. "Black people are seeking an end to the police state they have to endure," Coby Smith had told the *Memphis Press-Scimitar* earlier in the day. "They resent handouts given them, and that is one reason for the destruction they may cause."[3]

For Smith, as for many black activists in the late 1960s, the police state and the state of poverty in America were entangled issues. Black alliances were also deeply entangled in the late 1960s: Lawson, the well-known apostle of nonviolence, seemed an unlikely ally for the local Black Power duo of Smith and Cabbage. But Lawson's defense of the two men grew from his commitment to working alongside them in a citizen-led effort to battle poverty in South Memphis—an alliance forged despite their fundamental disagreement about the role of nonviolence in the black freedom movement. In the variegated milieu of black politics in late 1960s Memphis, antipoverty efforts functioned to create both alliances and conflicts between the nonviolent wing of the movement associated with Lawson and his Black Power allies in the Black Organizing Project.

While these two camps maintained critical differences, primary sources from antipoverty organizations in Memphis and newly surfaced FBI documents reveal that the explosive events of late March and early April 1968 cannot be explained merely by differences among black activists.[4] The fracture within Memphis's black freedom movement—a rupture that nearly thirty years of scholarship has attributed chiefly to deepening fissures between advocates of Black Power and those espousing nonviolence during the Memphis sanitation strike of 1968—is better explained by two factors: political resistance at both the local and national levels to black-led antipoverty efforts, and a robust and likely illegal effort by the FBI to infiltrate and undermine both the Black Power and nonviolent wings of the black freedom movement.[5] Just as activists considered the antipoverty and black freedom movements "inextricably tied together," the political efforts to halt both movements in Memphis were also inextricably bound.[6]

Poverty in America, Poverty in Memphis

In his first State of the Union address on January 8, 1964, President Lyndon Baines Johnson called for a War on Poverty to improve the lives of the 40 million Americans living in households with incomes of less than $3,000 per year.[7] In August 1964, one month after passage of the Civil Rights Act of 1964, the president signed into law the Economic Opportunity Act (EOA). The EOA dedicated the federal government to funding a fight against the poverty afflicting more than 22 percent of the US population. The legislation established the Office of Economic Opportunity (OEO) to carry out "job training, youth employment, adult education, rural economic development, services for migrant farm workers, [and] Legal Services," among many other programs, and Congress appropriated $947 million to implement this robust set of new initiatives.[8] Sargent Shriver was hired to "jumpstart the new agency," and the president's innovative plan channeled federal funding directly to local communities for implementation of these government-funded programs.[9]

Title II of the EOA enabled the creation of Community Action Agencies (CAAs) to oversee and govern Community Action Programs (CAPs) in neighborhoods across the United States.[10] Historian Gail Murray has suggested that these independent neighborhood agencies were intended to provide federal funds directly to neighborhood people and thus avoid obstruction by local or state government agencies, effectively enabling local people to carry out antipoverty projects designed and governed by poor citizens themselves. But the legal language establishing this framework for CAAs and CAPs was a source of deep controversy from the outset. Seeking to achieve "maximum feasible participation of residents of the areas and groups served," the law effectively entitled millions of people—in urban areas, largely black and brown people—to federal subsidies for self-governing neighborhood uplift programs.[11] Johnson's adviser Daniel Patrick Moynihan argued that the intent of this language was not that the poor would actually serve on Community Action Committees; instead, policymakers would "act on their behalf." But in Memphis, this language became a source of major conflict between civil rights activists and the municipality as soon as War on Poverty funding began to flow into the Bluff City.[12]

As historian Laurie Green has argued, the sanitation strike of 1968 was only "the most visible marker of the deep poverty and poor health care that existed in majority black [Memphis] neighborhoods."[13] In 1965, the year that federal funds for the War on Poverty first arrived in Memphis, the city's median income was $4,903—more than $1,500 below the national median of $6,439.[14] Twenty-eight percent of all Memphians lived below the poverty line of $3,000, making Memphis the largest "pocket" of concentrated poverty in the state of Tennessee. Of the city's nonwhite population, 58 percent lived in poverty in 1965. Malnutrition of infants racked these communities: in 1965 the mortality rate for black babies in Memphis was 61 per 1,000; for white babies, the mortality rate was 24 per 1,000.[15] The OEO concluded that poverty in Memphis was among the worst in the nation.[16]

Black Memphians saw Johnson's War on Poverty as an opportunity to directly address these problems. In January 1965 the Memphis Urban League hosted a two-day workshop to outline a plan for attacking poverty in the city. The Reverend James M. Lawson Jr. was assigned the task of compiling suggestions from attendees about how to organize local leaders in the War on Poverty. Suggestions included the following:

1. That all efforts be made to spread the news of antipoverty projects and programs among the really poor.
2. That Negroes be a part of committees and personnel responsible for planning and operating antipoverty projects.
3. That people residing in poverty pockets be included on advisory committees working with sponsors on the War on Poverty.[17]

Memphis Mayor William Ingram praised the Urban League's workshop and promised "to integrate committees and administrative personnel . . . to carry out government sponsored projects and programs designed to aid the poor in this area." Ingram pledged that "representation in the war on poverty would come from pockets of poverty," and he called the program "one of the best improvement projects ever attempted."[18]

But the Memphis branch of the NAACP criticized Ingram's antipoverty plan. At a workshop hosted by LeMoyne College in February 1965, the NAACP publicly registered the first of many complaints about the lack of black Memphians on Memphis's War on Poverty Committee (WOPC).[19] According to Baxton Bryant, executive director of the Tennessee Council on Human Relations, the committee had "two 'glaring' deficiencies": no representation from the "militant Negro community," and no actual representation from the poor. Bryant called it "inconceivable" that the committee did not even include any moderate African American leaders such as Russell B. Sugarmon Jr., Maxine and Vasco Smith, or Jesse Turner.[20]

The federal OEO also became "critical of the setup" in Memphis.[21] Mayor Ingram had appointed sixty-six people to the WOPC, naming himself as chair, and he had appointed local school board member Francis Coe to serve as the primary liaison between the OEO and Memphis's WOPC.[22] But after a month of no movement, Coe resigned and "lambasted the setup," charging the mayor with exercising "too much control" over the committee. Debates swirled over the intent and effect of the legislative language calling for "maximum feasible participation from the poor," with Coe maintaining that the OEO had "sent down a directive with instructions for the city to follow" to ensure adequate representation of the poor. Ingram, she said, had simply failed to follow through.[23]

An OEO representative from Atlanta arrived in August to investigate the complaints and found that Coe's charges were "legitimate." The OEO threatened to cut the city's initial $110,000 War on Poverty grant unless the mayor relinquished "direct control" over the committee. James M. Lawson Jr. and local attorney A. W. Willis Jr., both initial appointees to the Memphis WOPC, were removed from the committee in the fall of 1965 at Ingram's behest. "You were one of the first mayors in the country to recognize the possibilities of the anti-poverty program," Lawson wrote in an open letter to Ingram published by the *Memphis World*, "but instead of encouraging a committee to work and operate with an imaginative program, you have kept the city embroiled in controversy." Lawson concluded that the mayor's actions would "make the Memphis War on Poverty no more than a rear-guard skirmish after the battle has been lost."[24] After three months of negotiations between the local NAACP and the municipality led by Memphis Eighth District congressman George Grider, a compromise was reached whereby neighborhood councils would be established in low-income sectors across the city. Each neighborhood council would elect a representative to serve on the citywide WOPC, and this citywide committee would then elect its own chair.[25]

In March 1966 MAP-South—one of these citizen-led neighborhood councils that was chaired by Lawson—applied for $234,000 in federal aid. MAP-South had previously applied to become a "delegate agency" to receive funding directly from the OEO in late 1964, but the skirmishes between black activists and the city had stalled the funding. Nevertheless, the citizen group pressed ahead and made plans to tackle the serious poverty facing the residents of South Memphis. The *Memphis Press-Scimitar* reported in the summer of 1965 that the population in the MAP-South area was 38,721, of which 37,159 were black. The median family income in the area was $2,344, with 67 percent of families in the MAP-South area having household incomes of less than $3,000.[26] Characterizing MAP-South's program as "community re-development by community residents," the *Press-Scimitar* described the strategy of hiring "practical social workers . . . [who] would be paid up to $18.75 weekly to work with their neighbors in the war on poverty . . . these workers would be trained to do case work designed 'to involve people in the area in taking more leadership in solving their own problems.'"[27]

The ongoing "political controversy" over the city's slow pace of implementation meant that funding for MAP-South's program did not flow until January 1967.[28] Lawson's role as chair of MAP-South was critical. It signaled, in the words of historian Shirletta Kinchen, "a connection between the issues of civil rights and economic justice" in Memphis. But this fusion of economic justice and civil rights also meant that local politicians viewed antipoverty work as being linked directly to civil rights.[29] Known internationally as a militant black activist, Lawson had spent eighteen months in prison in 1951 and 1952 for refusing to fight in the Korean War. Living as a nonviolent black activist in a Cold War–Jim Crow society, Lawson called the laws of conscription and the laws of segregation "a complete denial of the meaning of freedom . . . the free man must maintain his right to determine those laws that are absolutely contrary to the meaning of freedom and justice."[30] This perspective made Lawson "a visionary of the civil rights movement," but it also contributed to the "notoriety" of his antipoverty efforts in Memphis.[31]

Nevertheless, the OEO chartered MAP-South in January 1967, and federal funding for neighborhood-based antipoverty organizing began to flow to South Memphis under Lawson's leadership. Black army veteran Washington Butler was hired as executive director of the citywide WOPC in the spring of 1967, and he soon became an outspoken advocate for neighborhood efforts that allowed the poor "to help themselves."[32] Autry Parker was hired as the first executive director of MAP-South in early 1967, and the South Memphis antipoverty effort was off to a strong start. MAP-South's first annual report in 1967 showed a contact list of more than 5,000 residents, 73 block clubs, and an attendance of 1,621 at 685 meetings.[33] But just as this robust antipoverty work was taking off in South Memphis, so too were the agency's political problems.

Black Power and Nonviolence in Memphis

In July 1967, as police clashed with black communities in cities across the nation, President Johnson appointed a group of eleven Americans to the National Advisory Commission on Urban Disorder. The commission, which produced the now famous Kerner Report, stated: "Our nation is moving toward two societies, one black, one white—separate and unequal." Although police in Memphis did not clash with black communities on the same scale as the conflicts in Watts, Newark, and Cleveland, in the nearby middle Tennessee city of Nashville, black youths battled with police in the neighborhood surrounding historic Fisk University. The fight followed a series of speeches delivered by Stokely Carmichael at three local colleges in April 1967. "You ought to organize and take over this city," Carmichael told the crowd at Tennessee State, "but you won't because you don't want power." The night of Carmichael's final speech at Vanderbilt University in Nashville, a Jefferson Street restaurant owner called the police and asked them to remove a young patron from his establishment. The young man's forceful removal touched off a battle that lasted through the night, with black youths fortifying themselves at Fisk University as they fought with police.[34]

In Memphis, amidst these simmering tensions, Lawson had just hired two Black Power advocates to work as neighborhood organizers for MAP-South. Charles Cabbage, foremost among this emerging group of young black leaders, had attended Carver High School in Memphis before matriculating at Morehouse College in Atlanta. After graduating in 1967, Cabbage returned to Memphis that summer. He met with Lawson and Willis to outline his plan to establish the Black Organizing Project (BOP), an umbrella group for a number of smaller, loosely affiliated groups—the most notable being the Invaders. Self- described as the "military end" of the BOP, the Invaders got their name from a late 1960s TV program. Kinchen argues that the Invaders offered "an alternative model of manhood" to the traditional black male leadership of A. W. Willis Jr., Benjamin J. Hooks, Vasco A. Smith, and Russell B. Sugarmon. Focusing on "high school students and college underclassmen," the Invaders "understood that the threat of violence, or just the threat of revolution, could be a weapon itself."[35]

During his meeting with Cabbage in the summer of 1967, Lawson asked questions about the organizing philosophy of the BOP, and he remembered Cabbage replying: "We intend to organize young people and we intend to fight the system. And we will use Molotov cocktails, we will steal and cheat and lie, we'll do anything we need to do in order to change the way things are." Lawson, a seasoned leader in the student movement of the early 1960s, recalled that this was his first encounter with "young adults who . . . were concerned for change and spoke in those terms."[36] Lawson's relationship with BOP cofounder Coby Smith had soured earlier, after Smith had refused to abide by Lawson's nonviolent organizing ethic. But despite these obvious differences, Lawson hired both Cabbage and Smith to work for MAP-South as federally funded block organizers.[37]

When MAP-South held its initial "general meeting" in April 1967, the *Tri-State Defender* called it the first time "in the city's history in which the victims of poverty will be asked to describe their situation and encouraged to give suggestions on how to relieve them. All segments of the area's residents," the article continued, from "businessmen, ministers, professional people, factory workers, domestic servants, laborers, and the unemployed are urged to be present."[38] But by 1967, this federally subsided organizing in black communities had made some Americans "livid."[39] Mississippi senators James Eastland and John Stennis organized a congressional investigation into the use of War on Poverty funding for civil rights and antipoverty work, a clear sign that the federal tide was turning against the Economic Opportunity Act of 1964. Locally, Republican Dan Kuykendall's 1966 triumph over sitting Eighth District Democratic congressman and Johnson ally George Grider signaled the end of the political coalition shepherding the EOA and landmark civil rights legislation through Congress. The newly minted congressman Kuykendall joined a Republican assault on the EOA, describing the War on Poverty as the "federal financing of agitators."[40]

In this increasingly hostile political climate, and with the events at Fisk University fresh in the minds of Memphians, the *Memphis Commercial Appeal* reported that Charles Cabbage and Coby Smith were "associated with organizations advocating violence." Local WOPC executive director Washington Butler immediately "ordered" that Cabbage and Smith be "removed from the Memphis Area Project South payroll . . . on grounds of being identified with organizations whose purposes 'don't coincide' with the War on Poverty."[41] It was amidst these accusations that Lawson rose to the defense of Cabbage and Smith. He argued that the two young men were essential to the fight against poverty in Memphis, and he told his colleagues in MAP-South that Cabbage and Smith had reached a population that button-down ministers and middle-class lawyers could not. But perhaps most important, Lawson concurred with them on a critical point made by Cabbage: "Black people need to control their own communities."[42] This idea of community control was, in fact, precisely the reason why the seasoned civil rights veteran had hired the two young organizers. Despite being motivated by different philosophies, Lawson, Smith, and Cabbage agreed on MAP-South's basic goal: black actualization and community uplift through institutional development, strategies central to twentieth-century black organizing in the United States.

At the hearing organized by Lawson for Cabbage and Smith at Centenary Church on August 10, 1967, WOPC director Butler and MAP-South director Parker defended the firing of the two young men on the grounds that they were associated with the Student Nonviolent Coordinating Committee (SNCC)—the group held responsible for the recent uprising in Nashville. But at Lawson's behest, local attorney Lucius Burch cross-examined Smith and Cabbage in front of the MAP-South advisory committee to demonstrate their importance to antipoverty work in South Memphis.[43] Calvin Taylor remembered that Smith was interviewed first, and Burch emphasized Smith's character by underlining the fact that he had been the first African American to enroll at Southwestern at Memphis (now Rhodes College). But according to Taylor, when Burch put Cabbage on the stand, Cabbage nearly "blew it." Cabbage and Smith had been accused of organizing rent strikes among South Memphis residents—an accusation that was, in fact, true. And as Taylor recalled, the two young men "were going about telling people they could organize such things as rent strikes . . . [and] this is where we . . . really got hung. We came out character-wise good and reference-wise great, but we got hung because Cabbage admitted that he was organizing people for rent strikes and he admitted it on the basis that these people needed this material and help in order to get their living conditions upgraded. Cab [said people] cannot live in a house with no plumbing, no running hot and cold water . . . and rats everywhere. And Cab admitted that he was organizing the rent strikes."[44]

Despite their call for rent strikes, Lawson argued, Cabbage and Smith were indispensable to MAP-South. He observed that "one of the failures of MAP-South" before Cabbage and Smith were hired was that "the grassroots effort, the door-to-door effort," was not effective. Cabbage and Smith, however, served the critical role of going door-to-door at night to enlist a more elusive but essential MAP-South demographic: men who spent time in pool halls and dive bars.

But their high profile as advocates of Black Power made retaining Cabbage and Smith difficult, especially as the local police cracked down on the Invaders. Police arrested Cabbage and fellow Invader John B. Smith in the summer of 1967 after an incident in which a white gas station attendant refused to return their gas cap. Although it later became clear that they had not broken any laws, a local judge claimed the two men "were trying to start a riot, that they were trouble-makers, and possible SNCC people." Lawson recalled that this story was reported "all across the paper the next day." But even after their arrest, the two young men refused to be subservient or show deference to the Memphis police. They were "not polite to the police," Lawson remembered. "They looked the police in the eyes. They told the police, 'You are wrong.'" When Coby Smith arrived at the station to bail Cabbage out of jail, "he looked the police in the eyes and talked straight to them. So he was marked as well."[45]

Despite these difficulties, Lawson was authorized to rehire the two young men as MAP-South employees in the fall of 1967 at a wage of $30 per week. They were also awarded back pay.[46] Though the relationship between Lawson and his Invader allies was strained, it was collaboration nonetheless. "Without Jim Lawson," Cabbage later said, "there is a very real possibility that we would not have been able to pull off the Black

Organizing Project. We would not have been able to live . . . we would have had to take jobs, but we had jobs working for MAP-South."[47]

The shared work of Lawson, Smith, and Cabbage challenges the idea that there was a clear divide between "traditional civil rights leadership" and "black power advocates"; it suggests instead that conflicts among black activists in the Memphis movement were not irreconcilable.[48] Debates about armed self-defense, revolutionary violence, and nonviolence were central in the black freedom struggle of the twentieth century. And as recent literature on the "black tradition of arms" suggests, most black Americans were not ideologically bound to one strategy or another; rather, they opted for any strategy that produced tangible results.[49] In Memphis, however, an overemphasis on differences within the black community—in particular, an emphasis on divisions between advocates of Black Power and advocates of nonviolence during the 1968 sanitation strike—has been sustained in nearly three decades of scholarship. This long-standing narrative, the idea that fractures within the Memphis movement led directly to the cataclysmic events of 1968, has ascended to the level of historical fact and shifted focus away from state-led efforts to quash black organizing in the late 1960s.[50]

Lawson and members of the Invaders clearly shared a commitment to neighborhood-based antipoverty organizing. And when the Memphis sanitation strike began in March 1968, advocates of both Black Power and nonviolence were allied in an effort to end what Lawson has called "plantation capitalism"—the concerted maintenance of a sizable black underclass by a white political class in control of a nearly all-white police force. The efforts of Lawson and the Invaders to challenge this plantation capitalism through the sanitation strike of 1968 were ultimately thwarted by a sophisticated state surveillance apparatus, a government-led spying effort that enabled both local and federal authorities to identify key differences within the black organizing class in Memphis and effectively exploit those cleavages to disrupt antipoverty efforts to dramatic effect.

Nonviolence and Black Power on "Tough Thursday"

The War on Poverty in Memphis had no bigger theater than the sanitation strike of 1968. Despite the raft of scholarship on the strike, questions remain about the relationship among King, his Memphis lieutenant James M. Lawson Jr., and members of the Invaders. Specifically, historical reckonings of March 28, 1968—known as "Tough Thursday"—have produced more questions than answers. While scholars have certainly moved beyond the earliest accounts of the march put forth by David Tucker and Joan Turner Beifuss, here I hope to clarify some of the questions that persist about Tough Thursday. In particular, my goal is to better explain the complex interplay of Black Power and nonviolence during the Memphis sanitation strike as it occurred amidst the War on Poverty.[51]

Lawson—chair of the Community on the Move for Equality (COME) strategy team—was the primary architect of the march on Tough Thursday. Despite their many differences, Lawson clearly had a working relationship with several members of the Invaders by the time the march took place—in fact, Lawson's acceptance of the strategy team chairmanship was contingent on Charles Cabbage's appointment to COME. The differences between Lawson and Cabbage over revolutionary violence and nonviolence were publicly aired during the strike, and this certainly contributed to the escalating tension in Memphis in the weeks before the march. But these disagreements over strategy did not cause the collapse of the Tough Thursday march. The demonstration's ultimate undoing resulted in part from the work of a young FBI informant named James Elmore Phillips.[52] A student at LeMoyne College in 1968, Phillips was at the center of Memphis's black youth movement in the late 1960s. FBI reports also indicate that he was a key facilitator in the window-breaking incidents that brought the long-percolating tensions between white police and civil rights activists in Memphis to a boil.[53]

Cabbage and the Invaders saw the sanitation strike as an opportunity to recruit members and acquire resources. But Lawson and his ministerial allies Malcolm Blackburn, Ezekiel Bell, and Harold Middlebrook also saw the strike as an opportunity to mobilize the youths being recruited by the Invaders. Each camp saw cooperation and self-interest as inseparable, but like their alliance in the War on Poverty, this shared work was beset with disagreement from the start. At the first COME strategy meeting on March 1, 1968, Lawson interrupted Cabbage's comments to place their long-standing disagreement over nonviolence at the center of strike strategizing. "We have to operate in a nonviolent manner," Lawson told Cab-

James Lawson during the 1968 sanitation strike. (Courtesy Special Collections Department, University of Memphis)

bage, at which point an FBI informant reported that "Charles Cabbage interjected and accused Lawson of 'selling out to the union.'"[54]

Nevertheless, Cabbage played an important, formal role in organizing youth for COME, a strategy that led FBI agents to conclude that the Invaders were "gaining numerous young supporters."[55] But enlisting these "young supporters" in the strike's larger nonviolent strategy proved more difficult. While Cabbage and John B. Smith inspired hundreds of young Memphians with their speeches throughout March 1968, it was clear that these students were not organized in a way that resembled the disciplined nature of Lawson's famous 1960 Nashville sit-down campaign. And yet, under the auspices of the Lawson-led COME, Cabbage and Smith enlisted dozens of high school and college students to join in the daily pickets organized by COME. But Cabbage and Smith were working with many more students who were not participating in these disciplined, nonviolent demonstrations.

Lawson remained steadfast in supporting Cabbage's youth organizing efforts, but their relationship grew increasingly strained as the strike wore on. In a public interview on March 8, Lawson told local media outlets that his group would be "bringing in the 'black power' boys" for a "united front," stating that Stokely Carmichael had done much to "unify Negroes all over the eastern seaboard; and if it was necessary to insure a unified Negro effort in Memphis he, Lawson, would bring Carmichael to Memphis."[56] But Cabbage, having further cemented his reputation as a youth leader in the fight against poverty, "bitterly resented" media characterizations of Lawson as in "control" of the black community.[57] "Cabbage now appears to be extremely jealous of James Morris Lawson," an FBI report stated in mid-March, noting that it was Lawson "who ironically . . . put Cabbage . . . on the payroll of the Memphis poverty agency, known as the Memphis Area Project–South."[58]

This oft-cited divide between advocates of Black Power and advocates of nonviolence in the Memphis sanitation strike cannot be dismissed, but Lawson's continued willingness to support Cabbage's youth organizing suggests that the movement was not neatly bifurcated. This overlap between the nonviolent and armed wings in the Memphis movement was a feature common to local movements across the country. Cabbage and Smith had made a "concerted effort . . . to have all junior high and high school negro students in Memphis to stay away from school to support the sympathy march" led by Martin Luther King on March 22.[59] The city's black high schools had been, according to the FBI, "saturated with leaflets urging all students to remain away from school," and there was speculation that 20,000 students had been invited to participate in the planned march.[60] Black high school and college students—the very group Cabbage and the Invaders had been cultivating at the behest of Lawson and others—constituted a sizable portion of the marchers recruited by COME.

The centrality of the Invaders and Cabbage to COME's youth strategy also refutes Calvin Taylor's strange claim that Lawson told King there was no "black power element" in Memphis.[61] To wit: King's Southern

Christian Leadership Conference (SCLC) lieutenant James Bevel gave an address at LeMoyne College on March 20 that an FBI informant described as a "most virulent black Power Talk."[62] But even the Invaders were surrounded by another smaller group of youths led by John Henry Ferguson and Willie James Jenkins that the FBI described as "all militant." FBI reports indicated that this group was "very definitely not a part of the Cabbage-Smith BOP Group," and they expressed concern that "from this group will come those who will engage in sporadic acts of vandalism throughout Memphis."[63] Cabbage and the Invaders, at the behest of COME, had clearly been encouraging black Memphis youths to participate in the strike. The young people were now responding.

James E. Phillips and "Tough Thursday"

The War on Poverty in Memphis and the events leading up to the mass march on Tough Thursday are critical to understanding the march itself. Charles Cabbage, Coby Smith, John B. Smith, and other Invaders had stirred students to action in the month leading up to the planned march, but it is incorrect to attribute the day's unraveling to these men alone. The march's failure, in truth, flowed from a variety of factors. Moving the event from March 22 to March 28 likely contributed to the unusually large size of the crowd (5,000). King's late arrival created too much idle time for the massive group, and once the looting began, a group of Beale Street regulars clearly contributed to the problem. James Lawson—the man King called the "leading theoretician of nonviolence"—also failed on many fronts in preparing for the march, making mistakes that were uncharacteristic for the seasoned organizer. The march did not have enough marshals for its size, and issuing four-foot-long wooden sticks connected to "I Am a Man" placards was a tactical misstep—particularly because hundreds of fairly disorganized youths had been invited to attend the march.

Moreover, FBI documents suggest that counterintelligence program (COINTELPRO) informant James Elmore Phillips was a key instigator in the events that led to the collapse of the march. Estimating that half of the 5,000 marchers were "teenagers of school age," FBI informant Ernest Withers—also one of America's most famed civil rights photographers—reported that "common criminals" and "people who have been in and out of penal institutions" were interspersed throughout the march.[64] Withers told FBI agents that "John Smith and some of his associates were in his opinion inciting violence and that they were indiscriminately giving out the 4 foot poles to various teenage youngsters in the area." According to Withers, Smith told "these youngsters, identities not known, not to be afraid to use the sticks, he did not elaborate as to what he meant."[65] A different FBI source reported that James Phillips and Samuel Carter spoke between 8:30 and 9:30 a.m. at Clayborn Temple, which was march headquarters. The two young men stated: "They were going to 'tear this SOB town up today.' Phillips made some general statements about some high school students being 'chicken' and staying in school rather than marching and he stated that the white people who were participating in the march were fools for marching because if any trouble started that the Negro Marchers would turn on them first."[66]

An FBI report after the march stated the following: "Source two stated that the march started at approximately 11 o'clock a.m., and that [James] Phillips and [Samuel] Carter [of LeMoyne College] and some unknown associates remained behind. As the March progressed north of Linden on Hernando, Phillips and another associate from LeMoyne College, understood to be in the BOP group, Clinton Ray Jameson, went back into an alley and obtained some sticks and bricks."[67]

Michael K. Honey writes that Phillips was among the "new recruits" to the Invaders, those who joined the group upon King's announcement of a planned march in Memphis. Although it unclear whether Phillips was a COINTELPRO informant at the time of the march, by the end of April 1968, he was providing information directly to COINTELPRO agents in Memphis. It is obvious that Phillips was intent on creating chaos and violence at the march, suggesting that he and other new Invaders were motivated by King's presence to foment a serious disruption—which is precisely what happened on March 28, 1968.[68]

In 1979 the Senate Select Committee on Assassinations looked squarely at the question of whether the FBI had paid "members of the Invaders . . . or act[ed] through its informants in the Invaders, to incite the violence on March 28 that led Dr. King to return to Memphis." The committee concluded that "nothing in the . . . investigation, file review or interview of [an Invaders] informant indicated that FBI informants were used as agent provocateurs during the March 28 violence."[69] However, this conclusion was predicated on an important caveat. The committee cited "two serious discrepancies" in interviews with an Invaders informant, one of five informants the committee found to be working within the Invaders, and these discrepancies "tarnished the evidence given by both the Bureau and the informant." The committee was left with "a measure of uncertainty about the scope of FBI involvement with the Invaders."[70]

Other documents that were thought to be destroyed after the King assassination but were actually retained by a former Memphis police officer also suggest that COINTELPRO agents S. A. Howell Lowe and William Lawrence, both stationed in Memphis, operated independently of other FBI agents in gathering information about the King assassination throughout 1968. The intelligence they gathered was provided by a small group of informants who were interviewed outside the scope of the larger FBI investigation, and James Phillips—the self-declared Invader who called for violence immediately before the march and gathered sticks and bricks only moments before windows were broken—was among this group. It is possible that FBI agents were attracted to Phillips only after observing his role in the events of March 28, but by the end of April 1968, Phillips was one of at least five movement activists providing information directly to COINTELPRO agents in Memphis.

The role of Calvin Taylor also remains suspect. In an interview with the Memphis Search for Meaning Committee in 1968, Taylor claimed he read about the events of March 28 in the local paper.[71] "BOP member Calvin Taylor took no responsibility for the disruption," Kinchen writes, "but confessed that his organization created the tension that day."[72] Yet, in a 1988 interview for "Eyes on the Prize," Taylor directly contradicted that story. "I remember they asked me at the Senate investigation hearing," Taylor recalled, "'Did you throw a rock?' And I said, 'In all honesty, yes, I did throw a rock.' So that's what I did. I picked up a rock, a brick or bottle or two or three or four. I don't know how many. . . . You know, I, I do remember tossing a brick or two and I do remember, uh, standing on a car urging people to, you know, to, to maintain their ground."[73] Taylor's conflicting testimony about this critical moment raises major questions about the "serious discrepancies" cited by the Senate Select Committee. Even more perplexing is Taylor's claim that Lawson told King there was no Black Power movement in Memphis. In truth, and as noted earlier, Lawson and other leaders in the COME ministerial alliance—Harold Middlebrook, Ezekiel Bell, and Malcolm Blackburn—all supported Black Power advocates in mobilizing high school and college students. Lawson also worked with King's SCLC staff to bring in James Bevel. Thus, Taylor's role in the Invaders may warrant further research, but it is clear that Phillips was at the center of the disruption in 1968 and was providing information to COINTELPRO agents by April.

Black Power, Black Poverty, and the Surveillance State

In the summer of 1968, just a few months after King's death and the resolution of the sanitation strike, members of the Invaders received War on Poverty funding to carry out twenty-seven programs for youth under the auspices of the Neighborhood Organizing Project (NOP). "A year removed from the controversial dismissal of Cabbage and Smith as MAP-South employees," Kinchen writes, "the War on Poverty Committee decided to take another chance on Black Power."[74] Like MAP-South, the NOP sought to be a "community-development program" centered on "unification, uplift, and providing opportunities for the most unstable and unemployable elements of Memphis society."[75] And despite their clashes during the sanitation strike, the city's Black Power vanguard aligned with Lawson and MAP-South once again in pursuing a politics of black self-organization and community uplift.

But this unified strategy of black uplift was precisely the problem— at least for white officials. On August 23, 1968, the *Memphis Press-Scimitar* erroneously reported that the WOPC was paying rent for the Invaders' office space. Just a week after the article appeared, local FBI agents reported that "the Memphis Office plans to increase the amount of derogatory information obtained through investigations concerning black power militants at Memphis, Tennessee, presently being given to a reliable and trusted newspaper source at Memphis, Tennessee. The purpose of this is to assist this newspaper source in writing articles embarrassing to local black militants."[76]

The FBI's purpose was "to counteract and discredit black power activities at Memphis" and "embarrass the BOP without possible compromise of the bureau's interest or sources of information."[77] A note written by FBI director J. Edgar Hoover stated that "authority is granted to furnish public source information and leave material, which will not jeopardize your sources, concerning the black organizing project (BOP)."[78] Even though the claim that federal money was being used to pay the Invaders' rent was false, it sparked Shelby County commissioner Stanley Dillard to call for "a complete investigation of WOPC and its programs."[79] While the formal investigation into the Memphis WOPC by OEO regional officers in Atlanta found that it was "poorly administered," many WOPC efforts in Memphis met the critical federal criterion of job creation.[80] But because both federal and local officials remained intent on undermining the black organizing enabled by War on Poverty programs, the FBI's clandestine campaign to publicly discredit Black Power organizing cannot be seen as simply coincident with Memphis's War on Poverty programs. The FBI's effort to undermine Black Power was a central strategy for disrupting the widespread black organizing against poverty in America.

By the end of 1969, the War on Poverty had become a casualty of President Richard Nixon's New Federalism—a policy pledge to shift all War on Poverty programs from local to state control.[81] And indeed, in March 1970 recently appointed OEO director Donald Rumsfeld announced that the "Oklahoma Plan" would transfer all antipoverty programs to state administration.[82] By late 1970, the antipoverty efforts resisted by the Ingram administration in 1965 had finally succumbed to a president intent on "shutter[ing] the command center of the War on Poverty."[83] The *Memphis Press-Scimitar* reported in October 1970 that WOPC executive director Washington Butler, "clad in a blue and white dashiki," had called the recent restructuring of War on Poverty programs "extra-legal," characterizing those efforts as an attempt to "impugn the intelligence, integrity, honesty and professional character" of everyone involved with Memphis's War on Poverty program—including "the poor people" of Memphis themselves. Prominent NAACP official Jesse Turner Sr. provided a direct loan of $50,000 to keep local antipoverty efforts moving, but the federal blow was too much to withstand.[84] Federal funding for the "central administrative staff, Memphis Area Project South, family planning, the Youth Opportunity Program, and the three neighborhood centers and the emergency food program" was terminated on October 31, 1970.[85]

As Gail Murray has written, because "civil rights goals and community organizing of the poor overlapped" so clearly in Memphis—especially during the sanitation strike of 1968—the abrupt conclusion of the city's War on Poverty cannot be disentangled from broader political efforts to undermine the black freedom movement.[86] The clear collapse of this important phase of black organizing was not simply the result of differences over strategy and ideology within the black community—differences that were magnified during the sanitation strike of 1968. In Memphis, the unraveling of black organizing in the late 1960s flowed largely from white politicians' uneasiness with the decentralized structures of antipoverty efforts such as MAP-South and the NOP, structures that placed power and money directly in the hands of black people. This federally mandated and decentralized arrangement ran completely contrary to the traditional structure of political power in Memphis, an arrangement that had, for decades, afforded a powerful white mayor complete control over white commissioners who served at his pleasure—a legacy of E. H. Crump's long informal reign in Memphis.[87] By placing money and political power in the hands of black Memphians, CAAs and CAPs bucked this centralized system of strong white control and led Memphis officials first to hesitancy and ultimately to hostility toward federally subsidized, citizen-led organizing in black Memphis neighborhoods.

But most important, the central state played a major role in disrupting this new wave of black organizing in Memphis. Administratively, the OEO became a target for "law and order" candidate Richard Nixon, who saw a mandate to end the federal subsidization of projects led by "lawless" Black Power advocates.[88] But the FBI's long-standing effort to undermine the credibility of Martin Luther King intersected powerfully with a deepening FBI commitment to undermine Black Power groups in the late 1960s. This unprecedented level of FBI surveillance and infiltration was, without question, a contributing factor to the volatile crucible that was Memphis's civic environment in March and April 1968. The continuous surveillance of both King and the Invaders during the sanitation strike provided valuable intelligence to FBI officials overseeing the extensive nationwide campaign to infiltrate and undermine the black freedom movement. Ernest Withers's recently released FBI file has only begun to illuminate the "shadowy interstices" of FBI infiltration "and those who inhabit them."[89] But these new materials have already challenged long-standing narratives suggesting that the unraveling of movement activity in late 1960s Memphis resulted from internal fissures in the black community. These new sources show us that the Memphis movement faced a sophisticated and centralized surveillance state that was well organized, powerful, and ultimately insurmountable.

Notes

1. Charles Brown, "Anti Poverty Group Demands Hearing for Two Controversial Workers," *Memphis Press-Scimitar*, August 11, 1967.

2. Calvin Taylor, interview by Bill Thomas, August 17, 1968, container 24, folder 116, Sanitation Strike Archival Project, Mississippi Valley Collection, Ned McWherter Library, University of Memphis.

3. Brown, "Anti Poverty Group Demands Hearing."

4. Historical narratives have done little to dispel the notion that Martin Luther King Jr. was forced to return to Memphis after Black Power advocates violently disrupted a massive march poorly organized by James M. Lawson Jr. It is easy to understand how people then—and now—arrived at the conclusion that tensions between the nonviolent Lawson and Black Power advocates caused the violence. Shirletta Kinchen writes, "Leaders [from the Invaders] openly touted their disdain for nonviolence and its tactics," with Cabbage and his allies calling for what they termed a "good riot." Shirletta J. Kinchen, *Black Power in the Bluff City: African American Youth and Student Activism in Memphis, 1965–1975* (Knoxville: University of Tennessee Press, 2015), 60. Kinchen rightly concludes that "Black Power activists understood that the threat of violence, or just the threat of revolution, could be a weapon itself" (ibid., 61). But words were one thing. Starting a riot was quite different. Nevertheless, prominent African American leaders in Memphis, including the Reverend Samuel Billy Kyles and city councilman Fred Davis, as well as Andy Young of the Southern Christian Leadership Conference, immediately blamed the Invaders for the unraveling of the events on March 28. Ibid., 65. Historians have done little to correct this understanding in recent years, with Tennessee civil rights historian Bobby Lovett writing, "King's people believed that local young militants started the riot." Bobby L. Lovett, *The Civil Rights Movement in Tennessee: A Narrative History* (Knoxville: University of Tennessee Press, 2005), 218. Historian Michael Honey reports that "King seemed genuinely depressed by Cabbage's account of failed

communications with Lawson, as he relied heavily on Lawson's organizing skill and history of building strong relationships with young people in the Movement." But Honey also notes that King did not view the Invaders as "'totally innocent.' Members of the Invaders had indeed encouraged young people to take rocks and sticks in their hands before the March 28 riot, then they stayed out of the march and claimed innocence." Michael K. Honey, *Going down Jericho Road: The Memphis Strike, Martin Luther King's Last Campaign* (New York: W. W. Norton, 2007), 373. This essay shows that members of the Invaders were in fact at the march with rocks and sticks, and some of them also provided information to the FBI.

5. Political resistance to the civil rights movement has been well documented over the years. However, scholarship on federal surveillance and efforts to infiltrate the movement with the intention of disrupting it continues to expand. David Garrow began to explore this terrain by publishing part of Martin Luther King's FBI file—a file we now know to be much more extensive. See David J. Garrow, *The Martin Luther King, Jr., FBI File* (Frederick, MD: University Publications of America, 1984), microform. More recent scholarship reveals that a sophisticated American surveillance state arose following World War II. Gary Gerstle writes that an "oligopolistic military industrial complex . . . gave rise to a largely clandestine national security apparatus in the 1950s and 1960s with the capacity, and often the authority, to put large swaths of the American population under surveillance." He notes that these efforts began in earnest during World War I. Gary Gerstle, *Liberty and Coercion: The Paradox of American Government from the Founding to the Present* (Princeton, NJ: Princeton University Press, 2015), 9. Seth Rosenfeld's book on the free speech movement in Berkeley is based largely on FBI surveillance files. It includes documentation of Black Panther Richard Aioki's role as both an FBI informant and a primary distributor of guns to the Panthers. See Seth Rosenfeld, *Subversives: The FBI's War on Student Radicals, and Reagan's Rise to Power* (New York: Farrar, Straus and Giroux, 2012), 445. Much more work remains to be done on the influence of the surveillance state and state infiltration on the black freedom struggle.

6. Annelise Orleck and Lisa Gayle Hazirjian, *The War on Poverty: A New Grassroots History, 1964–1980* (Athens: University of Georgia Press, 2011), 15.

7. The figure of 40 million is for the year 1960. Orleck and Hazirjian, *War on Poverty*, 5.

8. Ibid., 9.

9. Gail S. Murray, "Taming the War on Poverty: Memphis as a Case Study," *Journal of Urban History* 43 (2015): 3.

10. Kinchen, *Black Power in the Bluff City*, 102.

11. Orleck and Hazirjian, *War on Poverty*, 10.

12. Murray, "Taming the War on Poverty," 3.

13. Laurie B. Green, "Saving Babies in Memphis: The Politics of Race,

Health, and Hunger during the War on Poverty," in Orleck and Hazirjian, *War on Poverty*, 140.

14. Murray, "Taming the War on Poverty," 3.

15. Green, "Saving Babies in Memphis," 141. A St. Jude collaboration with MAP-South to improve infant mortality rates was a success, and Green argues that the St. Jude project "paralleled at least the stated (if often controversial) goals of the OEO, which funded the project." Ibid., 151.

16. Ibid.; Kinchen, *Black Power in the Bluff City*, 87–88.

17. *Tri-State Defender*, February 13, 1965.

18. "Successful 3-Day Workshop Staged by Urban League," *Memphis World*, January 16, 1965.

19. *Memphis World*, February 27, 1965.

20. "Dump CAC, Insists Anti-Poverty Unit," *Memphis Press-Scimitar*, August 14, 1965.

21. Ibid.

22. Murray, "Taming the War on Poverty," 4.

23. "Poverty War Set-up Here Hit by U.S.," *Memphis Press-Scimitar*, August 20, 1965, clipping, War on Poverty file, Memphis and Shelby County Room, Memphis Public Library.

24. "Lawson and Willis Hit Back at Mayor, Blast Ingram for Kicking Them Out," *Memphis World*, October 9, 1965.

25. Murray, "Taming the War on Poverty," 4–5.

26. Alan Bussel, "Anti-Poverty Plan for Big City Area," *Memphis Press-Scimitar*, July 13, 1965.

27. Ibid.

28. Green, "Saving Babies in Memphis," 142.

29. Kinchen, *Black Power in the Bluff City*, 88. As Orleck has argued, the War on Poverty often "pitted dyed-in-the-wool segregationist politicians against some of the same civil rights activists they had been fighting for the past ten years." Orleck and Hazirjian, *War on Poverty*, 15.

30. James M. Lawson, interview by Joan Beifuss, Bill Thomas, and David Yellin, September 18, 1968, 7, Sanitation Strike Archival Project, Mississippi Valley Collection, Ned McWhirter Library, University of Memphis.

31. Green, "Saving Babies in Memphis," 142.

32. Murray, "Taming the War on Poverty," 5.

33. Green, "Saving Babies in Memphis," 143.

34. Bill Carey, "A Vanderbilt Guest Starts a Riot," *Nashville Post*, April 2, 2008. See also Benjamin Houston, *The Nashville Way: Racial Etiquette and the Struggle for Social Justice in a Southern City* (Athens: University of Georgia Press, 2012), 164–86, 193–200; Scott Frizell, "Not Just a Matter of Black and White: The Nashville Riot of 1967," *Tennessee Historical Quarterly* 70, no. 1 (Spring 2011): 26–52.

35. Kinchen, *Black Power in the Bluff City*, 61.

36. James M. Lawson, interview by Anthony C. Siracusa, July 23, 2007, in author's possession.

37. While Lawson later acknowledged that he was intentionally trying to reach the "angry guys . . . searching for direction," Kinchen rightly argues that his decision to hire the two men "spoke to the minister's convictions concerning non-violence and the strength of redemption." Kinchen, *Black Power in the Bluff City*, 90–91. It is also likely that Lawson wanted to keep the two young men close. Green suggests that although the views of Cabbage and Smith "sometimes clashed with those of Lawson . . . he saw in them a means of connecting with unemployed youth." Green, "Saving Babies in Memphis," 152. Kinchen agrees, arguing that Lawson "recruited the two to aid in MAP-South's efforts to reinvigorate the south Memphis community and educate its residents on ways to improve their living conditions." Lawson appreciated "the young men's organizing experience, familiarity with the community, and youthful exuberance." Kinchen, *Black Power in the Bluff City*, 89.

38. "'Poor' Will Speak at MAP South Meet," *Tri-State Defender*, April 22, 1967.

39. Orleck and Hazirjian, *War on Poverty*, 16. See also Jason Morgan Ward, *Defending White Democracy: The Making of a Segregationist Movement and the Remaking of Racial Politics, 1936–1965* (Chapel Hill: University of North Carolina Press, 2011); Crystal Sanders, *A Chance for Change: Head Start and Mississippi's Black Freedom Struggle* (Chapel Hill: University of North Carolina Press, 2016).

40. Kinchen, *Black Power in the Bluff City*, 93.

41. K. W. Cook, "Poverty Group Learns Lesson," *Memphis Commercial Appeal*, October 18, 1967.

42. Kinchen, *Black Power in the Bluff City*, 52.

43. As Burch later recalled, "I don't like the idea of men getting fired on the basis of association." "Anti-Poverty Workers Reinstated," *Tri-State Defender*, September 2, 1967.

44. Taylor interview.

45. James M. Lawson Jr., interview by Tom Yellin and Joan Beifuss, September, 23 1969, 39, Sanitation Strike Archival Project, Mississippi Valley Collection, Ned McWhirter Library, University of Memphis.

46. "Anti-Poverty Workers Are Reinstated in Jobs," *Tri Sate Defender*, September 2, 1967.

47. Cabbage quoted in Shirletta Kinchen, "'We Want What People Generally Refer to as Black Power': Youth and Student Activism and the Impact of the Black Power Movement in Memphis, Tennessee, 1965–1975" (PhD diss., University of Memphis, 2011), 118.

48. Kinchen, *Black Power in the Bluff City*, 147.

49. Scholars have done important work in chronicling the preponderance of armed self-defense—often in close alignment with voter registration drives and nonviolent direct action campaigns—among black activists in the 1950s and 1960s. See Timothy B. Tyson, *Radio Free Dixie: Robert F. Williams and the Roots of Black Power* (Chapel Hill: University of North Carolina Press, 1999); Charles M. Payne, *I've Got the Light of Freedom: The Organizing Tradition and the Mississippi Freedom Struggle* (Berkeley: University of California Press, 1995); Christopher B. Strain, *Pure Fire: Self-Defense as Activism in the Civil Rights Era* (Athens: University of Georgia Press, 2005); Wesley C. Hogan, *Many Minds, One Heart: SNCC's Dream for a New America* (Chapel Hill: University of North Carolina Press, 2007). Another more recent cohort of scholars has directly engaged the questions of armed self-defense relative to nonviolence both during the civil rights era and in the years before it. See Simon Wendt, *The Spirit and the Shotgun: Armed Resistance and the Struggle for Civil Rights* (Gainesville: University Press of Florida, 2007); Akinyele Omowale Umoja, *We Will Shoot Back: Armed Resistance in the Mississippi Freedom Movement* (New York: New York University Press, 2013); Charles E. Cobb, *This Nonviolent Stuff'll Get You Killed: How Guns Made the Civil Rights Movement Possible* (Boston: Basic Books, 2014); Nicholas Johnson, *Negroes and the Gun: The Black Tradition of Arms* (Amherst, NY: Prometheus Books, 2014).

50. Kinchen rightly argues that "the young radicals and MAP-South leaders differed on method and approach, but they coalesced around the issue of poverty and infusing power into a community that felt powerless to solve its own problems." Kinchen, *Black Power in the Bluff City*, 96.

51. David Tucker flatly claims that "young militants left the line of march on Beale Street to join the window breaking and looting which turns a demonstration into a riot." David Tucker, *Black Pastors and Leaders: The Memphis Clergy, 1819–1972* (Memphis, TN: Memphis State University Press, 1972), 135. Most recently, Gail Murray turned the events of March 28 into a question, suggesting that, "correctly or not, many blamed (the Invaders) for the vandalism that ended King's first march in Memphis, as their leaders had publicly disavowed the tactic of nonviolence." Murray, "Taming the War on Poverty," 6.

52. An FBI memo prepared by COINTELPRO agents in late April states, "On April 23, 1968, SA's [special agents] William Howell S. Lowe and William H. Lawrence interview[ed] an individual identifying himself as James Elmore Phillips, Jr., who reside[s] at 1592 Short Street, Memphis, Tennessee, and who is a senior at Lemoye College, 807-25 Walker Avenue, Memphis, Tennessee." FBI Memo 44-1987, in possession of the author courtesy of former Memphis police officer Venson Hughes. As Hughes notes, "It seems to APPEAR that the only interviews these two ConIntelPro agents conducted were of informants. All other interviews done by other agents in the MEM office were done with a wide variety of subjects, done within a few days of the assassination and were

numerous for each agent. Lowe and Lawrence did their interviews a couple of weeks AFTER the assassination and interviewed only a very few subjects. So the ASSUMPTION is they were only talking to their informants. Not proof but a strong indication. . . . the abnormal circumstances make it stand out." E-mail message from Venson Hughes to Anthony C. Siracusa, July 21, 2016.

53. Phillips's role on March 28 must be placed in the broader context of a well-documented COINTELPRO campaign waged against King, a campaign the Department of Justice described as "very probably . . . felonious." *Report of the Select Committee on Assassinations of the U.S. House of Representatives* (Washington, DC: US Government Printing Office, 1979), sec. D, 407.

54. FBI memorandum, March 1, 1968, 10, Ernest Withers FBI file, https://archive.org/details/ErnestWithers, 231.

55. FBI memorandum, March 7, 1968, 8, Withers FBI file, 250.

56. FBI memorandum, March, 18, 1968, 6, Withers FBI file, 302.

57. FBI memorandum, March 14, 1968, 9, Withers FBI file, 279.

58. Ibid.

59. FBI memorandum, March 21, 1968, 2, Withers FBI file, 325.

60. Ibid., 3, Withers FBI file, 326.

61. Kinchen, *Black Power in the Bluff City,* 3.

62. FBI memorandum, March 21, 1968, 4, Withers FBI file, 327.

63. Ibid., 5, Withers FBI file, 328.

64. FBI memorandum, March 29, 1968, Withers FBI file, 338.

65. Ibid., 340.

66. Ibid.

67. Ibid., 341.

68. Honey notes that Charles Harrington, Charles Ballard, Hurley Gibson, and Don Neely also joined up with the Invaders. Neely, in particular, was known for causing trouble on Beale Street. Honey, *Going down Jericho Road,* 314. Phillips later worked for the Neighborhood Organizing Project and admitted that NOP workers sought to "shake down" white businesspeople and kept the money for themselves. Kinchen, *Black Power in the Bluff City,* 110.

69. *Report of the Select Committee on Assassinations,* sec. D, 412.

70. Ibid.

71. Kinchen, *Black Power in the Bluff City,* 64.

72. Ibid., 49.

73. Calvin Taylor, interview by Paul Steckler, October 17, 1988, Washington University Libraries, Film and Media Archive, Henry Hampton Collection, http://digital.wustl.edu/e/eii/eiiweb/tay5427.0183.159calvintaylor.html.

74. Kinchen, *Black Power in the Bluff City,* 102.

75. Ibid., 101.

76. FBI memorandum from SAC [special agent in charge] Memphis (100-4542) to FBI Director (100-448006), November 29, 1968, "Counterintelli-

gence Program Black Nationalist Hate Groups," 1. Incidentally, Calvin Taylor worked at the *Memphis Commercial Appeal* in the summer of 1968.

77. FBI memorandum from SAC Memphis (100-4542) to FBI Director (100-448006), December 11, 1968, "Counterintelligence Program Black Nationalist—Hate Groups; Racial Intelligence," 1.

78. FBI Director (100-448006) to SAC Memphis (100-4542), December 11, 1968, "Counterintelligence Program Black Nationalist—Hate Groups; Racial Intelligence (Black Organizing Project)."

79. As Murray has shown, the accusations were, "in fact, recycl[ed] charges from 1968 when the head of the Neighborhood Organizing Project was fired for allowing the Invaders to meet in its offices on Florida Street." Murray, "Taming the War on Poverty," 10.

80. As Murray notes, the "report fails to mention whether any of the poor themselves were interviewed about the program's accomplishments." Moreover, she cites "high employee turnover and low morale at project sites, insufficient reporting by Board committees, failure by Butler to establish priorities and time-lines for programs, lack of evaluative procedures, failure to maintain up-to-date inventory of program property, and an overestimation of volunteer contributions when applying for grants." But even when the OEO priority of "job creation" was achieved in impoverished neighborhoods, funding was often withdrawn. OEO funding for ten shops "that employed low-income teens" was likely cut "because they made dashikis," although investigators claimed they "did not meet 'guidelines for youth employment.'" Ibid., 11.

81. "The Nixon administration wanted control lodged with governors and mayors, state legislators and city councils." Ibid., 10.

82. Orleck and Hazirjian, *War on Poverty*, 18.

83. Rumsfeld quoted in Murray, "Taming the War on Poverty," 10.

84. Ibid.

85. "WOPC Board to Dissolve on Oct 31," *Memphis Press-Scimitar*, October 7, 1970.

86. Murray, "Taming the War on Poverty," 1.

87. It was not until the city's charter was reformed in 1968 that the five-member mayor-appointed commission was expanded to a thirteen-member elected council. See Wayne Dowdy, *Crusades for Freedom: Memphis and the Political Transformation of the American South* (Jackson: University of Mississippi Press, 2010), 111–15.

88. Because Title II of the EOA had "paved the way" for organizations like the Invaders-led NOP to receive federal funding, they were targeted by anti-EOA forces. Kinchen, *Black Power in the Bluff City*, 102.

89. Alfred McCoy, *Policing America's Empire: The United States, the Philippines, and the Rise of the Surveillance State* (Madison: University of Wisconsin Press, 2009), 12.

Beyond 1968

The 1969 Black Monday Protest in Memphis

James Conway

On July 28, 1969, the Memphis branch of the NAACP sent a letter to the Memphis Board of Education regarding statements made by superintendent of schools E. C. Stimbert, who did not agree with the federal court's desegregation order regarding the transfer of teachers into city schools. The letter contained fifteen questions concerning the percentages of new teachers, black and white, for the upcoming school year and the number of administrators, black and white, managing schools with integrated populations. The NAACP also wanted to know the racial percentages of recruiters and asked why experienced black teachers were transferred to white schools, while inexperienced white teachers were assigned to black schools. It further requested an explanation of how white children who lived in predominantly black areas were able to attend white schools. Finally, it asked when the board planned to appoint black administrators in proportion to the percentage of black students in the school system. The organization requested answers by August 1 so that it could determine its next course of action.[1]

The school board waited until August 12 to respond. Though defending Superintendent Stimbert, it sent the NAACP the requested information. It admitted that although black students in city schools accounted for more than 53 percent of the student body, there were many more white teachers than black ones. The board explained that 34 percent more white teachers than black teachers had been hired for the upcoming fall semester due to a decline in qualified black applicants. As for the very low number of black administrators, the board promised that four black administrators would be assigned to schools with predominantly white enrollments. Still, twenty-two white administrators were assigned to predominantly black schools. The board made no promise or commitment to appoint black administrators in proportion to the percentage of black students. It stated, "Teachers and other professional personnel will be employed solely on the basis of qualification and without regard to race or color."[2]

Unsatisfied with the board's response, the NAACP chose to take action. Members of the organization decided that instead of sending the board a list of fifteen questions, this time they would send a list of fifteen demands. They warned the board that they would ask parents to keep their children out of school if their demands were not met. The school board scheduled a meeting with the NAACP for Friday, October 10. On September 8 the NAACP issued a press release encouraging black Memphians to attend the meeting. NAACP education committee member Laurie Sugarmon stated that the NAACP would "reiterate its protest against the racist policies of the School Board, and present arguments in favor of immediate compliance with its demands for black representation at all levels of school administration."[3]

The NAACP had traditionally handled educational conflicts through the courts. Now, compelled by the shifting climate in black politics, the organization was asking parents and children to force changes in the school system. Their protest, which lasted less than two months, came to be known as Black Monday. Through downtown marches, boycotts, pickets, violence, and vandalism of schools and businesses, the NAACP was able to create a unified front. The black community forced rapid change in the Memphis school system. By the time the boycott ended, the school board had agreed to appoint two black advisers, a black assistant superintendent, and a black coordinator.[4] It later agreed to grant amnesty to students and teachers who had participated in Black Monday but had not engaged in any violence or vandalism. The Black Monday protest demonstrated that black Memphians had more control over their community than at any other time in the city's history.

Although the initial impetus for the protest was to create change in the Memphis school system, the boycott evolved to include a host of issues that affected all black Memphians. It became a battle not only for better education but also against racism. The Black Monday protest unified the entire black community. The NAACP pursued its demands, students used resistance, and teachers participated in spite of threats of termination. The cause merged with the St. Joseph Hospital labor strike, merchants were boycotted and picketed, and the United Black Coalition was formed. But the protest also showed the limitations of Black Power coalitions and exposed the differences between moderates and radicals.

The black community's protest in Memphis and the role of the NAACP after the assassination of Dr. Martin Luther King Jr. have been overlooked and understudied. From 1968 to 1973 the organization tackled prominent issues in the black community such as poverty, employment, and education. During that time, the Memphis NAACP repositioned itself at the forefront of the black freedom struggle by blending a more radical approach with its traditional emphasis on legal rights. It blurred the lines between civil rights and Black Power. Its aggressive tactics and public rhetoric departed from its previous style, but the NAACP was never as radical as mainstream Black Power groups.[5]

Other scholars of the civil rights movement in Memphis have marked the assassination of King as the city's pivotal point of massive protest.[6] But after 1968 the movement became larger and attracted more black citizens. The NAACP made strong appeals in impoverished areas and convinced those citizens that the organization had not abandoned them. The NAACP worked to ensure that it remained the largest civil rights organization in Memphis, sustaining its validity by creating positive changes in local black communities. The organization's direct action tactics, which brought protest into the city's poor areas, balanced the national strategy with local necessity.

Memphis was an NAACP town. The organization demonstrated and provided guidance during the sit-in movements in the early 1960s, and it spent the rest of the decade fighting segregation in court, creating biracial coalitions, and making public appearances before the City Council and school board. As city schools were gradually integrated and blacks were appointed to minor local government positions and later served on the City Council, Memphis experienced less racial confrontation than most other southern cities. Therefore, the NAACP accepted the tokenism dispensed by the white establishment.

In the late 1960s Black Power leaders emerged who sought control over their communities. They were unsatisfied with the small changes achieved by the Civil Rights Act of 1964 and the Voting Rights Act of 1965, the lack of attention paid to urban areas, and the gradualism encouraged by moderate blacks and whites. Token hiring practices in neighborhood stores and symbolic integration no longer satisfied blacks during this era. The celebrated rhetoric of Black Power was only one facet of protest in this period. The ways that communities organized to effect change during this time are often misunderstood or highly exaggerated, and they demand more attention.

Like the national organization, the Memphis NAACP tried to avoid the Black Power label. The branch was image conscious, and the term was not politically expedient. Just as the national office did not want to be grouped with radicals like Stokely Carmichael, the local group did not want to be identified with militant grassroots leaders such as Lance "Sweet Willie Wine" Watson and the Invaders. However, the NAACP shared Black Power activists' pluralist ideology about interest-group politics. As Simon Hall has argued, "So long as equal opportunities and respect were offered to all groups, amicable coexistence was possible, with a cohesive black community able to enjoy a 'representative share of both local and national decision-making power.'"[7]

In the Black Power era, the Memphis NAACP's style resembled the Southern Christian Leadership Conference's nonviolent, direct action strategy more than the radical militancy of the Black Panthers. On the surface, its activism did not mirror a classic version of black militancy; however, if one considers the scope of the organization and its place in the city of Memphis, it can only be viewed as such. Instead of asking for change, it demanded change. It demanded that white merchants in black neighborhoods double their workforce and hire more blacks in management positions. It demanded that the school board appoint black members so that black teachers, students, and parents would have representation. When those demands were not met, the NAACP boycotted and held demonstrations. It chose a fiery leader in Ezekiel Bell, whom the white press labeled a militant. It publicly used radical rhetoric when describing the white establishment. Although the organization never advocated violence, it was clear that if its demands were not met, violence could occur, and the NAACP would not hold itself responsible. It shut down schools

and businesses. It encouraged children to stay out of school and participate in demonstrations. Its actions were militant in the context of both
the organization and the city of Memphis.

That militancy brought thousands of supporters who participated
directly and indirectly in NAACP protests. The branch succeeded in getting a large number of black Memphians to register to vote. Membership increased during a time when people were questioning the relevancy
of the NAACP. With more than 10,000 members, Memphis became
one of the largest branches in the country. However, the branch ultimately suffered a decline in membership and support due to lengthy protests, divided leadership, arrests, and police and government harassment.
Although both the national office and the local branch supported court-
ordered school busing to achieve integration, it did not win broad support among Memphians, including black Memphians. Yet the branch
survived. The increase in black public officials in the 1970s and 1980s
can be traced to the NAACP's militancy in this critical period.

In 1954 the Supreme Court ruled in *Brown v. Board of Education*
that "separate but equal" schools were unconstitutional. Most white
southerners reacted by using delaying tactics to postpone integration or
doing nothing at all. In the 1950s the Memphis NAACP took a gradual
approach toward desegregation. After the city continuously ignored its
proposals, the NAACP sued in *Northcross v. Memphis Board of Education*.[8] In an attempt to circumvent these legal proceedings, the Memphis
Board of Education agreed to a gradual desegregation plan for the city's
school system: integrating one grade each school year, starting with first
grade. When school doors opened in 1961, thirteen children integrated
four of the city's elementary schools without violence or disruption.[9]

As the NAACP continued its court battles with the city school system, integration progressed at a slow pace. Ten years after *Brown*, only
344 (out of 61,841) black children attended white schools in Memphis,
and only fifteen schools were classified as desegregated. Yet by 1965,
black students accounted for approximately 50 percent of the Memphis
school population. The slow and gradual pace of integration was due in
part to delaying tactics by the Memphis Board of Education, but also to
years of residential segregation. For decades, the city's black and white
residents had lived in segregated zones, and children attended school in

those areas. Therefore, when the courts mandated that the city develop a true unitary school system, this was difficult to achieve because most white schools were not close to black neighborhoods, and the city did not have school buses to transport students.[10]

The black community was not interested in the Board of Education's excuses for the delay in integrating city schools. In September 1967 the local branch of the NAACP sent the school board a memorandum titled "Discrimination in the City of Memphis School System." It addressed many of the problems blacks faced in the school system, including over-crowding, unequal distribution of supplies, teacher assignment problems, and the small number of black administrators. The organization con-cluded the letter by calling on the board to "see that a Negro is hired, immediately as the head, or assistant to the head, of every department in the school system. We further call upon you to correct, immediately, the numerous inequities in the system that prevent Negro students receiving quality education. How can anyone expect Negro students to compete with such inferior education?" The board did not respond to the branch's memo.[11]

The next year the NAACP's attention was diverted by the sanita-tion strike and the Ghetto Development Project, a protest against local merchants. However, the NAACP reentered the education arena at the grassroots level at the end of 1968, when teachers challenged the school board. That November, the board sent city teachers a pamphlet entitled *Dialogue of Dignity.* Created by a biracial committee, the document's purpose was to provide guidelines for black and white teachers in inte-grated classrooms. Although well intended, it caused a firestorm among black teachers because the directives they received were different from those given to their white counterparts. The condescending document required both groups to teach and discipline children of the opposite race in different ways. For example, the pamphlet told white teachers to "maintain positive attitudes toward student achievement. Pupils can and will learn." It instructed black educators to "keep in mind the necessity for demonstrating a thorough knowledge of the subject matter."[12] Some of the black teachers sent a letter to Superintendent Stimbert express-ing their anger. They called the pamphlet an insult. "We feel that you implied that white teachers will have to do the best they can with their lot—uneducable, incorrigible Negro students—and that Negro teachers are ill-educated, grammatically incompetent, unprofessional and should rely on white co-workers to aid us in a job that you were perfectly willing to allow us to do alone so long as only black children were involved."[13] Vasco Smith commented that the pamphlet proved that Memphis was continuing to operate a segregated school system and that the board was still led by bigots. Despite the outcry, the school board did not take any action.[14]

Problems between teachers and the Board of Education became worse in the following year. In late 1968 Memphis added ten schools and nearly 9,000 students after annexing the Mitchell–Levi Road area just south of the city. The school board claimed that although it was acquiring the schools for the 1969 school year, no changes would be made until September 1970. That, however, did not apply to the status of the teachers in those schools. In March 1969 they were interviewed, vetted, and then notified by letter regarding their employment status for the upcoming school year. Of the 307 educators, about 20 lost their jobs, the majority of whom were black.[15]

The entire rehiring process upset the black teachers in the annexed area because, back in 1958 when the city annexed the predominantly white Frayser community, all the teachers had automatically been transferred to the city school system. They appealed to the NAACP for help. The organization consulted lawyers to see whether any action could be taken, as it seemed obvious that the school board was discriminating against the black teachers. A few months earlier Superintendent Stimbert, testifying in a case involving faculty desegregation, had stated in US District Court that he was opposed to any plan that emphasized "maximum mixing of the races" as a top priority.[16] But the Board of Education had not violated any laws. In fact, it was following court orders for the upcoming school year by transferring teachers into different schools to achieve 20 percent teacher integration. This measure was unpopular among both black and white teachers because it meant leaving schools they had grown attached to and working in communities of the opposite race. Many were upset because they were not informed whether they would be transferred or where they would be sent until about a month before school started. But what made blacks especially angry was the way the board handled the transfer process. Stimbert appeared to encourage white teachers to resist the ruling by stating that their only recourse was through the courts. One school board member allowed a group of white teachers who intended to oppose the law to meet several times at a vacant house he owned, where they discussed the possibility of creating a white teachers' union. The president of the Memphis Education Association was invited to attend these private meetings. More black teachers were transferred from black schools than whites from white schools, and some black principals argued that their best educators were being forced to leave their schools.[17]

Since both the county and the city Boards of Education were in compliance with federal law, the NAACP could do nothing more than voice complaints. It became obvious that any change would have to come from the top. Unlike the time after the *Brown* decision, the black community now had more power to openly challenge the city's school system.

On July 25 the school board met to discuss the grievances of black and white teachers and administrators. Although the meeting took place downtown on a Friday evening, more than 600 people attended, including NAACP executive board members Maxine Smith and Ezekiel Bell. Smith had been chosen to speak on behalf of the black teachers, but when she began, many of the white teachers rose from their seats and rudely walked out of the auditorium in protest. Reading from a written statement, Smith told the board members, "Many black teachers of the city school system feel that through the leadership of Mr. Stimbert and [board member] Mr. [Hugh] Bosworth, teachers and the citizens of Memphis are being misled regarding the information being given on the recent court desegregation order involving the transfer of teachers." Smith presented the board with a list of questions that included an inquiry about the percentage of black teachers that would be hired for the upcoming 1969–1970 school year. She wanted to know what criteria the board had used in the past for transferring teachers and the ratio of black and white teacher recruiters. She also asked, "When does the board propose to appoint black administrators, beginning at the very top level, in proportion to the percentage of black students in the system?"[18]

A few weeks later, NAACP members made an unscheduled appearance at Board of Education headquarters and told board president Edgar

Bailey that if he did not present the long-awaited answers, the group would stage a sit-in. Bailey defused the situation when he agreed to submit a written response the following week.[19] The board's response defended Stimbert's management of teacher transfers, but it also provided the organization with the requested information.

Unsatisfied with the board's response, the NAACP decided to take action. Dr. Vasco Smith, former vice president of the NAACP, explained how Laurie Sugarmon and his wife Maxine planned to proceed:

> [They] decided after many discussions of different ways that they could make an impression that they would really take a long risk. The schools are funded on the basis of average daily attendance, that's ADA, and that if there were some way that they could legally reduce the figures on average daily attendance without any difficulties occurring. . . . That was when they decided . . . they could ask the kids to stay out of school one day. . . . And if they could ask the parents to cooperate, that it would really bring about dramatic changes, and they also realized that this was risky.[20]

Keeping children out of school to affect the schools' funding could be an effective strategy, but it carried many risks. Historically, the NAACP had championed equal education—a moderate goal that many blacks and liberal whites could support. However, using children to force the school system to provide equal employment among teachers and administrators was quite different from fighting for integrated schools. There was no guarantee that the parents would support such a radical measure. And if they did allow their children to participate, how could anyone be assured that they would return to school the next day? What day of the week should be chosen for the protest? And how should this effort be presented to the community?

The local branch of the NAACP correctly assumed that the children would be easy to convince. During the 1968 sanitation strike, the Reverend Harold Middlebrook, a leader in Community on the Move for Equality (COME), had organized a large group of students from different schools to take an "illegal holiday" and participate in all-day activities that included marching, picketing, and blocking traffic. Students at Hamilton High School threw rocks at police, hitting at least one officer and smashing the windows of a squad car. The police attacked the students, injuring one girl. After the demonstration began, youths smashed windows downtown, which led the police to attack all the marchers.[21]

A new, young Black Power group called the Memphis Mobilizers officially announced its presence and its support for the Black Monday protest during an NAACP prep session on Wednesday, October 8, 1969. Youth coordinator Don "Joey" Williams said that NAACP executives had questioned whether it would be possible to close the schools within thirty days. When the Mobilizers were given a chance to speak, Williams told the large number of young people in attendance, "We will walk out every day until those crackers meet the NAACP's demands."[22] Herman O'Neal, the organization's minister of information, told the crowd, "We may have to close them down and teach our students in churches."[23] The Mobilizers insisted that they were capable of shutting down schools in black neighborhoods within the next two days. This would show the school board what would happen if their demands were not met. The children would show their support by attending the big showdown meeting between the local branch of the NAACP and the Board of Education that Friday. The NAACP, however, was not convinced that this new group could accomplish such a big task; it had few members, and its core leaders had been out of the city for a year. NAACP vice president Vasco Smith expressed his disbelief in the Mobilizers' ability to galvanize more than half of the city's school population. Williams recalled, "I will never forget, Vasco Smith's body language, his tone of voice . . . his vibe and everything. The skepticism; the apprehension. His attitude was 'well if you think you can do that, alright. Y'all go ahead on and give it a try.' But he was very pessimistic. He didn't believe it."[24]

The next morning the Mobilizers dispersed members and supporters to all the predominantly black schools throughout the city, and many students walked out. Before noon, 900 students walked out of Northside High School. The principal at Douglass High estimated that 500 of the 1,800 students "either did not come to school or left after arriving." Some of the students who did not leave vandalized the schools. At Humes High School, "students started pounding the tables, yelling, and turning over the tables and strewing food throughout the cafeteria. After littering the cafeteria, the students spilled over into the halls, turned over wastebaskets and disrupted classes." Sixty-eight windows were broken at Humes. Ultimately, nine of the schools in predominantly black neighborhoods reported damage. Many of the students were taken out of school by their parents to prevent them from getting hurt. Several police cars surrounded the schools, and the city's police helicopter "was kept busy reporting on groups of students gathering and roaming at different places." Before the day ended, twenty-one schools in black neighborhoods had closed.[25]

The next day, around 45,000 students left early or were reported absent. A meeting scheduled between the Board of Education and the NAACP was canceled. Board president Edgar Bailey stated, "The board of education will not meet with the NAACP or any other organization under the threat of boycott, unrest, or destruction of property." At a press conference, NAACP education committee chair Laurie Sugarmon fired back at Bailey, denying the organization's involvement in instigating the protest. She blamed the students' actions on the school board and said that because it had canceled their meeting, the NAACP was increasing its demands and calling for three members of the school board to be replaced, instead of two.[26]

Later that night, the NAACP held a mass meeting at Mount Olive Christian Methodist Episcopal Church, just south of downtown. Reverend Bell formally announced the plans for Black Monday. In addition to urging parents to keep their children home from school, the NAACP was planning demonstrations at the Board of Education building; at the homes, churches, and businesses of board members; and at some white schools. The organization called for an economic boycott of white merchants, which had proved to be a successful strategy during the previous year's Ghetto Development Project. Other suggestions included wearing only black clothing and shopping exclusively at black businesses. To keep blacks informed and children educated while they were out of school, the NAACP hosted Freedom Schools, which included a series of eight workshops. Maxine Smith blamed the school board for the school closures and violence and stated, "If they want to meet with us now, it will have to be on our conditions."[27]

On October 13, the first Black Monday, 62,518 students were absent from predominantly black schools. A local newspaper featured a picture of an elementary school where only nine of thirty-two students were present. No disturbances were reported. However, elsewhere in the county, about 400 students marched out of classes at the predominantly black Mount Pisgah School, protesting a faculty that included more white teachers than black. They were also upset because some teachers called their black students "niggers." Five of the students presented a list of grievances to the principal and gave him and the county school board three days to respond and make changes. The majority of the children returned to class before noon.[28]

The NAACP held workshops at many churches to discuss its fifteen demands with students and parents, as well as its plans for future action. At New Hope Baptist Church in the Orange Mound neighborhood, the Reverend James Slaughter urged about 200 people to commit themselves to a fight for "freedom and justice for blacks." Other members of the NAACP picketed the school board building from 11:00 a.m. to 3:00 p.m. At around 4:00 p.m., hundreds of teachers attempted to meet with the board to discuss some of the issues raised by the NAACP. The night before, they had sent Bailey a telegram informing him of their purpose and the time of their arrival.[29] However, police officers prevented them from entering the building. The infuriated teachers met at Parkway Gardens Presbyterian Church and issued a statement to the press, proclaiming, "Unless the board meets the demands of the black community on Wednesday, we will stay home on Monday, Oct. 20, and appeal for a general meeting of teachers."[30]

The NAACP had proved to the school board that it could mobilize a large group of people in a short amount of time. The impact of the students' absences on the schools' funding, along with the vandalism of school buildings, was enough for the school board to agree to a meeting with the local branch. Representatives of the two groups gathered on the night of October 16 at the new Holiday Inn located at Union and McLean. But instead of trying to reach a compromise, the school board president read a statement consisting of a list of rebuttals to each of the NAACP's fifteen demands. After Bailey finished, members of the local branch walked out in protest. NAACP president Ezekiel Bell told the press that the board's presentation was not only insulting but also "vague, negative, and utterly ridiculous."[31]

After leaving the hotel, the NAACP held a late meeting at Bell's church. The next day it held a press conference and announced the creation of the United Black Coalition (UBC). The coalition consisted of several organizations and clubs, including the NAACP; American Federation of State, County, and Municipal Employees (AFSCME); Shelby County Democratic Club; COME; Interdenominational Ministerial Alliance; Bluff City Council on Civic Clubs; Concerned Teachers of Memphis; Welfare Rights Organization; and Memphis Mobilizers. The NAACP's Laurie Sugarmon asserted, "We can no longer talk about separate issues in racial problems. All issues overlap—politics, unemployment, housing, poverty, education." Since the NAACP and AFSCME were the two main groups, the coalition's goal was to engage in a series of protests based not only on the school board's unwillingness to include black members but also on a labor strike at St. Joseph Hospital.[32] Reverend Bell told the press, "We have initiated efforts to bring together all elements in the black community to fight against white racism wherever it is found." Bell said the protest would include recurring Black Mondays and boycotts of white-owned businesses. To indicate the coalition's seriousness, Bell explained, "We will not buy anything for Thanksgiving, Christmas, or Easter. This is an all out war in terms of keeping money in our pockets." One reporter wrote, "This coalition may represent the most potent expression of 'black power' in the civil rights movement in Memphis since the marches and sit-ins in 1959 and 1960 and the sanitation strike last year."[33]

The UBC was a risky strategy for the NAACP and AFSCME. The relationship between civil rights and labor groups had an interesting history in Memphis. Although labor organizing was normal in the area, AFSCME was new, the chapter having been established in 1968 during the sanitation strike. It spent the next eighteen months successfully organizing and becoming the union for nonskilled workers employed at city hospitals and schools. However, St. Joseph was a private hospital owned by an out-of-state interest and administered by Catholic nuns and priests. The union and the NAACP were charting unfamiliar territory. One of the biggest questions they faced was how to proceed if one of them negotiated and reached an agreement. What would happen to the other party? Sensing trouble ahead, the Reverend Samuel "Billy" Kyles cautioned the two groups, "You can court but don't marry." He and some of the other members feared that fully committing to the hospital strike would result in a prolonged battle, as had occurred with the sanitation strike. They believed that the school board would negotiate promptly to prevent the loss of school funding, whereas gaining union recognition for the hospital workers was uncertain. According to Maxine Smith, both sides agreed that if one dispute ended before the other, the organization that reached an agreement would not have to continue protesting.[34]

The number of participants increased on the second Black Monday. More than 65,000 students were absent or left school to support the boycott. Black teachers made good on their threat, and 674 of them missed work. More than 560 black Memphians marched downtown toward City Hall, adding participants along the way. Many of them entered the chambers, surprising a joint meeting of the City Council and Shelby County Quarterly Court. The demonstrators were denied an instant hearing by the council and left in frustration, but they soon returned with more protesters who filled every available seat.[35]

The coalition held demonstrations at St. Joseph Hospital and in downtown Memphis during the week. Leaders gave speeches encouraging citizens to boycott and picket department stores. They increasingly spoke about police brutality in black communities. It was important that the UBC present a united front because it had to convince the black community, the white establishment, and the press that its members were in accord. Although the NAACP was a traditional civil rights organization, Maxine Smith told the press that there was room for young militant groups in the UBC. Invaders leader Lance "Sweet Willie Wine" Watson told a crowd at a rally, "We in the Black community are no longer divided." He added, "When you see us advance, follow us; when you see us stop, push us; when you see us turn around, kill us." Memphis Moblizers president Cordell Jackson stated, "We have no quarrels with the NAACP."[36] At an earlier meeting, Sugarmon told a group of 300 black teachers, "I never in my life before today believed I would see the day when all elements of the Negro community could be unified . . . the Negro community is more closely knit today than they have ever been before."[37]

The number of student absences decreased during the third week of the protest. However, the fourth Black Monday saw the biggest demonstration since King's memorial march the previous year and the second largest protest march in Memphis's history. Many of the demonstrators skipped school and work; an estimated 66,969 students and 660 teachers boycotted classrooms. Previous Black Mondays had affected only schools in black communities. This time, five white schools closed due to high absence rates.[38]

The effect of the protest spilled over into public and private businesses, because a large number of employees missed work to support Black Monday. Nearly 2,000 public works employees failed to report to work that Monday morning, including more than 1,300 of the city's 1,420 sanitation workers. Only two garbage trucks were dispatched throughout the entire city that day to cover the humane shelter and city hospitals. Sanitation officials told the press it could take up to three weeks to collect the backlog of trash, and they feared additional Black Mondays could affect the upcoming holiday schedule and have them trying to catch up well into the new year. An estimated 900 school cafeteria workers throughout the city (including at white schools) did not show up for work either. Teachers, substitute teachers, parents, and principals had to prepare food. At the Board of Education building, Ted McCloud, director of food services, washed dishes while the secretaries prepared sandwiches. At city hospitals, cafeterias were kept open despite the absence of half their dietary staffs. Hospital officials reduced the normal workload by using paper plates and plastic utensils to avoid dishwashing.[39]

Many of the employees who missed work were members of AFSCME. They identified not only with the UBC but also with striking workers at St. Joseph Hospital who were seeking union recognition. Although most private companies reported normal attendance that Monday, some of their employees missed work to show their support. Seventh grader Calvin Johnson recalled, "I think my dad may have went to work, doing construction work. I know my momma had to work at Baptist. She didn't go to work on those Mondays. A lot of folks in the neighborhoods didn't work on Mondays. Folks just took off. Didn't go to work, didn't go to school. Nobody in my neighborhood went to school that I knew that I remember."[40]

The fourth Black Monday showed that the United Black Coalition had the power to affect the entire city. It put city leaders on notice that this was more than a school issue. Since they could not get the UBC to settle with the school board and St. Joseph, city officials attempted to limit boycotts by passing ordinances and filing lawsuits. For instance, the City Council required organizations hosting downtown parades to provide at least seventy-two hours' notice before the event.[41]

Mayor Henry Loeb warned that the city was taking legal action to block city workers from walking off their jobs in the future. Public employees who did not attend work on Monday would be docked a day's pay and considered for suspension. City attorney James Manire claimed the workers were being used as pawns, and he filed a suit in Chancery Court to stop coalition leaders from encouraging city employees to miss work. He also threatened to sue several individuals (specifically AFSCME leaders) for financial damages.[42]

After announcing that city schools could lose more than $2 million and that their accreditation was in jeopardy, the school board filed an injunction in Chancery Court to prevent the UBC from encouraging Black Monday boycotts. The suit named specific coalition leaders and used handbills, a letter from Bell, and a telegram from labor leader Jesse Epps as evidence. The suit charged that the UBC had "urged, incited, and assisted school children to be absent from school." It claimed that the NAACP and others had encouraged pickets that "intimidated or threatened pupils or their parents and teachers" to keep them from entering schools. In addition to an injunction, the school board asked that an unspecified amount of damages be awarded.[43]

Despite the city's efforts, a fifth Black Monday protest was conducted on November 10, with 46,421 students missing school. But the main concern was a march planned for later that afternoon. Southern Christian Leadership Conference president Ralph Abernathy had traveled to Memphis to lead the protest. Fearing a confrontation, assistant city attorney Frierson Graves and city councilman Jerred Blanchard met with representatives of the UBC and worked out an agreement whereby demonstration leaders would approach a police barricade and be arrested for disorderly conduct. They agreed that the rest of the marchers would disperse peacefully after the arrests. Following the meeting, the coalition

Maxine Smith (center) leads Black Monday demonstrators on Beale Street in 1969. (Courtesy Memphis and Shelby County Room, Memphis Public Library)

explained the situation to the waiting participants. The march began at 5:20 p.m., and when more than 2,000 marchers crossed Linden Avenue, they were warned that anyone who proceeded would go to jail. At that point, fifty-three people (including Abernathy) approached the barricade and were arrested. Without incident, they were placed on a bus and transported to the city jail.[44]

Once all the leaders had been arrested, the rest of the demonstrators were left in the hands of march marshals. The police ordered the crowd to disperse and return to Clayborn Temple. But at that point, the frustration of Black Mondays boiled over. The marshals held hands to form a human chain, attempting to contain the crowd. After about thirty minutes, some youths penetrated the line and began to throw bricks and bottles at the barricade. This caused the police officers to fire waves of tear gas at the crowd. State Representative Alvin King—one of the fifty-three leaders arrested—said in anger, "The police came with barricades, a fogging machine, guns and gas masks. They were determined to try out their new equipment. They did."[45] Before the night ended, there were more than twelve incidents of looting, several break-ins, and one case of sniper fire. The Memphis Fire Department responded to six firebombing incidents.[46]

Later that night, the NAACP's executive committee held a closed-door meeting to discuss the progress made by the nine-member biracial committee created with city leaders to mediate the dispute. After talking for more than four hours, the executive committee voted seventeen to fourteen in favor of a ten-day moratorium on school boycotts. In a statement released after 12:30 a.m., the NAACP noted, "We do not deem it necessary for parents to continue to keep their children out of school. At the expiration of ten days, our Executive Committee will reappraise the progress being made by our negotiators and make appropriate recommendations." However, the statement added, "We intend to escalate activities in other areas until our demands on the School Board have been met."[47]

Ezekiel Bell, who had stated hours earlier that there would be no moratorium or cooling-off period, resigned immediately. Several others followed suit. Bell said the meeting had been "railroaded" and that some of the members were in collusion with Mayor Loeb to ensure that St. Joseph workers would not have a union. He accused Jesse Turner and Vasco Smith of influencing the vote. Bell argued, "There were people voting last night who had been dragged up from nowhere for the meeting. People were at the meeting last night who have not been to an NAACP meeting in three years and have never picketed in recent years." A disgruntled Bell told the press, "The NAACP is dead as a voice in this community."[48]

Bell became chairman of the United Black Coalition and founded a local chapter of the Southern Christian Leadership Conference. The UBC continued to ask students to stay home on Mondays. It organized demonstrations to support striking workers at St. Joseph Hospital and students who had been suspended for missing too many days of school. But as the protests continued, so did the violence and vandalism. Since its deal with the NAACP did not deter students from missing class or engaging in vandalism, the Board of Education and city officials once again used the law to try to stop the coalition. The school board filed a $10 million lawsuit in federal court against the UBC. Bailey cited losses due to vandalism, funding decreases because of low average daily attendance, and food waste in school cafeterias because of boycotts, walkouts, and closings. The suit charged that the UBC used children for the sole purpose of forcing St. Joseph Hospital to reach a settlement with AFSCME. It said the defendants "have begun a campaign of turmoil, unrest, violence, threats, vandalism and destruction of property in and around the public schools that has made the order of this court with the desegregation of public schools impossible to perform."[49]

On Tuesday, December 9, nearly three weeks after the UBC called for the end of school boycotts, coalition leaders (including NAACP members) were notified that they would be arrested for their roles in Black Monday marches and boycotts. Nineteen people were charged with violating Section 39-1011 of the Tennessee Code Annotated. Under that section of the law, it was a misdemeanor to persuade a child not to attend or to leave school; this law also covered contributing to the delinquency of a minor by interfering with school attendance and conspiracy to interfere with attendance. Some leaders were charged with multiple offenses. District attorney Philip Michael Canale recommended a bond of $500 for each indictment. However, Judge Odell Horton (the only black judge in Memphis) set the bail at $1 for each defendant.[50]

The Memphis Board of Education made assurances that there would be no reason for the NAACP or the UBC to call for any more Black Monday school boycotts. On December 18 it announced that two black advisers had been appointed to the board. One was Dr. Hollis D. Price, the sixty-five-year-old president of LeMoyne-Owen College who would be retiring from that position at the end of the year. The other was thirty-year-old attorney George H. Brown, who had taught geography at Carver High School for five months before starting his law practice. He was also a deputy director of the Equal Employment Opportunity Commission in Memphis. Brown's wife Margaret was an English teacher at Hamilton High School.[51]

The NAACP's and UBC's demands for more blacks in administrative positions seemed to be ignored when the recently deceased assistant superintendent was replaced by another white person. However, Stimbert announced that he had named William D. Callian Jr. as the acting coordinator of instruction. Stimbert's choice did not require a vote from the board. Callian became the first black man to be appointed to the coordinator level of the Memphis Board of Education's administrative staff.[52]

Although school attendance returned to normal, the rest of the school year was affected by Black Monday's aftermath. In addition to some teachers, at least one school principal had resigned. Twenty of the suspended students were allowed to check out books so they could keep up with their work, but they could not return to school until January. Five of them were forced to transfer to other schools. Even students who were not suspended felt like they faced reprisals from the school system through cuts to after-school events and activities. Almella Starks-Umoja, a graduating student at Booker T. Washington High School, remembered that some proms and ballets (after-school dances) were canceled. Calvin Johnson, a student at Porter Junior High, remembered, "We had no activities at all that year. In gym they used to teach us how to square dance and at the end of the semester they would have a big boy and girl sock hop where you square dance and stuff. All of that was cut out."[53]

The Memphis school board began to include more blacks in all facets of education. But as more whites left the city for the suburbs and put their children in private schools, they took their tax dollars with them, and the city schools declined rapidly. The next decade brought more turmoil to the school system because of the nationwide busing crisis. However, the Black Monday campaign exemplified the amount of control black Memphians had over their community. The gradualism of the previous decade had been destroyed by the latter part of the 1960s. Blacks in Memphis became more radical in their efforts to achieve political progress and combat racism, poverty, and discrimination. After this shift, white moderates' participation in the freedom struggle declined. Black leaders believed that blacks needed to control their own neighborhoods and institutions. At this historic juncture, the blurring of Black Power and traditional civil rights tactics allowed the NAACP to unify black Memphians and bring rapid changes to the city school system in a short time frame.

Notes

1. Rolland Haynes Jr., "No School on Mondays: Protest and Boycotts in the Memphis City Schools Fall 1969" (paper submitted to Dr. Charles Crawford, Memphis State University, December 12, 1977), 1–2, Maxine Smith Collection, box V, folder 17, Memphis and Shelby County Public Library.

2. Ibid., 5.

3. Smith Collection, box V, folder 22.

4. Calvin Taylor Jr., "Representation for Blacks Is Major Part of Plan Backed by Panel," *Memphis Commercial Appeal*, November 17, 1969.

5. A detailed study of Memphis's NAACP and Black Power can be found in James Conway, "Moderated Militants in the Age of Black Power: The Memphis NAACP, 1968–1975" (PhD diss., University of Memphis, 2015).

6. Those scholars include Laurie Green, *Battling the Plantation Mentality: Memphis and the Black Freedom Struggle* (Chapel Hill: University of North Carolina Press, 2007); Michael Honey, *Going Down Jericho Road: The Memphis Strike, Martin Luther King's Last Campaign* (New York: W. W. Norton, 2008); G. Wayne Dowdy, *Crusades for Freedom: Memphis and the Political Transformation of the American South* (Oxford: University of Mississippi Press, 2010); and Elizabeth Gritter, *Black Politics and the Memphis Freedom Movement, 1865–1954* (Lexington: University Press of Kentucky, 2014).

7. Simon Hall, "The NAACP, Black Power, and the African American Freedom Struggle, 1966–1969," *Historian* 69, no. 1 (February 2007): 53, http://onlinelibrary.wiley.com/doi/10.1111/j.1540-6563.2007.00174.x/pdf (accessed January 12, 2015).

8. Beverly Bond and Janann Sherman, *Memphis in Black and White* (Charleston, SC: Arcadia Publishing, 2003), 135; John Branston, "Integration and Innocence: Enlisted in a Cause They Barely Understood as First-Graders, Memphians Look Back at Segregation," *Memphis Flyer*, May 19, 2004; Dowdy, *Crusades for Freedom*, 80–83.

9. Elizabeth Gritter, "Local Leaders and Community Soldiers: The Memphis Desegregation Movement, 1955–1961" (senior honors thesis, American University, 2001), 89–91.

10. Daniel Kiel, "Exploded Dream: Desegregation in the Memphis City Schools," *Law and Inequality: A Journal of Theory and Practice* 26 (2008): 277; Christopher Silver and John V. Moeser, *The Separate City: Black Communities in the Urban South, 1940–1968* (Lexington: University Press of Kentucky, 1995), 51.

11. Memorandum from Memphis Branch NAACP to Memphis Board of Education, September 8, 1967, container 9, folder 68, Special Collections, University of Memphis.

12. *Dialogue of Dignity*, Memphis City Schools, 1968, container 11, folder 87, Special Collections, University of Memphis.

13. "Teachers Send Protest Letter to Board," *Tri-State Defender*, December 21, 1968, 1, 2.

14. Ibid.; "Teacher Pamphlet Draws NAACP Fire," *Memphis Press-Scimitar*, December 14, 1968, 5.

15. Clark Porteous, "Memphis Has Added 21,900 New Residents and 10 Additional Square Miles Today," *Memphis Press-Scimitar*, December 31, 1968, sec. 2, 13; "County Teachers Worried about Future as City Begins Taking over Schools in Annexed Areas!" *Memphis World*, March 29, 1969; "Netters in Plea for Dismissed Teachers!" *Memphis World*, May 3, 1969.

16. "Emphasis on Desegregation in Schools Hit by Educator," *Memphis Press-Scimitar*, December 20, 1968.

17. "475 Teachers Await Transfers," *Memphis World*, June 28, 1969; Branch Department, General Office Files, Tennessee, Memphis Garbage Strike, March 5–April 1, 1969, Records of the National Association for the Advancement of Colored People, Library of Congress, Washington, DC, part VI, C69; ibid., May 7–June 3, 1969; "Teacher Transfer at Boiling Point," *Memphis World*, July 26, 1969, 1, 4; "Teachers to Be Chosen by Lot," *Memphis Press-Scimitar*, June 20, 1969, sec. 2, 11.

18. "School Board Quizzed by NAACP Exec," *Tri-State Defender*, August 2, 1969, 3; "My Viewpoint: By State Representative James I. Taylor," *Tri-State Defender*, August 2, 1969, 6.

19. "School Officials Will Answer 10 NAACP Questions," *Memphis World*, August 23, 1969.

20. Gritter, "Local Leaders and Community Soldiers," 89–91.

21. Clark Porteous and Charles A. Brown, "Churchill Puts 116 on Probation," *Memphis Press-Scimitar*, March 6, 1968, 1, 18; Jimmie Covington, "King Implored by Ministers to Come Here," *Memphis Commercial Appeal*, March 14, 1968; George Bryan, "Truancy Crackdown Ordered by Judged to Curb Rowdyism in Garbage Strike Marches," *Memphis Commercial Appeal*, March 16, 1968; "Students Hurl Rocks at Police," *Memphis Press-Scimitar*, March 28, 1968.

22. "Students Support Threat Tactics," *Memphis Commercial Appeal*, October 10, 1969, 12.

23. Ibid.

24. Ibid.; Don Williams, interview by the author, Bartlett, TN, December 15, 2011; "Schools Meet Set Friday," *Memphis Press-Scimitar*, October 8, 1969, 15.

25. "Negro Pupils Start Boycott with Violence," *Memphis Press-Scimitar*, October 9, 1969; "NAACP Repeats Black Monday Call," *Memphis Commercial Appeal*, October 12, 1969.

26. "Demands against Memphis School Board Are Increased by NAACP," *Memphis Press-Scimitar*, October 10, 1969, 11.

27. David Vincent, "600 Chanters Stymie Talks on Schools," *Memphis Commercial Appeal*, October 11, 1969; Wayne Chastain, "Boycotting Pupils Refused

Entry," *Memphis Press-Scimitar,* October 11, 1969, 2; "NAACP Repeats Black Monday Call."

28. "62,518 Pupils Skip Classes in Dispute," *Memphis Press-Scimitar,* October 13, 1969; David Vincent, "School Board, NAACP Will Meet Tomorrow; Students Urged to Return to School Today," *Memphis Commercial Appeal,* October 14, 1969.

29. Calvin Taylor Jr., "Teachers Seek School Board Talks," *Memphis Commercial Appeal,* October 13, 1969.

30. Vincent, "School Board, NAACP Will Meet Tomorrow"; "62,518 Pupils Skip Classes in Dispute."

31. David Vincent, "Threat of Negro Boycott Looms as NAACP Bolts School Meeting," *Memphis Commercial Appeal,* October 16, 1969, 1, 10, 11; Charles A. Brown, "School Racial Situation Tense after Meeting," *Memphis Press-Scimitar,* October 16, 1969, 19.

32. In 1969 AFSCME led black workers at St. Joseph Hospital in Memphis in a strike for union recognition.

33. David Vincent, "New Coalition of Negro Groups Plan Mass March as First Step," *Memphis Commercial Appeal,* October 17, 1969.

34. Maxine Smith, interview by the author, Memphis, August 22, 2011.

35. Calvin Taylor Jr., "600 Teachers Vow to Skip School to Push NAACP's 'Black Monday,'" *Memphis Commercial Appeal,* October 20, 1969; Robert Kellett, "65,000 Absent from School as Coalition Gathers Boycott Momentum," *Memphis Commercial Appeal,* October 21, 1969; "Slim Crowd Turns out for March," *Memphis Press-Scimitar,* October 20, 1969; "Teachers Lead out in Black Monday March," *Tri-State Defender,* October 25, 1969.

36. David Vincent, "New Militancy, Scope Marks NAACP's Demands," *Memphis Commercial Appeal,* October 26, 1969.

37. "NAACP Group, Educators to Air Dispute," *Memphis Press-Scimitar,* October 15, 1969, 37.

38. Kay Pittman Black, "66,969 Pupils Out—A Record," *Memphis Press-Scimitar,* November 3, 1969; Richard Lentz, "City to Seek Court Action on Walkouts after 1,995 Join 'Black Monday' Marches," *Memphis Commercial Appeal,* November 4, 1969; "Thousands in March Here: Demands Schools, Unions Share," *Tri-State Defender,* November 8, 1969.

39. Lentz, "City to Seek Court Action on Walkouts"; "March Restricted to Midday Hours," *Memphis Press-Scimitar,* November 3, 1969.

40. Calvin Johnson, interview by the author, Memphis, August 19, 2011.

41. David Vincent, "Civic Leaders Meet with School Board," *Memphis Commercial Appeal,* November 8, 1969.

42. Lentz, "City to Seek Court Action on Walkouts."

43. "School Board Seeks Boycott Injunction," *Memphis Press-Scimitar,* November 6, 1969.

44. Wayne Trotter, "Tear Gas Follows Rocks as Police Stand Firm; March Leaders Arrested," *Memphis Commercial Appeal,* November 11, 1969; "After March Prevented, Scattered Incidents of Violence Occur," *Memphis Press-Scimitar,* November 11, 1969, 8.

45. Kay Evans, "Rep. King, Mrs. Hohenburg among Those Arrested," *Memphis Press-Scimitar,* November 11, 1969, 15.

46. "After March Prevented, Scattered Incidents of Violence Occur."

47. "Black School Boycott Is Suspended 10 Days," *Memphis Commercial Appeal,* November 14, 1969.

48. "NAACP Splits over Boycott Halt," *Memphis Press-Scimitar,* November 14, 1969, 1, 4; David Vincent, "Concern for Black Students Called Factor in NAACP Action," *Memphis Commercial Appeal,* November 15, 1969, 4.

49. "Schools Seek $10 Million Damages," *Memphis Press-Scimitar,* November 20, 1969, 1, 6; "Black Coalition Orders End to Boycotts after Board Files Suit," *Memphis Press-Scimitar,* November 22, 1969, 1, 10.

50. "Charges Served on Boycott Chiefs," *Memphis Press-Scimitar,* December 10, 1969, 1, 3.

51. Minutes of the Board of Education of the Memphis City Schools, December 18, 1969, Shelby County Schools, Memphis; Kay Pittman Black, "2 Negroes Named School Advisors," *Memphis Press-Scimitar,* December 18, 1969, 1, 4.

52. "Counce Promoted; Negro Gets Posts," *Memphis Press-Scimitar,* December 20, 1969, 5.

53. Wayne Chastain, "School Board Delays Filling Vacancies," *Memphis Press-Scimitar,* December 6, 1969; Almella Starks-Umoja, interview by the author, Memphis, August 17, 2011; Johnson interview.

Beauty and the Black Student Revolt

Black Student Activism at Memphis State and the Politics of Campus "Beauty Spaces"

Shirletta Kinchen

Maybelline Forbes graced the front page of the *Tiger Rag,* the student paper and student voice of Memphis State University (MSU), her left arm extended in the Black Power salute. Despite what some considered a militant gesture, the beautiful twenty-one-year-old biology major from nearby Bolivar, Tennessee, smiled broadly, posed unapologetically, and was visibly excited about her achievement. Forbes's excitement stemmed from her recent coronation as homecoming queen at the school's 1970 homecoming festivities. Her victory marked the first time in the history of the institution that an African American had won the title, and it was Black Power that made Forbes's victory a reality.[1]

Those unfamiliar with the spirit of the Black Power era, an age and a movement that emphasized a heightened perspective and level of consciousness about political, social, economic, and cultural blackness in all aspects of black life, might have argued that a homecoming parade was not an appropriate occasion for Forbes to take such a stance. They might have argued that her pose, which reflected the politics of the time, was an act unbefitting the parade and an unacceptable representation of the university by someone who was arguably the second most important and visible woman on campus. Indeed, comments made by several students in the *Tiger Rag* reflected their disapproval of Forbes's gesture during one of the biggest campus events of the year, and some of them actually questioned *how* Forbes had won the election for homecoming queen. That the majority of her support had come from black students and the so-called longhairs, a not so veiled reference to the campus's hippie counter-culture, worried many segments of the more conservative white student body. But in their rush to discredit Forbes and the black student movement that had backed her campaign, they neglected to consider the fact that even if their accusations of black students working together to get her elected were true (which they were), white students had been forming voting blocs for years, with the explicit intent of keeping black women from serving as homecoming queen.[2] There was no collusion or trickery on the part of the black students involved in helping Forbes obtain the crown. After her victory, Forbes argued that despite what ostensibly amounted to an apolitical position, the title of homecoming queen very much represented a cultural and political victory for all of Memphis State's black students.

Forbes's coronation followed a tumultuous yet defining academic year for Memphis State University, the black student population in general, and, more specifically, the school's Black Student Association, in which Forbes was actively involved. The snapshot of Forbes on the front page of the *Tiger Rag* was but a small visual representation of the larger story of the struggle of black students attending Memphis State in the late 1960s and early 1970s. Although a largely symbolic position, Forbes's historic win not only represented a triumph for black students but also symbolized the first significant change in the accepted beauty and cultural standards on campus. Before her victory, the campus culture had failed to showcase any black standards of beauty or provide African Americans with any significant cultural representations.[3]

Much of the scholarly attention on black student activism during the late 1960s and 1970s centers on the various protest efforts, including boycotts, strikes, marches, building takeovers, violent reprisals, and other forms of aggressive and direct action protests. Particularly as the scholarship developed and expanded its emphasis beyond black student activism during the modern civil rights movement and student participation in traditional civil rights campaigns to an exploration of black student activism on college campuses during the Black Power era, scholars such as Ibram X. Kendi (formerly Ibram H. Rogers), Stefan Bradley, and Martha Biondi have highlighted these more established modes of campus protest and activism.[4] However, many studies fail to fully assess the day-to-day struggles of African American students, specifically how they engaged in campus politics vis-à-vis campus clubs, organizations, and student body offices and positions. As student protest transitioned from lunch counters to college campuses in the late 1960s, and as college enrollment increased at predominantly white colleges and universities, many African American students became determined to gain access to and transform the traditional campus outlets for student life. Importantly, these outlets, which excluded black student participation, also became sites of protest and struggle.

This essay examines these alternative modes of black student protest on college campuses during the Black Power era. It considers how black students used these different avenues of protest to not only challenge their respective colleges to become more responsive to their demands for Black Studies programs, the recruitment of black students, and more black faculty and administrators—all of which were principal among the litany of black students' demands during the late 1960s and early 1970s—but also to press for access to the more mainstream and social aspects of student and campus life.

Primarily, this essay explores how black students at Memphis State University politicized what I call campus "beauty spaces" and how, in addition to the call for curriculum changes and other more mainstream demands, these spaces became contested areas for black student protest. I employ my own definition to describe the idea of "beauty spaces." For instance, campus queens and court positions, women's clubs and auxiliaries, and all-female pep squads are examples of "beauty spaces." At Memphis State and at many other historically and predominantly white educational institutions, these positions were clearly reserved for the white female student population, thereby setting an unwritten and unspoken standard of the beauty aesthetic—an aesthetic that clearly excluded black women. While revolutionizing the campus remained the primary goal for Memphis State's black student activists, that revolution, they argued, included breaking down the social barriers that prohibited black students from being active participants in the college experience. For black students, both men and women, penetrating these areas accessible only to white female coeds became a battleground for campus protest.

In retelling the story of this particular movement at MSU in the late 1960s and early 1970s, I retrace the early experiences of African American students during the university's desegregation in 1959 and their impact on the activism of the later generation of black students. I also examine the formation of the Black Student Association (BSA) and its leadership role in building and developing the consciousness of the black student body. I conclude with an analysis of the evolution of BSA protest efforts, paying specific attention to attempts to penetrate the campus beauty spaces, and end the essay where it began—with Maybelline Forbes's historic victory and its impact on Memphis State University.

Memphis State University in the Early 1960s

The period from the mid-1960s to early 1970s witnessed a flurry of campus activism, protest, and dissent. Distressed about the nation's involvement in Vietnam, racial strife, and gender and income inequality, among other political and social issues, college students (both black and white) around the country shifted the focus of their protest and activism from desegregating lunch counters and registering voters to transforming the culture and politics of higher education. Ibram X. Kendi, a scholar who has studied and written extensively about this transformative period in black student activism, suggests that during this time, African American students forced the "radical reconstruction of higher education."[5] By 1968, the apex of what Kendi defines as the "black campus movement," black students no longer utilized the same modes of protest that had characterized the struggle for civil rights in the early part of the decade. Framed by the radical nature of the Black Power movement, student protest had become more aggressive and more vocal.[6]

Unlike Maybelline Forbes and other African American students who were part of what historian Donna Murch calls the "Black Power generation," the first wave of African American students that arrived on predominantly white college campuses after the 1954 *Brown v. Board of Education* decision declaring segregation in public schools unconstitutional did not have an opportunity to be aggressive or vocal.[7] In fact, just surviving each day unscathed at hostile educational institutions across the South was a daily exercise in campus protest and student activism. Yet it was those students, including the eight African American students who enrolled at MSU in the fall of 1959, that provided the foundation for

Forbes's historic victory long before she enrolled at the university. MSU became the first institution in the state of Tennessee to admit black undergraduates. The local press referred to the five women and three men as the "Memphis State Eight," and their entrance into the segregated university inspired the city's black youths, who viewed these trailblazers as their own version of Arkansas Central High School's "Little Rock Nine."[8]

The legacy of the Memphis State Eight fueled the activism of black students who enrolled after 1960, and each successive wave of incoming African American students created its own pockets of protest. They were motivated by the early integration experiences of those eight students, especially as they and eventually others became the backbone of the city's successful desegregation movement.[9] With no local branch of the Student Nonviolent Coordinating Committee (SNCC) in the city, young black activists looked outward to the national movement for inspiration, but they also focused inward on the local achievements and examples set by the Memphis State Eight. Their triumphs as well as their travails as pioneers became a rallying point for future black students. These students vowed that they would not be subjected to the same hostile treatment and exclusion from campus life; nor would they allow themselves to feel like "appendages who were tolerated but not integrated into the whole."[10]

Formation of the Black Student Association

Black students at Memphis State were not the first or the only black students to be disillusioned by their college experience. As Joy Ann Williamson notes, black students at predominantly white institutions suffered from feelings of alienation, isolation, and exclusion from "student life associations and organizations such as fraternities and sororities, student government, or academic associations."[11] In part to deal with their frustration over this lack of institutional access, but also as a response to the increased racial consciousness driven by the rise of the Black Power movement, black students throughout the country began organizing black student unions (BSUs) and associations. These organizations served many functions, but they ultimately operated as the nerve center and central base for black student campus organizing.[12] Beginning in 1966—the same year SNCC's Stokely Carmichael and Willie Ricks publicly unveiled the Black Power chant in Greenwood, Mississippi—black students organized the first BSU on the campus of San Francisco State College. These organizations became the "central coordinating mechanism for Black Power protests" on predominantly white as well as historically black college campuses around the country.[13] This national movement encouraged black students at Memphis State to organize as well, as they had begun to realize "the injustice of not having black student representation."[14]

Memphis's black students did not reinvent the wheel in forming their BSA. Almost a year after the creation of San Francisco State's BSU, African American students at Memphis State embraced the same ethos as thousands of other black students around the country. A group of older male students at MSU began to gather and organize the younger blacks students with the goal of creating a BSA to serve as the official vehicle for the black student body. The organizers encouraged their black classmates not to accept outsider status and urged them to become "part of this campus life . . . and show more than a passive interest in campus activity."[15]

The older students who constituted the leadership of the BSA—James Mock, David Acey, Ester Hurt, and James Pope—were all military veterans, and they understood that Memphis State required a different type of revolution than that taking place on other campuses. Being older than most of their classmates, having traveled the world and interacted with people of different classes and ethnicities, they had acquired a certain level of race and class consciousness that had to be developed and nurtured in the other students. They argued that instead of criticizing black students for a lack of social, political, and racial consciousness, they had to meet the students at their level of consciousness before they could seriously engage other political issues. But most important, they had to determine what issues were most important to the black students at Memphis State.

Eventually, the BSA leadership discovered that culture, identity, and inclusion were the issues of greatest concern to the black students. Attracted to the cultural politics of the Black Power era, black students stressed a desire for their educational experience to reflect their culture and racial heritage. As William Van DeBurg argues in one of the first full historical treatments of the Black Power movement, the movement's "cultural connection was most clearly evidenced within the context of higher education."[16] While cultural politics constituted only one branch of the Black Power movement, its emphasis on racial pride and reshaping and redefining black cultural values connected both the hard-core and more casual proponents of the movement. This was especially true in the case of black students at Memphis State—a mixture of hard-core Black Power advocates and those not as ideologically wedded to every tenet of the movement.

Culture Shock? Black Student Protest in Beauty Spaces

Essentially, the BSA had a simple mission: integrate its members as Memphis State students without sacrificing their collective black identity. The black students searched the campus for positive black representations and meaningful social outlets. Although the absence of a Black Studies program and a lack of black representation in the classroom and in administrative positions were significant voids in their campus experience, black students emphasized their exclusion from social activities, demanding the "full integration of collegiate affairs," while complaining that they were "in Memphis State, but not of it."[17]

Nowhere was this more evident than in the campus beauty spaces. By 1968, the number of black male athletes on some of the school's sports teams had increased, but the number of black female athletes remained low; nor where there any black women on the sidelines as part of the cheerleading or pep squads.[18] The women's auxiliary of the Reserve Officers' Training Corps (ROTC), the Angel Flight, followed the example of its male counterpart in excluding blacks. Fraternities and sororities remained segregated as well.[19]

However, exclusion from white fraternities and sororities did not mean exclusion from campus Greek life. Since the founding of the first black Greek-letter organization (BGLO), Alpha Phi Alpha Fraternity, on the campus of Cornell University in 1906, African American students had found ways to channel campus exclusion into opportunities to serve the race.[20] At Memphis State, black women led the way in 1963 when they created their own social, service, academic, and beauty space, the Epsilon Kappa chapter of Delta Sigma Theta Sorority. The Epsilon Kappa chapter became the first BGLO chartered at Memphis State.[21]

Using the example of their early-twentieth-century predecessors and organization founders, Delta Sigma Theta members used their sorority as an instrument of racial uplift.[22] They also hoped to be trailblazers, leaving a positive imprint on the campus that would make it easier for other BGLOs to receive charters. In addition to serving the interests and standards of the national organization, Delta Sigma Theta members strongly believed that their function at Memphis State included bridging "the racial divide that existed in the wake of integration, by participating in not only events germane to black student's interests but to the common student body as well."[23] Also, they "pushed to participate in [integrated] pageants and talent shows such as the Delta Zeta Follies and All Sing with other white sorority contestants," which became one of the first examples of black student protest and activism creating access within spaces formerly reserved for white female students.[24] However, they could participate in those events only as members of BGLO sororities, not as members of organizations reserved for white students.

Despite the Deltas' early efforts to bridge the "racial divide" and a noticeable swell in Memphis State's black student enrollment, by the late 1960s, not much had changed in terms of creating an inclusive and culturally sensitive environment for black students, and particularly black women, at Memphis State. Black women found that other outlets aimed at showcasing femininity and beauty were off-limits to them. The *Tiger Rag* dedicated a section called the "Campus Cutie" to showcasing the most "attractive," socially active, and academically astute females students. Students were encouraged to nominate women who embodied the aforementioned attributes, and the staff of the *Tiger Rag* selected one Campus Cutie for each issue. Black students questioned the legitimacy of this process, because although they continued to submit nominations, no black women appeared in the section.[25]

BSA leader David Acey recalled years later: "There were all these beautiful black women on campus and there were no black cheerleaders. No black pom-pom girls, no nothing. No black girls anywhere."[26] That void became a battleground on which the BSA staked a central part of its platform to challenge the campus's rigid racial and cultural politics. On November 7, 1968, the BSA called a mass meeting at the campus's University Center to discuss several pressing issues, including the "integration of Angel Flight and a breakdown of the segregation practices by white fraternities and sororities."[27] The organization's coordinating committee decided, and the students in attendance agreed, to give the offending parties two months to respond to their demands.[28]

Notwithstanding the two-month moratorium, BSA members decided not to wait to confront staff members of the *Tiger Rag* about their discriminatory practices. Students made their way to the paper's office with the intention of making "the psychological presence of black students on campus apparent."[29] They demanded more coverage in the school's paper, specifically requesting a full page devoted to the issues, news, and accomplishments of black students. Editor Mary Welsh did not deny that the paper lacked black voices and coverage of black issues but claimed she thought black students did not "want their news covered in the *Tiger Rag*." The students did not believe Welsh and cited examples of censorship and marginalization of black reporters. They even accused the paper of abolishing the Campus Cutie pictures "when it heard that several beautiful black co-eds intended to apply."[30]

The students' concern about their white counterparts using the school paper and other parts of campus life to dictate the beauty standard came at a time when African Americans were beginning to eschew the dominant Eurocentric beauty standard and embrace a more Afrocentric aesthetic. Although the era's shifting black aesthetic and its political implications impacted black people of both genders, black women were more often reduced to fashion plates whose fashion choices and modes of styles were devoid of any political meaning. According to scholar Tanisha C. Ford, black women in particular "struggled to redefine themselves over and against layers upon layers of stereotypes about the black female body that circulated in both mainstream and activist culture."[31] Even activist and revolutionary Angela Davis, both famous and infamous for her natural Afro hairstyle as much as her politics, suggested that such an intense focus on her hair relegated her "politics of liberation to the politics of fashion."[32]

However, as Ford argues, fashion and beauty were inherently political and often integral to black women's activism during the black freedom struggle.[33] These new beauty ideals and the changing beauty dynamic also became hotly contested issues within the BSA and the black student body. Memphis State's basketball coach Moe Iba had already mandated that his black male players had to "get rid of those naturals [hairstyles]," creating a campus-wide controversy that filtered into the BSA's private discussions. The BSA held weekly forums that addressed various topics pertinent to black students. At its December 4, 1968, forum, BSA member and sociology major Charles Parnell chastised the black women on campus for ascribing to the so-called Eurocentric standards of beauty. He criticized black women who were "intent upon frying their hair," a colloquialism for the use of heating irons, combs, or lye-based products to straighten "kinky" or tightly coiled hair. "Straight hair," Parnell suggested, was "not a Negroid characteristic." As he continued his tirade against black women's beauty choices, he opined, "Black women do not have to straighten their hair to show their femininity. Black women are holding the black man back."[34]

Not all black students agreed with Parnell's vague and unfair charge that black women who embraced Eurocentric standards of beauty were somehow impeding black men's progress, especially since implicit in his criticism was the idea that advancement of the black race depended solely on the progress of black *men*. However unfair or untrue Parnell's statements were, the cultural politics of the Black Power era had a huge impact on the psychology of black hair. According to Ayana D. Byrd and Lori L. Tharps, black hair underwent its biggest transformation in American history during the mid-1960s. They contend that the way blacks wore their hair shifted from a matter of "style" to a political and cultural "statement." "Right or wrong," they argue, "Blacks and Whites came to believe that the way Black people wore their hair said something about their politics."[35] In 1966, four years before Memphis State crowned Maybelline Forbes as its first black homecoming queen, Robyn Gregory of Howard University became the first "Afro-wearing" homecoming queen.[36] So when black students urged black women on campus to stop "imitating something you'll never be," they inextricably linked the political and the physical and argued that women who rejected the mainstream beauty aesthetic were more politically attuned to the "black revolution."

BSA members sensed that the black revolution had finally made its way to Memphis State. Months had passed with no action on their

Homecoming queen Maybelline Forbes. (Courtesy Special Collections Department, University of Memphis)

demands for a Black Studies curriculum and black faculty or for the integration of beauty spaces. Tired of being patient, BSA leaders planned an aggressive protest to publicize the lack of black cheerleaders. Acey recalled recruiting young women who had been cheerleaders in high school to be on the MSU pep squad. Acey suggested that by recruiting black women with prior experience, they would avoid the excuse that they were unfit to cheer.[37] Calling their campaign "Black Power on the Hardwood," the BSA threatened to "perform with a band and freedom singers to prevent the basketball game from taking place"—a televised game against Metro Conference rival Louisville.[38] But someone informed the administration before the black students could act on their plan, which included wearing "Black Panther uniforms" to dramatize the absence of black women on the cheerleading and pep teams.[39]

Still, 1969 was a pivotal year for Memphis State's black students and a year that provided the crack that eventually opened the campus's beauty spaces to black women. Although the Black Power on Hardwood campaign was unsuccessful in terms of providing a visual protest to publicize the campus's inequality in beauty spaces, it acted as an opening salvo for a longer, more sustained movement. Despite claims that the black women were not properly trained, by the next game, two black female students were allowed on the cheerleading squad.[40]

But "token" positions on the cheerleading squad were hardly sufficient. By the spring of 1969, black students were tired of waiting for the administration to act in good faith on their demands, and on April 23 they confronted the university president. Their displeasure was exacerbated by the school's refusal to pay for a visit from Adam Clayton Powell Jr.[41] The confrontation resulted in a sit-in at the administration building, and 109 students were jailed for their participation.

In its aftermath, the students gained several concessions: a black dean, Black Studies courses, and more black athletes on the sports teams. But in line with one of its slogans—"We want our own thing"—the BSA did not simply sit back and wait for the beauty spaces to open organically. BSA members turned their attention to the beauty spaces the administration could not regulate: *Tiger Rag,* sororities, Angel Flight, and campus beauty queens. In May 1969 the BSA held the first "Extravaganza in Black," a celebration of black culture that became an annual affair. The event's centerpiece—the Miss Black Memphis State pageant—marked the first time that black women could showcase their beauty in an open campus forum. Claudia Conner won the crown, and, in a sense, her victory and the ceremony itself broke the seal on one of the most coveted beauty spaces—pageant queen.[42] Even this commemoration of black women on campus and the creation of this parallel space—using beauty, fashion, style, and culture—became its own form of protest.

The Extravaganza in Black, the Miss Black Memphis State pageant, and years of protests finally bore fruit when BSA member Janice Jones won a coveted spot on the Angel Flight squad. Taking seriously her role as the first African American women selected for the squad, Jones vowed that the door would not shut behind her. The *Tiger Rag* captured Jones's excitement and her promise to "raise much hell" on the squad.[43] The newspaper finally accepted more ethnic standards of beauty and culture when Sandra Price became the first black Campus Cutie in October 1969.[44] The *Tiger Rag* also included more articles related to black culture, black dress, and black affairs. Although the BSA was never specifically credited with prompting these changes at Memphis State, its efforts created an awareness of the plight of black students there.

The BSA's goal of full integration without cultural dilution dictated that the organization continue to push the boundaries. Also, black students persistently linked their activism and the integration of beauty spaces with what they called the "black cause." Some female BSA members objected to the involvement of women in the Miss Black Memphis State pageant who were not politically active in the BSA. "Some of the people who ran [for Miss Black Memphis State] had not contributed to the black cause at this school at all. Somebody should have won who went to jail with the 109 students or at least, had shown that she was 'black-spirited,'" a female BSA member complained.[45]

Building on the success of the Extravaganza in Black and the Miss Black Memphis State pageant, BSA leaders pressed to "get in the system," a claim rarely made by black student organizations during the Black Power movement. And getting into the system meant securing a position for a black woman in the most visible campus beauty space.[46] Ironically, this campaign maintained a very patriarchal tone. Men in the BSA leadership made most of the important decisions about these female-only positions. Acey recalled the BSA's decision to use the election of home-coming queen to get into the system:

> We looked around and we saw all these white sororities on cam-pus, homecoming they got signs everywhere. So we called a meet-ing . . . BSA. So we said, "OK, anybody here want to be queen? There are six of ya'll, one of ya'll are going to be the queen . . . so what are we going to do?" We had some straws. We said, "Who-ever pull the longest straw will be the queen. There won't be no dissension, won't be nothing . . . we're going to come out of here as one. Whoever pulls the longest straw will be the queen." When Maybelline Forbes pulled the longest straw, the men cautioned the other women to "keep cool," patronizingly reminding them, "All ya'll [are] queens."[47]

Despite that proclamation, only one woman could actually win the crown, and the organization used its newfound power to get Forbes elected. While the white organizations openly campaigned for their candidates, the BSA kept the name of its candidate quiet and used its own private networks to rally black students and their allies on campus to vote for Forbes. Her victory shocked the predominantly white student body and the city. Forbes's life was threatened, and she was told that if she boarded the queen's float, she would not make it off alive. The BSA understood that for the larger black student body, the issues of inclusion and identity hinged not simply on Black Studies courses and black staff but also on Forbes's treatment in the campus beauty space. The BSA demanded that Forbes be treated with the same "dignity and respect as previous Home-coming Queens" and stated that anything short of that would be a "pub-lic slap in the face."[48]

Forbes, who identified herself as a "civil rights activist" in the *Tiger Rag*'s write-up, pointed first and foremost to her arrest the previous spring during the BSA's 1969 administration building protest to establish her activist credentials. This clearly signaled that her position was more political than aesthetic. In her new role, Forbes promised to represent the school at all times but cautioned that she would "never deny her black-ness."[49] The adversarial relationship between the *Tiger Rag* and the black students continued when the paper openly questioned how Forbes had won. The BSA leadership did not hide their agenda. "Black Power was used to elect Maybelline, just as the white people have used white power to elect their queens," Acey told the paper.[50] Forbes's win not only signaled a shift in what it meant to be a female coed and a black student at Memphis State; it also changed the homecoming queen election process. Candidates no longer had to be backed by an organization to participate in the election; the Student Government Association opened up the field to every female student wishing to run.

A year later, and despite the rule change, Sandra Price made the front page of the *Tiger Rag* under the headline "Black Is Beautiful . . . And Powerful Too" after she was elected homecoming queen.[51] The title of the article acknowledged two important things that neither the paper nor the campus's white majority had recognized before: the viability of blacks, specifically black women, as a standard of beauty that others could admire, and that the consecutive victories by BSA-supported candidates had cemented the organization's place as one of the most powerful blocs at Memphis State—a status achieved in part through protests to gain access to beauty spaces. Whereas men were the vocal component of the BSA's movement, women provided the visual evidence of the organization's success. And for an organization that emphasized inclusion in the system, arguably no position better represented that system than homecoming queen.

The Memphis State BSA used culture, beauty, and femininity as a tool of protest and as an entry point to change the campus's racial dynamics. Black students at MSU linked campus success to the ability to fully integrate into these various campus spaces. By politicizing these positions, they publicized the organization's overall agenda and in the process became a powerful campus constituency. Following Maybelline Forbes's promise not to deny her blackness, the BSA made the same pact—continuing to connect beauty, power, and protest when it proclaimed, "Being Black is Beautiful, we will not settle for less. Why should we?"[52]

Notes

1. "Black Queen Reigns over Homecoming," *Memphis State University Tiger Rag*, October 20, 1970.

2. Ibid.

3. Ibid.

4. Martha Biondi, *The Black Revolution on Campus* (Berkeley: University of California Press, 2014); Stefan M. Bradley, *Harlem versus Columbia: Black Student Power in the Late 1960s* (Urbana-Champaign: University of Illinois Press, 2012); Ibram H. Rogers, *The Black Campus Movement: Black Students and the Racial Reconstitution of Higher Education, 1965–1972* (New York: Palgrave Macmillan, 2012).

5. Rogers, *Black Campus Movement,* 3.

6. William L. Van DeBurg, *New Day in Babylon: The Black Power Movement and American Culture, 1965–1975* (Chicago: University of Chicago Press, 1993), 69–70.

7. Donna J. Murch, *Living for the City: Migration, Education, and the Rise of the Black Panther Party in Oakland, California* (Chapel Hill: University of North Carolina Press, 2010), 4.

8. Shirletta J. Kinchen, *Black Power and the Bluff City: African American Youth and Student Activism in Memphis, 1965–1975* (Knoxville: University of Tennessee Press, 2016), 20.

9. Ibid.

10. Memphis State University Black Student Association, *Black Thesis* 1, no. 1 (1968), Special Collections, University of Memphis; Joy Ann Williamson, "In Defense of Themselves: The Black Student Struggle for Success and Recognition at Predominately White Colleges and Universities," *Journal of Negro Education* 68, no. 1 (Winter 1999): 92–105.

11. Williamson, "In Defense of Themselves," 5.

12. Ibram H. Rogers, "The Marginalization of the Black Campus Movement," *Journal of Social History* 42, no. 1 (Fall 2008): 175–82.

13. Van DeBurg, *New Day in Babylon,* 71.

14. "Black Students Open Office, Schedule Year's Events Program," *Memphis State University Tiger Rag,* April 22, 1969.

15. Ibid.

16. Van DeBurg, *New Day in Babylon,* 65.

17. Memphis State University Black Student Association, *Black Student Appeal* 1, no. 25 (April 1969), Special Collections, University of Memphis; Memphis State University Black Student Association, *Black Thesis: The Realm of the Black Mind* 2, no. 3 (1968), ibid.

18. Memphis State University Black Student Association, *Black Thesis* 3, no. 4 (1969), Special Collections, University of Memphis.

19. Ibid.

20. Gregory S. Parks and Stefan M. Bradley, *Alpha Phi Alpha: A Legacy of Greatness, the Demands of Transcendence* (Lexington: University Press of Kentucky, 2011), 2–5.

21. Jeffrey Harris, "A History of the Development of Greek Life, Religious Organizations and the Black Student Association" (seminar paper, University of Memphis, 2009), 10 (copy in author's possession).

22. Paula S. Giddings, *In Search of Sisterhood: Delta Sigma Theta and the Challenge of the Black Sorority Movement* (New York: William Morrow Paperback, 1994), 46–48.

23. Harris, "History of the Development of Greek Life."

24. Ibid.

25. Kinchen, *Black Power and the Bluff City,* 229.

26. David Acey, interview by the author, Memphis, June 9, 2009.

27. Memphis State University Black Student Association, *Black Thesis: The Realm of the Black Mind* 2, no. 3 (1968).

28. Ibid.

29. Ibid.

30. Ibid.

31. Tanisha C. Ford, *Liberated Threads: Black Women, Style, and the Global Politics of Soul* (Chapel Hill: University of North Carolina Press, 2016), 1.

32. Angela Davis, "Afro Images: Politics, Fashion, and Nostalgia," in *Soul: Black Power, Politics, and Pleasure,* ed. Monique Guillory and Richard C. Green (New York: New York University Press, 1998), 23.

33. Ford, *Liberated Threads,* 3–6.

34. Memphis State University Black Student Association, *Black Thesis: The Realm of the Black Mind* 2, no. 3 (1968).

35. Ayana D. Byrd and Lori L. Tharps, *Hair Story: Untangling the Roots of Black Hair in America* (New York: St. Martin's Griffin, 2002), 51.

36. Susannah Walker, *Style and Status: Selling Beauty to African American Women, 1920–1975* (Lexington: University Press of Kentucky, 2007), 167.

37. Acey interview.

38. Mr. Youngson, "Message to Dr. C. C. Humphreys," November 7, 1968, Special Collections, University of Memphis; Memphis State University Black Student Association, *Black Thesis* 1, no. 2 (n.d.), ibid.

39. Acey interview.

40. Ibid.; Mr. Youngson, "Message to Dr. C. C. Humphreys."

41. Acey interview.

42. Ibid.

43. "Black Students Start New Year," *Memphis State University Tiger Rag,* September 30, 1969.

44. "Campus Cutie," *Memphis State University Tiger Rag,* October 14, 1969.

45. "Speaking Out," *Memphis State University Tiger Rag,* May 20, 1969.

46. Acey interview.

47. Ibid.

48. "Black Queen Reigns over Homecoming."
49. Ibid.
50. Ibid.
51. The same year, the school hired its first black athletic coach, Pete Mitchell.
52. "Black Queen Reigns over Homecoming."

After Stax

Race, Sound, and Neighborhood Revitalization

Zandria F. Robinson

Scores of people descended on an iconic block in South Memphis on an unseasonably warm October day in 2016.[1] They were gathered for the Soulsville Festival, the brainchild of Tonya Dyson, a young entrepreneur, soul singer, and music educator in Memphis. The festival, then in its second year, was the first of its kind to explicitly pay homage to the city's legacy of soul by showcasing new homegrown musical talent. In the shadows of the festival's jubilance were the enduring inequities left by a protracted urban renewal process, deindustrialization, globalization, and the dismantling of one of the neighborhood's key anchor institutions—Stax Records. Though many of the neighborhood's other anchor institutions, including churches, a historically black college, and long-running businesses, remained after the shuttering of Stax, the neighborhood's constituents had experienced decades of economic decline.

The "Soulsville" moniker functions on multiple levels. It is the neighborhood's colloquial name that emerged in the heyday of Stax Records, a counter to Hitsville and Motown that marked the neighborhood's significance in the production of American soul music. It is the twenty-first-century reclamation of "Soulsville" by the foundation of the same name established to memorialize Stax Records on its original site. Yet it is also a powerful idea, one wrapped in color-blind nostalgia, about the possibilities for interracial relations and cooperation in the post–civil rights era. The festival encapsulated the tensions between these different conceptions of Soulsville as neighborhood and musical legacy, as well as the racial and economic friction that continues to shape the neighborhood as it undergoes revitalization.

The product of more than a decade of revitalization efforts, Soulsville now houses a museum that commemorates the record label's rise and fall, an academy that trains young musicians, and a charter middle and high school, all of which fan out from the original Stax Records location. Soulsville's reimagining is explicitly rooted in contested claims to and definitions of the soul sound—what it is, to whom it belongs, and how it should be used. The reconstitution of the Soulsville brand has had mostly flat and uneven economic effects on the surrounding neighborhoods that validate and authenticate it, even as there is new interest in collecting stories, information, and input from South Memphis residents. The Soulsville case presents a different way to discuss gentrification, neighborhood change, and race and class politics in twenty-first-century America in general and in the post–civil rights urban South in particular.

Though the decline of Stax and of its neighborhood are correlated, the former did not cause the latter. Instead, racism, institutionally embedded in local urban policy in a globalizing world, limited and forestalled black power. In the aftermath of this cultural and material destruction of a neighborhood and the consequent destabilization of one of its chief cultural and economic exports, a new kind of power based in sound, nostalgia, and color-blind racial ideologies emerged: *sonic politics.*

This essay examines how sonic politics—ideas about race, place, and the ownership of sound—have shaped neighborhood change in Soulsville and the surrounding South Memphis neighborhoods in tandem with local urban policy, particularly since 1980. As the South Memphis neighborhood is redeveloped by and for competing interests, including the tourism industry, nonprofit organizations, community organizations, social preservationists, foundations, and, most importantly, residents, the battle over the right to the soul sound—the neighborhood's most enduring and profitable commodity—reveals race and class inequities that shaped Soulsville long before Stax. These competing interests continue to influence the neighborhood's future a generation after the record label's demise. People's differing claims to the soul sound help us make sense of the process and consequences of neighborhood redevelopment, revealing how sound and nostalgia solidify and obscure the marginalization of black residents, especially poor and older black residents. In an increasingly complex ownership landscape, who has a right to the place, the sound, and the economic benefits to be reaped from both?

This work is part of a larger project that draws on three years of ethnographic fieldwork, including oral histories with community members and participant observation in community groups and neighborhood institutions, as well as analyses of neighborhood census data over time. Drawing on late geographer Clyde Woods's notion of blues epistemology, the project considers the relationship among black economic self-determination, external economic repression, and the development of a neighborhood-based soul sound that changed the local economy and popular music.[2] Three sources of data are relevant to the conversation: perceptions of neighborhood residents and community organizations, perceptions of individuals acting within one or more of the three parts of Soulsville, and descriptive quantitative data about neighborhood change. As an ethnographer, I am interested in the relationship between everyday interactions and social structures, and my time in South Memphis brought this relationship into sharp relief. I spent time with community groups made up of longtime residents as they strategized plans for the neighborhood, both their own plans and plans in response to redevelopment decisions and efforts by other groups. I also spent time with residents who were not formally organized in community groups but nonetheless had ideas about the neighborhood and revitalization processes. I talked frequently, both informally and formally, with Soulsville Foundation and Stax Music Academy staff; taught in a summer program at Soulsville; participated in a design charette for the Stax Museum of American Soul Music; facilitated lectures and conversations with students and parents at the Stax Music Academy and performed other mentoring work there; and talked with parents and teachers of students at the Soulsville Charter School. People's ability to influence structural change or maintain existing structures is ultimately shaped by race and class disadvantage and advantage, but this does not mean that residents were powerless against the forces of revitalization. Instead, community advocates marshaled ideas about authenticity that connected their past experiences in the neighborhood with their right to shape its present and future.

I begin with an examination of the neighborhood's history before and during the rise of Stax, tracing its early evolution from an overflow space for a black population that had outgrown its allotted segregated space in North Memphis and Orange Mound into a center for black business and culture. I then chronicle the overlapping changes in the neighborhood from the 1960s to the present, juxtaposing Stax's heyday with the initial decline of the neighborhood wrought by desegregation processes and neglectful urban policy. Finally, I highlight the relationship between discourses of neighborhood revitalization and the politics of neighborhood change, including housing destruction, school closures, and declining anchor institutions.

Before Stax

In the late nineteenth and early twentieth centuries, African Americans migrating from the Mississippi Delta and surrounding rural communities were segregated into South Memphis as other black communities in North Memphis and Orange Mound battled overcrowding. Political scientists Christopher Silver and John V. Moeser refer to the kind of neighborhood arrangements prevalent in southern cities like Memphis and Atlanta before the 1970s as "separate cities."[3] Unlike in the ghettos of midwestern and northeastern cities, black population expansion in southern cities almost always meant land expansion as well. That is, whereas exponentially increasing black populations in Chicago, for instance, were crowded into the same Black Belt land mass, the sheer number of black urban southerners, and the explicit commitment to segregation, meant that urban policy needed to ensure separate spaces. This policy of spatial expansion in tandem with black population expansion continued until the 1960s, when desegregation and urban renewal allowed southern cities to begin to mirror the spatial organization and ghettoization patterns of their northern metropolitan counterparts. Before the 1970s, though, Silver and Moeser argue that it was in these separate spaces that black communities devised the organizational structures that would power the civil rights movement.

The settling of African Americans in South Memphis was a function of black population growth outpacing the space allotted for black residents. During and after Reconstruction, the city's white elite, anxious to manage the growing black population and simultaneously maintain a biracial system of segregation, ushered black people into communities south of downtown that extended eastward from the Mississippi River.

As a result, South Memphis developed and expanded south of the central business district and downtown area along the river, eventually reaching the Mississippi state line through annexation. It also expanded eastward to North and South Parkways, had an interstate built through it, and was flanked in some places by the region's railways. Today, this collection of neighborhoods contains nearly one-fifth of the population residing within the city limits. It is also home to black populations that bear the legacy of the systemic racial inequality that affected neighborhood development and urban policy.

Despite the ramshackle nature of the land, its spatial organization, and the erected housing, South Memphis became a thriving entrepreneurial black community, a separate city with broad political and economic power. It grew and expanded southward as the city of Memphis annexed land down to the Mississippi state line to accommodate the growing black populations and ensure that they did not seep into white neighborhoods in East Memphis. For a few decades, even with its relatively larger size, South Memphis surpassed its generally wealthier counterpart North Memphis in percentage of home ownership, with more than half of black residents owning their own homes in 1940. In particular, it boasted a prosperous, semi-integrated tract of wealthy and professional African Americans, including the family of Robert Church Sr., who was much lauded as the South's first black millionaire.

Yet whites felt threatened by the neighborhood's success from the outset. Individual whites, white politicians, and wealthy whites with the power to influence urban policy ensured that black people were unable to realize the self-determination that their political and economic power otherwise would have allowed. The history of South Memphis is punctuated by key incidents of whites using physical, political, and social violence to destroy blacks. The first was the massacre of black people and anchor institutions right after freedom in 1866, followed by the murder of three black grocers—Thomas Moss, Calvin McDowell, and Henry Stewart—in 1892. The 1950s saw the destruction of the Church family mansion on Lauderdale Street and surrounding middle-class communities on Vance Avenue and their replacement with housing projects. Finally, there was the closing and razing of Stax in the 1980s. The neighborhood's revitalization since the 1980s, particularly by white interests, carries this baggage of the violent and systematic destruction of black communities.

The aftermath of Reconstruction is replete with narratives of white people destroying entire black communities, particularly economically successful ones, but the case of South Memphis reflects the ruthlessness of white power in the face of black existence even before Reconstruction took hold. In 1866, before much of South Memphis had been incorporated into the city limits, the community became the site of one of the most significant white massacres of blacks in history. After an altercation between black Union soldiers and white police officers, the latter group facilitated a white mob that burned more than two dozen churches, homes, and schools; raped five women; killed forty-six black men, women, and children; and robbed and assaulted scores of others over the course of a couple of days in early May.[4] The unprecedented violence arose from hostile Irish immigrants and other white groups taking action against black populations in South Memphis and reflected the highest of anxieties about class, masculinity, and race in the months after the end of the Civil War. No one was punished for the hundreds of thousands of dollars in property damage or the loss of life. The aftermath of the massacre encouraged city officials and planners, already committed to segregation, to develop a system of racialized spatial organization that kept white and black groups separate.

The violence of the 1866 massacre reverberated throughout black communities up and down the Mississippi River and beyond. Yet black strivings for self-determination continued. By 1890, South Memphis's black communities, some of which had been incorporated into the city, had settled into a rhythm, if an uneasy one, with their white counterparts. White hostility toward black people persisted, however, always on the brink of violence as white groups became increasingly resentful of black power. Still, a black professional and small-business-owner class had emerged and in some cases lived alongside white middle-class people. Thriving black institutions, including the church, the press, and schools, were a testament to black existence and resistance in postmassacre, post-Reconstruction Memphis.

The emergence and success of black businesses meant competition for white businesses, which had relied on the destruction and marginalization of black property and business as central to their business models. Moreover, partially out of necessity, black people had begun to pool their resources to support their communities. People's Grocery, for instance, opened in 1889 and was essentially a food cooperative owned by multiple partners, including Thomas Moss, who was also a postman. Located in a South Memphis neighborhood called the Curve, which was still outside city limits in 1890, People's Grocery was a destination for black people inside and outside the city. It had begun to compete successfully with a neighboring white-owned grocery and was thus a source of enmity for whites. When People's Grocery employees defended a black boy from attack by whites outside the store, they became a target for those who were eager to destroy the store and what it symbolized about black power and economic freedom in South Memphis. In the end, the black grocers who had defended themselves from attacks on their bodies and property were kidnapped and lynched by a white mob. People's Grocery, located around the corner from where Stax would be sited some sixty-five years later, was sold to its white competitor, one of the central instigators of the violence.

Ida B. Wells decried the violence and its racist capriciousness in an editorial for her paper the *Free Speech and Headlight of Memphis,* in which she reported Thomas Moss's last words: "Tell my people go West." Some black people who had the means to do so did move west and headed to Oklahoma, despite propaganda from the white media that described the territory as a lawless space of Native American violence. More than 5,000 black people left the city as a result of the violence, deploying their economic and political power as citizens, laborers, and consumers to vote with their feet. Because of Wells's activism in the aftermath of the lynchings, her newspaper office was burned by whites and a bounty was put on her head. Though white mob violence abated somewhat in the early twentieth century as segregation more strictly separated blacks and whites (particularly blacks from poor whites), white political violence rose in the era of machine boss Edward H. Crump and caused a similar kind of destruction of black community power.

Crump's rise was aided in part by the Church family, whose sophisticated political and business acumen buoyed black power in South Memphis and the façade of black power in Memphis at large. However, as historian Preston Lauterbach notes, Crump, in tandem with a Republican Party eager to oust black partisans, conspired to dismantle the Churches' political power structure.[5] The destruction and exile of the Church family neutralized the political threat of wealthy African Americans in local and state power structures, ensuring that black power remained conscripted to the separate city for most of the twentieth century.

Between the 1930s and 1950s, Memphis began an aggressive annexation campaign, acquiring areas to the north, south, and east of the city limits to increase the tax base, regain white populations that had left the city for the suburbs, relocate black families who had been displaced by so-called slum clearance, and, most important, maintain segregation. As the city expanded geographically, it also limited the spatial footprint of African Americans, using federal funding to destroy single-family homes and construct segregated buildings consisting of several hundred units each. After establishing the first such housing in North Memphis, the city turned to South Memphis in 1940. The decade saw a dramatic increase in public housing construction in South Memphis, and one of the first was the William H. Foote Homes on Lauderdale, across from the Church mansion. As a result of the influx of public housing rental units, by the end of the decade, black home ownership in South Memphis, once well over 50 percent, had dropped to 29 percent. Conversely, home ownership in North Memphis, with its smaller African American footprint and exponentially fewer public housing units, increased. Thus, black populations were constrained in general, and the percentage of middle-class African Americans in the city was specifically limited. By destroying pathways to the attainment of middle-class status through the destruction of single-family housing and the construction of public housing, the city of Memphis systematically disenfranchised African Americans and stunted economic growth in near perpetuity.

It was in fact the quest to keep African Americans out of East Memphis and from expanding in North Memphis that made Stax's siting in the abandoned Capitol Movie Theater on McLemore possible. Capitol was a white theater, even though by the 1940s, several of the streets that intersected McLemore between Bellevue and Mississippi were home to African American families. In most cases, empty properties and blight were caused by white flight from the relatively integrated neighborhood to newly established white communities in the east, some of which were still outside the city limits. Like People's Grocery and the Church mansion before it, Stax became a bastion of community-based economic power that was ultimately undone by white people and political structures resistant to black self-determination. Although Stax has been memorialized and reanimated through the education of young people, these processes have not translated into socioeconomic opportunity.

Stax in Black South Memphis

In the northeast corner of South Memphis, the block bounded by Bellevue and Mississippi on the east and west and by McLemore and Walker on the south and north was a thriving, if changing, community in 1960. Despite empty homes and businesses as a result of two decades of black displacement, white flight, and the concentration of government-funded low-income housing throughout South Memphis, the neighborhood was becoming a thriving enclave of working-class and middle-class African American residents. The neighborhood was home to a range of businesses and churches, many of which predated Stax, as well as the city's historically black LeMoyne-Owen College. Still, the neighborhood's anchor institutions, which had served as economic, intellectual, and cultural engines despite the community's changing configuration, were given new legitimacy when the record label occupied the empty theater. Even though Stax founders Will Stewart and Estelle Axton were white, and even though the theater had been white, by 1960, South Memphis was a definitively black neighborhood, and Stax quickly became a label driven by black artists and black music.[6] Indeed, the label benefited from the presence of these institutions and from the residents who brought them to life. The neighborhood's gospel roots, nurtured at community churches such as Metropolitan Baptist and Second Congregational, were harnessed by Stax artists in the service of a new sound and a new historical moment in the nation and the neighborhood.

By the 1970s, the music industry was one of the largest employers of African Americans in the city of Memphis, contributing tens of millions of dollars annually to the local economy. As a city, Memphis was a leader in the global music industry, recognized not only for its distinct contributions to sound but also for its prolific production of recordings at multiple iconic studios and labels across the city. Stax contributed to the music industry's centrality in Memphis, as well as to the city's role as a globally recognized music hub, employing scores of African American people over time. In less than two decades, the label had created an iconic sound that temporarily transformed the neighborhood and forever transformed global music culture. It broke sales records, made legends, and generated neighborhood-based black economic power in the twilight of the Jim Crow era. Stax musicians and staff, many from the South Memphis neighborhood and others from nearby small towns in Mississippi and Tennessee, made soul music that traveled the nation and the globe. In a segregated society dependent on the marginalization of African American labor, the soul sound was once a source of economic stability and an articulation of freedom for African Americans.

Although Stax artists enjoyed wide acclaim both nationally and internationally, in Memphis, the label, its artists, and neighborhood residents were seen as disruptive to the city's white power structures, which were rooted in entrenched machine politics, labor disenfranchisement, and racial intimidation. Black strivings for economic self-sufficiency, which increased under the leadership of Al Bell at Stax beginning in 1969, were met with resistance. After all, black economic aspirations and attainment were supposed to be constrained, and wealth diluted if not eradicated, by segregation and the concentration of low-income housing in the community. However, urban policy that limited black economic resources and political power in some ways further enshrined the inherent assets of the separate city. In the Stax years, South Memphis became its own chocolate city, a cultural juggernaut that transmitted out to other chocolate cities from Harlem to Watts. The neighborhood's human capital, its most enduring asset, was essential to its success.

Stax's unprecedented and distinctive success ironically set the stage for its spectacular fall. The orchestrated destruction of Stax was a continuation of the racist urban policy that Crump had initiated in the 1930s and 1940s, as well as the city's history of antiblack violence in the face of black economic ascendancy. White financiers, in collusion with other white city elites, were fed up with "niggers riding around in Cadillacs with white girls," so they froze Stax's assets and called in a $100,000 loan for immediate repayment. The label was compelled to file for bankruptcy, folded, and lost access to many of its master recordings, an economic resource for its artists and the Soulsville community. In December 1975 federal marshals seized the building and led Bell out at gunpoint. Closed and shuttered, the building fell into disrepair and was soon sold to the Church of God in Christ for $1, on the condition that it raze the building, which it did in 1989. Just as Crump had ordered the burning of the Church mansion—an act largely seen as political violence against the entire African American community—white elites ensured the destruction of a resurgent source of black pride and power on another South Memphis block, using black religious folks—the music's sonic foundation—as the symbolic axe.

South Memphis had been designed by white planners, politicians, and elites to fail black people. The community nevertheless thrived for short periods through individual and group ingenuity and resistance in spite of these predetermined conditions. For Stax and black Memphians, Martin Luther King's assassination had invigorated their commitment to resistance, as the Stax sound and politics moved definitively toward an epistemology of Black Power. This critical turn, coupled with the label's increasing economic success, would not be tolerated by whites who were intent on keeping black people spatially and socially "in their place." The destruction of Stax, the city's neglect of the neighborhood, and desegregation pushed some black middle-class people out of the neighborhood and has continued to deter economic and population growth since 1980. The people who stayed, their children, and their grandchildren struggled to make sense of the loss and salvage what they could.

Soul Power, Sound Power

In early 2012, nearly forty years after Stax went bankrupt and closed, President Barack Obama, campaigning for his second term, made a fundraising stop at Harlem's Apollo Theatre. In front of the packed house, Obama offered up the opening line from Memphis soul singer Al Green's "Let's Stay Together." "I'm," he sang—and then paused as the crowd erupted in cheers—"so in love with you." Although Green recorded for a competing label, the collective sound produced by Hi Records, Stax

Records, and Royal Studios had become synonymous with a global soul sound that came from Memphis. Loud acclaim continued for several seconds before the president could begin his remarks, and YouTube videos of the brief performance received more than 10 million views. Using the popular classic song in a black space, Obama took ownership of the soul sound to mark his racial authenticity and tap into a collective African American and national consciousness.

The next year, Stax was in the White House when "living legends" such as Mavis Staples were backed by the "future of Stax," young musicians from the Stax Music Academy. The performance, aired across the country on PBS, was exemplary of the Soulsville brand's narrative that, despite the demise of the label, the sound lives on. In the nation's capital—the original chocolate city turned latte metropolis—the performance offered up the music, the sound, the legacy, and the legacy's future as a kind of cultural currency for the city of Memphis.

The soul sound, and Memphis's place in creating it, has been definitively enshrined as the city's chief cultural export. Sound shapes our lives in important ways that are at once aesthetic and political, and the soul sound is no exception.[7] Sound matters for movement politics and identities,[8] for ideas about race and authenticity,[9] and for nation-making projects.[10] At the White House, as in other showcase performances, the sound's role as the soundtrack for and articulation of a black resistance politics was de-emphasized. Instead, in a "postracial" moment with a black First Family, the soul sound was deployed as a sanitized version of where we had been, a testament to how far we had come, and a promise for the future.

The road to the White House performance, and to its version of the sonic and political history of South Memphis, had begun in the early 1990s, shortly after the Stax building was torn down. Preservationists and philanthropists, spurred by the global popularity of the music that had come from McLemore Avenue, worked to memorialize what had been there. It seemed that, except for the sound, everything of value was gone—the building had been razed, and the rights to the music were now owned largely by California-based Concord Records. The power, profitability, and local and global resonance of the sound jump-started a long process of neighborhood reclamation, revitalization, and change.

Not everyone agrees on what the sound means, how it should be used, and, perhaps most important, who should use it. Because Concord Records owns the masters, stakeholders are battling over what is left: the right to control *ideas* about the soul sound. Museum and music academy officials often talk about the sound as a site of racial harmony, a common language that people can speak across races, and their approach suggests that we should apply this use of the soul sound to today's racial troubles. Investors and politicians see the grittiness of the soul sound as a marker of race and place authenticity and thus as public and private property that should generate income for the city and financiers. Residents, especially those who stayed, believe the sound is an archive of African Americans' struggle for racial equality and a sonic history of black South Memphis's strivings for political and economic sustainability in the face of orchestrated efforts to destabilize the community. They believe the sound belongs primarily to the people of the neighborhood, past and present, and that its use should be directed toward the psychological, political, and economic empowerment of the black people Stax once symbolized.

Post-Soulsville

One of the first cities to build housing projects, Memphis was also among the first to demolish them with a new wave of federal funding from Hope VI beginning in the 1990s. The Department of Housing and Urban Development had replaced the discourses of "slum clearance" popularized in the 1930s and the "urban renewal" of the 1960s (colloquially called "Negro removal") with language such as "revitalization" and "preservation." For more than fifty years, scores of black people had been pushed into the nondescript brick buildings surrounded by iron gates in South Memphis. But by the 1990s and early 2000s, new policies aimed to reduce density and improve neighborhood quality of life pushed people out.

Much of the overall population decline in South Memphis from 1990 to the present can be attributed to the reduction of available housing units in the community. Newer facilities—mixes of single-family homes, town houses, and apartments—replaced most, but not all, units. Further, continued white flight to the east, coupled with a new housing voucher program that allowed residents of government housing to move outside of housing projects, opened up housing stock in new places and encouraged population decline. Rates of home ownership increased, but largely as a result of the reduction in the ratio of rental units to single-family, owner-occupied homes.

The institutionalization of Hope VI facilitated, influenced, and was shaped by the neighborhood's changing spatial arrangements and demographics. City officials used population declines in South Memphis to justify closing elementary, middle, and secondary schools. As South Memphis's historically black Booker T. Washington High School was being honored with a visit from President Obama in 2011 for winning the Race to the Top competition, many of its students were being displaced from Cleaborn Homes, the largest housing project in the city. As other low-income housing was demolished and more people left the neighborhood, more schools were closed. Vance Middle School, near the original site of the Church mansion, was closed owing to underutilization of its building space, and the remaining students were sent to nearby Booker T. Washington in the 2015–2016 academic year. This loss of housing and these school closures are reflective of the city's long-term disinvestment in the neighborhood's black residents, even as revitalization dollars continue to shape who and what will remain. As longtime residents age and younger families choose neighborhoods with more resources, amenities, and stability, the population decline will continue. This will enable more powerful stakeholders to make economic decisions about space and to profit unevenly from revitalization efforts that are made possible by the poorest people. These processes may deliver the final, fatal blow to the South Memphis community as a current and future space of black pride, self-determination, and socioeconomic success.

This material reality of a community of black people surviving in distress and rupture surrounds the Soulsville campus. Yet, the discursive reality that Soulsville creates sublimates this material reality. As an anchor institution in its own right, Soulsville presents a linear story of triumph, of the legacy, and the future of a legacy, that is in some ways at odds with the lived experiences of South Memphis residents.

Soulsville Town Center was a mixed-use retail and business building erected across from the Stax Museum in 2009. It was supposed to serve as another anchor for the neighborhood and to house businesses, offices, and services for the community's most vulnerable residents. The building never achieved its intended goals. In August 2015 it was sold at auction to a philanthropist and former Hollywood filmmaker with connections to St. Jude Children's Hospital. The LeMoyne-Owen Community Development Corporation, which owned the space, had struggled to come up with the money to prevent the sale, and the development corporation was blamed for the building's failure. According to some residents, though, LeMoyne-Owen had been shut out of the auction process. For long-time residents suspicious of the process and cautious about partnerships with philanthropists, even those who seem well-intentioned, the outcome seemed too convenient.

In a meeting that included few residents but several architects, financiers, philanthropists, and other elite and generally white decision makers, the new owner shared his vision of the redesigned Town Center, which would include a movie theater, counseling services, and a rock-climbing wall. For some residents, the event signaled a new era of gentrification (as opposed to revitalization) in their neighborhood—one that would likely displace many poor people and threaten some of the more stable residents as well. Their organizing efforts drew on the soul sound to lay claim to neighborhood legacies and legitimize their respective visions for the neighborhood.

According to the Soulsville Foundation, its three entities—the Stax Museum of American Soul, the Soulsville Charter School, and the Stax Music Academy—represent the past, present, and future of Stax, respectively. Yet each entity almost exclusively memorializes soul. From the Stax hits played on a loop over the museum's external speakers to millennial and Z generation musicians' constant reprisal of those hits to the rigidly operated and hypersegregated charter school, Soulsville elites are implicitly committed to narrating a past that yields a postracial future—one in which the material realities of the neighborhood and the broader social movements of black resistance, such as Black Lives Matter, do not exist. In Soulsville, the soul sound is memorialized in these three institutions, and this memorialization is tied to philanthropists' and funders' interest in nostalgic and sanitized narratives of racial harmony through music.

Today, a broad cross section of Memphis's power elite recognizes the profitability of the soul sound, particularly if it is shorn of the roots of its radical critique of racism. Memories of the soul sound, like that called up by President Obama's performance, and ideas about the music, place, and race are the dominant economic currency, exchanged annually for millions of tourist dollars. Stax is now a museum in South Memphis, a monument to the heyday of the neighborhood and the label. Distinctly post–civil rights forms of African American musical expression, including neo-soul, punk rock, and hip-hop, are often seen as a threat to this soul sound narrative—and its economic profitability—by local politicians, businesses, and music elites. While city elites have used the soul sound to tell a story about racial harmony and music as the great equalizer, longtime residents emphasize the sound as an archive of triumph despite dogged and violent racial discrimination.

Residents and in some cases Soulsville staff have contested the official memorialization of Stax with their own memory projects. As the neighborhood declined in the 1990s and revitalization plans got under way, residents redefined what it means to live in and be committed to South Memphis. They inserted themselves into discussions about the Soulsville Foundation's projects and became indispensable to the process, even as tensions about ownership, history, and race shaped these negotiations. In community meetings and events, longtime Soulsville residents emphasized that it was the people who made the neighborhood and thus Stax and the soul sound. They called for the memorialization of not only the music and musicians but also the everyday South Memphis residents who facilitated the community's resistance to white racism. Residents see themselves as citizens of soul, cocreators of the neighborhood and its sound, and caretakers of its legacy. And they are invested in preserving the neighborhood's people, encouraging younger generations not to sell or rent their homes and to re-create the thriving small-business landscape that defined many pockets of South Memphis over time.

The Afterlife of Soul

The South Memphis neighborhood that was once home to Stax Records and now houses the Stax Museum of American Soul is the stage on which different power brokers use rhetorical and sonic strategies to claim ownership of the soul sound and the neighborhood's future. From Soulsville, a sound emerged that is "burned into our consciousness"; it is "what we hear today on the radio" and "the soundtrack for liberation."[11] These actors, which include longtime neighborhood residents, newcomers, nonprofit organizations, community development corporations, and the Soulsville Foundation itself, draw on sonic politics to lay claim to the soul sound and shape neighborhood revitalization efforts in Soulsville according to their respective tunes. At the center of their claims are divergent definitions of the soul sound, notions of ownership, and perspectives on the use of the sound.

By the time a replica of Stax was erected—complete with the Capitol Theater's marquee and the sloping floors of its aisles, which became Studio A—many people who had lived in the neighborhood during the Stax years had left South Memphis and headed east in the city or south to expanding DeSoto County in Mississippi. The museum commemorates the Stax years, the academy trains new musicians in Stax classics, and the charter school boasts 100 percent college acceptance for its largely black student body. Housing projects have been demolished, a community development corporation provides musicians with rehearsal space in the revitalized home of blues pianist Memphis Slim, and the Town Center's redesign will soon be under way. The Memphis soul sound floats through the neighborhood every day from speakers atop the Stax Museum of American Soul Music; it is the foundation for a new, resurrected, and re-imagined Soulsville that uses the soulful sound of past racial struggles to drown out present parallels.

Even if the sound endures, we are witnessing the soul sound's after-life, which is inextricable from the neighborhood's afterlife as an authenticator of memorialization projects. As a contested tool of political power and a building block for a new movement of young black creatives in Memphis, the soul sound is a commodity that provides historical legitimacy to social, political, aesthetic, and cultural movements. Young artists, including residents of the neighborhood and those who live in bordering neighborhoods and frequent South Memphis businesses, argue for the sound's use once again as a distinctively black economic engine for community empowerment, resistance to racism, and social change. It is not yet clear whether their vision for the neighborhood, which depends on the training and retaining of young residents, will come to fruition. But it is certain that for most residents, the renewal of a black South Memphis, complete with the power to self-determine, is central to the afterlife of the soul sound in the community.

Notes

1. South Memphis is a broad term for several neighborhoods that stretch from the southwesternmost corner of the city, north along the river to downtown Memphis, and east from the river to US 78. This chapter focuses on the neighborhoods around the site of the Stax Museum of American Soul Music, whose residents are most involved in conversations and negotiations about changes brought about by the Soulsville Foundation's presence.

2. Clyde Woods, *Development Arrested: The Blues and Plantation Power in the Mississippi Delta* (New York: Verso, 2000).

3. Christopher Silver and John V. Moeser, *The Separate City: Black Communities in the Urban South* (Lexington: University Press of Kentucky, 1995).

4. Steven Ash, *A Massacre in Memphis: The Race Riot that Shook the Nation One Year after the Civil War* (New York: Hill and Wang, 2013).

5. See Preston Lauterbach, *Beale Street Dynasty: Sex, Song, and the Struggle for the Soul of Memphis* (New York: W. W. Norton, 2015).

6. The notion of "black" music or "race" music is a function of the music industry's construction of a biracial, segmented market of sound that ultimately benefited white artists and music executives.

7. Jennifer Lynn Stoever-Ackerman, Liana Sylva, and Aaron Trammell, *Sounding Out! The Sound Studies Blog,* http://soundstudiesblog.com/ (accessed 2014).

8. Shana Redmond, *Anthem: Social Movements and the Sound of Solidarity in the Diaspora* (New York: New York University Press, 2014).

9. Charles Hughes, *Country Soul: Making Music and Making Race in the American South* (Chapel Hill: University of North Carolina Press, 2015).

10. Jocelyne Guilbaut, *Governing Sound: The Cultural Politics of Trinidad's Carnival Musics* (Chicago: University of Chicago Press, 2007).

11. Robert Gordon, *Respect Yourself: Stax Records and the Soul Explosion* (New York: Bloomsbury USA, 2013), xii.

Black Workers Matter

The Continuing Search for Racial and Economic Equality in Memphis

Michael K. Honey

> You are reminding, not only Memphis, but you are reminding the nation that it is a crime for people to live in this rich nation and receive starvation wages. . . . Now the problem is not only unemployment. Do you know that most of the people in our country are working every day? And they are making wages so low that they cannot begin to function in the mainstream of the economic life of our nation.
> —Martin Luther King Jr., March 18, 1968

Speaking at Mason Temple to an overflow audience of hundreds of black men on strike and thousands of people supporting them, Dr. King declared, "You are going beyond purely civil rights to questions of human rights." King had come to Memphis as part of his Poor People's Campaign, seeking to create a mass coalition of the poor that included African Americans, Mexican Americans, Native Americans, and whites. Congress and the nation, he said, should guarantee a basic standard of living—decent housing, health care, education, and meaningful employment—for all. King called this "phase two" of the freedom struggle. In Memphis, he declared, "Now our struggle is for genuine equality, which means economic equality."[1]

King called on the city government to recognize Local 1733 of the American Federation of State, County, and Municipal Employees (AFSCME) and allow the checkoff of union dues from workers' paychecks, something Mayor Henry Loeb had vowed he would never do. The struggle for labor rights and decent employment in Memphis, King insisted, remained central to improving the lot of the working poor. After raising the applause lines higher and higher, King paused for a moment and then made a stunning proposal: "I tell you what you ought to do, and you are together enough to do it: in a few days you ought to get together and just have a *general work stoppage* in the city of Memphis." The audience responded with thunderous cheers as people leaped from their seats and raised their fists in jubilation. King had struck a chord: everyone knew that African Americans did most of the heavy, hard work in Memphis and always had. Black workers, black students, black teachers, and black ministers and their congregations could shut the city's economy down. When King returned to the microphone, he promised to return in a few days to lead a mass march and a mass strike.[2]

General strikes have happened rarely in American history, with mixed results, but King's proposal could have worked. Instead, a freak snowstorm prevented his return. When he finally arrived back in Memphis on March 28, a handful of young people at the rear of a mass march on Beale Street broke some store windows. March organizers thought police agents might have been responsible, and the window breaking triggered a riot by the police. They attacked people in the streets, in a restaurant, and in parking lots; they blasted marchers hiding inside Clayborn Temple with tear gas. In a local housing project, a white officer pushed the barrel of his shotgun into the stomach of sixteen-year-old Larry Payne, who had his hands in the air, according to witnesses, and fired. With Payne's death, riots spread, and Mayor Loeb brought in the National Guard. Memphis suddenly looked like a war zone, as troops with drawn bayonets roamed the streets.[3]

His national reputation as a proponent of nonviolence on the line, King returned on April 3. Speaking again at Mason Temple, he invoked a long history of human rights revolutions and called on people to follow the "dangerous unselfishness" of Jesus. He recalled that a pilgrim from the disparaged people of Samaria, traveling the dangerous Jericho Road, had saved the life of a beaten and robbed man of another race left by the side of the road. King urged the black middle class to be like the Good Samaritan and stand with an outcast group: poor sanitation workers. In concluding this, his last speech, King made a promise for the ages: "I may not get there with you. But I want you to know tonight that we as a people will *get* to the Promised Land!"[4]

On April 4, 1968, an assassin murdered King. Ever since, we have sought to absorb the true meaning of King's legacy. Some saw King's death and the subsequent failure of the Poor People's Campaign as the end of the civil rights movement. Yet King's last campaign also represents a powerful moment that linked labor rights, civil rights, calls for peace, and Black Power demands to a multiethnic constituency with a broad agenda for change. In Memphis, in contrast to every other southern city, a cadre of white trade unionists, revolted by Mayor Loeb's anti-union stance, militantly supported the sanitation workers. On April 8 nearly 40,000 people, including many trade unionists, came to Memphis from all over the nation to honor King and support his last campaign. National pressure from President Lyndon Johnson on down forced the city to recognize a public employees' union, to negotiate better wages and a contract, and to deduct union dues from workers' paychecks. When the city signed a contract with AFSCME on April 16, Local 1733 organizer T. O. Jones exclaimed, "We have lost many things. But we have got the victory."[5] For the next twenty years, Local 1733 shaped the political and economic life of Memphis, leading to a higher-paid public employment sector that ultimately included police, firefighters, and public school employees. Ironically, the police force became one of the city's most powerful public unions. Nationally, public employee unionism became the fastest-growing union sector, and AFSCME helped rebuild a declining labor movement and bolster civil rights demands.[6]

King's last campaign should shift our understanding to a legacy that goes beyond civil rights and encompasses a broader framework of human rights and economic justice that is still highly relevant. James Lawson, the black minister who led the Memphis strike, points out that, as an advocate of nonviolence, King aimed to overturn *all* violence, including the violence of racism, war, and economic deprivation.[7] King's plunge into labor struggles also had a long pedigree, one that should inform our understanding of the civil rights revolution and its legacy. King had supported unions since his work in a tobacco field as a teenager, and he had been a preacher of the black social gospel all his life. He came to maturity in the 1940s and 1950s, when American unions reached their peak of membership and power. He admired how they pioneered the sit-down strike and other forms of direct action in the 1930s. King worked closely with the left wing of unions in a labor–civil rights coalition from the Montgomery bus boycott onward, and in 1967 he keynoted the Labor for Peace conference in Chicago to stop the Vietnam War. In a meeting of teamster shop stewards in New York City, King called for a "second phase" of the black freedom movement.[8] His work was firmly rooted in beliefs and experiences that led to his call for a new movement for "economic equality" in Memphis.[9]

What has happened to King's dream of economic equality? If it has not been achieved, why not? What has become of the black working poor he strove to liberate? By looking at events before and after that April 4, 1968, moment in Memphis, we can more readily understand the importance of King's last campaign and more easily place the long black freedom struggle into the context of the long march of black labor history.

Plantation Capitalism and Black Labor Organizing

In Memphis and throughout the Mississippi Delta, slavery provided the taproot of capital accumulation, based on the exploitation of African American labor. In the postslavery era, segregation and the denial of education to African Americans kept black workers doing poorly paid, backbreaking labor. Racial division undergirded an economic system based on cheap labor in part by making it extremely difficult to organize unions. Scholar-activist W. E. B. DuBois saw the division of workers by race as the downfall of the labor movement in the South.[10] James Lawson called this linkage of racism to labor exploitation "plantation capitalism." Black Memphians identified the mentality that went with the economics of America's racial capitalism as the "plantation mentality," and that system pervaded race relations throughout the surrounding countryside.[11] Cheap wages and exploited labor imposed a heavy burden on the region. Employers insisted on low wages, which created underconsumption and weak internal economic markets. Low wages and incomes kept living standards and educational levels down; this underdevelopment of the region's people kept most of them in poverty.[12]

In Memphis, white workers in the trades used unions to freeze black workers out; white working-class citizens sided with white politicians and white employers against the interests of working-class and poor African Americans. Nonetheless, the Jim Crow system of white supremacy could more accurately be called "white business supremacy." From before World War I to the 1954 *Brown v. Board of Education* desegregation decision, Edward H. Crump, a white politician from a Mississippi plantation, pursued his business interests in Memphis and created a tidy city based on one-man tyranny, making Memphis a hard nut to crack for union and civil rights organizers. In the 1930s and 1940s Memphis did not need the Ku Klux Klan: white police officers, many of them secret KKK members, carried out a reign of terror against both black and white workers who tried to organize unions. Police also brutalized and murdered black people in the street at random and expelled anyone, white or black, who spoke out against the Crump regime or tried to organize. Crump made segregation profitable for the city's white elite.[13]

For most of its history, white economic and political elites dominated Memphis, but not without resistance from working people. When I first moved to Memphis as a civil liberties organizer in 1970, I had the impression that, prior to the 1968 sanitation strike, workers had not significantly challenged the city's low-wage, segregationist labor system. Historical documents and my interviews with veteran union organizers proved me wrong. Although Boss Crump and white employers largely prevailed, the 1930s industrial union movement did penetrate Memphis. From 1935 to 1955, during the era of the Congress of Industrial Organizations (CIO), many international unions rejected segregation; a few organizers from those unions dared to organize in Memphis, often at the risk of their lives. In the 1940s surprising alliances emerged, often fueled by leftist union organizers, black and white, who led campaigns for labor rights, civil liberties, and black civil rights.[14]

At the end of World War II, unions represented about 32,500 industrial workers and a similar number of craft workers in Memphis. In the postwar era, CIO unions provided a core of voters who helped elect racially "moderate" Democratic liberals such as Tennessee senators Estes Kefauver and Albert Gore Sr. and Memphis congressman George Grider. New Deal laws and court rulings enforced union rights, and by the 1960s, Tennessee had one of the highest rates of unionization in the South (around 20 percent). All this aligned white and black workers against the old cheap labor system.[15] It soon became an era of "opportunities lost," however; McCarthyism, anticommunist hearings, and union purges largely destroyed white labor allies of the civil rights movement.[16] King later built national alliances with leftist-led civil rights unions that had survived the purges, and he became a favorite speaker at their conventions, but few of those unions had any power in the South.[17]

White craft unionists kept generations of black workers out of the skilled trades, while white industrial employers and many white workers tried to keep blacks locked into the lowest-paid, most dangerous, least desirable factory jobs. Yet interviews with black Memphians revealed that many of them made significant gains through industrial unions. For example, Hillie Pride started out making 10 to 15 cents an hour at the Firestone factory during the Depression, but through unionization he ended up making $20 an hour in the 1970s. An important core of Memphis industrial workers gained citizenship rights on the job. Black workers in CIO unions could vote and hold union offices—rights that were usually impossible to obtain in the Jim Crow system. With higher wages, limited hours of work, and access to pensions and health care, unionized black industrial workers built the black middle class in Memphis.[18]

After World War II and into the 1960s, black auto and rubber worker George Holloway, furniture workers Leroy and Alzada Clark, and food and tobacco workers Leroy Boyd and Earl Fisher, along with a small number of white equal rights unionists, challenged racism at the point of production. Unions and black community organizations helped build a black political base that challenged Crump and then the remnants of the Crump system after he died. Many in the organized black working class could afford to buy homes and send a new generation of black students to college. Some of those union-raised students, including Coby Smith of the activist Memphis Invaders, went on to challenge Jim Crow across the board in the 1960s.[19]

Many industrial unions and practically all craft unions failed to break down the occupational segregation and exclusion that dictated low wages for black workers. And unions largely failed to organize service workers and public employees before the breakthrough in 1968. Laurie Green documents that into this void came working-class black women and welfare rights activists who provoked ferment that led to widespread community action. According to Alzada Clark, a leader in the United Furniture

Workers Union and a black community organizer, despite their limitations and failures, unions often provided a base for electoral and community organizing, fund-raising, and political lobbying. The lesson of her life, she said, was that "together we could accomplish a lot, separately we couldn't accomplish much." King brought the same message to striking sanitation workers: "We can all get more together than we can apart . . . and this is the way we gain power." They both knew, however, that the hard-won values of solidarity and self-organization could be lost.[20]

The Poor People's Reckoning: 1968 and Its Aftermath

By the time King came to Memphis to support the sanitation strike, an important segment of black workers in the city—though certainly not a majority—had obtained an economic foothold through unionization. Yet the plantation mentality and its political economy of low wages and bad jobs still crippled black lives. At the time of the sanitation strike, 57 percent of black families in Memphis lived below the poverty line (compared with 14 percent of white families). Over 80 percent of employed black men worked in unskilled and low-wage jobs in the city's agriculturally based cottonseed oil, compress, packaging and processing, and hardwood industries.[21] White men made their way into supervisory and white-collar jobs, while white women increasingly obtained secretarial and sales jobs. But these jobs were largely closed to black men and women, most of whom remained locked into unskilled, low-wage jobs in factories, on the streets, in steam laundries, and in the homes of whites.[22]

In the surrounding Mississippi Delta, an economic disaster unfolded. Machines harvested only 5 percent of cotton in 1950, but that figure reached 50 percent by 1960 and 95 percent by 1970.[23] Even as the 1960s witnessed the growth of a potential new black middle class consisting of college students, millions of unemployed, underemployed, and underpaid black workers piled up in the cities. Unemployed agricultural workers streamed into Memphis. One of them was James Robinson, born in 1937 in Earle, Arkansas, the epicenter of mass violence against the Southern Tenant Farmers' Union in the 1930s. Like his sharecropper father, James grew up baling cotton and went to a one-room school with fifty students and one teacher. He fled the countryside for a unionized factory job in Michigan, only to end up in a dead-end job in the low-wage Memphis service economy. Unions had reached into some major national industries, but they had failed to organize the service economy, where most blacks remained stuck at the bottom. Robinson remembered sanitation as "the worst job I ever had. . . . We were workin' every day then for welfare wages."[24] Extending unionization to desperate public workers is exactly the challenge that T. O. Jones, James Robinson, Joe Warren, and other sanitation workers took upon themselves.

These workers suffered every day from the plantation mentality and the politics of "white backlash." Barry Goldwater's opposition to the Civil Rights Act gained him much white support in Memphis and the South during his presidential run in 1964; Alabama's inflammatory segregationist George Wallace ran for president in the 1968 Democratic primary, gaining even more white support; and Republican Richard Nixon won the general election for president based on his "southern strategy" of using "law and order" and anti–civil rights rhetoric to get white Democrats to switch to the Republican Party. In 1968 Memphis whites voted overwhelmingly for both Nixon and right-wing Republican Dan Kuykendal, who replaced a moderate Democrat representing Memphis in Congress.[25]

In this context, heavily influenced by the anticommunist, anti–civil rights, "New Right"—and white—agenda, Henry Loeb had taken office as mayor in 1966. His family's Loeb Laundries had employed black laundresses at minimal wages and for years had beat back efforts to unionize them. Loeb, like his Republican colleagues, believed that effective governance required no unions, low wages, and austerity budgets. As head of the Public Works Department, Loeb had refused to improve equipment, to recognize unions as legitimate bargaining units, or to allow a union dues checkoff—a necessity among low-wage workers who could barely spare a dime. On February 1, 1968, faulty equipment on a garbage truck killed Echol Cole and Robert Walker, two young sanitation workers, and a series of other incidents pushed the workers beyond their limits. They blamed Loeb. When 1,300 black male workers went on strike on February 12, Loeb and the city's main newspaper, the *Commercial Appeal,* refused to bend from an antiunion, austerity agenda. White racial conservatism and low-wage thinking ultimately led Memphis to a condition akin to civil war. The crisis of 1968 culminated a long history of trying to keep black labor cheap and disposable, while segregation had encouraged a deadly climate of hatred and conformity, all of which provided the backdrop for King's murder.[26]

What did we learn from the traumatic events of 1968? Did AFSCME's ultimate victory change the trajectory of low wages and the plantation mentality that plagued Memphis? William Lucy believed it should have. A brilliant young African American organizer for AFSCME, Lucy became a key leader during the Memphis sanitation strike and later led the national Coalition of Black Trade Unionists. He guided Local 1733 as it obtained a contract, union dues checkoff, and improved wages and conditions. He believed the Memphis community as a whole had a vested interest in improving the lot of marginalized and underpaid public employees like the sanitation workers. When wages went up in low-wage service industries, that money poured almost directly into retail sales, restaurants, and real estate. "In a city like Memphis you've got families, one worker works in public works and the other works in the city hall. Or one works in public works and the other works at the city hospital or the school board." Many of these new consumers were women who worked in hospitals, schools, and service occupations. Lucy believed, "in the long run, it was in everybody's collective interest that trade union organizing took place" because it would raise the living standards, taxes, and economic activity of the city.[27]

Lucy said the strike produced a powerful "spirit of Memphis" that AFSCME celebrated nationally, and it spread throughout US public employment in the 1970s and 1980s. AFSCME became the fastest-growing union in the nation and helped launch thousands of black families into the middle class. The Memphis strike, in this sense, can be viewed as an important labor and civil rights success. But few southern white employers viewed unionization this way, and most of them remained opposed to the union vision of shared economic interest and development.

In Memphis, community movements exploded and police retaliation raged in the aftermath of the strike. In 1969 the Reverend James Lawson and many others went to jail as masses of students participated in a general strike against an at-large electoral system that prevented even a single African American from serving on a school board that governed a major-

Marching for economic justice during the sanitation strike. (Courtesy Memphis and Shelby County Room, Memphis Public Library)

ity-black school population. By the time I came to Memphis as an organizer in 1970, the overwhelmingly white police force was on a rampage
of revenge, beating and killing young black men and women with impu-
nity. In 1971 sixteen white police officers engaged in a car chase involving
a frightened sixteen-year-old named Elton Hayes. After his car crashed,
they surrounded Hayes and beat him to death. While the late 1960s and
early 1970s produced a kind of nirvana for Memphis music through Stax
Records and many brilliant black performers, it was also a time of deadly
resurgence of police brutality and white supremacy.[28]

The rise of black political power provided the countervailing force.
Throughout Memphis history, African Americans never lost the right to
vote, and it provided them with leverage that few black people in the
South possessed. As the Voting Rights Act of 1965 took effect, the percentage of black voters in Memphis increased every year and achieved
more victories. By 1974, a widespread community movement by black
Memphians and a few white allies elected Harold Ford to replace Kuykendal, making him the first African American from the Mid-South to
serve in Congress since Reconstruction. Memphians also elected black
women legislators such as Minerva Johnican and white allies such as Pam
Gaia. NAACP leader Maxine Smith gained election to the school board
after the city broke the back of white supremacy by replacing at-large
elections with electoral districts.[29]

Black political power continued to be a potent force in Memphis,
but race and class disparities, low wages, and white flight dragged the city
schools down.[30] And just as black power emerged at the ballot box and
civil rights took hold in the workplace, a new tragedy unfolded for black
workers.

Deindustrialization and the Shift to the Right

In the 1970s and 1980s King's dream of economic equality evaporated
and a new version of the cheap labor system emerged. Workers in Memphis—and in every other American city—experienced a profound and
wrenching transformation. A lengthy contraction of the US economy
began in 1973, induced by oil shocks and the negative effects of massive government spending on the Vietnam War. Even newly elected black

mayors pulled back from unionization, including Atlanta's Maynard Jackson, who went all-out to defeat an AFSCME strike of sanitation workers in 1974. Companies aggressively sought to cut costs. RCA, which had moved a television factory to Memphis to flee unionization in the North, found that black workers were not "docile," as the Chamber of Commerce had long advertised. When workers demanded their rights, RCA closed its doors and went to Mexico.[31] One factory after another closed, ultimately including the best-paying and unionized Firestone Tire and International Harvester.

A white right-wing political upsurge accelerated, based on a well-planned and well-funded effort by some of the richest capitalists in America. Their goal: to return the country to an era of low taxes, low wages, little regulation, and no unions. The ultra-Right rebuilt itself with big money and undermined the labor–civil rights solidarity for which Dr. King and so many others had given their lives, setting off union-busting efforts in almost all basic industries. President Ronald Reagan matched his anti-union and anti–civil rights rhetoric by firing 11,000 air traffic controllers who went on strike in 1981. This gave a green light to employers everywhere to justify union busting. Commentators attributed this to competition from the "global economy"—shorthand for American corporations that shut down their factories and went abroad to exploit cheaper wages.[32]

During 1980, as the Reagan campaign for president heated up, the Memphis Furniture Company launched an antiunion, anti–civil rights backlash. Owned by a family whose roots went back to slaveholders in Mississippi, the company had broken a hard-fought strike of mostly black women in 1949. In the wake of the civil rights movement of the 1960s, black women joined the United Furniture Workers Union and regained a contract. But when contract negotiations reopened, the company tried to take away union dues checkoff and contractual rights, setting off a strike. The company bused strikebreakers into the plant and used Memphis police to intimidate the striking workers. Supported by Coretta King, the energized black women held rallies, mobilized black support, and won—only to see Memphis Furniture close its doors and sell its assets to another company.[33]

As the "Reagan Revolution" produced a counterrevolution against labor and civil rights, the unfolding loss of unions and manufacturing jobs had dire consequences. Whereas unionized jobs at Firestone and other factories had once allowed workers to buy homes and send their children to college, and civil rights upheavals had opened new opportunities to organize the black working poor in the service economy, Memphis now became known for having the poorest black underclass of any city of its size in the nation. Unemployment, impoverishment, drug use, and mass incarceration hollowed out family and economic structures in Memphis's black community.[34] Scholar Manning Marable called it a "crisis of the black working class," as black communities across the nation lost unions, political organizations, and family-waged jobs. He identified rising rates of poverty, permanent unemployment, cuts in public-sector funding, police violence, and "hyperincarceration" as part of the dreadful but increasingly normal landscape of black lives. Meanwhile, the white working class also lost its grip on jobs and a decent life, as white politicians pitted them against the black and multiracial poor. Many people of color experienced what Marable termed "the highest stage of underdevelopment," as the capitalist economy discarded them entirely. Writer Roger Wilkins called them society's "throw-away people."[35]

In the 1990s, during the presidency of William Clinton, black lives in Memphis seemed to matter more. An uptick in jobs, greater investment in people and communities, and a more compassionate tone in government emerged. In 1991, as a majority or near-majority of African Americans became voters in Memphis, they elected former school superintendent Willie Herenton as the city's first black mayor. Thus began a sixteen-year odyssey in which some things got better and some things got worse, while Herenton increasingly ruled like an autocrat. Assessing the fortunes of African Americans in Memphis in 2000, political scientist Sharon D. Wright described Memphis politics as an example of "the hollow prize"—that is, African American politicians strive for and achieve political power, only to discover a lack of economic wherewithal to bring about significant change for the masses once they take office.[36]

The Not-New Economy of Poverty

In 2008 Memphis economist David Ciscel and I compared the city's racial and economic statistics forty years after King's death. We found a city transformed for the worse in many ways. Although medical services, transportation, warehousing, service, and wholesale jobs grew, "the work was hard, the pay was low, jobs were non-union and work was scheduled totally by the employer." Work became temporary, with few ladders into higher-paying jobs. On the positive side, many black workers had gone beyond laboring jobs, but they had few unions and little power. We concluded, "there is less ability to struggle for economic equality in today's economy than in the economy of Martin Luther King's era."[37]

Twenty-first-century social and economic policies led to a true crisis for many in Memphis's black community. The return to privatizing, "free market," and deregulation policies under President George W. Bush (2001–2009) led to a near meltdown of the American economic system. It hit Memphis especially hard. Real estate and banking firms, particularly Wells Fargo, lured thousands of people, many of them poor African Americans, into untenable mortgages and loans. Inner-city Memphis and Frayser in the northern suburbs proved particularly vulnerable, as the housing market for working-class African Americans collapsed upon itself. The bursting jobs and housing bubble left a landscape littered with thousands of vacant homes, failing schools, poverty, and destitution.[38] Job losses proved stunning. From 1990 to 2011, the number of manufacturing workers in Shelby County fell by 50 percent. Although deindustrialization depressed all working-class incomes, African Americans suffered unemployment at twice the rate of whites. Black median incomes, which had been increasing for a generation after World War II relative to white incomes, now fell back to half that of whites. Nearly 83 percent of city schoolchildren—most of them black—suffered from economic disadvantages and needed free school lunches.[39]

In 2009 the Obama administration launched an investment program to stabilize the collapsing American economy. Some new jobs came to Memphis, but so did austerity budgets and renewed interest in the old tradition of cheap wages. Even as companies complained that the city lacked a well-educated, skilled workforce, a Memphis journalist wrote in 2011, "cost cutting, and not creating jobs with middle-class wages for low-skilled workers, is key as manufacturers seek to be competitive with their counterparts in China and elsewhere."[40] Investments by Electrolux, Mitsubishi Electric, and a few other multinational corporations provided some desperately needed jobs in the city, but without union wages.

Meanwhile, reduced tax revenues and state and federal funds sent the city government into an economic crisis. It could not afford to fix potholes, pay its pension obligations, fund its schools, protect public safety, or address the problem of widespread poverty.[41] The City Council cut subsidies for employee health care, raising health insurance premiums for workers by 24 percent, in an effort to shore up a troubled pension fund. After police and firefighters lost their lawsuit challenging a 2011 salary cut of 4.6 percent, they staged "blue flu" and "red rash" stay-at-home strikes in the summer of 2014.[42]

In the context of austerity budgets, Local 1733 of AFSCME became a prime target. City Council members made repeated attempts to eliminate AFSCME's union-waged jobs and working conditions by contracting out sanitation work to private companies. However, the city was still required by law to make contracts and perform oversight, and some studies concluded that privatized jobs might actually cost more in overhead than city jobs. Beginning in 2010, Wisconsin's Republican governor Scott Walker set off a mania for public employee union busting by eliminating the very things Local 1733 had won in the sanitation strike of 1968: union dues checkoff and long-term contracts. Working-class wages and political power collapsed. In Memphis, toppling Local 1733 would similarly destroy one of the most important labor advances made in Dr. King's day: the growth of public employee unions that disproportionately represented black workers. Destroying the base of unionized labor would undermine living wages and pensions and result in a loss of control over one's work for millions of working-class families. Gail Tyree, a longtime union and African American community organizer, pointed out that such policies would be disastrous for working-class incomes in Memphis. "If they can dig up the root of the tree, they can topple that tree," said Tyree.[43] Destruction of public employee unions would return Memphis to the old model of cheap labor.

The Kellogg's Lockout: Defending the Black Middle Class

A more recent drama in Memphis speaks volumes about how changes in the labor landscape have continued to erode the fortunes of black workers. Kellogg's, the world's largest cereal company, based in Battle Creek,

Michigan, announced in 1957 that it would spend millions to build a new plant on seventeen acres at the corner of Frisco and Airways in Memphis. City and state governments backed the effort with massive subsidies. The company had a unionized workforce in Michigan, where unions were strong, and it pledged that union workers would build and run the new facility in Memphis. Kellogg's said nothing about looking for cheap labor, thus breaking the "plantation mentality" syndrome. Kellogg's ushered in a generation of unionized workers—almost all of them white—with family-waged jobs and pensions upon retirement.[44]

Fast-forward to the Kellogg's factory in October 2013. The damage inflicted by forty years of union decline was obvious. The company had once employed between 500 and 700 workers, but automation had cut that number to about 220. The civil rights revolution had also created a workforce that was more than 80 percent black, and these workers had become the mainstay of the black middle class. During negotiations for a renewal of their local contract, workers in the plant accepted twenty-two of the company's twenty-four bargaining positions. However, the company demanded that the Memphis local accept two-tiered employment, which would have brought new workers in at a much lower wage and off-loaded health insurance costs onto the workers. These two demands would have revised the union's national contract, something the local union had no authority to negotiate. Kellogg's had four major plants in the United States but targeted only the one in Memphis—the only plant with a majority of black workers—to make these changes, apparently expecting that Memphis workers would be the weakest link in the union's chain of locals as the company attempted to undo the national contract.[45]

When the workers in Memphis refused to go along with these demands, Kellogg's hired an antiunion firm to bring in replacement workers, who were put up at a Hilton Hotel; it also rented a parking lot near the plant to be used for mobilizing scab labor. Kellogg's immediately cut off health insurance for the locked-out workers, leaving one of them stranded in a hospital with no medical insurance. For more than a year, workers walked the picket line in the cold and the rain, as workers lost their homes and cars and could not pay for their medicine.[46]

This all came as a shock to union president Kevin Bradshaw. As a black college graduate, he had gone to work at Kellogg's because of its strong union wages and benefits. People in the plant regularly worked seven days a week, with twelve-hour shifts and sometimes double shifts, but they made a good living with overtime wages. They produced the profitable Raisin Bran, Rice Krispies, and Fruit Loops brands. By 2013, however, Wall Street's imperative to maximize profits and stockholder dividends had overtaken an earlier business ethic that supported family-waged jobs. The company's CEO made millions, and Kellogg's took in more than $4 billion each quarter. Nonetheless, returning to the old argument that southerners should work for lower wages, Kellogg's wanted to pay incoming workers at its Memphis plant the average wage in the local labor market—less than half of what the current Kellogg's workforce was making. The company also wanted incoming workers to pay a great deal more for their medical benefits. This two-tiered system would bring new workers down to the level of most black workers in Memphis, who barely survived with nonunion wages and benefits.

"Kellogg spent over $50 million to lock us out," recalled Bradshaw. The company's demands were about money, of course, but according to Bradshaw, "It is a race issue. This was the only Kellogg local attacked." When the plant first opened, whites had been the overwhelming majority; now that blacks were in the majority, the company wanted to lower their wages and benefits. Local civil rights activists and black church leaders saw it as a civil rights issue and supported the union. It became one of the most grueling and consequential conflicts in Memphis labor history since 1968.

The Kellogg's workers fought an uphill battle. At first, many people thought the union workers had gone on strike, and the company encouraged this unfavorable publicity. "We want to work. Kellogg won't let us. This is not a strike," protested Bradshaw.[47] "What's unusual is the company's hardball approach," a labor relations expert concluded. "This is about as mean and nasty as it gets." At the same time as the Kellogg's lockout, Tennessee's Republican governor and US senator successfully pressured workers in Chattanooga to vote against unionization at an auto plant. Kellogg's thought workers in Memphis would fold, undermining the union's national contract and setting up older employees to be replaced with a new tier of lower-paid workers.

African American Glen Mason had worked at Kellogg's for thirty-eight of his fifty-nine years, producing Rice Krispies and Frosted Flakes. After the lockout, he decided to retire. "I can't work for that company anymore," he told a reporter. "I've never seen the company stoop so low as it has done this past year. I don't feel like I could go back and be a good employee, having been treated the way we were treated." Mason had dropped out of LeMoyne-Owen College to work at Kellogg's, figuring that a unionized factory job would give him better opportunities than a college education. He bought a home and raised six children, sending four of them to college, on union wages. He became president of Local 252G of the Bakery and Confectionary Workers Union. He and his union had made various concessions on wages and hours over the years, but the company and the union had always kept bargaining, even while working without a contract. Mason concluded, "This is about corporate greed. That's shameful." Scheduled to retire with full benefits in October 2013, Mason was instead locked out of his job and saw his income cut to virtually nothing while he walked the picket line.[48]

The fate of black workers, even those with good jobs, now hung by a thread. Workers had no choice but to resist because, according to Bradshaw, "We didn't want to give away the things we've negotiated over the last 58 years." Corporate capitalism's imperatives put all those benefits at risk for white workers as well as for African Americans. Kay Davis, a white Mississippian who had started working at Kellogg's shortly after it opened, agreed that work at the company was good but very tough. "Doctors know all the people at Kellogg's have high blood pressure, bad knees, and bad backs" from overwork. "We had three or four drop dead at work." She recalled many fights over the years to obtain and maintain good wages and benefits for all, regardless of race. Her mother had fought for union rights in Mississippi and suffered for it, and Kay felt proud of what the workers had done.[49]

Based on a strong history of union solidarity, Kellogg's workers refused to buckle. In a rare win for the labor movement, the National Labor Relations Board and federal courts stepped in during August 2015, ultimately ordering Kellogg's to end its lockout and pay the workers back wages.[50] Although the workers kept their jobs, their trust in management had collapsed. The national union subsequently accepted some of the demands the Memphis workers had fought to oppose—namely, the use of "casual" workers who received lower wages and fewer health benefits than longtime workers. Meantime, at the shop floor level, great damage had been done in the company's search for profits: many of its union workers retired as soon as they could.[51]

Where Do We Go from Here?

The Kellogg's scenario took place within a larger political context affecting all workers, but especially black workers. In days of old, southern plantation owners, manufacturers, and real estate and banking interests ran Memphis, using poll taxes, racial violence, undereducation, and miseducation to divide workers along racial lines and to beat down unions. Through most of that history the Democratic Party was the white supremacist party in the South, but by the twenty-first century, the Republican Party had taken its place in the former Confederate states. Fomenting black and Latino disfranchisement, electoral gerrymandering, nonunion labor, and sharp racial divisions became its trademarks. In Tennessee, white Republican rule increasingly encircled the state's one predominantly black electoral district comprising Memphis and Shelby County. While claiming to support "states' rights" against federal power, Republicans passed laws that took away local autonomy, making it illegal for Memphis and Shelby County to pass local minimum wage laws, control their schools, and make economic improvements through taxation.[52]

We like to think that history is always moving toward a better day, but history also shows that we can fall back into the same old patterns. I spent part of February 2016 in Memphis, exploring what had happened to King's dream of economic equality. People holding a variety of views said that Memphis was at a crucial point, one that would either lead to improvements or drag the city into the abyss. Hopeful signs persist. Many white businesspeople in Memphis have turned in the direction of cross-racial cooperation. The success of the National Civil Rights Museum, located in what used to be the Lorraine Motel, has changed the city's racial tenor. I experienced this in 2008, when the city turned out in force to commemorate forty years since King's death. As I drove into the city, banners advertising the events surrounding that anniversary adorned the city's light poles. The media, arts, and political communities all turned out in a great celebration of what is known in the South as "civil rights tourism." It provided a breathtaking contrast to Memphis in the 1970s, when white officials wanted to tear down the Lorraine Motel and either ignore or forget what happened in 1968.[53]

In 2016 many Memphians felt guardedly optimistic about the city's future. When I interviewed housing developer and white businessman Henry Turley, he rhetorically asked, "What if that 1968 strike happened now?" Answering his own question, he said, "We'd make a quick deal. The gentry would require it. We no longer cling to the old system." Depriving people of education and rights was "no longer good economics," he concluded. He hoped that Memphis would continue to move forward into the "knowledge economy." Turley warned, however, "We are burdened by southern history."[54] That history has left the city with an intractable poverty problem based on racism and cheap wages—or, often, no wages. This trend extends beyond the urban core into the next ring of suburbs.

The Benjamin Hooks Institute for Social Change at the University of Memphis has done more than any group to collect and publicize the depressing statistics on the growing poverty and community disinvestment in Memphis. It found that, as of 2013, one-third of African Americans in Memphis lived in poverty; the poverty rate among black children was the highest in the United States and five times the rate among white children; one in three black males had a lifetime risk of going to prison; some 50 percent of black males aged sixteen to sixty-four lacked jobs; and black incomes and wealth remained only a fraction of white incomes and wealth.[55] University of Memphis sociologist Elena Delavega published devastating facts showing that, in 2014, Memphis had "the unfortunate top spot" in the overall child poverty and infant mortality rates among cities its size. Speaking to me in 2016, she warned that these unfortunate conditions were worsening.[56]

Despite such statistics, Hooks Institute director and attorney Daphene McFerren remained guardedly optimistic about the future. White and black alike, she believed, recognized the need to address the systemic issues holding back all people in the city and the Mid-South region. Facing up to these problems required facing up to the past, the effects of which live on in the present. "You can't separate our poverty today from the under-accumulation of black wealth based on our history," she said. Some white businesspeople understood this, and the success of civil rights tourism provides one example that rather than denying the tragic assassination of Dr. King, the city could look at the other side of 1968: King's empowering message of equal rights and economic justice that offered hope for a different kind of community in Memphis. McFerren felt that "something is in the air," and a more progressive, proactive community was coming of age. At the same time, she observed, black middle-class nostalgia for the civil rights era was not helpful in forging a better future, for "often, that legacy is not translating into action." King's admonition that "we go up together, or we go down together" seemed obvious to McFerren. Speaking of the perennial problem of racism in Memphis, she said, "You work hard to hurt someone, and in doing that you hurt yourself." She concluded, "We will either tip forward or we will tip back."[57]

Otis Sanford, an African American who served as editor of the city's once rabidly segregationist *Commercial Appeal,* reflected on the changes that have occurred in Memphis. He recalled that the city seemed to enter a time warp after King's assassination, as race relations reached an all-time low. On one level, things are better today, he said, citing economist David Ciscel's estimates that up to one-third of the Memphis black population now lives at a middle-class level. The post-King crisis might seem to be over for some, but Sanford also observed that, for black Memphians—as for almost all working Americans—one job loss or one major illness could plunge a middle-class family into poverty. Half or more of the Memphis black community remains on the knife edge of poverty, castoffs from the economy of twenty-first-century global capitalism.[58]

In the wake of the 2007–2008 economic crisis, A. C. Wharton followed Willie Herenton into office as the second black mayor of Memphis. Wharton had spent years as a legal services lawyer working with poor people and had seen some terrible conditions, including police officers using dogs to assault African Americans in the county jail. Witnessing the poverty of the incarcerated population, he concluded that "people don't have legal problems, they have economic problems." Low incomes, lack of education, bad housing, poor skills, and the other burdens of poverty translate into trouble with the police, jail time, and mass incarceration.

Wharton went into politics to try to alter the situation, but he found the realities of office-holding daunting. As Memphis mayor, Wharton ran into numerous obstacles during the worst economy since the Great Depression. Massive federal funding cuts, a weak tax base, heavy pension obligations, and high expenditures for social services and education hampered the city budget. As he tried to cut budgets, eliminate jobs, constrain wages, and minimize pension and health care costs, he came into direct conflict with Local 1733 and the other public employee unions. They resisted, and Wharton paid the price at the polls, losing his reelection bid in 2015.[59]

Wharton saw a difficult but not impossible path ahead for Memphis. Like McFerren, he came to believe that civil rights victories had "lulled us into a false sense of achievement." People had understandable pride in the progress made in Memphis, but it often blinded them to stark economic realities. "We have no 'Whites Only' signs anymore, but economic barriers continue to hold everyone back," he said. Wharton blamed not just poverty but also vast income disparities that worsened the heavy burdens of Memphis history. He saw the city's main task as raising incomes of the working and unemployed poor and stabilizing working- and middle-class incomes in order to build a vibrant economy based on consumer spending, education, and good jobs. Was it possible to do this, he asked himself? That would be up to the leaders of the future to decide.[60]

In 1961 Martin Luther King prophetically warned the AFL-CIO that the ultra-Right, if not checked by a people's movement, would threaten "everything decent and fair in American life."[61] In 2016 labor and civil rights advocates shuddered as the presidential election threw hopes for amelioration and improvement in Memphis into the air once again. Leading up to the election, the US Supreme Court gutted the Voting Rights Act, and Republican state legislatures created roadblocks to voting and used gerrymandered districts to keep incumbent white Republicans in power. During the campaign of Republican Donald Trump, old-fashioned white supremacy tactics of fear and intimidation exploded, along with misogyny and attacks on immigrants, not only in the South but across the country. For years, southern employers and many political leaders in Memphis and elsewhere had insisted that low wages, low taxes, and a lack of unions provided the basis for economic growth. That philosophy seemed to be back, and it could have an especially devastating effect on black workers in Memphis.

Fifty years after King's death, the "crisis of the black working class," to use Manning Marable's memorable phrase, remains at the center of our continuing quest for equal rights. King stressed that "there is no intrinsic difference" between workers and that we should reject those who "impose disunity" on workers based on their skin color or immigrant heritage; instead, we should pursue "a dream of a nation where all our gifts and resources are held not for ourselves alone but as instruments of service for the rest of humanity." To know the history of black workers in Memphis is to recognize why King's dream of racial and economic equality continues to resonate. Many people are still asking, as Dr. King did, "Where do we go from here?"[62]

Notes

1. Martin Luther King Jr., *All Labor Has Dignity,* ed. Michael K. Honey (Boston: Beacon Press, 2011), 172, 175.

2. See Michael K. Honey, *Going Down Jericho Road: The Memphis Strike, Martin Luther King's Last Campaign* (New York: W. W. Norton, 2007), 297–304, for a description of the March 18 speech and audience response.

3. Ibid., 347–58, 359–60.

4. King, *All Labor Has Dignity,* 182–95.

5. Honey, *Going down Jericho Road,* 493.

6. AFSCME played a key role in the expansion of public employee unions and the Coalition of Black Trade Unionists. By the 1980s, it "became one of the AFL-CIO's largest and most dynamic affiliates." Robert H. Zieger, *For Jobs and Freedom: Race and Labor in America since 1865* (Lexington: University Press of Kentucky, 2007), 227.

7. Honey, *Going down Jericho Road,* 92; Thomas F. Jackson, *From Civil Rights to Human Rights: Martin Luther King, Jr., and the Struggle for Economic Justice* (Philadelphia: University of Pennsylvania Press, 2011).

8. King used his "first phase, second phase" analysis in a speech to teamster shop stewards on May 2, 1967. See King, *All Labor Has Dignity,* 123–36.

9. For details on King's relationship to unions, see the introduction and introductory notes in *All Labor Has Dignity.*

10. W. E. B. DuBois saw slavery's distinction between "black labor" and "white labor" as so divisive that in the postslavery era, few white workers could

even imagine joining up with African Americans as allies. See W. E. B. DuBois, *Black Reconstruction in America, 1860–1880* (New York: Atheneum, 1935), chaps. 1, 2. See also Sven Beckert, *Empire of Cotton: A Global History* (New York: Alfred A. Knopf, 2011); Edward E. Baptist, *This Half Has Never Been Told: Slavery and the Making of American Capitalism* (New York: Basic Books, 2014).

11. John Handcox, of the Southern Tenant Farmers Union, told me that white landlords and merchants became angry when he used his ability to add and subtract and to read and write to challenge their figures when it came time to pay his bills as a sharecropper and tenant. Michael K. Honey, *Sharecroppers' Troubadour: John L. Handcox, the Southern Tenant Farmers' Union, and the African American Song Tradition* (New York: Palgrave Macmillan, 2013).

12. Gavin Wright, *Old South, New South: Revolutions in the Southern Economy since the Civil War* (New York: Basic Books, 1986), and James C. Cobb, *The Selling of the South: The Southern Crusade for Industrial Development, 1936–1980* (Baton Rouge: Louisiana State University Press, 1982), 113–21, document how white southern employers and politicians sought industry on a low-wage model, used racial division, and kept jobs nonunion. David Roediger, *Seizing Freedom: Slave Emancipation and Liberty for All* (London: Verso, 2014), provides insight on DuBois's view that racism was the Achilles' heel of the American labor movement but shows that cross-racial rebellions occurred nonetheless. On the political economy of racism, see Michael Honey, "Racism and the Labor Market in the American South: Memphis, Tennessee, in the Segregation Era," in *Racism and Power Relations in the Labour Market*, ed. Marcel van der Linden (Amsterdam: International Institute of Social History, 1994), 213–36.

13. On the suppression of labor and civil rights in Memphis in the Crump era, see Michael Honey, *Southern Labor and Black Civil Rights: Organizing Memphis Workers* (Champaign: University of Illinois Press, 1993), chap. 1.

14. Ibid. Other works show the pattern of organizing against low wages and segregation in the pre–civil rights era. See, for example, Robin D. G. Kelley, *Hammer and Hoe: Alabama Communists during the Great Depression* (1990; reprint, Chapel Hill: University of North Carolina Press, 2015); Glenda Gilmore, *Defying Dixie: The Radical Roots of Civil Rights, 1919–1950* (New York: W. W. Norton, 2008); John Egerton, *Speak Now against the Day: The Generation before the Civil Rights Movement in the South* (New York: Alfred A. Knopf, 1994).

15. See Honey, *Southern Labor*, 213–14, on Memphis union membership. David M. Tucker, *Memphis since Crump: Bossism, Blacks, and Civic Reformers, 1948–1968* (Knoxville: University of Tennessee Press, 1980), documents the rise of some racially moderate political leaders in the wake of Crump's death.

16. Robert Korstad and Nelson Lichtenstein, "Opportunities Found and Lost: Labor, Radicals, and the Early Civil Rights Movement," *Journal of American History* 75 (December 1988): 786–811; Honey, *Southern Labor*, chaps. 8, 9.

17. See King, *All Labor Has Dignity*.

18. See Michael Honey, *Black Workers Remember: An Oral History of Segregation, Unionism, and the Freedom Struggle* (Berkeley: University of California Press, 1999).

19. Coby Smith's father was a union steward at International Harvester. Honey, *Going down Jericho Road,* 85.

20. Laurie Green, *Battling the Plantation Mentality: Memphis and the Black Freedom Struggle* (Chapel Hill: University of North Carolina Press, 2007); Honey, *Going down Jericho Road,* 367–68.

21. Wright, *Old South, New South,* shows how low wages kept the South and its people in a backward state. The 57 percent figure is from Honey, *Southern Labor,* 282, based on an article by Ray Marshal and Arvil Van Adams titled "Negro Employment in Memphis."

22. Honey, *Southern Labor,* 282–83; Honey, *Black Workers Remember,* 288–90.

23. Honey, *Black Workers Remember,* 288.

24. Ibid., 304.

25. G. Wayne Dowdy chronicled the rise of a more liberal politics in Memphis from 1948 to 1968 in *Crusade for Freedom: Memphis and the Political Transformation of the American South* (Jackson: University Press of Mississippi, 2010). However, the white South was moving in a different direction, creating increasing contradictions between white and black voters. See Wanda Rushing, *Memphis and the Paradox of Place: Globalization in the American South* (Chapel Hill: University of North Carolina Press, 2009).

26. See Honey, *Going down Jericho Road;* Joan Beifuss, *At the River I Stand* (Memphis, TN: B and W Press, 1985); Michael Honey, "Martin Luther King, Jr., the Crisis of the Black Working Class, and the Memphis Sanitation Strike," in *Southern Labor in Transition, 1940–1995,* ed. Robert H. Zieger (Knoxville: University of Tennessee Press, 1997), 146–75.

27. Honey, *Black Workers Remember,* 316, 317.

28. Robert Gordon, *Respect Yourself: Stax Records and the Soul Explosion* (New York: Bloomsbury, 2013); Charles L. Hughes, *Country Soul: Making Music and Making Race in the American South* (Chapel Hill: University of North Carolina Press, 2015).

29. Elizabeth Gritter, *River of Hope: Black Politics and the Memphis Freedom Movement, 1865–1954* (Lexington: University Press of Kentucky, 2014).

30. Marcus Pohlmann, *Opportunity Lost: Race and Poverty in the Memphis City Schools* (Knoxville: University of Tennessee Press, 2008).

31. Jefferson Cowie, *Capital Moves: RCA's Seventy-Year Quest for Cheap Labor* (New York: New Press, 1999).

32. Hedrick Smith, *Who Stole the American Dream?* (New York: Random House, 2012); Joseph McCartin, *Collision Course: Ronald Reagan, the Air Traffic Controllers, and the Strike that Changed America* (New York: Oxford University Press, 2011).

33. Honey, *Black Workers Remember,* 342–48, 363–68. On the economic effects of Reagan's policies on African Americans, see, for example, Alphonso Pinkney, *The Myth of Black Progress* (Cambridge: Cambridge University Press, 1984).

34. Honey, *Black Workers Remember,* 367.

35. Manning Marable, *How Capitalism Underdeveloped Black America: Problems in Race, Political Economy, and Society,* updated ed. with a foreword by Leith Mullings (Chicago: Haymarket Books, 2015), 21–60. Roger Wilkins, a former Justice Department official, recorded "Throwaway People" on the National Public Broadcasting System in the 1980s.

36. Sharon D. Wright, *Race, Power and Political Emergence in Memphis* (New York: Garland Publishing, 2000).

37. Michael Honey and David Ciscel, "Memphis since King: Race and Labor in the City," *Poverty and Race* 18, no. 2 (March–April 2009): 8–11. For a more lengthy treatment, see Michael Honey and David Ciscel, "Race and Labor in Memphis since the King Assassination," in *Life and Labor in the New New South,* ed. Robert H. Zieger (Gainesville: University of Florida Press, 2012), 236–57.

38. Personal interview with David Ciscel, Memphis, May 13, 2015. In 2013 Steve Lockwood, CEO of the Frayser Community Development Corporation, took me on a tour of abandoned homes in working-class neighborhoods devastated by the housing crisis. African Americans lost a huge amount of assets to the housing bubble, and efforts to revive the housing market have been crucial to pulling Memphis out of the recession.

39. David Ciscel, "Memphis in 2018," unpublished paper in author's possession.

40. Tom Bailey Jr., "Manufacturing in Memphis—The City Gains Another Heavy Manufacturer with Mitsubishi Electric. Is This the Beginning of a Trend?" *Memphis Commercial Appeal,* May 15, 2011. Mitsubishi built a $200 million plant on the Memphis riverfront, hiring 1,250 workers to make ovens; the corn-milling company Cargill invested $72 million to update its plant; and City Brewery planned to develop an older Coors plant with 500 workers.

41. "State of the City/Potholes to Poverty," January 30, 2014, at infoweb, Memphis Public Library.

42. Timberly Moore, "'Blue Flu,' 'Red Rash' Cases Subside," *Memphis Commercial Appeal,* July 20, 2014.

43. Personal interview with Gail Tyree, Memphis, February 9, 2015; Zack McMillan, "Cutting against History's Grain—Sanitation Workers Are Volatile Budget Target," *Memphis Commercial Appeal,* June 19, 2011; Amos Maki, "Deal between City, Union Could Be Costing Millions—Outdated Sanitation Equipment Requires More Manpower," *Memphis Commercial Appeal,* June 11, 2011.

44. "Kellogg Will Make Cereal on Airways," *Memphis Commercial Appeal,* September 20, 1957; Clark Porteous, "Contract for New Kellogg Factory: Start at Once," *Memphis Press-Scimitar,* March 27, 1958. Porteous wrote: "Kellogg expected to employee 300–400 people, who Mayor Orgill said would be 'eas-

ily trained and hard-working labor,' and the next ten years would witness the greatest industrial development in Memphis history." Companies received massive subsidies to move to southern cities. When Kellogg planned another site in 1958, it struck a deal: it would not pay real estate or personal property taxes on the full value of the land for five years, it would receive $3.5 million in federal and state funds for job training, and Tennessee would fund $400,000 to improve access to the site and up to $750,000 in other improvements. "Kellogg," *Memphis Commercial Appeal*, January 23, 1958.

45. Wayne Risher, "Kellogg Lockout Goes On," *Memphis Commercial Appeal*, October 24, 2013.

46. Personal interview with Kevin Bradshaw, Memphis, February 8, 2016.

47. Risher, "Kellogg Lockout Goes On."

48. "Faith in Memphis Panel: Memphis Lockout," *Memphis Commercial Appeal*, February 22, 2014; Wayne Risher, "NLRB Move Buoys Kellogg Workers' Hopes," *Memphis Commercial Appeal*, March 29, 2014; David Waters, "Not All Employees at Kellogg Return to Work," *Memphis Commercial Appeal*, August 13, 2014.

49. Telephone interview with Kay Davis, July 9, 2016.

50. Wayne Risher, "NLRB Backs Kellogg Workers," *Memphis Commercial Appeal*, May 8, 2015.

51. Davis interview.

52. Personal interview with David Ciscel, Memphis, February 10, 2016.

53. See Rushing, *Memphis and the Paradox of Place*, on civil rights tourism, identity, and the contradictions of Memphis's economic development. On the civil rights museum, see Michael Honey, "Doing Public History at the National Civil Rights Museum," *Public Historian* 17, no. 1 (Winter 1995): 71–84. AFSCME played a large role in saving the Lorraine and spurred state and local governments to fund the civil rights museum.

54. Personal interview with Henry Turley, Memphis, February 10, 2015.

55. Benjamin Hooks Institute for Social Change, "A Call for Collective Action: Tackling Social Challenges in Memphis," October 2014, 4–6.

56. Elena Delavega, "2015 Memphis Poverty Fact Sheet," Mid-South Family and Community Empowerment Institute, University of Memphis.

57. Personal interview with Daphene McFerren, Memphis, February 11, 2016.

58. Personal interview with Otis Sanford, Memphis, February 11, 2016; Ciscel interview, February 10, 2016.

59. Personal interview with Gail Tyree, Memphis, February 9, 2016.

60. Personal interview with A. C. Wharton, Memphis, February 9, 2016.

61. Speech to the AFL-CIO Constitutional Convention, December 11, 1961, in King, *All Labor Has Dignity*, 38.

62. Ibid., 43; Martin Luther King Jr., *Where Do We Go from Here: Chaos or Community?* (1967; reprint, Boston: Beacon Press, 2010).

Coda

Charles W. McKinney Jr.

Where, on a timeline of Memphis history, would you place the following scenario? *In the wake of the killing of an unarmed black person, black Memphians organized mass-based protests, community meetings, and voter registration drives. These actions represented a collective response to the persistence of police brutality, economic and residential segregation, racist urban policy, and the palpable ambivalence of the city's political leadership. These sustained efforts to confront racial inequality resulted in both increased political influence and heightened retaliation from the white power structure.* Would you place it in the nadir of American race relations—perhaps early in the twentieth century? How about in the 1940s? Certainly this sounds like something that could have occurred in the 1960s. Or perhaps you would be inclined to place it somewhere in the post–civil rights period.

Regrettably, it is a scenario with an all-too-familiar feel. It is the summation of a recognizable cycle: black death, collective action, tentative progress, backlash. This scenario can be placed on multiple points of the city's historical timeline. It is thus a grim testament to the enduring—some would say intractable—nature of racial inequality in the Bluff City. These lines could be referring to the murder of Ell Persons and the subsequent response, which Darius Young describes. They could be telling the story of Fred Jackson's murder and its aftermath—a story relayed in Laurie Green's essay. The pattern holds for other incidents as well. Whether it is the exclusion of black women from high-paying union jobs, the shooting of a civil rights activist, the coordinated effort to intimidate law-abiding black citizens, or the jagged enforcement of segregation in the wake of a natural disaster, the cycle remains consistent. For black folks in Memphis, the constancy of racial subordination pervaded every facet of life. As one historian put it, "there was neither escape from, nor redress for, the ubiquitous, arbitrary, and cruel reality of senseless white power."[1]

However, just as the above scenario reflects the enduring nature of the racial subordination and inequality black Memphians confronted, it also represents an opportunity to contend with the equally enduring reality of black insurgency—rooted in a deep and abiding determination to pursue equality. Black folks in Memphis responded to the "ubiquitous, arbitrary, and cruel" with bold directives, meticulously planned actions, slow-cooked resistance, and impromptu responses—all buttressed by a dynamic sensibility that enabled them to craft theories of thought and action that anchored their struggle. As we see throughout *An Unseen Light,* violence perpetrated against black Memphians begat political organization and incremental increases in political power. Throughout the twentieth century, employment discrimination begat mass mobilization, which emboldened individuals and their organizations. Black people from all walks of life shaped the pursuit of greater freedom by laying claim to their humanity and mounting an array of seen and unseen actions.

Much, if not most, of the history written about black activism in Memphis tends to focus on particular moments of tension or controversy—we could call these historical flashpoints. However, *An Unseen Light* reveals how these flashpoints turned out to be quite a bit more complicated. The essays in this volume suggest that although flashpoints can focus intense energy and attention on specific issues, they often obscure the complex set of social, political, racial, and tactical dynamics that constitute the tensions of domination, survival, and insurgency. When we reinterpret these moments in Memphis history, we are better able to make sense of their meanings and to understand the truly complicated calculus of social change in the Bluff City.

The killing of Darrius Stewart by a Memphis police officer in July 2015 provided a powerful reminder of the legacies of authority and struggle that lie at the heart of the city's history. Stewart became one more victim in a barrage of state-sanctioned killings of black people dotting the country that year. As historian Chris Johnson powerfully observed, Stewart was killed "one year to the day after Eric Garner was choked to death gasping for life, three months after Walter Scott was shot in the back while running to save his life, four days after Sandra Bland died in a jail cell after fighting to save her life, one week before Ralkina Jones begged police for life . . . and died of poisoning two days later."[2] Later that year, the grand jury in Shelby County declined to indict the officer responsible for Stewart's death, despite a recommendation from the county's district attorney that he be charged with involuntary manslaughter. Few people were surprised when, the following year, the Department of Justice also declined to prosecute the officer, citing "insufficient evidence."[3] Stewart's unjust killing plunged Memphis into the national conversation about police brutality, racial profiling, and the state's inability to address the "ubiquitous, arbitrary, and cruel" nature of the city's racial status quo.

It would be easy to mythologize this moment, to construct a "flashpoint" reading that framed the response to Stewart's killing as the spontaneous, incendiary reaction of an aggrieved subset of the black community. Instead, we find a resurgent movement, intentionally built and tactically savvy, anchored by #BlackLivesMatter (#BLM). Founded in the wake of George Zimmerman's acquittal in the murder of Trayvon Martin in 2012, the creators of #BLM (three black, queer women) shaped an organization dedicated to rebuilding the black liberation movement that reshaped the nature of American life in the middle of the twentieth century. However, in a significant break from past practices, #BLM activists sought to craft a movement that viewed the work of liberation expansively, with an agenda that affirmed and supported black women, transgender people, and queer folks—portions of the black community that disproportionately suffered the ravages of racial violence and discrimination. Activists who founded the Memphis chapter of #BLM in 2014 took this perspective to heart. #BLM would quickly gain members and momentum in the city by hosting a series of marches, protests, and forums. In August 2015 a consortium of local churches and progressive nonprofit organizations created the Memphis Grassroots Coalition.[4] This new cadre of organizers represented an emerging generation of activists, many of them millennials, who were not beholden to older, more traditional civil rights organizations.

The presence of this new, energized assemblage of progressive organizations explicitly invested in black freedom provided the central organizational momentum for a movement seeking to address a host of issues relevant to the lives of black Memphians. Economic inequality took up a central place in organizing efforts across Memphis, a city that had recently been ranked the poorest metropolitan area in the nation.[5] The Fight for $15 movement and the Workers Interfaith Network confronted the grinding poverty in the city by advocating for living wages and protecting low-income workers from wage theft. The renewed focus on income inequality—fueled by the financial crisis of 2008 and the persistence of underemployment and unemployment—also emboldened the black business community to demand a dramatic increase in the percentage of city and county contracts procured by black-owned businesses. In a city that is 63 percent African American, black-owned businesses earned less than 1 percent of the city's total business revenue in 2012.[6]

In early July 2016, almost a year to the day after the death of Darrius Stewart, #BLM activists helped mobilize a protest march in response to the killing of two more black people at the hands of the police. Replicating a tactic deployed across the nation, a few hundred people (which eventually swelled to more than a thousand) made their way to the DeSoto Bridge over the Mississippi River, shutting down both lanes of Interstate 40 for nearly four hours. The march garnered national attention for its powerful affirmation of black life. It also caught the eye of national news outlets because protesters and police officers managed to navigate a potentially violent confrontation with no arrests.[7] During the march, interim police director Mike Rallings and protest leaders agreed to set up a community forum for city residents to express their concerns to both Rallings and Memphis mayor Jim Strickland.[8]

The community forum, convened a scant twelve hours after the bridge protest, proved to be a raucous affair. Tensions ran high as people, many of whom lived in neglected communities across the city, expressed their doubts that anything productive would come from the hastily assembled public forum. Some detractors yelled that the meeting was simply a publicity stunt designed to feign concern over the city's inability to address long-standing structural challenges. These doubts were well founded; they resulted from the observations of men and women who were grappling with persistently high poverty rates, little access to jobs that paid a living wage, and other challenges related to ongoing inequality.[9] However, the meeting also provided a crucial snapshot of the issues motivating black folks across Memphis. In an effort to address the myriad concerns expressed by Memphians, Mayor Strickland offered to respond to all the written questions he received. Those questions spanned the entire range of the black freedom struggle: What are you doing about police brutality? What's being done to engage elite white Memphis to hold them accountable? What do you do daily to improve the safety and livelihood of urban communities? What are you doing to make our kids safe? What is being done to aid inner-city schools? Other questions were related to job training, youth programs, public works spending, and a living wage.[10]

An Unseen Light moves us away from a flashpoint rendering of these events toward a fuller view—one that places the violence, protests, and negotiation of the contemporary moment within the longer struggle to reshape the Bluff City's racial terrain. By following the analytical frame set forth in this volume, we can recognize this moment for what it actually is—a resurgence of the black freedom struggle. The protests against police brutality and the systematic harassment of poor and working-class blacks have energized black folks and their allies across the city. The protests waged throughout Memphis also reflect a crucial expansion of the city's freedom agenda. In numerous instances, #BLM has partnered with organizations such as SisterReach and Planned Parenthood to assert that reproductive justice, LGBTQ rights, and access to affordable health care must be integral parts of any authentic freedom struggle.[11] Elected officials, from the mayor to the district attorney to members of local elected bodies, are facing increased scrutiny—a hallmark of movement activity. Tami Sawyer, a key figure in the #BLM movement in Memphis, was a candidate for a seat in the Tennessee House of Representatives in 2016. Running a grassroots campaign as an unrepentant advocate for black people, she garnered 44 percent of the vote.[12] Sawyer's campaign served as a powerful reminder that, from the end of the nineteenth century onward, movement activists in Memphis have always navigated the fluid relationship between electoral politics and community organizing.

As we approach the fiftieth anniversary of Martin Luther King Jr.'s assassination, Memphis once again finds itself an epicenter of movement activity. Sadly, were he alive today, King would recognize many of the structural obstacles that undermine the lives of black folks in the city. He would recognize a national poverty rate among black people that is virtually unchanged from 1968. He would recognize the ongoing problem of police brutality. He would recognize the policy choices of a president and a federal bureaucracy that are openly hostile to the material well-being of black people. He would certainly recognize the persistence of segregation and the shadow it casts over every aspect of life, from birth to death, for black Memphians. He would recognize the appalling disparities between schools populated by white students and those populated by black students. He would recognize the tortured inertia of religious and political moderates. Finally, as someone who spent the last thirteen years of his life labeled a "security risk," he would recognize the heightened levels of surveillance perpetrated against activists and organizations—this time, in the name of "homeland security."

However, other dynamics at play in the Bluff City might give King reason to feel a guarded optimism. A small but growing assemblage of neighborhood organizations, churches, nonprofits, and other institutions are deeply involved in the work of social change. Activists throughout the city are creating spaces for people to engage in the debates and dialogues necessary to build investment within the city's civic universe. Grassroots organizations are holding elected officials accountable for their actions. People of all ages are taking stock of their lives under the Trump administration, and they are stepping up their political activity accordingly. In the face of enduring inequality, black folks and their allies are deeply invested in what King once called "the long and bitter, but beautiful struggle for a new world."[13]

With any luck, King would recognize these lights—no longer unseen.

Notes

1. William Chafe, Raymond Gavins, Bob Korstad, et al., eds., *Remembering Jim Crow: African Americans Tell about Life in the Segregated South* (New York: New Press, 2014), 5.

2. Chris Johnson, "Killed on Holy Ground," http://gawker.com/killed-on-holy-ground-dispatch-from-a-sea-of-blue-1734459652 (accessed June 1, 2017).

3. Jody Callahan, "Grand Jury Declines to Indict Officer in Teen's Shooting; Officer Remains Off Duty," *Memphis Commercial Appeal,* November 3, 2015; Katie Fretland, "Department of Justice Declines to Prosecute Officer in Darrius Stewart Case," *Memphis Commercial Appeal,* September 27, 2016.

4. Brittney Gathen, "Memphis Grassroots Coalition Debuts on 31st Day after Darrius Stewart's Death," *Tri-State Defender,* August 7, 2015. Coalition members include the Mid-South Peace and Justice Center; #BlackLivesMatter–

Memphis chapter; Abyssinian Baptist Church (Earle Fisher, pastor); First Baptist Church, Lauderdale (Noel Hutchinson, pastor); Freedom's Chapel Christian Church (Roz Nichols, pastor); Gifts of Life Ministries (Andre Johnson, pastor); Fight for 15; Stand for Children; Just City; Memphis School of Servant Leadership; Manna House; Memphis Artists for Change; SisterReach; and PERL (People for the Enforcement of Rape Laws). Micaela Watts, "Groups Combine Efforts in Order to Say Her Name, Louder," https://www.memphisflyer.com/NewsBlog/archives/2016/10/05/groups-combine-efforts-in-order-to-say-her-name-louder (accessed June 1, 2017).

5. Wendi Thomas, "Inequality in Memphis: The Working Poor," https://mlk50.com/inequality-in-memphis-the-working-poor-f4650c16b086 (accessed June 1, 2017).

6. Madeline Faber, "Fenced Out," https://www.memphisdailynews.com/news/2016/jan/30/fenced-out/ (accessed June 1, 2017).

7. Jody Callahan, "Marchers Shut Down I-40 Bridge at Memphis during Black Lives Matter Rally," http://archive.commercialappeal.com/news/tennessee-black-caucus-calls-for-calm-amid-racial-unrest-3714d93e-1078–6a7d-e053-0100007f134e-386214081.html (accessed June 2, 2017).

8. "Woke: Was the Protest on the Bridge a Sign of Real Change to Come?" *Memphis Flyer,* https://www.memphisflyer.com/memphis/woke-was-the-protest-on-the-bridge-a-sign-of-real-change-to-come/Content?oid=4761617 (accessed June 3, 2017).

9. The overall poverty rate for African Americans in Memphis was 30.1 percent in 2015. For black Memphians under the age of eighteen, the rate jumped to 47 percent. See "Trends in Memphis Poverty," http://www.memphis.edu/socialwork/pdfs/2016memphisdetailedpovertytableswebversion.pdf (accessed June 5, 2017).

10. Office of Mayor Jim Strickland. "Q and A from July 11 Community Meeting," http://memphistn.gov/Portals/0/pdf_forms/AmaniQA.pdf (accessed June 5, 2017).

11. Tom Charlier, "Memphis Groups Demand Justice, Human Rights for Poor," *Memphis Commercial Appeal,* February 23, 2017.

12. David Royer, "Sawyer Announces Run for State House Seat," *Memphis Commercial Appeal,* http://archive.commercialappeal.com/news/government/politics/sawyer-announces-run-for-state-house-seat-2fff5a0e-0d4f-2058-e053-0100007ffe35-375092661.html (accessed June 6, 2017); Kim Chaney, "Incumbent John DeBerry Wins," Local Memphis.com, http://www.localmemphis.com/news/local-news/incumbent-john-deberry-wins-the-democratic-primary-for-tennessee-house-district-90/524252342 (accessed June 6, 2017).

13. Speech by Martin Luther King Jr., "Beyond Vietnam," April 4, 1967, Riverside Church, New York City.

Contributors

Beverly Greene Bond is associate professor of history at the University of Memphis. She is a native Memphian. The city's history has figured in essays on the origins of public education in Memphis and Shelby County, Tennessee; on Sarah Roberta Church, granddaughter of the prominent Robert R. Church family; and on nineteenth-century African American enslaved people, antebellum free women of color, and freed women in Memphis and across the state. Her publications include *Memphis in Black and White, Images of America: Beale Street, Tennessee Women: Their Lives and Times—Volume I, Tennessee Women: Their Lives and Times—Volume II, Dreamers. Thinkers. Doers: A Centennial History of the University of Memphis,* and *University of Memphis.*

James Conway is associate professor of history at Tarrant County College. He earned his PhD from the University of Memphis in 2015. Dr. Conway's research interests include twentieth-century United States history and African American history with an emphasis on the civil rights and Black Power movements at the local level.

Aram Goudsouzian is chair and professor of the Department of History at the University of Memphis. He is the author of book chapters and articles on the history of race, culture, and politics in the United States. His books include *Down to the Crossroads: Civil Rights, Black Power, and the Meredith March against Fear, King of the Court: Bill Russell and the Basketball Revolution, Sidney Poitier: Man, Actor, Icon,* and *The Hurricane of 1938.*

Laurie B. Green is associate professor of history at the University of Texas at Austin, with courtesy appointments in the Center for Women's and Gender Studies and in the departments of American Studies and African and African Diaspora Studies. She earned a joint MA in history and archival management at New York University before completing her PhD at the University of Chicago. Her 2007 book *Battling the Plantation Mentality: Memphis and the Black Freedom Struggle* garnered the 2008 Philip Taft Labor History Book Award. In 2014, the University of Minnesota Press published *Precarious Prescriptions: Contested Histories of Race and Health in North America,* which she coedited with Martin Summers and John Mckiernan-González. Her current research focuses on the politics of race, hunger, and poverty in the US in the 1960s and 1970s.

Elizabeth Gritter is assistant professor of history at Indiana University Southeast in New Albany, Indiana. She is the author of *River of Hope: Black Politics and the Memphis Freedom Movement.* She heads the Institute for Local and Oral History at Indiana University Southeast and directs the school's campus oral history project.

Michael K. Honey holds the Fred T. and Dorothy G. Haley Endowed Professorship in the Humanities at the University of Washington, Tacoma. He is the author of *Going Down Jericho Road: The Memphis Strike, Martin Luther King's Last Campaign,* winner of awards from the Robert F. Kennedy Book Foundation, the Organization of American Historians, the Southern Historical Association, and the United Association of Labor Educators. His other books include a collection of King's labor and economic justice speeches, *All Labor Has Dignity,* a biography of John Handcox called *Sharecropper's Troubadour,* and two books on Memphis: *Black Workers Remember: An Oral History of Unionism, Segregation and the Freedom Struggle* and *Southern Labor and Black Civil Rights: Organizing Memphis Workers.*

Charles L. Hughes is the director of the Memphis Center at Rhodes College, and author of the acclaimed book, *Country Soul: Making Music and Making Race in the American South.* He has written and spoken extensively on music, race, and the South.

Jason Jordan is assistant professor of history at the University of New Haven. He holds a PhD and MA in history from the University of Illinois at Urbana-Champaign as well as a BA in history from Rhodes College in

Memphis. His research focuses on race, politics, and black activism in the Jim Crow South.

Shirletta Kinchen is assistant professor of Pan-African Studies at the University of Louisville. Her research focuses on the intersections of Black Power, local grassroots activism, black student and campus activism, and black youth politics during the civil rights and Black Power movements. She is the author of *Black Power in the Bluff City: African American Youth and Student Activism in Memphis, 1965–1975.*

Steven A. Knowlton is Librarian for History and African American Studies at Princeton University Library. Winner of the Justin Winsor Library History Essay Award, he has published in *Tennessee Historical Quarterly, Libraries: History, Culture, and Society, Raven: A Journal of Vexillology, College and Research Libraries, Library Resources and Technical Services,* and *Serials Review,* among others.

Charles W. McKinney Jr. is the Neville Frierson Bryan Chair of Africana Studies and associate professor of history at Rhodes College. He is the author *of Greater Freedom: The Evolution of the Civil Rights Struggle in Wilson, North Carolina* and various articles and book chapters on civil rights organizing in the rural South and black women's activism. He has a BA from Morehouse College and a PhD from Duke University.

Brian D. Page received his MA in history from the University of Memphis and his PhD in history from the Ohio State University. He is currently a professor of history at Florida SouthWestern State College. He has published articles on the African American community in Memphis, Tennessee, in the *Tennessee Historical Quarterly* and the *Journal of Urban History.*

Zandria F. Robinson is author of *This Ain't Chicago: Race, Class, and Regional Identity in the Post-Soul South,* which won the 2015 Eduardo Bonilla-Silva Outstanding Book Award from the Division of Racial and Ethnic Minorities of the Society for the Study of Social Problems, and coauthor of *Chocolate Cities: The Black Map of American Life* with Marcus Anthony Hunter. Her work has appeared in *The New Encyclopedia of Southern Culture,* the *Annual Review of Sociology* (with Marcus Anthony Hunter), *Oxford American,* and *Rolling Stone.*

Anthony C. Siracusa is a native Memphian who specializes in the intersection of religion, race, and politics in modern United States history. He has written regularly about Memphis for the *Memphis Commercial Appeal* and the *Memphis Flyer,* and his work has appeared in the *Journal of Civil and Human Rights, Tennessee Historical Quarterly,* and the *West Tennessee Historical Society Papers.* An advocate for biking and walking, he is the recipient of a Thomas J. Watson Fellowship to explore bicycle cultures across four continents.

Elton H. Weaver III is an assistant professor of history at LeMoyne-Owen College. He received his PhD from the University of Memphis. His research explores the life of Charles H. Mason and the geneses of the Memphis-based Church of God in Christ.

David Welky is professor of history at the University of Central Arkansas. He is the author of *The Thousand-Year Flood: The Ohio-Mississippi Disaster of 1937, Marching Across the Color Line: A. Philip Randolph and Civil Rights in the World War II Era, A Wretched and Precarious Situation: In Search of the Last Arctic Frontier,* and other books on twentieth-century American history.

Darius Young is as an associate professor of history at Florida A&M University. He received his PhD in history from the University of Memphis. His research focuses on the early civil rights movement, with an emphasis on black political movements during the first half of the twentieth century. He is finishing his first book on the black political leader, Robert Church Jr., and has been published in *The Griot: The Journal of African American Studies.* He has won awards from the Southern Regional Education Board, the Gilder Lehrman Institute of American History, and the Benjamin L. Hooks Institute for Social Change. In 2014, Florida A&M named him the University Teacher of the Year.

Index

CIVIL RIGHTS AND THE STRUGGLE FOR BLACK EQUALITY
IN THE TWENTIETH CENTURY

SERIES EDITORS
Steven F. Lawson, Rutgers University
Cynthia Griggs Fleming, University of Tennessee
Hasan Kwame Jeffries, Ohio State University

In Peace and Freedom: My Journey in Selma
Bernard LaFayette Jr. and Kathryn Lee Johnson

Democracy Rising: South Carolina and the Fight for Black Equality since 1865
Peter F. Lau

Civil Rights Crossroads: Nation, Community, and the Black Freedom Struggle
Steven F. Lawson

Selma to Saigon: The Civil Rights Movement and the Vietnam War
Daniel S. Lucks

In Remembrance of Emmett Till: Regional Stories and Media Responses to the Black Freedom Struggle
Darryl Mace

Freedom Rights: New Perspectives on the Civil Rights Movement
edited by Danielle L. McGuire and John Dittmer

This Little Light of Mine: The Life of Fannie Lou Hamer
Kay Mills

After the Dream: Black and White Southerners since 1965
Timothy J. Minchin and John A. Salmond

Faith in Black Power: Religion, Race, and Resistance in Cairo, Illinois
Kerry Pimblott

Fighting Jim Crow in the County of Kings: The Congress of Racial Equality in Brooklyn
Brian Purnell

Roy Wilkins: The Quiet Revolutionary and the NAACP
Yvonne Ryan

Thunder of Freedom: Black Leadership and the Transformation of 1960s Mississippi
Sue [Lorenzi] Sojourner with Cheryl Reitan

For a Voice and the Vote: My Journey with the Mississippi Freedom Democratic Party
Lisa Anderson Todd

Art for Equality: The NAACP's Cultural Campaign for Civil Rights
Jenny Woodley

For Jobs and Freedom: Race and Labor in America since 1865
Robert H. Zieger